The Concept of
Neutrality in
Classical Greece

The Concept of
Neutrality in
Classical Greece

Robert A. Bauslaugh

UNIVERSITY OF CALIFORNIA PRESS
Berkeley · Los Angeles · Oxford

University of California Press

Berkeley and Los Angeles, California

University of California Press, Ltd.
Oxford, England

© 1991 by
The Regents of the University of California

Library of Congress Cataloging-in-Publication Data

Bauslaugh, Robert A.
  The concept of neutrality in classical Greece / Robert A. Bauslaugh.
      p.   cm.
  Includes bibliographical references.
  ISBN 0-520-06687-1 (alk. paper)
  1. Greece—Neutrality—History.   I. Title.
JX1550.B38   1990
341.6′4′0938–dc20   90-10880
                                               CIP

Printed in the United States of America
1 2 3 4 5 6 7 8 9

The paper used in this publication meets the minimum requirements of American
National Standard for Information Sciences–Permanence of Paper for Printed
Library Materials, ANSI Z39.48-1984. ∞

To the memory of my father,
George Arnold Bauslaugh

Contents

Preface

The role of nonbelligerent parties in the interstate politics of ancient Greek warfare has been a neglected subject. In the preface to their authoritative study of neutrality in modern international law published in 1935 and 1936, P. Jessup and F. Deák acknowledged that "there are vast sources untapped by the present writers." "Here," they say, "is much work, first for the historian and then for the international lawyer."[1] Yet during the more than fifty years since this statement was made, no one has produced a comprehensive study of neutrality in ancient Greek history, despite the fact that the existence of neutral parties is constantly assumed without question.[2]

1. P. C. Jessup and F. Deák, *Neutrality: Its History, Economics and Law in Four Volumes*, vol. 1 (New York, 1935), xiv.

2. See, for instance, F. E. Adcock and D. J. Mosley, *Diplomacy in Ancient Greece* (New York and London, 1975), 146, 207–8, 234, who remark about the fifth century B.C.: "In 415, after the Athenians had sent out their first expedition to the west against Syracuse, ... they called upon Rhegium to help its kinsmen in Leontini. Rhegium, however, declared that it would observe neutrality until the Italiots had determined what their policy was to be" (146). Regarding the fourth century, see, among others, C. D. Hamilton, *Sparta's Bitter Victories: Politics and Diplomacy in the Corinthian War* (Ithaca, N.Y., and London, 1979), 217: "Thebes had already learned the significance of the site [i.e., of Corinth], when Pausanias, taking advantage of Corinthian neutrality in July 395, had marched his Peloponnesian army across the isthmus to meet with Lysander at Haliartus." So too on the Hellenistic period, P. Klose, *Die völkerrechtliche Ordnung der hellenistischen Staatenwelt in der Zeit von 280 bis 168 v. Chr.* (Munich, 1972), 164, observes: "Immerhin war die Neutralität im politischen und rechtlichen Sinne seit langem erfasst, insbesondere das Recht neutraler Staaten auf Respektierung ihrer unparteiischen Haltung und ihrer Integrität im Prinzip anerkannt."

This neglect is, however, easy to understand, for there exists a major stumbling block created by the question of definition. In modern international law, neutrality is a legal position involving a wide range of specific rights and obligations, the majority of which reflect practices accepted between the sixteenth and twentieth century. Thus, scholars generally consider neutrality's incorporation into the body of modern international law as a basically practical response to contemporary experience and therefore, in its modern juridical definition, distinctly different from any analogous status accorded nonbelligerents in earlier periods of history.[3] Jessup and Deák, accordingly, dismiss antiquity with a sweeping generalization:

> Concepts of nationality, of diplomatic immunities, of treaties, and of other portions of modern international law find counterparts long before the dawn of the Christian era. But all of these precursors must be viewed with careful appreciation of their setting in history unless a false picture is to be drawn. Modern international law presupposes the existence of a family of states whose interrelations it regulates. That is why the modern international legal system had to wait upon the emergence of the modern state.[4]

This view is typical. R. Kleen, for example, claims at the beginning of his two-volume *Lois et usages de la neutralité* that since—as he believes—neutrality as a principle of law was unknown to the ancients, the seemingly neutral position of states that did not take part in a war represents nothing more than indifference or chance. Hence Kleen holds that the study of antiquity and the citation of ancient evidence are pointless for understanding the concept of legal neutrality that evolved in "a more advanced age."[5] Likewise, H. H. Andrae, in his "Begriff und Entwicklung des Kriegsneutralitätsrechts," maintains that until the rise of modern states neutrality was purely a factual condition without rights and obligations agreed upon by belligerents and nonbelligerents.[6] Many other studies could be cited; but the point is clear. By insisting that legal definition is a necessary precondition for the existence of "true"

---

3. E.g., Jessup and Deák, *Neutrality*, vol. 1, 3–19.
4. Ibid., 3–4.
5. R. Kleen, *Lois et usages de la neutralité d'après le droit international conventionnel et la société des nations*, vol. 1 (Paris, 1898), 1–3.
6. H. H. Andrae, "Begriff und Entwicklung des Kriegsneutralitätsrechts" (Diss., Göttingen, 1938), 1.

neutrality, commentators have simply eliminated discussion of neutrality prior to the seventeenth century.[7]

Behind this exclusion of antiquity is an unacknowledged (and indeed unquestioned) belief that the incorporation of neutrality as a legally defined status in international law is evidence of the superiority of the modern world over all previous ages—proof, in fact, of the modern world's progress toward more civilized international relations. The international law of neutrality is thus viewed as something newly created in the wake of the modern world's acceptance of international law itself. This notion is particularly clear in standard histories of international law like that of L. Oppenheim, which casually dismisses the ancient world with the statement:

> Since in antiquity there was no notion of an International Law, it is not to be expected that neutrality as a legal institution should have existed among the nations of old. Neutrality did not exist even in practice, for belligerents never recognized an attitude of impartiality on the part of other States. If war broke out between two nations, third parties had to choose between belligerents and become allies or enemies of one or the other.[8]

But is this kind of sweeping generalization really correct? What is the evidence for such a conclusion? Is it legitimate to demand the

7. The scholarship is extensive and virtually unanimous; for rare exceptions, see C. Phillipson, *The International Law and Custom of Ancient Greece and Rome*, vol. 2 (London, 1911), 301–3, 381–82; S. Séfériadès, "La conception de la neutralité dans l'ancienne Grèce," *Revue de droit international et de legislation comparée* 16 (1935): 641–62; G. Nenci, "La neutralità nella Grecia antica," *Il Veltro: Rivista di civiltà italiana* 22 (1978): 495–506. N. Politis, *Neutrality and Peace*, trans. F. C. Macken (Washington, 1935), 11, speaks of "traces" of a law of neutrality in ancient India and Greece but offers no discussion (on India, see K. Sastry, "A Note on Udasina: Neutrality in Ancient India," *Indian Yearbook for International Affairs* [1954], 131–34). Other studies, even when promising treatment of antiquity, typically provide only a few well-known examples in support of the conclusion that there is little to learn; e.g., M. J. MacQuelyn, *Dissertatio iuridica politica de neutralitate tempore belli* (Lyons, 1829), 1, 10–11, 21; B. Bacot, *Des neutralités durables: Origine, domaine et efficacité* (Paris, 1943), 23–34; B. Jankovic, "De la neutralité classique à la conception moderne des pays non-alignés," *Revue égyptienne de droit international* 21 (1965): 90.

8. L. Oppenheim, *International Law*, vol. 2, 7th ed., ed. H. Lauterpacht (New York, 1952), 624, representing a long tradition; see also, for example, R. Ward, *An Enquiry into the Foundation and History of the Law of Nations in Europe from the Time of the Greeks and Romans to the Age of Grotius* (Dublin, 1795), 108–9; T. J. Lawrence, *The Principles of International Law*, 3d ed. (London, 1906), 475; W. E. Hall, *A Treatise on International Law*, 8th ed., ed. A. P. Higgins (London, 1924), 691; A. Berriedale Keith, ed., *Wheaton's Elements of International Law*, 6th ed. (London, 1929), 912.

presence of legal definition as the sine qua non for studying neutrality? Is it true that if there is not *de iure* neutrality, there cannot in its absence be any neutrality? Or, more broadly, should we accept the idea that the dichotomy of friend and enemy was a fundamental reality in interstate relations of antiquity? Are modern legal historians right in dismissing any and all examples of nonbelligerent and neutral behavior as nothing more than the result of de facto circumstances that involve neither recognized status nor consistent principles?

Suppose we strip away the veneer of "legality" from modern regulation of nonbelligerent and neutral parties. Are the underlying concepts fundamental to neutrality as a "legalized" position to be found only in the modern world? Is neutrality really new? Or is this "finest most fragile flower of international law"[9] nothing more than the expression in legal terms of extremely old notions of justice and reciprocity between states? Or to put it differently, in what way does juridical definition alter the situation confronting nonbelligerents in their relationship with belligerents? How much better off for its legal status was, for example, Belgium in the First World War or Cambodia in the Vietnam conflict than Melos in the Peloponnesian War or the Achaean League in the Third Macedonian War? These are questions that have simply not been asked by legal scholars or historians.[10]

It must also be remembered that in modern international law neither the definition nor the specific rules of neutrality are static. Exactly how neutrality is defined and what rules apply change constantly in response to historical circumstances. In any context, however, the specific definition of neutrality and its practical existence are based on a remarkably consistent set of principles. Specific rights and obligations may therefore vary according to existing cultural and political forces, but the underlying principles remain recognizably the same. For example, the Hague Conventions of

9. P. Lyon, "Neutrality and the Emergence of the Concept of Neutralism," *The Review of Politics* 22 (April 1960): 259.

10. R. Ogley, *The Theory and Practice of Neutrality in the Twentieth Century* (London, 1970), examines the violation of both Belgium (61–75) and Cambodia (197–203). He concludes: "It is doubtful whether *anything* could have saved Belgian neutrality in a war between France and Germany in 1914" (62); and observes prophetically (writing in 1970): "Cambodia remains perched in precarious fashion on the sidelines of a war that still threatens to engulf it" (201). The similarities between the failed neutrality of these two modern states and that of the Melians and Achaeans are striking and ominous.

1899 and 1907 specified numerous legal requirements for both
neutral and belligerent states in accordance with the optimistic
mood of respect for international law that prevailed prior to the
outbreak of World War I; yet the principles upon which the specific
neutrality legislation of 1899 and 1907 was based were essentially
the same as those underlying the rules set forth in the *Consolato
del Mare* of 1494, which was based, in part, on ancient Rhodian
sea law.[11]

But the questions remain. Were there any recognizable principles
that applied to nonbelligerency and neutrality in ancient Greece?
And what, if any, are the common elements in the ancient and
modern concepts? Only one thing seems certain at the outset of
this investigation. When the *Consolato del Mare* version of Rhodian sea law specifies rules for handling the maritime goods of
nonbelligerents, when Machiavelli, arguing from evidence steeped
in Roman history, condemns neutrality as bad policy for a prince,
and when Hugo Grotius, the father of modern international law,
includes discussion of the rights and duties of nonbelligerents (his
medii) on the basis of ancient precedent, it should be clear that
there is something fundamentally inadequate in the widespread
notion of neutrality as unworthy of serious investigation prior to
the evolution of modern international law.[12] What is needed is a
different approach. C. Phillipson, a lawyer himself, seems to have
recognized this. Phillipson argued that what was needed was a shift
from a strictly legal focus to a broader historical analysis, observing

11. On the relationship, see N. Ørvik, *The Decline of Neutrality, 1914–1941*,
2d ed. (London, 1971), 33–35, who concludes: "The Hague Conventions mark
the top, the very climax of legalized neutrality. From *Consolato del Mare*, piece
by piece had been added to the law of neutrality, until the 1907 Convention
disposed of most of the controversial points in the relations between belligerents
and neutrals" (32–33). For the conventions, see J. B. Scott, *The Hague Conventions and Declarations 1899 and 1907* (London, 1909); for the *Consolato*, S. S.
Jados, *Consulate of the Sea and Related Documents* (Tuscaloosa, Ala., 1975).

12. See *Consolato del Mare*, sec. 276: "If an intercepted vessel belonged to
friendly nationals and the cargo aboard it belonged to unfriendly nationals, the
admiral in command of the armed vessel may force the patron of the merchantman
to surrender all enemy goods to him," and so on (trans. Jados, *Consulate of the
Sea*, 192; see pp. xi–xii on Rhodian sea law); N. Machiavelli, *The Prince* (1513):
"It will always happen that the one who is not your friend will want you to
remain neutral, and the one who is your friend will require you to declare yourself
by taking arms" (trans. M. Lerner, *The Prince and the Discourses* [New York,
1950], 83); H. Grotius, *De iure belli ac pacis libri tres*, vol. 3 (Paris, 1625), xvii,
dealing with "those who are of neither side in war" (trans. F. W. Kelsey, *Classics
of International Law* [London, 1925], 783).

that "in the investigation and weighing of ancient practices the
main point is ... not so much the nature of the ultimate sanction
and in what sphere it resided, but whether and to what extent
regularization of procedure obtained, and how far it was protected
and insisted upon."[13]

To get at these issues a systematic and comprehensive review of
the evidence is necessary, despite the many problems presented by
the limited sources available. The hope is that a careful study of
nonbelligerency and neutrality in classical Greece will not only
shed light on ancient attitudes toward states that refused to participate in specific conflicts but also provide insight into how the Greek
states conducted themselves under the harsh disruption of warfare
and its test of self-imposed restraints. Furthermore, the identification of either principles or regularized procedures connected with
uncommitted states may provide additional insight into the realities
and limitations inherent in any formulation of international law.

It should be understood that by necessity this study examines
classical Greek history from an unusual perspective. Instead of
concentrating on the best-known and most powerful states, which
normally determined or dominated events, the investigation focuses
on states that sought to remain aloof from the conflicts of the
period. These would-be nonparticipants were often lesser states,
which struggled not for supremacy but survival. Reconstruction of
their diplomatic history at times leads to quite different views of
well-known events and to unexpected conclusions about the complex dynamics of interstate relations during periods of warfare.
Many questions are raised, not all of which can be answered with
assurance. Often the sources fail to provide the critical information
required; and all too frequently the information that is provided
proves to be frustratingly ambiguous. Nevertheless, the role of
nonbelligerent states in the international affairs of classical Greece
cannot be denied; and it should not continue to be ignored, for the
history of Greek diplomacy is in no way complete without a
thorough examination of the position and influence of states that

13. Phillipson, *International Law and Custom*, vol. 2, 302; cf. the objection of
P. Bierzanek, "Sur les origines du droit de la guerre et de la paix," *RHDFE* 4th
ser., 38 (1960): 122: "Au xixe et au début du xxe siècle, l'école positiviste montrait
une tendance à traiter le droit international d'une manière dogmatique et formelle,
ce qui ne favorisait pas non plus les études sur l'évolution des institutions de ce
droit et détachait la règle juridique de la réalité politique dans laquelle elle s'était
formée et développée."

refused to commit themselves to one belligerent party or another.

I am indebted to a number of institutions for support during the preparation of this study. The American Council of Learned Societies, the National Endowment for the Humanities, the University Research Committee of Emory University, the Society of Fellows in the Humanities of Columbia University, the Graduate Division of the University of California, Berkeley, and the Mabelle McCleod Lewis Memorial Fund of Stanford University have all generously funded my research, which began as a doctoral thesis entitled *Neutrality in Ancient Greece: Its History to the End of the Fifth Century B.C.* and submitted to the Graduate Group in Ancient History and Mediterranean Archaeology at the University of California, Berkeley, in 1979.

From the beginning, I have profited greatly from discussions with my teachers, colleagues, and students, and I am extremely grateful for the critical contributions they have made in reaction to the "neutral" interpretation of historical events that I presented to them. In particular, I would like to thank my thesis advisers, Erich Gruen, Raphael Sealey, and Ronald Stroud, for their steadfast advice, support, and criticism; Robert Connor for his many searching questions of the issues involved in the study; Malcolm Wallace for editorial suggestions and criticism; the anonymous readers of the University of California Press and editors Doris Kretschmer, Mary Lamprech, and Marian Shotwell for their careful and constructive work on the manuscript; and, finally, Cambridge University, the Faculty of Classics, for granting me visiting status during 1988–89 and Colin Shell for allowing me to use the computing facilities of the Department of Archaeology during final revision of the manuscript.

Cambridge, June 1989   R. A. B.

Abbreviations

ATL	B. D. Meritt, H. T. Wade-Gery, and M. F. McGregor, *The Athenian Tribute Lists*, vol. 1 (Cambridge, Mass., 1939), vols. 2–4 (Princeton, 1949–53).
CAH	*Cambridge Ancient History.*
Edmonds, *FAC*	J. M. Edmonds, *The Fragments of Attic Comedy*, vol. 1 (Leiden, 1957).
Jacoby, *FGH*	F. Jacoby, *Die Fragmente der griechischen Historiker* (Berlin and Leiden, 1923–55).
HCT	A. W. Gomme, A. Andrewes, and K. J. Dover, *A Historical Commentary on Thucydides*, 4 vols. (Oxford, 1947–71).
IG	*Inscriptiones Graecae* (Berlin, 1983–).
*LSJ*⁹	H. G. Liddell and R. Scott, *A Greek-English Lexicon*, 9th ed., rev. by H. S. Jones (Oxford, 1940).
Meiggs and Lewis	R. Meiggs and D. Lewis, *A Selection of Greek Historical Inscriptions to the End of the Fifth Century B.C.* (Oxford, 1969).
RE	Pauly-Wissowa-Kroll, *Real-Encyclopädie der klassischen Altertumswissenschaft* (Stuttgart, 1894–).

Dittenberger, *SIG³*	W. Dittenberger, *Sylloge Inscriptionum Graecarum*, 3d ed. (Leipzig, 1915–24).
Bengtson, *SVA²*	H. Bengtson, *Die Staatsverträge des Altertums: Die Verträge der griechisch-römischen Welt von 700 bis 338 v. Chr.*, 2d ed. (Munich, 1975).
Tod	M. N. Tod, *A Selection of Greek Historical Inscriptions*, vol. 2: *From 403 to 323 B.C.* (Oxford, 1948).

Introduction

Formal abstention during interstate conflict—neutrality, in the terminology of modern international law—is a surprisingly common feature of ancient Greek warfare. There are many examples: the Milesians in the mid-sixth century B.C.; the Argives in 480; the Melians, Therans, Achaeans, and others in 431; the Agrigentines, Camarinaeans, and the majority of South Italian cities in 415; the Boeotians and Corinthians in 399; the Megarians from the 390s onward; the united Greek alliance in 362; Athens in the 340s; and a substantial number of states in the final struggle against Philip II in 338. The simple fact is that among surviving accounts of virtually every major conflict of the classical period there are references to states that remain—or seek to remain—in a posture friendly yet uncommitted to the belligerents. The evidence, though woefully scattered and fragmentary, nevertheless reveals time and time again that the diplomatic concepts influencing the actual interstate dynamics of classical warfare were far more complex and subtle than a simple dichotomy of friends and enemies. But the question here is specific: Just how did the states of the classical period go about abstaining from a given conflict?

What exactly did it mean for a state to refuse to take sides, in effect, to adopt a "neutral" position? Were there specific rights and obligations that accompanied such a policy? Were there recognized principles or even specific regulations that applied? Did a would-be neutral state need to obtain acceptance of its position from the belligerents, or could it assume their respect on the basis of nothing more than a unilateral declaration? Moreover, to look at the problem historically, do we find anything during the classical period that might be termed "evolution"? In other words, does the position of nonparticipants remain largely undefined and subject to nothing more than the ad hoc circumstances of each successive conflict, or do practices and attitudes evolve through time? Furthermore, and perhaps most important of all, can we see in the study of states that refused to commit themselves any of the essential features and principles of neutrality as it has come to be defined in modern international law? Is there, we may ask, any common foundation that might be considered absolutely essential to the acceptance of neutrality regardless of its specific historical context? And if there seems to be such a foundation, then for neutrality not only to exist but to succeed, what are the critical elements of interstate relations that must be recognized irrespective of the presence or absence of a well-defined structure of international law?

It is no easy task to study the position of states that remained aloof during the wars of the classical period. Ancient Greek had no single word for the diplomatic concept of neutrality; and while this does not mean that either the idea of nonbelligerent status or the identification of states and individuals that fell into this category could not be communicated, it does mean that descriptions of such parties and their policy were by necessity adapted from common speech to fit the specific context of a given reference.

Thucydides, for example, employs a wide range of descriptions for nonparticipants (see Chapter 1 below), including some phrases that are unmistakable, such as *ekpodōn histantes amphoterois* ("those standing aloof from both sides") or *symmachoi ontes mēdeterōn* ("those who were allies of neither side"), and some that can be frustratingly vague, like *hoi hēsychian agontes* ("those remaining at peace"). Fortunately, in most instances, the absence of standard nomenclature does not present a serious obstacle for the study. The real difficulty lies not in the identification of a state's nonbelligerency but rather in the reconstruction and interpretation of the underlying principles of interstate behavior and diplomacy. To understand what those principles were during different periods and how they affected the policy decisions of individual states, we have to evaluate not only the information provided by the ancient sources but also the bias of the sources themselves.

For the study of neutrality the surviving ancient sources present a number of complicated problems. Perhaps the most frustrating is simply disinterest. Instead of providing information about non-combatants, the sources in most cases either ignore them entirely or provide only incidental and superficial references. When there is mention, it is often so vague that it fails to illuminate the exact position and policy of the bystanders. Herodotus (8. 73.3) mentions only in passing—with explicit condemnation—Peloponnesian states that failed to take sides in 480/479 (see 5.2 below); Thucydides (4. 78.2–3) never defines the position of the Thessalians, although their official policy was certainly uncommitted after 431 (see 6. 3.B below); Xenophon (*Hell*. 5. 1.1) abruptly introduces the Aeginetans in the context of 389 with the cryptic remark that they had previously maintained normal relations with the Athenians (see 8. 3.D below)—to mention just three examples. The point is, and this must be emphasized, that ancient authors normally pay attention only to unexpected neutrality, the change from nonparticipation to active belligerency, or sensational acts of violence committed against nonbelligerents. The unusual, not the ordinary, interested literary minds. In addition to these problems there is the basic issue of subjectivity. Unfortunately, in the event that any discussion of neutrals and neutral policy is offered, the sources all too often display strong personal bias and provide an obviously prejudiced assessment of the motives and legitimacy of neutrals. This makes reconstructing the exact policy and status of states that attempted to remain aloof from a given conflict all the more difficult, a problem that is, of course, compounded by the absence of technical language.

Faced with this formidable array of obstacles, we have to proceed with extreme care, for at issue is not only *what* our sources say about neutral behavior but also *why* they say what they do. In order to reach any valid conclusions about neutral states we therefore need to examine very carefully not only the references themselves but also the historical context in which they appear and the rationale for their inclusion in each source's narrative. Only when we have done this may we attempt to reconstruct the diplomatic principles that applied specifically to neutrality, and only thereby can we achieve a better understanding of the policy whenever it appears.

At the outset we need to be clear about what exactly is meant

by neutrality. In modern international law, neutrality is a legal
status available to any sovereign state during the armed conflicts
of other states. As Phillipson defined it at the end of the First World
War, "neutrality is the condition of states which stand aloof from
a war between other states; they may continue such pacific intercourse with belligerents as will not consist of giving direct aid to
either side in the prosecution of the hostilities. Thus the essential
significance of neutrality lies in the negative attitude of holding
aloof, and not in the positive attitude of offering impartial treatment
to the adversaries."[1] Phillipson emphasizes this distinction because
there has been, at least since the sixteenth century, considerable
uncertainty about whether complete abstention or merely impartial
treatment is absolutely necessary for proving a legitimate neutral
attitude.[2] In fact, the truth seems to lie somewhere in between, for
as R. L. Bindschedler explains in the *Encyclopedia of Public International Law*, "the laws of neutrality constitute a compromise
between conflicting interests of the belligerents and the neutral
States."[3] Far from being absolute and static the legal expression of
rights and obligations attached to neutrality is in reality the outcome of constant renegotiation influenced to a large degree by the
relative power of belligerents and neutrals. Hence greater restriction
of neutral activity and insistence upon formal abstention follow
when the relative power of the collective belligerent forces is superior to that of the neutrals, but greater freedom, especially of trade,
and stricter respect for the territorial integrity, property, and life
of the neutrals result when the collective power of the neutrals is
greater than that of the belligerents.

To estimate the extent of recognition of neutrality in the diplomacy of classical Greek states we cannot, therefore, simply apply

1. F. Smith, *International Law*, 5th ed., rev. and enl. by C. Phillipson (London,
1918), 293.
2. See Jessup and Deák, *Neutrality*, vol. 1, chaps. 1–2, on the emergence of a
law of neutrality and treaty developments. The problem is well summarized in
W. P. Cobbett's *Cases on International Law*, vol. 2: *War and Neutrality*, 5th ed.,
ed. W. L. Walker (London, 1937), 340: "The controlling principle of the modern
law may be that no active aid in the war may be given to a belligerent at the
expense of the other by a Power which desires to retain the status of neutrality,
yet, even assuming that the eighteenth century rules as to prior Treaty engagements
had become obsolete through a century of disuse and the disapproval of juristic
opinion, on principle a prior Treaty agreement, recognized by all affected parties,
is capable of modifying the general law."
3. R. L. Bindschedler, "Neutrality, Concept and General Rules," in *Encyclopedia of Public International Law*, Instalment 4, ed. R. Bernhardt (New York, 1982),
10.

a checklist of the currently accepted legal requirements of neutrality, as though the list's contents would be definitive for identifying the presence of neutral policy in antiquity. The evaluation of classical practices through some two hundred years of warfare conducted in constantly shifting balances of power requires special concern for the underlying principles that influenced specific notions of neutrality and determined whatever specific requirements applied to neutral status in a given conflict.

The following investigation will begin with an examination of the language used to identify and describe uncommitted parties in times of conflict (Chapter 1). This leads to a discussion of the principal sources of information for studying neutral parties (Chapter 2). Consideration of institutions and customary practices that contributed to the recognition of uncommitted states in the diplomacy of the classical period follows (Chapter 3) by way of providing some background and context for a discussion of the realities confronting would-be neutrals (Chapter 4). Since no comprehensive collection of the evidence for abstention has ever been published, a diachronic reconstruction of the details of specific instances of certain and suspected neutral policy between the late seventh century and the battle of Chaeronea in 338 is presented (Chapters 5–9). On the basis of this evidence, the study concludes with answers to the questions of how neutral policy was perceived, what kind of detailed expression it came to have in classical Greek diplomacy, and why it developed the way it did.

οἱ δὲ Λακεδαιμόνιοι δικασταὶ νομίζοντες τὸ ἐπερώτημα σφίσιν ὀρθῶς ἕξειν, εἴ τι ἐν τῷ πολέμῳ ὑπ' αὐτῶν ἀγαθὸν πεπόνθασι, διότι τόν τε ἄλλον χρόνον ἠξίουν δῆθεν αὐτοὺς κατὰ τὰς παλαιὰς Παυσανίου μετὰ τὸν Μῆδον σπονδὰς ἡσυχάζειν καὶ ὅτε ὕστερον ἃ πρὸ τοῦ περιτειχίζεσθαι προείχοντο αὐτοῖς, κοινοὺς εἶναι κατ' ἐκεῖνα, ὡς οὐκ ἐδέξαντο, ἡγούμενοι τῇ ἑαυτῶν δικαίᾳ βουλήσει ἔκσπονδοι ἤδη ὑπ' αὐτῶν κακῶς πεπονθέναι ...

The Spartan judges decided that their question—whether they had received any help from the Plataeans in the war—was a proper one to ask. Their grounds were that, in accordance with the original treaty made with Pausanias after the Persian War, *they had all the time (so they said) counted on Plataean neutrality*; later, just before the siege, they had offered them *the same conditions of neutrality implied by the treaty*, and this offer had not been accepted; the justice of their intentions had, they considered, released them from their obligations under the treaty, and it was at this point that they had suffered injury from Plataea.

Thucydides 3. 68.1–2; translation by Rex Warner (my italics)

PART ONE

The Classical Concept of Neutrality

CHAPTER ONE

Ancient Greek Diplomatic Terminology for Abstention from Conflict

Ancient Greek never had anything like the extensive vocabulary for diplomatic categories known in the modern world. However, this does not mean that classical diplomacy was rudimentary and unsophisticated or that it was unable to differentiate clearly between such groups as belligerents and nonbelligerents. The problem seems to lie not in any limited conceptualization of the categories but in a basic indifference to the idea that exclusively diplomatic terminology was necessary. Hence, whether an individual privately or a state publicly remained uncommitted during a conflict, it could simply be said of them that they "kept quiet" (*hēsychian ēgagon*) or "remained at peace" (*eirēnēn ēgagon*) while others took sides. Depending on the context, this phrase might signify any number of positions, ranging from indecisive inaction to formal policy. So to begin with, it must be understood that the vocabulary for talking about parties that abstained from war was neither specialized nor exclusively restricted to diplomacy.

Already in Homer's *Iliad* the existence of a party (Achilles and his Myrmidon troops) that refused to take sides in a conflict (the ongoing Trojan War) created an extraordinary diplomatic situation that challenged the linguistic capabilities of eighth-century Greek. In epic poetry there is virtually no specialized vocabulary for diplomacy. For example, *polemos*, which came later to have the exclusive meaning of formal armed conflict between states, is in Homer an entirely unspecialized word meaning not only interstate conflict (e.g., *Il.* 1. 61) but also any kind of battle or fight (e.g., 1. 226) and even single combat (7. 174). *Spondai*, literally "libations" but, by extension from the drink offerings that accompanied sworn agreements, also "truce" or "treaty," appears only in its original religious sense (e.g., *Il.* 2. 341) and never by itself with diplomatic meaning. On the contrary, the word used in epic for formal articles of agreement (*synthesia*: e.g., *Il.* 2. 339) is not the term known from the fifth century onward (i.e., *synthēkai*) but is instead nothing more than a vague commonplace applicable to just about any whole created from composite parts (as English *synthesis*). Perhaps most tellingly, the word for ally (*symmachos*) never appears. What we see in this linguistic deficiency is that at the time of the composition of the Homeric epics (eighth century B.C.), an abstaining party simply could not be described in terms of diplomatic categories, for neither those categories nor virtually any other of the formal structural details of interstate relations had yet been introduced and formally incorporated into the language.[1]

As a recognizable group, nonparticipants in conflict first appear in the political poetry of the sixth century.[2] Solon (eponymous archon at Athens ca. 594/593) berates those who believe that they

---

1. See E. Audinet, "Les traces du droit international dans l'Iliade et dans l'Odyssée," *RGDI* 21 (1914): 29–63; L.-M. Wéry, "Le fonctionnement de la diplomatie à l'époque homerique," *RIDA* 14 (1967): 169–205 (= E. Olshausen and H. Biller, eds., *Antike Diplomatie*, Wege der Forschung 462 [Darmstadt, 1979], 13–53); D. Cohen, "'Horkia' and 'horkos' in the *Iliad*," *RIDA* 27 (1980): 49–68; P. Karavites, "Diplomatic Envoys in the Homeric World," *RIDA* 34 (1987): 41–100. Cohen states: "It should be pointed out that the use of legal terms like 'treaty' and 'truce' is not meant to imply that such concepts are present in Homer as part of a clearly formulated system of formal law. The relatively clear separation that we make today between law and custom, and law and morality, is not found in the Homeric world and thus such terms are not to be taken in their modern technical senses" (49 n. 1).

2. In earlier poetry, a fragment of Callinus of Ephesus (fl. first half of the seventh century) criticizes youths who sit at peace (*en eirēnē histasi*) while the land is full of war (Stob. *Anth.* 15.19 = Callinus frag. 1, J. M. Edmonds, ed., *Elegy and Iambus*, vol. 1, Loeb Classical Library [Cambridge, Mass., and London, 1931], 44–45). This may refer to a group that believed—wrongly in Callinus' view— that they could safely abstain from involvement; but these would-be nonpartici- pants may simply be foolishly wasting time, oblivious to the reality that war has already reached their country and made further procrastination suicidal. If the latter interpretation is correct, the Callinus fragment then belongs with other archaic period exhortations to young men aimed at promoting their participation in state-sponsored warfare (see, for example, the poetry of Tyrtaeus at Sparta; L. B. Carter, *The Quiet Athenian* [Oxford, 1986], 8–9). Already in epic the potentially disastrous effects of abstention or even delayed involvement are empha- sized by Phoenix in the tale of Meleager (*Il.* 9. 527–605), the point of which is to convince Achilles to end his abstention and return to battle.

will remain safe simply by avoiding involvement when factional
fighting erupts within the *polis*. So inexorable, he warns, is the
momentum of violence during *stasis* that

> thus does city-wide evil come into every house, and the outer doors
> will no longer be able to hold it back; but it leaps the high hedge
> and finds every man, even if he flees into the farthest recess of his
> bedchamber.[3]

According to later sources, Solon's solution to dealing with an
element of the populace that abstained during *stasis* in the expectation that that policy would provide immunity against injury from
either of the warring factions was to outlaw specifically the option
of individual political neutrality. His law, famous in antiquity and
often discussed since,[4] identified the offending group as "whosoever

3. Trans. Edmonds, *Elegy and Iambus*, vol. 1, 118–21.

> οὕτω δημόσιον κακὸν ἔρχεται οἴκαδ' ἑκάστῳ,
> αὔλειοι δ' ἔτ' ἔχειν οὐκ ἐθέλουσι θύραι,
> ὑψηλὸν δ' ὑπὲρ ἕρκος ὑπέρθορεν, εὗρε δὲ πάντως,
> εἰ καί τις φεύγων ἐν μυχῷ ᾖ θαλάμου.

(Solon frag. 4. 26–29, M. L. West, ed., *Iambi et Elegi Graeci*,
vol. 2 [Oxford, 1972] [= Dem. 19 (*False Leg.*). 254])

4. For the law, see Arist. *Ath. Pol.* 8.5; Cic. *Att.* 10. 1.2; Au. Gell. 2. 12, who
cites Favorinus' adaptation of the law to domestic quarrels (12.5) and provides
the most detailed ancient reference:

> Among those very early laws of Solon which were inscribed upon
> wooden tablets at Athens, and which, promulgated by him, the Atheni-
> ans ratified by penalties and oaths, to ensure their permanence, Aristotle
> says that there was one to this effect: "If because of strife and dis-
> agreement civil dissension shall ensue and a division of the people into
> two parties, and if for that reason each side, led by their angry feelings,
> shall take up arms and fight, then if anyone at that time, and in such a
> condition of civil discord, shall not ally himself with one or the other
> faction, but by himself and apart shall hold aloof from the common
> calamity of the State, let him be deprived of his home, his country, and
> all his property, and be an exile and an outlaw."   (trans. J. C. Rolfe,
> *Aulus Gellius*, Loeb Classical Library [New York and London, 1927])

For subsequent references and comment, see Plut. *Sol.* 20.1; *Mor.* 550C, 823F,
965D; Diog. Laert. 1. 58; Cantacuzen 4. 13; Nicephorus Gregora 9. 6 *fin* (cf. also
Dio [quoted below in note 7]). References to Solon's law from the sixteenth
through the eighteenth century include B. Ayala, *De iure et officiis bellicis et
disciplina militari libri III*, bk. 1 (Douay, 1582), 17 (trans. J. P. Bate, *Classics of
International Law*, vol. 2 [Oxford, 1912], 14); D. Hume, *Enquiry Concerning the
Principles of Morals* (London, 1751), Conclusion, sec. 9, part 1, in *Hume's Moral
and Political Philosophy*, ed. H. D. Aiken (New York, 1948), 254–55. The law's
authenticity has been debated intensely. Among those denying it are R. Sealey,
"How Citizenship and the City Began in Athens," *AJAH* 8 (1983): 97–129;
E. David, "Solon, Neutrality and Partisan Literature of Late Fifth-Century

failed to take arms with one side or the other" and punished their failure to align themselves with loss of all civic rights (*atimia*).[5]

Solon's strongly negative attitude toward any politically neutral element in the *polis* contrasts sharply with the very positive characterization found in Theognis of Megara (fl. 540s). Theognis gives the following advice to his friend Kyrnos when the state is torn by *stasis*:

> Be not overly vexed while your fellow citizens are in an uproar, Kyrnos, but follow the middle path as I do.[6]

Not surprisingly, Theognis employs exactly the kind of rhetoric we would expect from a proponent of neutrality. The description of the policy as a "middle path" rather than (as in Solon) a "standing aside" associates it with moderation and adherence to the Mean rather than with the more negative ideas of separation and exclusion.

Sources after the archaic period often identify abstaining parties from these perspectives. For example, Xenophon follows the line of Theognis when he identifies the neutral policy of the Achaean

---

Athens," *Mus Helv* 41 (1984): 129–38; J. Bleicken, "Zum sogenannten Stasis-Gesetz Solons," *Symposium für Alfred Heuss*, Frankfurter Althistorische Studien 12 (Kallmünz, 1986): 9–18; Ch. Percorella Longo, "Sulla legge 'soloniana' contro la neutralità," *Historia* 37 (1988): 374–79; accepting it, J. A. Goldstein, "Solon's Law for an Activist Citizenry," *Historia* 21 (1972): 538–45; V. Bers, "Solon's Law Forbidding Neutrality and Lysias 32," *Historia* 24 (1975): 493–98; B. Manville, "Solon's Law of *Stasis* and *Atimia* in Archaic Athens," *TAPA* 110 (1980): 213–21; P. J. Rhodes, *A Commentary on the Aristotelian Athenaion Politeia* (Oxford, 1981), 157; J. M. Rainer, "Über die *Atimie* in den griechischen Inschriften," *RIDA* 33 (1986): 89–114. On balance the case against authenticity is indecisive and ignores the important implication of the Solonian fragment quoted above in note 3, where Solon himself expresses deep concern about citizens who believe it is safe to abstain from *stasis*.

5. ὁρῶν δὲ τὴν μὲν πόλιν πολλάκις στασιάζουσαν, τῶν δὲ πολιτῶν ἐνίους διὰ τὴν ῥαθυμίαν [ἀγα]πῶντας τὸ αὐτόματον, νόμον ἔθηκεν πρὸς αὐτοὺς ἴδιον, ὅς ἄν στασια-ζούσης τῆς πόλεως μ[ὴ] θῆται τὰ ὅπλα μηδὲ μεθ' ἑτέρων, ἄτιμον εἶναι καὶ τῆς πόλεως μὴ μετέχειν. (Arist. *Ath. Pol.* 8. 5).

6. Μηδὲν ἄγαν ἄσχαλλε ταρασυομένων πολιητέων,
     Κύρνε, μέσην δ' ἔρχευ τὴν ὁδὸν ὥσπερ ἐγώ.
                         (Theog. 219–20)

Compare the similar language and sentiment in Theognis 331–32, 399–400, 945–46; see also the oracle reportedly given to Solon (*hēso mesēn kata nēa, kybernētērion ergon euthyōn* "sit in the middle of the ship, steering like a pilot" Plut. *Sol.* 14.6). D. B. Levine, "Symposium and the *Polis*," in *Theognis of Megara*, ed. T. Figueira and G. Nagy (Baltimore and London, 1985), 180–81, unfortunately ignores the positive characterization of neutrality in Theognis.

city-states with the verb *emeseuon* ("they were following a middle policy," i.e., "they were neutral").[7] Thucydides, on the other hand, introduces a great variety of expressions (see the full list below) of both types, ranging from *ekpodōn histantes amphoterois* ("standing aloof from both sides") to *ta mesa tōn politōn* ("the middle segment of the citizenry" [i.e., belonging to neither faction]).[8] Herodotus even merges the two perspectives in the phrase *ek tou mesou katēmenoi* ("standing aloof in the middle").[9]

In most instances, however, the sources identify parties that stand outside of a given conflict simply in terms of their inactivity. They "keep quiet" (*hēsychian agousi*) or are "holding (or maintaining) peace" (*eirēnēn echousi* or *agousi*). Unfortunately, these expressions can be frustratingly vague for the purpose of understanding what such a posture might mean in its relationship to the parties at conflict. Worse still, neutral parties very rarely characterize their policy for themselves. Instead, what we normally get is the perception of others and the inevitable subjectivity that accompanies their attitude toward the nonparticipants.

On the rare occasions when uncommitted parties characterize their position for themselves, as in the fragment of Theognis quoted above or in the speech that Thucydides attributes to the Corcyraeans (2. 32–36), they naturally use language that supports and emphasizes the formal legitimacy and fairness of their position. This is especially clear in Thucydides' presentation of opposing Corcyraean and Corinthian speeches given at Athens in 433 (1. 32–43). The Corcyraeans content that they have previously been allies of no one (*symmachoi oudenos hekousioi genomenoi* 1. 32.4) because they considered it wise (*sōphrosynē*) to pursue a policy of avoiding active involvement with other states (i.e., pursuing *apragmosynē* 32.5). However, the danger of the present war with Corinth and its allies has now made them realize that this policy was a mistake (*hamartia* 32.5); and, they argue, since they have not been allied with either the Peloponnesians or Athenians (*mēdamou sym-*

---

7. Xen. *Hell.* 7. 1.43 (cf. Dio 41. 46: [Καῖσαρ] ὑπώπτευσέ σφας μεσεύειν τε καὶ ἐφεδρεύειν τοῖς πράγμασιν, οἷά που ἐν στάσεσι φιλεῖ γίγνεσθαι "[Caesar] suspected that they had adopted a neutral attitude and were watching the course of events, as often happens in civil strife" [trans. E. Cary, *Dio Cassius*, Loeb Classical Library (New York and London, 1927)]).

8. *ekpodōn* (Thuc. 1. 40.4); *ta mesa* (3. 82.8).

9. Hdt. 4. 118.2; 8. 22.2, 73.3 (cf. 3. 83.3).

machousi 35.2), Athens is free to accept them as allies without violating the existing peace (*Lakedaimoniōn spondas* 35.1).

What makes this speech especially important for understanding the contemporary diplomatic situation is its extraordinarily sensitive manipulation of political language. Through their careful choice of words, the Corcyraeans reinforce the legitimacy, and thus the acceptability, of their previous policy by characterizing it with highly charged political vocabulary transferred from the context of internal political debate into the realm of foreign affairs (note especially *sōphrosynē* and *apragmosynē*).[10] As V. Ehrenberg pointed out long ago,

> *apragmosynē* involved anti-imperialism, non-aggressive policy, quiet attitude and therefore peace. Even the word which in general expressed the Greek ideal of moderation, modesty and wisdom, *sōphrosynē*, gained political meaning and sided with *hēsychia* against the restlessness of the imperialists. To Thucydides *sōphronein* was almost identical with being a conservative and an enemy of the radical democrats.[11]

In essence then, Thucydides represents the Corcyraeans as seeking to legitimize their diplomatic objectives by usurping the "hottest" political buzzwords of the day and applying them to the defense of their foreign policy, past and present.

The language of the opposing Corinthian speech also contains

---

10. Of numerous studies, see particularly W. Nestle, "Ἀπραγμοσύνη," *Philologus* 81 (1925): 129–40; V. Ehrenberg, "*Polypragmosynē*: A Study in Greek Politics," *JHS* 67 (1947): 46–67; H. North, "A Period of Opposition to Sophrosynē in Greek Thought," *TAPA* 78 (1947): 1–17; G. Grossman, *Politische Schlagwörter aus der Zeit des peloponnesischen Krieges* (Zurich, 1950), 126–37; K. Kleve, "*Apragmosynē* and *Polypragmosynē*: Two Slogans in Athenian Politics," *Symbolae Osloenses* 39 (1964): 83–88; A. W. H. Adkins, "*Polupragmosunē* and 'Minding One's Own business': A Study in Greek Social and Political Values," *CP* 71 (1976): 301–27; J. W. Allison, "Thucydides and *Polypragmosynē*," *AJAH* 4 (1979): 10–22; P. Harding, "In Search of a Poly-pragmatist," in *Classical Contributions: Studies in Honour of Malcolm Francis McGregor*, ed. G. S. Shrimpton and D. J. McCargar (Locust Valley, N.Y., 1981), 41–50; Carter, *Quiet Athenian*. Also noteworthy is C. Collard, ed., Euripides, *Supplices*, vol. 2: *Commentary* (Groningen, 1975), 192–94, who cites the perceptive comments of R. A. Neil, ed., *The Knights of Aristophanes* (Cambridge, 1901), 41–42 (on line 261) and Appendix II, "Political Use of Moral Terms," 206–9.

11. Ehrenberg, "*Polypragmosynē*: A Study of Greek Politics," 52; on the diplomacy of Corcyra, Ehrenberg concludes: "Neutrality is conceived here as a form of political inactivity. Not to take sides, which seemed wrong in domestic policy, had become impracticable in foreign policy." J. Wilson, *Corcyra and Athens: Strategy and Tactics in the Peloponnesian War* (Bristol, 1987), unfortunately pays no attention to these issues. For further discussion, see 5.3.C below.

much contemporary political rhetoric transferred into the realm of interstate diplomacy; but for the specific investigation of neutrality, the critical point is that the Corinthian envoys concede—albeit grudgingly—that the *policy* of the Corcyraeans is itself legitimate enough. What they condemn is the Corcyraeans' alleged abuse of an acceptable policy for unjust and illegitimate ends, pointing out that the Corcyraeans "say that 'a wise discretion' (*to sōphron*) has hitherto kept them from accepting an alliance with anyone (*symmachian oudenos dexasthai*); but the fact is that they adopted this policy with a view to villainy (*kakourgia*) and not from virtuous motives (*aretē*)."[12] In the case of Corcyra, say the Corinthians, "this legitimate-sounding nonalignment" (*touto to euprepes aspondon* 37.4) is only a specious cover for wrongdoing (*hopōs adikōsi*). The diplomatic reality lying beneath this rhetorical blanket is clear: the international community of states accepts the existence of a category of states that stand aloof from the major alliances; and the legitimacy of that policy has to be conceded. However, what can be rigorously contested is the specific behavior of the Corcyraeans while they claim to be pursuing this policy. Furthermore, in the absence of standard diplomatic definitions and terminology, the speakers have considerable freedom to manipulate the language used for identifying the position of an uncommitted state. The resulting vocabulary therefore reflects the attitude of the speaker toward the specific policy of the state involved; and because the language itself is strongly politicized, the description becomes tainted with the speaker's personal prejudices.

The subjective content of the language is immediately noticeable. For example, along with such a noncommittal identification of would-be neutrals as "those remaining inactive" (*hoi hēsychian* or *eirēnēn agontes* or *echontes*), speakers supporting the legitimacy of abstention employ vocabulary with positive overtones, such as "those maintaining peace with all parties" (*hoi eirēnēn agontes pros hapantas*), "allies of neither side" (*mēdeterois symmachousi*), or those "for whom there existed friendship with both sides" (*toutois d' es amphoterous philia ēn*). The last of these characteriza-

12. Trans. C. F. Smith, *Thucydides*, Loeb Classical Library, rev. ed. (Cambridge, Mass., and London, 1928). Φασὶ δὲ ξυμμαχίαν διὰ τὸ σῶφρον οὐδενός πω δέξασθαι· τὸ δ' ἐπὶ κακουργίᾳ καὶ οὐκ ἀρετῇ ἐπετήδευσαν, ξύμμαχόν τε οὐδένα βουλόμενοι πρὸς τἀδικήματα οὐδὲ μάρτυρα ἔχειν οὔτε παρακαλοῦντες αἰσχύνεσθαι (Thuc. 1. 37.2).

tions has especially important meaning and will be discussed at
length below (see 3.4). For the moment, it should suffice to emphasize that the "friendship" (*philia*) referred to here is not the same
as the private relationship based on an emotional state of mind but
involves a quite different, formal diplomatic relationship between
states.

Since, however, it was painfully obvious that when a state
sought to abstain from a given conflict, it would naturally also
desire to be exempted from violent treatment by either belligerent,
some kind of obligation had to be created that could restrain the
belligerents. To achieve this end, that is, to secure recognition and
thus attain the status of what we would call a neutral party, the
abstaining states (and/or those who supported their policy) resorted
to rhetoric that they hoped would engender restraint on the part
of the belligerents. Hence, the characterization of nonparticipants
as parties seeking to maintain "peace" or "friendship" (or both;
e.g., Diod. 13. 85.2: *hēsychian echein kai philous einai . . . en eirēnē
menontas*) became a correspondingly important linguistic means
employed by would-be neutrals to achieve and protect their policy
(see, for example, 6.5 below [Corcyra's declaration of *philia* toward
the Peloponnesians in 427]).

Among the subjective political terms used to characterize the
attitude of neutral parties the adjective *koinos* (in the sense of
"impartial") deserves special comment. In modern international
law the status of neutrality carries with it a strict obligation of
impartiality. Despite their own rhetorical emphasis on the relationship of "friendship" for the belligerents, both ancient and modern
states standing aloof from conflicts have virtually always recognized
that maintaining an impartial posture can be crucial to the success
of their policy. This is, for instance, the delicate situation reflected
in the careful wording of George Washington's declaration of
American neutrality published in 1793: "The duty and interest of
the United States require that they should, with sincerity and good
faith, adopt and pursue a conduct friendly and impartial toward
the belligerent powers."[13] Very similar rhetoric appears in the
description of diplomacy in fifth- and fourth-century Greece. Thucydides, for example, reports that in 427 the Spartans condemned
the Plataeans, who surrendered after a long siege of their city, in

13. *American State Papers*, 2d ed. (Boston, 1817), 44–45.

part on the grounds that

> when, before the siege was undertaken, [the Spartans] had proposed to [the Plataeans] that they be impartial (*koinoi*) in accordance with the earlier agreement, [the Plataeans] rejected it.[14]

Similarly, in a speech written for the Plataeans after the Thebans had expelled them from their city in 373, Isocrates attempted to arouse Athenian indignation against Thebes by accusing that state of failure either to support Athens or, at least, to adopt a self-restrained policy of impartiality in the Athenians' ongoing struggle with Sparta:

> The Chians and Mytilenaeans and the Byzantines remained loyal; but these [Thebans], though they lived in so great a city, did not even have the courage to remain impartial (*koinous*) but stooped to such cowardice and treachery that they even swore to join [the Spartans] in attacking you who had saved their city.[15]

These examples show at least that impartiality could be made to be the critical feature of a state's abstention; and in a more subtle and potentially insidious way, the word *koinos* carries with it an important overtone derived from its regular association with the absolutely essential impartiality demanded of the law and of judges.[16] Since a fair and impartial legal and judicial structure had a very basic association in the classical Greek mind, transference of the idea to neutrality in interstate diplomacy must surely represent—as the history of neutrality shows—a seemingly fair, but in fact impossibly restrictive, requirement intended more for

14. καὶ ὅτε ὕστερον [ἃ] πρὸ τοῦ περιτειχίζεσθαι προείχοντο αὐτοῖς, κοινοὺς εἶναι κατ' ἐκεῖνα, ὡς οὐκ ἐδέξαντο (Thuc. 3. 68.1). The reference to an earlier agreement is presumably to the covenant made with the Greek general Pausanias after the Persian defeat in 479 mentioned just before the sentence quoted. Unfortunately the Greek text is corrupt here; most editors follow Badham's conjecture *kat' ekeinas*, which C. F. Smith translated "in accordance with the earlier agreement," adopted here.

15. καὶ Χῖοι μὲν καὶ Μυτιληναῖοι καὶ Βυζάντιοι συμπαρέμειναν, οὗτοι δὲ τηλικαύτην πόλιν οἰκοῦντες οὐδὲ κοινοὺς σφᾶς αὐτοὺς παρασχεῖν ἐτόλμησαν, ἀλλ' εἰς τοῦτ' ἀνανδρίας καὶ πονηρίας ἦλθον, ὥστ' ὤμοσαν ἦ μὴν ἀκολουθήσειν μετ' ἐκείνων ἐφ' ὑμᾶς τοὺς διασώσαντας τὴν πόλιν αὐτῶν (Isoc. 14 [*Plat.*]. 28).

16. See *LSJ*, 9th ed. s.v. *koinos* IV: 3; for examples of the identification of *koinos* with judgment, see, for instance, Isoc. 7 (*Areop.*). 20, 70; 8 (*Peace*). 11; Plut. *Arist.* 21.2; but cf. Thuc. 5. 79.1 (δίκας διδόντες τὰς ἴσας), 4 (ἴσαν ἀμφοῖν), which represent variations echoed in subsequent authors, e.g., Xen. *Hell.* 5. 3.10: οἱ μὲν γὰρ δὴ φυγάδες ἀξίουν τὰ ἀμφίλογα ἐν ἴσῳ δικαστηρίῳ κρίνεσθαι; Isoc. 4 (*Paneg.*). 176: ἴσως καὶ κοινῶς ἀμφοτέροις; 12 (*Panath.*). 130: κοινοτάτης καὶ δικαιοτάτης.

the purpose of challenging the legitimacy of the neutral's position and justifying its violation than for supporting the neutral's claim to unmolested exemption.

It should be clear from this brief overview of the language used to identify and describe nonparticipants that although no standard nomenclature ever evolved, the lack of specialized terminology did not in itself prevent anyone either from identifying parties whose policy put them in a separate category of uncommitted nonbelligerents or from characterizing their policy. It therefore follows that even though the available vocabulary may have been used in most instances without relation to a specific policy, there is no reason to deny that in the proper context a variety of words and phrases could be used to communicate accurately the special sense of a formal diplomatic posture.

The question remains, however, Why did diplomatic terms like "alliance" (*symmachia*) and "friendship" (*philia*), not to mention international political concepts like "self-determination" (*autonomia*) and "freedom" (*eleutheria*), exist in ancient Greek, while there were no terms to indicate specifically and unambiguously the wartime position of parties that adopted a position that was neither hostile nor supportive of the opposing belligerents? If neutrality (as we call it) came to be a generally recognized and valued concept in the framework of classical Greek diplomacy, would not linguistic specificity follow?

At the very least, the overall lack of specific terminology suggests that the formal diplomatic idea (in its modern sense) either was not fully understood or, even if it was, failed to achieve any commonly recognized definition. And even if we concede that judging ancient practice by a modern standard would be an unfair test of the definition of formal abstention in classical Greek diplomacy, the great variety of expressions used to identify abstaining parties does seem to indicate that there was no precise and exclusive concept of neutrality. This certainly does not mean that states (or individuals) could not pursue this policy, but only that the exact meaning of the policy was not automatically defined by the terminology applied to it. Instead, what we appear to have is something more fluid, in which the designation of rights and obligations does not have permanent specification and structure but achieves detailed form from the particular context out of which the policy arises.

ANCIENT GREEK DESCRIPTIONS OF NEUTRAL PARTIES

Solon (as quoted by Aristotle)

ὃς ἂν στασιάζουσαν τῆς πόλεως μὴ θῆται τὰ ὅπλα μηδὲ μεθ᾽ ἑτέρων *Ath. Pol.* 8.5 (cf. Plut. below).

Theognis

Μηδὲν ἄγαν ἄσχαλλε ταρασσομένων πολιητέων, Κύρνε, μέσην δ᾽ ἔρχευ τὴν ὁδόν, ὥσπερ ἐγώ 219–20 (cf. 331–32 = Stob., *Anth.* 15.6: Ἥσυχος ὥσπερ ἐγώ, μέσσην ὁδὸν ἔρχεο ποσσίν).

Εἶμι παρὰ στάθμην ὀρθὴν ὁδόν, οὐδετέρωσε κλινόμενος, χρὴ γάρ μ᾽ ἄρτια πάντα νοεῖν 945–46 (but cf. his concern over public opinion in 367–70).

Herodotus

ἐκ τοῦ μέσου κατήμενοι 4. 118.2; 8. 22.2, 73.3 (cf. 3. 83.3).

ἡσυχίην ἦγον (ἔχειν) 1. 169.2; 7. 150.2, 3.

Thucydides

ἄσπονδον 1. 37.4.

ξύμμαχοι οὐδενόσπω ... γενόμενοι 1. 32.4.

ἐκποδὼν στῆναι ἀμφοτέροις 1. 40.4.

ἡσυχίαν ἄγειν (ἔχειν) 5. 94.

ἐς ἡσυχίαν 3. 64.3.

ἡσυχάζειν 2. 7.2; 3. 68.1, 71.1; 5. 84.2; 7. 12.1, 58.1.

κοινούς 3. 68.1.

μηδὲ μεθ᾽ ἑτέρων (εἶναι) 2. 67.4, 72.1.
    οὐδὲ μεθ᾽ ἑτέρων εἶναι 6. 44.3; 7. 33.2.
    οὐδετέρων ὄντες 5. 84.2.

μηδετέροις ἀμύνειν 3. 6; 6. 88.2.
    μηδετέροις ξυμμαχοῦσι 5. 98.
    ξυμμάχους εἶναι μηδετέρων 1. 35.1; 5. 18.5, 94, 112.3; 8. 2.1.

ξυμμαχίαν οὐδενὸς δέξασθαι 1. 37.1.
    ξύμμαχοι ... πλήν 2. 9.2, 4.

οὐ ξυναράμενοι τοῦ Ἀττικοῦ πολέμου, ἀμφοτέροις δὲ μᾶλλον ἔνσπονδαι ὄντες 5. 28.2 (cf. Andoc. 3 [*On the Peace*]. 27).

παντάπασιν ἀφειστήκει τοῦ πολέμου 7. 7.2.

τούτοις δ᾽ ἐς ἀμφοτέρους φιλία εἶναι 2. 9.2.

φίλους μὲν εἶναι ἀντὶ πολεμίων, ξυμμάχους δὲ μηδετέρων 5. 94.

Euripides

προσῆκον γ' οὐδὲν Ἀργείων πόλει.
κἂν μὲν πίθῃ μοι, κυμάτων ἄτερ πόλιν
σὴν ναυστολήσεις. εἰ δὲ μή, πολὺς κλύδων
ἡμῖν τε καὶ σοὶ συμμάχοις τ' ἔσται δορός Supp. 472–75.

Aristophanes

οὐδ' οἶδε γ' εἷλκον οὐδὲν Ἀργεῖοι πάλαι.
ἀλλ' ἢ κατεγέλων τῶν ταλαιπωρουμένων,
καὶ ταῦτα διχόθεν μισθοφοροῦντες ἄλφιτα Peace 475–77.

Andocides

εἰρήνην ἄγειν (ἔχειν) 3 (On the Peace). 28.

Xenophon

εἰ δέ τις παρὰ ταῦτα ποιοίη, τὸν μὲν βουλόμενον βοηθεῖν ταῖς ἀδικουμέναις πόλεσι, τῷ δὲ μὴ βουλομένῳ μὴ εἶναι ἔνορκον συμμαχεῖν τοῖς
ἀδικουμένοις Hell. 6. 3.18 (cf. Thuc. 6. 88.2).

ἡσυχίαν ἄγειν (ἔχειν) Hell. 6. 1.14.

εἰρήνην ἄγειν Hell. 6. 1.18.

ἐμέσευον Hell. 7. 1.43 (cf. Dio 41.46).

Isocrates

κοινός 14 (Plat.). 28.

Oxyrhynchus Historian

ἐφ' ἑαυτῶν μένοντες οὔτε ἄνδρας οὔτε ναῦς ἔδωκαν καὶ οὐδενὶ συνεμάχ-
[ουν] Jacoby, FGH IIA, no. 105: 3 (P Oxy. VI 857).

Decree of Greek States ca. 362

ἡσυχίαν ἄγειν (ἔχειν) Dittenberger, SIG³ no. 182, line 9 (= Tod,
no. 145; Bengtson, SVA² no. 292).

Demosthenes

ἐπὶ πολλῆς ἡσυχίας 14 (Symm.). 8.

Polybius

ἡσυχίαν ἄγειν (ἔχειν) 4. 31.5, 36.8; 9. 32.12, 39.5; 29. 8.5, 7.

πρὸς ἡσυχίαν ὁρμήσατε 9. 39.7.

τῶν ἄλλων Ἑλληνικῶν πράξεων οὐδ' ὁποίας μετεῖχον 5. 106.7.

Diodorus

ἡσυχίαν ἄγειν (ἔχειν) 11. 3.3, 5; 12. 42.4; 13. 85.2; 16. 27.4, 33.2, 3.

ἡσυχίαν ἔχειν καὶ φίλους εἶναι Καρχηδονίοις ἐν εἰρήνῃ μένοντας 13. 85.2.

ἡσυχίαν εἵλοντο 18. 11.1.
μένειν ἐφ' ἡσυχίας καὶ τηρεῖν τὴν πρὸς ἀμφοτέρους εἰρήνην ἅμα καὶ φιλίαν 19. 77.7 (cf. 20. 81.2, 4).

εἰρήνην ἄγειν 13. 4.2.
κοινὴν εἰρήνην ἄγειν πρὸς ἅπαντας 20. 46.6.

σύμμαχοι ... πλήν 12. 42.5 (cf. 20. 99.3; Plut. Dem. 22.8).

τὴν ἐλευθερίαν διεφύλαττον 14. 84.4.

τούτων μὲν οὐδετέρῳ προσέθετο 20. 105.1.

Plutarch

ἄτιμον εἶναι τὸν ἐν στάσει μηδετέρας μερίδος γενόμενον Sol. 20.1.

παραλογώτατον δὲ τοῦ Σόλωνος, ἄτιμον εἶναι τὸν ἐν στάσει πόλεως μηδετέρᾳ μερίδι προσθέμενον μηδὲ συστασιάσαντα Mor. 550C.

[Σόλων] ἔγραψεν ἄτιμον εἶναι τὸν ἐν στάσει πόλεως μηδετέροις προσθέμενον Mor. 823F (cf. 824B).

[Autobulus] δῆλός ἐστι ... ὡς μηδετέροις προσθήσων ἑαυτόν. ἢ φαύλως εἰκάζομεν, ὦ φίλε Ὀπτᾶτε, κοινόν σε καὶ μέσον ἔσεσθαι ... [Optatus] πάλαι γὰρ ὁ Σόλωνος ἐκλέλοιπε νόμος, τοὺς ἐν στάσει μεδετέρῳ μέρει προσγενομένους κολάζων Mor. 965D.

Dio Cassius

πολλοὺς μὲν τῶν ἐκ τοῦ μέσου καθημένων προσχωρῆσαι 9. 21.

[Καῖσαρ] ὑπώπτευσέ σφας μεσεύειν τε καὶ ἐφεδρεύειν τοῖς πράγμασιν, οἷά που ἐν στάσεσι φιλεῖ γίγνεσθαι 41. 46.

The collection of expressions provided in the above list shows that no standard terminology for abstaining parties ever evolved in the classical period. Instead, authors used a wide range of words and phrases borrowed from everyday language as appropriate to the particular context of the reference. On the basis of the greatest frequency of occurrence, *hēsychian agein* or *echein* (together with *hēsychazein*), literally "to keep peace" or "to stay quiet," comes the closest to being conventional language for identifying specifically neutral parties. However, as a characterization of diplomatic policy, this phrase is entirely noncommittal. It communicates noth-

ing more than the passive inactivity of the nonparticipant and thus
provides no information about the nature of the relationship
between the party "remaining at peace" and the belligerents. By
itself, the phrase is, in fact, too vague even to indicate the existence
of formal diplomatic policy unless the author supplies a supporting
description that clarifies that the inactivity is the result of policy
and not chance or indifference. Fortunately, in most cases this
distinction is easily recognized. Take the following examples.

In Herodotus, Hecataeus urges Aristagoras to build a fort on
the island of Leros and keep quiet (*hēsychian agein*) there (5. 125);
the Persian fleet keeps quiet (*hēsychian agei*) at Aphetae the morn-
ing after many ships are sunk in the Hollows of Euboea (8. 14.1);
and Candaules' wife keeps quiet (*hēsychian echei*) for the moment
when she sees Gyges slip from her bedroom (1. 11.1). These examples communicate nothing more than simple inactivity. However,
Herodotus also states that Xerxes reportedly asked the Argives to
remain at peace (using both *hēsychian agein* and *hēsychian echein*)
when he invaded Greece (7. 150.2–3) and reports that because of
their treaty with Cyrus, the Milesians supported neither side but
remained at peace (*hēsychian ēgagon*) when the Persians invaded
Ionia (1. 169.2). Here there is real diplomatic policy. Likewise, in
Thucydides *hēsychian agein/echein* varies in meaning according to
the context. For example, the Macedonian cavalry, after initially
attacking Sitalces' expedition, find themselves so far outnumbered
that they cease their opposition and keep quiet (*hēsychian agousi*
2. 100.6); but the Melians reportedly ask the Athenians to allow
them to remain at peace (*hēsychian agousi*) and be friends instead
of enemies, but allies of neither side (5. 94).

Numerous other examples could be cited. But the point is that
although in the vast majority of instances the use of *hēsychian
agein/echein* has no relationship to diplomatic posture, it nevertheless can and repeatedly does communicate the idea of inaction due
to policy. And when this special idea is meant, it repeatedly appears
to represent something very much like the modern idea of neutrality.[17]

17. Most translators recognize this special contextual meaning and render the
phrase (together with the verb *hēsychazein*) accordingly, despite the *opinio com-
munis* among legal historians that no such idea existed. Take, for example, Thuc.
2. 72.1, which is translated "at least (as we have also advised you formerly) be
quiet, and enjoy your own in neutrality; receiving both sides in the way of

SUMMARY

The linguistic limitations of ancient Greek are a feature constantly acknowledged in modern analyses of classical institutions. G. Herman, for example, emphasizes in his recent study, *Ritualised Friendship and the Greek City*, that in classical and later Greek there existed no exclusive vocabulary for the notion of a bribe:

> What is remarkable about these words [i.e., those used to communicate the idea] is their ambiguity. For they signify at one and the same time the concept of bribe and the (to us) logically opposed concepts of "gift," "money" and "reward." In other words, there was in the Greek language no vocabulary of bribery distinct from that of gift-exchange itself; the same set of words served to denote both practices.[18]

Likewise, J. de Romilly begins her analysis in *Thucydides and Athenian Imperialism* with the cautionary explanation that

> there is no word in Greek to express the idea of imperialism. There is simply one to indicate the fact of ruling over people, or to indicate the people ruled over as a group: that is the word *archē*. Nevertheless, imperialism, and especially Athenian imperialism, is a very precise idea for a Greek.[19]

And so it is for formal abstention from warfare. Euripides' Creon may not demand Athenian "neutrality" by name in his state's struggle with Argive Adrastus; but, through his Theban herald, he nevertheless makes the desired policy perfectly clear:

> But I and all the Cadmean people warn you not to receive Adrastus into this land. ... Do not take up the dead by force, since you have nothing to do with Argos. And if you are persuaded by me, you

---

friendship, neither side in the way of faction" (Hobbes); "but if you prefer to be neutral, a course which we have already once proposed to you" (Jowett); "do what we have already required of you—remain neutral, enjoying your own" (Crawley); "then do what we have already asked you to do: remain neutral and live independently" (Werner). Compare the noncommittal translation of C. F. Smith: "otherwise keep quiet, as we have already proposed, continuing to enjoy your own possessions." But elsewhere Smith specifically equates *hēsychian agein* with neutral policy, as in Thuc. 5. 94 (on which see Smith's note on 5. 98). So too Gomme, *HCT*, vol. 4, 167, who comments that *hēsychian agontas* in 5. 94 is "a clear case of this meaning 'to be neutral'."

18. G. Herman, *Ritualised Friendship and the Greek City* (Cambridge, 1987), 75.

19. J. de Romilly, *Thucydides and Athenian Imperialism*, trans. P. Thody (Oxford, 1963), 13.

will steer your city apart from the stormwaves; but if not, there will
be a great tempest of war for us and for you and for our respective
allies.[20]

In short, Athens' neutrality will maintain peace; alignment will
bring war.

There is no doubt that Argos was a recognized neutral state
during the Archidamian War (431–421; see 6.1 below). Thucydides
duly reports this, but the exact language he uses to describe the
Argives' diplomatic position is remarkably vague by modern standards: "The Argives had not taken part in the Athenian [i.e.,
Archidamian] War, and being at peace with both sides, had reaped
much profit from them."[21] There is nothing technical in the language here, yet the description seems quite obviously to indicate a
recognized, formal position, which Thucydides' contemporaries
would understand and could identify, characterize, and even
conceptualize—all in the absence of specialized vocabulary. If not,
how can we explain Thucydides' concern to clarify that the presence of an Argive citizen, Pollis, on a Spartan embassy to the
Persian king in 430 was "unofficial" (idia 2. 67.1), that is, not a
violation of the expected behavior (the obligation) of the officially
neutral state of Argos? Aristophanes plays to his audience's understanding of this and has Hermes complain in the Peace:

> These Argives, too, they give no help at all.
> They only laugh at us, our toils and troubles,
> And all the while take pay from either side.[22]

Surely, the audience must laugh, if they can, at the contradiction

---

20. ἐγὼ δ' ἀπαυδῶ πᾶς τε Καδμεῖος λεώς
     Ἄδραστον ἐς γῆν τήνδε μὴ παριέναι·
     εἰ δ' ἔστιν ἐν γῇ, πρὶν θεοῦ δῦναι σέλας,
     λύσαντα σεμνὰ στεμμάτων μυστήρια
     τῆσδ' ἐξελαύνειν, μηδ' ἀναιρεῖσθαι νεκροὺς
     βίᾳ προσήκοντ' οὐδὲν Ἀργείων πόλει.
     κἂν μὲν πίθῃ μοι, κυμάτων ἄτερ πόλιν
     σὴν ναυστολήσεις· εἰ δὲ μή, πολὺς κλύδων
     ἡμῖν τε καὶ σοὶ συμμάχοις τ' ἔσται δορός.
                                    (Eur. Supp. 467–75)

See Collard, Euripides, Supplices, vol. 2, 233–36; he interprets the herald's speech
as follows: "Athens' neutrality will maintain peace, intervention will bring war"
(233).
     21. οἵ τε Ἀργεῖοι ἄριστα ἔσχον τοῖς πᾶσιν, οὐ ξυναράμενοι τοῦ Ἀττικοῦ πολέμου,
ἀμφοτέροις δὲ μᾶλλον ἔνσπονδοι ὄντες ἐκκαρπωσάμενοι (Thuc. 5. 28.2). Cf. 2.9.2.

of Hermes simultaneously blaming Argive neutrality and envying its success and profit!

If the fifth-century Greek audience could not conceive of neutrality as a possible diplomatic option, then the Argives' abstention would have made them, in effect, "enemies" of both belligerents, with no rights, no obligations, and certainly no enviable "profit" from the policy. But, obviously, the position of Argos was official and recognized; and Creon's threatening demand acquires far greater dramatic force when we understand that it represents a real option within the realm of Argive-Athenian diplomatic experience. No specialized vocabulary is required to communicate this reality. The audience would comprehend without it, just as they could distinguish between "gifts," "rewards," and "bribes." Unquestionably, the ancient Greek language remained, in comparison with modern languages, poorly supplied with specific diplomatic terminology, and not just for policies like neutrality or nonalignment but also for the conceptual framework of their existence, such as nonaggression or imperialism. All of these ideas remained within the confines of the existing nonspecific vocabulary, not unthought or nonexistent, but simply understood from the surrounding context without lexical specificity. "To remain at peace" or "to keep quiet" or any other of the many common expressions used only identified neutral policy when supported by information that indicated that this special meaning was intended.

However, the need for clarification from context makes the task of recovering the original intention of many possible references much more difficult than it would be in the presence of specific vocabulary. Moreover, the attitude of the source describing the policy also has important implications for the words selected to characterize neutrals and neutrality; and, of course, failure to maintain critical objectivity proves unfortunately to be in no way restricted to the comic characters of Aristophanes. Even without a

---

22. Trans. B. B. Rogers, *Aristophanes*, vol. 2, Loeb Classical Library (Cambridge, Mass., and London, 1924).

οὐδ' οἶδε γ' εἷλκον οὐδὲν ἀργεῖοι πάλαι
ἀλλ' ἢ κατεγέλων τῶν ταλαιπωρουμένων,
καὶ ταῦτα διχόθεν μισθοφοροῦντες ἄλφιτα.
(Ar. *Peace* 475–77)

On Argive policy, see Chapter 4 below, pp. 71–72, with note 2, and 6.1.

specific term, opponents of neutrality knew exactly what they loathed about abstention and abstaining parties, and proponents knew just as well what they approved and desired. In the volatile world of classical diplomacy there never was what we might call a semantic problem, since the overriding concern was not to find a specific term to express the abstract concept of neutrality but only to describe its presence when abstention played some practical or sensational role in the course of interstate affairs.

CHAPTER TWO

The Ancient Sources

Given the paucity of surviving documentary evidence, it is inevitably on literary sources that the reconstruction of the position of states that stood aloof during periods of warfare depends most heavily. For the classical period, Herodotus, Thucydides, Xenophon, and the Attic orators provide the bulk of contemporary information. Of later sources, the universal history compiled by Diodorus Siculus supplies some valuable evidence, but like Plutarch and other writers of the Roman period, Diodorus focuses almost exclusively on the major Greek city-states and their relationship to broad moral issues and dramatic events. Thus the issue of nonparticipation and often even the identity of the abstaining parties, since these matters normally involve insignificant states moving in the shadows of the warring powers, receive little or no attention. On the other hand, there is a tendency among the sources that do provide coverage of these topics, with the notable exception of Thucydides, to disapprove of any form of noncommittal abstention if it conflicts with the interests of the leading states and their hegemonial ambitions.

Herodotus is the earliest and, in some ways, most difficult historical source to evaluate. The problem is that Herodotus presents a visible, but blurred, mixture of historical information and personal commentary. For example, in his narrative of the Argives' policy in 480/479, he tells the reader, "I am obliged to report those things which are reported, but I am certainly not obligated in any way to

be convinced by them, and this statement holds for every story"
(7. 152.3). To emphasize this point he immediately recounts a
polemical accusation to the effect that the Argives actually invited
the Persians to attack mainland Greece because they thought nothing could be worse than the plight of their state, which had been
brought on by the crushing defeat the Spartans had dealt them a
few years earlier at Sepeia.[1]

Argive policy during Xerxes' invasion receives lengthy attention
from Herodotus, including highly critical versions (7. 150.3, 152.3);
yet Herodotus never commits himself to any one of the versions
he relates and concludes in the end that although in his opinion
the Argives acted shamefully, their offense was less serious than
the misdeeds of other states (7. 152.2). Such a statement suggests
that Herodotus was willing to accept the argument that under
certain circumstances a policy of neutrality could be justified, even
during a crisis as serious as Xerxes' invasion, but also that he
personally disapproved of the neutrals of 480/479. This is perfectly
clear from his expressed opinion that the Argives' policy was
shameful (*aischros*) and from the fact that he at least entertained
the suspicion that the Argives did not truly remain aloof and
impartial but, in fact, secretly supported the Persian cause (9. 12).

The excuses of Peloponnesian states that failed to join the Greek
alliance are similarly dismissed as disingenuous (8. 72). Herodotus
says outright that by adopting a neutral position these cities were
siding with the Persians (*ek tou mesou katēmenoi emēdizon* 73.3).
Judging from these explicit statements, it seems clear that regardless
of how the policy had been viewed previously and what diplomatic
justification may have been offered at the time, any state's refusal
to provide active support during such a deeply threatening conflict
as Xerxes' invasion of Greece was for Herodotus nothing less than
a shameful act of betrayal.

Thucydides was obviously interested in the diplomatic dynamics
of neutral policy. Moreover, he seems to have concluded that the
fate of would-be nonparticipants represented especially good evi-

---

1. Ca. 494 (see Hdt. 6. 75–84, which is discussed by R. A. Tomlinson, *Argos
and the Argolid from the End of the Bronze Age to the Roman Occupation*
[London, 1972], 93–97); on Herodotus' method, see, among others, F. J. Groten,
"Herodotus' Use of Variant Versions," *Phoenix* 17 (1963): 79–87; and L. Pearson,
"Credibility and Scepticism in Herodotus," *TAPA* 72 (1941): 335–55, though
neither study discusses the reports covered here. For Argive relations with Persia,
see 5.2 below.

dence of the truth of his contention that war was a "violent schoolmaster" (*biaios didaskalos* 3. 82.2). Observing how vulnerable and easily exploited those few states that attempted to remain aloof from an all-out conflict like the Peloponnesian War were, he recognized with brilliant insight how the interplay between those who were involved in the fighting and those who sought to remain on the sidelines reflected the war's degenerative effect on the conventional restraints that normally governed both private and public action. He therefore used the examination of the plight of neutrals as a measure of the changing attitudes of contemporaries toward the acknowledged institutions of their culture. And in a broader sense, Thucydides seems to have believed that evaluation of the fate of neutrals could provide critical evidence for understanding the progress and outcome not just of the Peloponnesian War but of any war.

Thucydides approaches the subject on two distinct, but closely parallel, levels: the sphere of personal conduct and the realm of public policy. For example, he specifically concludes that because of the extreme violence and civil upheaval that accompanied the internal revolution in Corcyra, the adoption of a neutral position provided neither advantage nor safety. Thus, he observes, "those citizens in the middle [i.e., aligned with neither faction] were destroyed by both sides, either because they would not share in the fight or out of jealousy that they should survive."[2] Even though this represents just one aspect of the effect of civil war, it is nevertheless a critical observation, because it not only demonstrates in concrete terms the extreme degree of mistrust and savage lawlessness that accompanied extreme *stasis* but also dispels any unrealistic notions about the possibility of anyone avoiding the severity of the consequences of civil war. The implied conclusion is that due to the exacerbating pressure of the war, abstention not only failed to provide any protection but even, paradoxically, furthered the momentum of violence, since the abstaining individuals were respected by neither side but instead fell victim to the irrational and unrestrained anger of both warring factions (*apaideusia orgēs* 3. 84.1). When the modern international law of neutrality was in its early stages of evolution, the English jurist C. Malloy, for one,

---

2. τὰ δὲ μέσα τῶν πολιτῶν ὑπ' ἀμφοτέρων ἢ ὅτι οὐ ξυνηγωνίζοντο ἢ φθόνῳ τοῦ περιεῖναι διεφθείροντο (Thuc. 3. 82.8).

expressed essentially the same sentiment, as follows: "As the neuter neither purchases friends nor frees himself from enemies, so commonly he proves prey to the victor; hence it is held more advantage to hazard conquest with a companion than to remain in a state wherein he is in all probability of being ruined by the one or the other."[3] Thucydides, like Solon before him (see pages 4–6 above), saw far too much ill-treatment of nonparticipants to believe that in the chaotic circumstances of civil war such a policy could be safely pursued.

A very similar conclusion emerges from examination of Thucydides' handling of the role of abstaining parties in interstate diplomacy. With characteristic self-restraint Thucydides mentions neutral states only when their position is relevant to the military narrative of the war; and the frequency and length of discussion can be simply characterized as inversely proportional to the success of the policy of the neutrality—that is, the more secure and undisturbed the policy, the less frequently Thucydides mentions the state. The result is that Argos, the cities of Achaea, Rhegium, and Acragas, the Thessalian Confederacy, and the majority of other states that can be identified as nonparticipants receive scant attention, while the circumstances surrounding the failed and violated policies of Plataea, Melos and Camarina figure prominently.[4]

It is no coincidence that several of the most celebrated passages in the *History*—the Corcyraean and Corinthian debate at Athens (1. 32–36, 37–43; especially 35.1–2, 40); the confrontation between the Spartan king Archidamus and the Plataeans (2. 71–74; especially 71.1–2) as well as their trial (3. 53–68; especially 64.3, 68.1); the Melian Dialogue (5. 85–113; especially 94–99, 112); and the conference at Camarina (6. 76–88; especially 80.1–2, 88.1–2)—contain careful and incisive consideration of this issue. By repeatedly introducing highly dramatic passages focused on the relationship between belligerents and nonbelligerents, Thucydides provides ongoing analysis of the realities of interstate responsibilities in war.

---

3. C. Malloy, *De iure maritimo et navali*, 3rd ed. (London, 1682), bk. 1, chap. 9, sec. 9, p. 125 (quoted in the *Oxford English Dictionary*, 1971, s.v. "neutrality").

4. Compare the treatment of Plataea (see 6.4 below), Melos (7.1 below), and Camarina (7.2 below) with Thucydides' virtual silence about other staunchly neutral states (e.g., Argos, Achaea [6.1 below], Acragas [7.3 below], or Thessaly, Crete, Persia [see 6.3 below]), which, due to the success of the policy, provided no adequate grounds for the type of meaningful analysis Thucydides desired.

At the same time, he betrays less of the personal subjectivity recognizable in Herodotus (e.g., 8. 73.3). On the surface, final judgment appears in each case to be left up to the reader. There is, however, a consistent pattern of presentation in the second half of the *History* that seems—in its consistency and repetition—to reflect Thucydides' personal feelings about attempted abstention from the conflict.

In the Melian Dialogue, Thucydides has the Melians warn that refusal to accept their proposed neutral policy (*hēsychian agontes ... symmachoi de mēdeterōn* 5.94) would be dangerous for Athens, because it would convert all neutral states (*hosoi nun mēdeterois symmachousi*) into enemies (*polemioi*), since they would no longer be able to trust the Athenians to restrain their aggression. The Athenians allegedly responded that, on the contrary, fear of Athens' power caused by the subjugation of Melos would serve as a strong deterrent preventing both subject states from contemplating revolt and independent states outside Athens' sphere of influence (*hosoi ēpeirōtai pou ontes tōn eleutherōn ... tous nēsiōtas te pou anarktous*) from joining in the opposition, and would therefore strengthen Athens' position (5. 99; cf. 6. 87.4). Ironically, the outcome proved that there was a measure of truth in both arguments. While Athens maintained its naval superiority, no state—not even Sparta—was willing either to attempt to aid Melos or to make any declaration of war because of the island's fate. At the time, the whole affair seems to have meant little to the majority of Athenians, who in the following year, when their imperialistic confidence was at its highest point, could even listen to comedic jests about subjecting the gods to a deadly "Melian famine."[5]

Thucydides saw greater significance in Athens' refusal to respect the Melians' neutrality. From the exaggerated attention and the significant position he accords the narrative of Athens' subjugation of this strategically insignificant island, it seems clear that he viewed the incident as a threshold where Athenian imperialism passed beyond the point of being restrained by any of the traditional rules of interstate behavior. And the inherent danger of such excess began to appear—in a form much like that in which the Melians had warned it would—almost immediately after the Athenians

---

5. Ar. *Birds* 185–86; cf. Phrynichus, *The Solitary*; Edmonds, *FAC*, vol. 1, 458–59, Phrynichus frag. 23 (ca. 414); for discussion, see 7.1 below.

launched their grandiose expedition to Sicily. When they arrived on the coast of Italy, Thucydides notes, the Athenians expected the support or at least the neutrality of states that were not the declared objective of their expedition (6. 21.1–2, 42.2). What they found was that the West Greek city-states were deeply mistrustful; with few exceptions they rushed to support the Syracusans the moment the Athenians faltered. Thucydides emphasizes this situation by providing speeches from a conference that allegedly occurred at Camarina during the winter of 415/414 in which both the Athenians and the Syracusans attempted to convince the vacillating Camarinaeans to become actively involved in the war.

The speech attributed to Hermocrates of Syracuse (6. 76–80) stresses that no Athenian assurances can be trusted in light of Athens' unrestrained aggression, which, he argues, threatens Camarina just as seriously as Syracuse (78). To aid neither side on the grounds of alliance with both (to mēdeterois boēthein hōs amphoterōn ontes symmachoi 80.1), he warns, is equivalent to supporting the Athenians; thereby one risks punishment if the Syracusans and their allies prevail. Euphemus responds (82–87) with the claim that the Athenian expedition is necessary in order to protect Athens against the possibility of Sicilian support for the Peloponnesian alliance (83.2–84.3) and insists that the Camarinaeans are not in any danger of subjugation by Athens because it would not be in Athens' self-interest to injure any state that showed itself hostile to Syracuse (85.1–2).

Much of what is said in these speeches amounts to amplification and confirmation of earlier views of neutrality presented from the prewar confrontation of Corinth and Corcyra onward. For example, when Thucydides has Hermocrates remind the Camarinaeans that the Rhegians, despite ethnic ties, have remained aloof from the conflict, the word he uses echoes the Corcyraeans' description of their traditional nonalignment (compare the characterization of the Rhegians [sōphronousin 6. 79.2] and the policy of Corcyra [sōphrosynē 1. 32.4]). In a negative use of the description, Hermocrates also argues that states are deluding themselves if they wish for Syracuse to be defeated "in order that we may learn moderation" (hina sōphronisthōmen 78.2) while they themselves remain safe. This is exactly the way Euphemus uses this description: once, when he characterizes the involuntary discretion (ho akōn sōphronein 6. 87.4; i.e., their current unwillingness to oppose

Athens) of states outside of Athens' orbit along with their inactivity (*apragmonōs* ibid.; cf. Corcyra's *apragmosynē* 1. 32.5) and a second time, to make the point that such a policy was unthinkable for an aggressively imperialistic state like Athens. "Do not," he says, "setting yourselves up like the officials who enforce moderate behavior (*hōs sōphronistai* 87.3), attempt to dissuade us ... but to the extent that it is advantageous to you, make use of our restless 'busybodiness' (*tēs hēmeteras polypragmosunēs* ibid.)."

What the consistency of Thucydides' descriptive terminology does is to focus clearly the contrast between the positive connotations of contemporary diplomatic rhetoric used to characterize neutral policy and the repeatedly negative outcome of attempts to adopt such a policy. The cumulative effect is powerful. While it may seem to be a "wise discretion" (*sōphrosynē*) to remain aloof from the conflicts of others, the dramatic accounts of the failure of that choice warn that such a position is in reality extraordinarily dangerous because it not only results in vulnerable isolation but also suffers from sharply differing interpretations that can be manipulated in such a way that a would-be neutral state is confronted with the no-win choice of "damned if it does" (e.g., Melos or Camarina) and "damned if it doesn't" (e.g., Plataea or Corcyra).

There is, however, another very different view of the position of abstaining states that comes out in Thucydides. At the beginning of the *History* Thucydides supports his contention that the Peloponnesian War was the greatest conflict in Greek history with the statement that from the outset the rest of the Hellenic race either took sides immediately or planned to do so.[6] At least part of Thucydides' interest in the fate of those states that did not immediately commit themselves must be related to the conviction that the war eventually involved virtually every *polis* in the Greek world. Certainly the combination of his studied silence about the successful neutrality of, for example, Argos and Acragas and the extraordinarily vivid dramatization of the disasters that befell Plataea and Melos subtly reinforces and legitimizes his original claim. However, Thucydides also appears to have gleaned a potential message from

6. Θουκυδίδης Ἀθηναῖος ξυνέγραψε τὸν πόλεμον τῶν Πελοποννησίων καὶ Ἀθηναίων, ὡς ἐπολέμησαν πρὸς ἀλλήλους, ἀρξάμενος εὐθὺς καθισταμένου καὶ ἐλπίσας μέγαν τε ἔσεσθαι καὶ ἀξιολογώτατον τῶν προγεγενημένων, τεκμαιρόμενος ὅτι ἀκμά-ζοντές τε ἦσαν ἐς αὐτὸν ἀμφότεροι παρασκευῇ τῇ πάσῃ καὶ τὸ ἄλλο Ἑλληνικὸν ὁρῶν ξυνιστάμενον πρὸς ἑκατέρους, τὸ μὲν εὐθύς, τὸ δὲ καὶ διανοούμενον (Thuc. 1. 1.1).

the fact that the eventual polarization of uncommitted states was almost universally to the benefit of Athens' enemies.

At the beginning of the eighth book, Thucydides states that following the Athenians' disastrous defeat in Sicily states throughout Greece that had previously maintained a neutral position (*hoi mēdeterōn ontes symmachoi* 8. 2.1) now voluntarily joined in opposition to Athens, "for they believed, one and all, that the Athenians would have come against them, if they had succeeded in Sicily."[7] What Thucydides seems to be saying is that Athens, by effectively eliminating all confidence that it would accept any restraints on its power—especially through acts like the annihilation of a hapless neutral state like Melos—significantly weakened, rather than strengthened (as argued in the Melian Dialogue), its military position. The implication is that respect for the position of neutral states, when joined with Athens' indisputably superior power, might have forestalled hostile polarization and thus served Athenian interests. If this is so, then Thucydides is actually suggesting that Athens' disregard for conventional restraints like respect for abstaining parties was the wrong policy, symptomatic of the Athenians' unrealistic assessment of the limitations of their own power and their miscalculation of the potentially disastrous result that the polarization of neutrals could bring.

In the end, therefore, it seems that Thucydides considered this anomalous policy as a double-edged sword, simultaneously dangerous, even potentially fatal, for those who pursued it, and yet also useful, even necessary, for belligerents, whose interests, indeed whose very victory or defeat, were served by convincing uncommitted states, whose polarization might prove disastrous, that it would in fact be the best and securest policy (i.e., *sōphrosynē*) to abstain from the conflict and remain at peace.

Xenophon shared none of Thucydides' interest in the analysis of interstate relations. His *Hellenica*, which deals essentially with mainland Greek history from 411 to 362, is filled with transparent pro-Spartan bias and is virtually devoid of investigation into the underlying causes or transcendent issues of the events reported.[8]

---

7. οἱ μὲν μηδετέρων ὄντες ξύμμαχοι, ὡς, ἤν τις καὶ μὴ παρακαλῇ σφᾶς, οὐκ ἀποστατέον ἔτι τοῦ πολέμου εἴη, ἀλλ' ἐθελοντὶ ἰτέον ἐπὶ τοὺς Ἀθηναίους, νομίσαντες κἂν ἐπὶ σφᾶς ἕκαστοι ἐλθεῖν αὐτούς, εἰ τὰ ἐν τῇ Σικελίᾳ κατώρθωσαν (Thuc. 8. 2.1). For discussion, see 7.5 below.

8. Despite some notable attempts to apologize for Xenophon (e.g., W. P.

Xenophon ignores, for example, the whole evolution of the diplomatic concept of Common Peace (*koinē eirēnē*) during the early fourth century, omits altogether the crucial foundation of the Second Athenian Confederacy in 378, and goes out of his way to malign and demean the role of Thebes in the history of the period.[9]

Where the issue of states attempting to abstain from war arises, Xenophon combines a distinct lack of interest in either the rhetoric or the diplomatic dynamics of abstention with apparent antagonism toward the concept itself—even to the point of equating it with betrayal. His analysis of the origins and events of the Corinthian War (395–386) provides good evidence of these shortcomings. Between 403 and 396 both Thebes and Corinth attempted to avoid confrontation with Sparta by refusing to participate in Spartan-initiated conflicts, thereby pursuing a policy of passive resistance to Sparta's increasingly aggressive and belligerent foreign policy. Thus both held aloof during Sparta's war with Elis (ca. 402/401), during the Spartan invasion of Attica (403), and in the Spartans' anti-Persian campaign in Asia Minor (396/395).[10]

Sparta's reaction to this resistance to its leadership was increasingly hostile and oppressive, but Xenophon neither provides any clear context for the policy of these states nor explains the reasons and diplomatic justification given for their refusal. The result is a serious distortion, for, as it stands, Xenophon implies that these states were not seeking to avoid conflict but acted in a deliberately hostile and confrontational way that led eventually to war with Sparta. Worse still, when a Corinthian faction seeks to extricate Corinth from the war being waged almost exclusively in its terri-

---

Henry, *Greek Historical Writing* [Chicago, 1967]; J. K. Anderson, *Xenophon* [London, 1974]), few would deny that Xenophon's bias and lack of analytic interest create serious problems for understanding the period covered in the *Hellenica*. See the detailed assessment of P. Cartledge, *Agesilaos and the Crisis of Sparta* (London, 1987), 61–66.

9. See, for example, T. T. B. Ryder, Koine Eirene: *General Peace and Local Independence in Ancient Greece* (Oxford, 1965), who calls Xenophon "the historian who in his *Hellenika* ignored the common pattern of the Common Peace treaties" (93) and complains that Xenophon "obscures the true nature of the Common peace treaties" (120); or J. Buckler, *The Theban Hegemony, 371–362* (Cambridge, Mass., 1980), 263–68, who warns: "Xenophon's prejudice against Thebes is as extreme as his bias in favor of Sparta" (264) and concludes: "On the whole, this part of the *Hellenika* is a poor piece of historical writing. Grave though its faults are, however, it remains the principal source for the Theban hegemony" (267–68). See also the criticism of Cartledge, *Agesilaos*, 62.

10. For discussion, see 8.2 below.

tory, Xenophon characterizes their efforts as aimed at betraying
the state to Sparta (*Hell.* 4. 4.2). The obvious possibility that
neutrality, and not betrayal, was the real goal of the Corinthian
peace movement is never even suggested.[11]

A number of other specific examples could be cited, which, like
those already discussed, and together with them, make the investigation of how various states sought to remain aloof from the
conflicts of the early decades of the fourth century far more complicated and uncertain than it should be.[12] Xenophon lived through
the turmoil of these years and could not have failed to observe the
growing desire for greater independence among the smaller city-
states of Greece, particularly in the Peloponnesus, where it
increased steadily as the power of both Sparta and Athens declined.
Widespread agitation for increased acceptance of neutrality can be
understood clearly from the description of events, but Xenophon
himself ignores the important implications of this diplomatic movement. For example, Xenophon could have used Plataea's unsuccessful struggle to balance itself between Sparta and Thebes in 386–378
(as Thucydides used Plataea's similar predicament in the Peloponnesian War) as a model of the weaker states' failure to achieve
recognition as neutrals in the continuing warfare of the major
hegemonial states. Instead, he leaves the diplomatic situation so
unclear that the exact policy of the Plataeans can hardly be reconstructed at all, and he provides so little evidence of the increased
agitation for neutrality beginning in 371 that virtually none of the
details can be recovered.[13]

In the first century B.C. Diodorus Siculus compiled the World
History (his *Bibliothēkē*), which narrates the entire period treated
by Herodotus, Thucydides, and Xenophon combined. Diodorus
normally does not indicate his sources and makes a number of
chronological errors in adapting material written according to subject matter (*kata genos*) to his own annalistic format arranged by

11. See 8.3.A below.
12. Consider, for instance, the problems involved in reconstructing from Xenophon's account the policies of Megara and Aegina during the Corinthian War (see
below 8.3.C and D, respectively) or in understanding the diplomacy of Sparta's
Peloponnesian allies in the 370s and 360s (see 8.4.B and 9.2.B–C below).
13. Compare the brief but suggestive accounts of Pausanias (9.1.4) and Isocrates (14 [*Plat.*]); for difficulties that arise in assessing Theban-Plataean relations,
see M. Amit, *Great and Small* Poleis: *A Study in the Relations between the Great
Powers and the Small Cities of Ancient Greece* (Brussels, 1973), 106–14.

archon years.[14] Since he was often completely uncritical in his adaptation of sources, in places where his narrative displays obvious bias (take, for example, his commonly anti-Spartan slant) it is always difficult to be certain whether the prejudice is his own or that of his source. Information about the policy and status of states that remained aloof in war must therefore be treated with caution and be verified, wherever possible, before being accepted as reliable. Unfortunately, in numerous places where his treatment of international policy and diplomacy can be compared with evidence from other sources, it is clear that Diodorus has seriously misstated the true situation.

For example, in his account of the Persian Wars, Diodorus makes only a passing remark about the neutral policy of Argos. The Argives, he reports, agreed to join the Greek alliance only on the condition that they share in the command, to which the Greeks responded that "if they considered it more terrible to have a Greek general than a barbarian master, they would be right to do nothing (i.e., *echein hēsychian*)" (11. 3.4–5). Neither the outcome of this confrontation nor any one of several other versions of the justification of Argive neutrality (duly reported by Herodotus) finds its way into Diodorus' account. The reader does not know whether the Argives joined the Greek alliance or fought for Xerxes.

The same kinds of problems arise in regard to neutrals in the Peloponnesian War. Diodorus casually dismisses Melos as an ally of Sparta (12. 65.1–2), misdates the Athenian reduction of the island to 418 (12. 80.5), and never even mentions the issue of neutrality. During the Sicilian expedition, the neutral position of Italian city-states is accurately reported (12. 3.4–5), but neutral Acragas is incorrectly said to have allied itself with Athens (12. 4.2 [as though Diodorus' source believed the argument of Hermocrates quoted by Thucydides and discussed above]). Likewise, the neutrality of Camarina, Messene, and the Sicel cities of the interior of Sicily is accurately recorded (12. 4.2), but Camarina is later (12. 12.4) included among states supporting Syracuse, without any of Thucydides' careful and necessary explanation of the circumstances surrounding the Camarinaeans' change in policy.

14. See R. Drews, "Diodorus and His Sources," *JP* 83 (1962): 383–92; id., "Ephorus and History Written κατὰ γένος," *AJP* 84 (1963): 244–55; id., "Ephorus' κατὰ γένος Revisited," *Hermes* 104 (1976): 497–98.

For the fourth century, Diodorus nevertheless becomes increasingly important both because of the unreliability of Xenophon's *Hellenica* and, for the period after 362, because he provides the only historical narrative that is extant. In most cases, however, this only confuses the situation. For example, Diodorus' account of the revolution at Corinth in 394 is even more simplistic and misleading than Xenophon's. In Diodorus' version, the conflict was a simple split between the pro-Spartan oligarchic faction and their democratic opponents supported by Argos and Athens (14. 8.6). Nothing is said about the original goal of peace or the independent posture (which even Xenophon acknowledges) of those who first sought simply to extricate Corinth from the war.

Despite his uncritical approach, Diodorus includes much valuable information about neutrality. He preserves the only accounts of the diplomacy surrounding the Carthaginian offer to respect the neutrality of Acragas in 406 (13. 85.2), the neutral posture adopted by some city-states following the battle of Cnidus in 394 (14. 84.4), and Phocian efforts to secure the neutrality of other states during the Third Sacred War of ca. 356/355–346 (16. 27.4, 33.2).[15] These few instances undoubtedly represent just a fraction of the evidence available in the sources from which they were extracted; but since the sources are now lost, anything preserved in Diodorus must be treated with special respect. Sadly, the importance of Diodorus seems to lie primarily in his inclusion of many facts of whose value he himself seems to have been ignorant.

The Attic orators also provide some valuable glimpses of contemporary attitudes toward neutrality. The evidence they provide, however, must be treated with great caution. The aim of the orators was to win in court and to influence public opinion and policy. Historical accuracy and truth are subordinate to and often shamelessly violated for these purposes. Being Athenians, the orators rarely represent the rights of other city-states in matters of foreign policy. For example, Isocrates brushes off the celebrated infamy of Athens' brutal subjugation of Melos in 416 by implying that the Melians were allies of Athens (cf. Diodorus above) who had revolted from the alliance and by claiming that it was not evidence of bad rule if some of those at war with Athens were shown to have been severely punished (4 [Paneg.]. 100–101). Elsewhere Melos

15. On Carthage, see 8.1 below; on the Asiatic reaction to Cnidus, 8.3.F below; on Phocian diplomacy in the Third Sacred War, 9.4 below.

is casually mentioned as nothing more than an example of an excessively expensive siege (15 [*Antid.*].113). Nowhere in Isocrates' writings is there any hint that Melos was an independent state struggling to preserve a neutral diplomatic position, which the Athenians crushed in a spasm of aggressive imperialism.[16]

Of all the orators, Demosthenes provides the best evidence of how the policy of neutrality was viewed by those for whom it created the worst disadvantage. The simple truth is that in his acute frustration at the reluctance of other Greek states to join Athens in opposition to Philip II, Demosthenes increasingly portrayed as active support for Macedon what was in reality only abstention.[17] Fortunately, we can trace the development of Demosthenes' attitude in part in the surviving public speeches. For instance, in 341, when the outcome of Athens' struggle remained in doubt, Demosthenes could still characterize the diplomatic situation without imputing it to wholesale "Philippizing":

> We [i.e., the Greek states] are in such a miserable position, we have so entrenched ourselves in our different cities, that to this very day we can do nothing that our interest or our duty demands; we cannot combine, we cannot take any common pledge of help or friendship; but we idly watch the growing power of this man, each bent (or so it seems to me) on profiting by the interval afforded by another's ruin, taking not a thought, making not an effort for the salvation of Greece. For that Philip, like the recurrence of attacks of a fever or some other disease, is threatening even those who think themselves out of reach.[18]

But in later years, especially after the struggle against Philip had been lost, Demosthenes' bitterness toward the states that refused to oppose Philip brought the accusation that it was all the result of Philip's corruption of the leaders in those states:

> But all the cities were demoralized. The active politicians were venal and corrupted by the hope of money ... and the people in general

---

16. See especially Isoc. 14 (*Plat.*). 39–40.

17. For discussion, see 9.5 below. For typical accusations of corrupt motives directed at politicians in other states who refused to join in active opposition to Philip, see Dem. 9 (*Third Phil.*). 37–40, 53–69; [Dem.] 10 (*Fourth Phil.*). 4–5; 18 (*De cor.*). 18–19, 48, 61. For a detailed reconstruction of how Demosthenes manipulated diplomatic failure into evidence of treachery, see H. Montgomery, *The Way to Chaeronea: Foreign Policy, Decision Making and Political Influence in Demosthenes' Speeches* (Oslo, 1983), 78–94.

18. Dem. 9 (*Third Phil.*). 28–29, trans. J. H. Vince, *Demosthenes*, vol. 1, Loeb Classical Library (Cambridge, Mass., and London, 1954).

were either blind to the future or ensnared by the listlessness and indolence of their daily life; in all the malady had gone so far that they expected the danger to descend anywhere but upon themselves, and even hoped to derive their security at will from the perils of others. In the result, of course, the excessive and inopportune apathy of the common people has been punished by the loss of their independence, while their leaders, who fancied they were selling everything except themselves, discover too late that their own liberty was the first thing they sold.[19]

Even if we agree that Demosthenes was *ex post facto* correct to see that by adopting a neutral attitude toward the struggle between the Athenians and Philip the Greek states were in reality surrendering their independence, the fact remains that at the time, *in medias res*, many leading politicians believed that neutrality was the best policy. It remains to be seen whether or not there is any compelling evidence that their policy arose from corrupt motives or was simply a miscalculation of the ultimate aims that lay behind Philip's assurances of respect for neutrals.[20]

SUMMARY

Aside from literary sources there is little evidence to help one to reconstruct the details of neutral policy in classical Greek diplomacy. A single fourth-century decree from Argos, now lost, records a joint declaration of Greek states "sharing the Common Peace" to the effect that they will remain neutral in the Persian king's struggle with his rebellious satraps if he also refrains from interfering in Greek affairs;[21] but it is the only document of its kind known; and although extant treaties of *philia* (discussed in 3.4 below) provide epigraphical testimony of the diplomatic framework in which the option of formal abstention becomes possible, none includes an explicit guarantee of the right of neutrality. In fact, most of what can be categorized as documentary evidence comes

19. Dem. 18 (*De cor.*). 45–46, trans. C. A. Vince and J. H. Vince, *Demosthenes*, vol. 2, Loeb Classical Library (Cambridge, Mass., and London, 1926).

20. J. Cargill, "Demosthenes, Aischines, and the Crop of Traitors," *The Ancient World* 11 (1985): 75–85, defends Demosthenes, but he fails to see development in Demosthenes' attitude and overlooks the categorical nature of the condemnation; Aeschines (3 [*In Ctes.*]. 130), for example, can remind the Athenians that Demosthenes' suspicion reached such a fever pitch that he opposed consulting Delphi on the grounds that the Pythia had "Philippized."

21. Tod, no. 145; see 9.3.A below.

from quotations in the literary sources.[22] Thus the study of classical neutrality depends almost exclusively on the collection and interpretation of references in the ancient sources, which unfortunately tend either to ignore the uncommitted or to report on their policy with undisguised disapproval.

Lack of objectivity does not, however, completely eliminate all details of classical Greek neutrality. Even Xenophon, whose reporting on diplomacy is otherwise woefully vague and inadequate, manages to provide such valuable details as the neutral position of the Achaean cities prior to the aggression of Epaminondas in 367 and the neutrality clause in the first Common Peace of 371.[23] The inclusion of these and similar facts could not be avoided; yet surely much other information has been lost—not to say suppressed—because of the attitude of the sources.

The central problem with the sources is their failure to follow up on Thucydides' acute insight into neutrals and neutrality. Far from being unworthy of mention (or, as in Herodotus, worthy only of contempt), the policy and predicament of neutrals offered, on many occasions, an accurate reflection of the realities of a given interstate conflict. Rather than being excluded and therefore irrelevant to the narrative of war, neutrals experienced—indeed suffered—the vicissitudes of interstate attitudes toward abstention and the restraint of power. The fate of Melos in the Peloponnesian War illuminates the escalating disregard for traditionally respected limits, but the obscurity of Megara, the Achaean cities, and other real and would-be neutrals during the fourth century creates just the opposite effect of rendering even the major events less comprehensible because the true complexity of the diplomatic situation has been so poorly reported. But the reality is that aside from isolated glimpses the sources pay no attention to neutrals. Only when the policy fails or when belligerent aggression eliminates the option do we hear about these parties. Success requires no notice; and we should always remember that this inverse relationship— namely, the less successful, the more notice—influences all available information and has the potential to distort conclusions about the classical perception and details of neutral policy.

---

22. E.g., the terms of the Thirty Years' Peace (446): Thuc. 1. 35.1, 40.2–3; the Peace of Nicias (421): Thuc. 5. 18.5; the first Common Peace (371): Xen. *Hell.* 6. 3.18.

23. On Achaea, see 9.2.B below; on the Common Peace of 371, see 8.5 below.

CHAPTER THREE

The Origins and Background of the Classical Concept of Neutrality

Classical Greek diplomacy was far more sophisticated than a simple dichotomy of friends and enemies. From the emergence of city-states as autonomous political entities, formal foreign relations existed and involved a complex spectrum of responsibilities that depended on both specified and understood obligations. Fundamental to this development was the acceptance of certain rules of interstate behavior. Although they depended on the voluntary restraint of all parties involved, the rules were nonetheless understood to be universally valid and ultimately enforceable because they represented the will of the gods. Admittedly, these interstate rules did not evolve into a written international law, but due to mutual respect born of shared culture and as a result of reverence for the gods, they exerted a surprisingly powerful hold over the thinking and actions of the classical Greeks. And whenever the rules were violated or called into question, an injured party could specifically refer to them under the name *nomoi Hellēnes.*

In our study it is necessary to review, even if very briefly, the diplomatic context in which any neutral policy had to be pursued. Greek warfare was far from chaotic and unrestricted—brutal, yes, but totally unrestrained, no. The question here is not whether states had a variety of diplomatic options available to them when confronted by the outbreak of warfare but rather whether the option of abstention was clearly enough defined and widely enough accepted to provide protection against belligerent hostility. In short, was there anything in classical Greek diplomacy that supported and gave legitimacy to the position of uncommitted parties?

I. THE EXEMPTION OF HERALDS AND HOLY PLACES IN WAR

The Greeks accepted the principle that heralds sent between belligerents should come and go in safety. This scruple held not only among the city-states in their relations with one another but also for non-Greek peoples. Herodotus makes this point most emphatically in the famous tale of Xerxes' refusal to retaliate against Sparta and Athens for the murder of his heralds on the grounds that he would not stoop to violate the "laws of mankind" (*ta pantōn anthrōpōn nomima* (7.136). Respect for heralds was, then, a universally accepted rule of ancient Greek warfare.[1] As a letter ascribed to Philip II plainly states, "violation of the rights of heralds and ambassadors is regarded by all men as an act of impiety, and by none more than by you [i.e., Athenians]" ([Dem.] 12 [*Philip's Letter*]. 3; cf. Eur. *Heracl.* 271). What is much less well understood is how the divine sanction protecting heralds also gave linguistic substance to one aspect of the classical perception of nonbelligerents.

In Diodorus we learn that the god especially associated with heralds was Hermes, who received in this role the epithet Hermes Koinos (5. 75.1). The explanation given is that the epithet arises from the fact that the benefit is common (*koinos*) to both parties when peace is exchanged for war. Of course, this is true. But *koinos* is also used in diplomatic contexts to communicate the idea of impartiality (see pages 10–12 above); that is, this divinely facilitated

1. Phillipson, *International Law and Custom*, vol. 1, 306; L.-M. Wéry, "Le meutre des hérauts de Darius en 491 et l'inviolabilité du héraut," *AntCl* 35 (1966): 468–86; D. Lateiner, "Heralds and Corpses in Thucydides," *CW* 71 (1977): 99–100; Karavites, "Diplomatic Envoys in the Homeric World," 41–100. Karavites argues: "Though the modern concept of stipulated conventions of diplomatic immunity did not obtain in the ancient world, the idea of diplomatic inviolability buttressed by religious sanction was definitely and effectively present" (100). An important distinction must be made here between heralds and ambassadors. The exemption of the former was unquestioned, but not that of the latter. The safe conduct and right of passage of embassies was certainly not above dispute, and execution of ambassadors did occur (though ransom was no doubt more common; see, for instance, Hdt. 7. 137, Thuc. 2. 67, [Dem.] 12 [*Philip's Letter*]. 3; cf. Pl. *Laws* 12. 941A). See also D. J. Mosley, *Envoys and Diplomacy in Ancient Greece* (Wiesbaden, 1973), 81–89, 97; D. Kienast, *RE Suppl.* 13 (1973), 499–627, s.v. *presbeia*.

common good was impartial to either party and therefore equally beneficial to both. Hermes was above the conflict, detached, immune to its violence; and heralds, his spiritual agents, because of their special intermediary function, served all parties equally, without bias.

Exemption of a few individuals because of the necessary diplomatic role they played was easy enough for the Greek states to accept, even if notorious violations did occur. Much more challenging to the self-restraint of belligerents was the strong religious scruple that in theory restricted warfare to the secular realm. Piety was a powerful force that influenced the collective behavior of Greek communities just as it did individuals, and there is abundant evidence that in war as well as peace territory consecrated to the gods was considered inviolable (asylos). Even unintentional transgression of this restriction could have serious consequences. For example, during one of their annual pillaging raids on the fields of Miletus, the Lydian forces of Alyattes accidentally set fire to the temple of Athena at Assesos. According to Herodotus (1. 19–22), Alyattes himself immediately fell ill and only recovered after he had rebuilt the temple. Naturally, examples of intentional violation are usually associated with extreme retribution. The Argives, for instance, told Herodotus (6. 84.1) that the madness of King Cleomenes of Sparta and his evil end were the result of his repeated disregard for religious scruples, including in particular his ordered burning of a sacred grove filled with Argive soldiers (1.80).

Occasionally the issue was disputed. During the Archidamian War, the Boeotians were so angered over the Athenians' fortification of the precinct of Apollo at Delium and the use of its sacred water by the army that they refused to allow the Athenians a truce to collect their dead, since the Athenians, they proclaimed, "had not done right in transgressing the usages of the Hellenes (ta nomima tōn Hellēnōn); for it was an established custom of them all, when invading one another's country to abstain from the sanctuaries therein" (Thuc. 4. 97.2–3).[2] But in their defense, the Athenians claimed that they had not violated the nomos of the Hellenes (ho nomos tois Hellēsin 98.2), since they had done no injury to the temple but acted only to defend the precinct from the Boeotians, who, they alleged, had repeatedly attacked temples in

2. Trans. Smith.

foreign territory. And in any case, they argued, since the absolute necessity of war, and no impious intention, compelled their transgression, the indulgence of the gods might be expected, whereas the Boeotians, by withholding the bodies of the dead, were guilty of far more serious impiety (98.6–7).

So, opinion about just what constituted unlawful treatment of a sacred site could differ,[3] but the principle of exemption itself was beyond question.[4] And what really matters here is that the Greeks and their civilized neighbors accepted this principle on the basis of a universal faith that protection of certain persons (e.g., heralds) and certain places (e.g., sanctuaries) was critical to the very existence of civilized life and therefore should impose restraint even on warring parties. Darius, for example, instructed Datis to respect Delos when the Persian fleet entered the Aegean in 490. In Herodotus' account Datis announced to the anxious Delians: "Holy men, why have you departed in flight and so misjudged my intentions? For it is both very much my own desire, and the King's command to me, to do no harm to the land in which the two gods were born, neither to the land itself nor the inhabitants. Now, therefore, return to your homes and dwell in your island" (6. 97.2). Perhaps this was mere propaganda, but the concept of respect for holy places was clearly recognized. The dispute at Delium attests to this, as do such extraordinary incidents as the sudden panic that swept Olympia in 420, when rumor spread that the Spartans might attack (Thuc. 5. 50.1–4), and the bitter objections within the Arcadian League in the late 360s, which led to the league's withdrawal from Olympia and a halt to further use of sacred treasures for maintenance of the league army (Xen. *Hell.* 7. 4.12–34).

Acceptance of certain venerable places as immune from war was not entirely the outcome of religious piety. The status of the Panhellenic sanctuaries in particular represented an important compromise involving specific obligations as well as privileges. On the

3. Lateiner, "Heralds and Corpses in Thucydides", 102–3, stresses: "The negotiations at Delion illustrate in the realm of international diplomacy that which *stasis* in Corcyra indicates for the Hellenic city torn by internal dissension: the destruction of common bonds and mutual respect. ... In the farcical arguments at Delion between heralds and about corpses, Thucydides describes in a specific incident the trivialization of politics and the diminution of religious and moral values caused by the Peloponnesian War."

4. This explains, for example, why the people of Ephesus reportedly hastened to dedicate their city to the goddess Artemis and even extended a rope between the city wall and the temple of Artemis when Croesus attacked (Hdt. 1. 26).

side of obligation, the principle of complete and permanent detachment from normal interstate relationships, guaranteed by perpetual disarmament, was fundamental to the legitimacy of the sanctuary's respected status.[5] These appear to have been universally accepted conditions matched on the secular side by acceptance of the sanctuary's inviolability, a vital concession that both protected and institutionalized the sanctity of all properly consecrated territorial units.[6] But if the sanctuary won permanent respect, it did so by strongly emphasizing its impartial, Panhellenic nature. Whether the administration of a sacred place resided with a particular city-state or with a group of states (i.e., an amphictyony), the sanctuary normally stressed its openness to all parties. The *Homeric Hymn to Apollo*, for example, includes this admonition to the priests: "Watch over my temple and welcome the tribes of mankind gathering here and most of all [obey] my will, but if you transgress my commands, whether in word or deed, and are insolent, as is the custom of mortal men, then others will hereafter be your rulers" (538–44).

Of course, it was no secret that the Delphians were not entirely impartial nonparticipants in the affairs and conflicts of the Greek

5. In the case of the sanctuary of Apollo at Delphi, a specific group of states, known as the Anthelan Amphictyony (Bengtson, *SVA*[2] no. 104), took responsibility for enforcing the inviolability. The sanctuary's military defense was entrusted collectively to the members of the amphictyony, who swore (according to Aeschin. 2 [*On the Embassy*]. 115) that "if anyone would violate the shrine of the god or be accessory to such violation, or make any plot against the holy places, they would punish him with hand and foot and voice, and all their power" (trans. C. D. Adams, *The Speeches of Aeschines*, Loeb Classical Library [Cambridge, Mass., and London, 1919]). Note the similarity to the oath providing protection for Elis (Strabo 8.3.33 [357]). However, Olympia's record of inviolability was not perfect. There was serious fear that the Spartans would attack during the Peace of Nicias (Thuc. 5. 50.1–4), in 365 the sanctuary was seized by the Arcadians, and in 364 a battle was fought within the Altis (Xen. *Hell*. 7. 4.14, 28–32). Still, religious objections from within the Arcadian alliance eventually halted the use of the sacred treasures for the maintenance of Arcadian troops (*Hell*. 7. 4.33–34). It should be stressed that these were extraordinary violations of customary respect for the sanctuary.

6. This status also allowed certain of the most respected sanctuaries to serve important diplomatic and cultural needs, including (1) the preservation of treaties (e.g., Bengtson, *SVA*[2] nos. 110, 111, 120), (2) the judicial enforcement of treaties (e.g., Bengtson, *SVA*[2] no. 111, and P. Siewert, "L'autonomie de Hyettos et la sympolitie thespienne dans les *Helléniques* d'Oxyrhynchos," *REG* 90 [1977]: 463 n. 4), (3) the giving of supposedly impartial advice regarding international acts intended or already committed (especially Delphi, through the voice of the oracle), (4) the holding of combined religious and competitive festivals open to all Greeks, and (5), though only rarely, the arbitration of international disputes (L. Piccirilli, *Gli arbitrati interstatali greci*, vol. 1: *Dalle origini al 338 a.c.* [Pisa, 1973], no. 8).

world. They not only granted special favors to individuals and states—such as the right of first consultation—but also reportedly meddled and intrigued on numerous occasions in both the internal and the interstate affairs of the Greek states.[7] Paradoxical though this may seem, it was a reality that existed and was tolerated for the simple reason that Pythian responses were always represented as the voice of the oracular god and never of the Delphians themselves. For the ancient patrons of the sanctuary, this must have been a crucial distinction. In its guise as the medium of Apollo, the Delphic sanctuary was allowed virtually complete freedom to champion or condemn any political (or religious) cause, private or public, local or international. The critical distinction seems to have been that the Delphians themselves remained formally detached and never entered into any alliances or denied the right of consultation to any party for undisguised partisan reasons. Because of this, their right of inviolability could not be (and indeed was not) challenged.

As W. K. Pritchett emphasizes in his book *The Greek State at War*,

> the important point is that Delphi was giving oracles to both sides. Such statements as that of W. G. Forrest (*CR* 72 [1958] 68): "while it is possible for Delphi to be neutral in any war, neutrality must mean advice to neither, not advice to both," are pertinent only if

---

7. Perhaps because of this, maintaining the independence of the famed oracle was not easy. Rivalry over control led to the First Sacred War (early sixth century?; see A. R. Burn, *The Lyric Age of Greece* [London, 1960], 200–203; L. H. Jeffery, *Archaic Greece: The City-States, c. 700–500* [London, 1976], 73–74, 81 n. 3), the Second Sacred War (ca. 449; see G. F. Hill, *Sources for Greek History between the Persian and Peloponnesian Wars*, new ed. by R. Meiggs and A. Andrewes [Oxford, 1951], 344; Gomme, *HCT*, vol. 1, 337–38; H. W. Parke and D. E. W. Wormell, *The Delphic Oracle*, vol. 1 [Oxford, 1956], 184–86), and the Third (356–346; see Parke and Wormell, vol. 1, 216–32), the latter of which was ruinous to Delphi and the rest of Greece alike. Especially aggravating to the problem was the seemingly inexorable polarization of the Greek world around Sparta and Athens during the fifth century, which resulted in determined efforts to politicize the Panhellenic sanctuaries. Resistance of these pressures was difficult and never wholly successful. Delphi's own unique prestige made this inevitable; yet, remarkably, the principle of political nonalignment was not disputed even by the parties attempting to undermine the sanctuary's impartiality. That would have been blatant sacrilege and everyone knew it. See, for instance, the guarantees written into the Peace of Nicias in 421 (Thuc. 5. 18.1–2). Nevertheless, R. Flaceliere, *Greek Oracles*, trans. D. Garman, 2d ed. (London, 1976), 60, is no doubt right to conclude as follows about Delphi: "Even had it remained utterly impartial it would have been suspected of putting the interests of one state, or group of states, above those of another; and from what we know of the history of ancient Greece there is little to suggest that the oracle *was* impartial."

we assume that Delphi was a power in Hellenic politics. Conversely, the fact that Delphi gave oracular responses to, and received dedications from, both sides suggests that her role remained religious.[8]

Pritchett's distinction is surely correct, and it should be stressed that the protected exemption in warfare of sacred places remained fundamentally different from any analogous position assumed or sought by individuals or states where no such special status existed.

The difference can be seen quite clearly in a legendary account about the distinction between the Eleans and the sanctuary of Zeus at Olympia, which they controlled and administered. In the fourth century a story circulated, perhaps first told by Ephorus, that in the time of the return of the Heraclidae all of Elis acquired a status of inviolability (asylia) that forbade as sacrilege any warlike act committed against the Eleans or even unfriendly passage through their territory. The Eleans were said, for their part, to have lived peacefully in total demilitarization and to have remained steadfastly aloof from interstate politics.[9] Since this tale is plainly contradicted by the fact that Elis was (and seemingly always had been) an entirely normal city-state, an explanation is added that attributes the Eleans' eventual abandonment of their inviolable status either to an alleged attack by Pheidon (i.e., Argive impiety) or to a territorial dispute with the neighboring Arcadians (i.e., the impiety of traditional enemies). The Eleans were compelled, so the story goes, to give up their status, arm themselves, and enter into alliances with other city-states.[10]

---

8. W. K. Pritchett, *The Greek State at War*, vol. 3 (Berkeley, 1980), 68.

9. διὰ δὲ τὴν τοῦ Ὀξύλου φιλίαν πρὸς τοὺς Ἡρακλείδας συνομολογηθῆναι ῥᾳδίως ἐκ πάντων μεθ' ὅρκου τὴν Ἠλείαν ἱερὰν εἶναι τοῦ Διός, τὸν δ' ἐπιόντα ἐπὶ τὴν χώραν ταύτην μεθ' ὅπλων ἐναγῆ εἶναι, ὡς δ' αὕτως ἐναγῆ καὶ τὸν μὴ ἐπαμύνοντα εἰς δύναμιν· ἐκ δὲ τούτου καὶ τοὺς κτίσαντας τὴν Ἠλείων πόλιν ὕστερον ἀτείχιστον ἐᾶσαι, καὶ τοὺς δι' αὐτῆς τῆς χώρας ἰόντας στρατοπέδῳ τὰ ὅπλα παραδόντας ἀπολαμβάνειν μετὰ τὴν ἐκ τῶν ὅρων ἔκβασιν·   (Strabo 8.3.33 [357–58] [= Jacoby, FGH 70, Ephorus frag. 115])

Cf. Polyb. 4.73.9–74.2; Diod. 8.1.1–2; Jacoby, FGH 257, Phlegon frag. 1, lines 1–9.

10. In fact, the sources quoted in the previous note provide four possible dates for when the Eleans renounced their inviolability: after the usurpation of Pheidon of Argos (Strabo [= Ephorus]); in connection with the Spartan invasion of 402/401 (Diodorus; see also Diod. 14. 17.11); and either in connection with the seizure of Olympia by the Arcadians (365–363) or as a result of an earlier dispute between the Eleans and Arcadians, which Polybius has wrongly associated with the fourth century (Polyb.). Clearly no reliable conclusion can be reached.

This entire story is obviously fictitious, but it makes one very clear point. Even though the Eleans were administrators of Olympia, their status was fundamentally different from that of the sanctuary, for in their separate identity as a regular city-state, the Eleans were free to involve themselves fully in the vicissitudes of interstate life but had no privileged exemption from its hazards (despite legends to the contrary). The Panhellenic sanctuary, on the other hand, was by definition a sacred and inviolable entity, strictly demilitarized and formally aloof from interstate politics. Hence, if we are seeking to understand how the Greeks perceived abstention from war on the part of regular states, their acceptance of the exemption of sacred places is not evidence in itself but does provide an important model that existed in the diplomatic background of interstate conflicts.

And it may be added that the sponsorship of Panhellenic games by a number of sanctuaries did serve a potentially useful international purpose. As Isocrates writes ca. 380,

> the founders of our great festivals are justly praised for handing down to us a custom by which, having proclaimed a truce and resolved our pending quarrels, we come together in one place, where, as we make our prayers and sacrifices in common, we are reminded of the kinship which exists among us and are made to feel more kindly towards each other for the future, reviving our old friendships and establishing new ties.[11]

That this is not just idle sentimentality from Isocrates can be seen in the continued celebration of the Panhellenic festivals during the Peloponnesian War, with respect for the sacred truce of the Isthmian Games reported by Thucydides as late as 412 (8. 9.1, 10.1).

II. THE FORCE OF ACKNOWLEDGED RULES OF WAR

In the *Odyssey* (16. 424–27), Telemachos bitterly rebukes Antinoos for ingratitude by reminding him how Odysseus had once given refuge to Antinoos' father and saved his life when the people (*ho dēmos*) of Ithaca were angry that he had joined Taphian pirates in a raid on the Thesprotians, with whom the Ithacans were on good terms (*arthmioi*). This is an important claim, for it involves the

---

11. Isoc. 4 (*Paneg.*). 43, trans. G. Norlin, *Isocrates*, vol. 1, Loeb Classical Library (Cambridge, Mass., and London, 1928).

understanding that Antinoos' father had violated an unwritten, but in some sense keenly felt, obligation of intercommunity conduct, for which he might have been severely punished. The potentially disastrous consequences of violating certain fundamental rules and failing to make amends were driven home by the fate of Troy itself;[12] but there are other examples, perhaps the most memorable of which appears in the confrontation between Odysseus and Polyphemus, a monster whose archetypal barbarism was revealed in his contemptuous disdain of all obligations of civilized behavior— for the Cyclops, hospitality (*xenia*) meant that you ate your guests! In the tale of Polyphemus' crime and punishment lies a clear message, a warning to the audience, that violation of the customary rules and restraints of civilized behavior leads inexorably to ruin.[13]

Admittedly, the Homeric epics present a fictionalized account of an earlier era. Nevertheless, it seems certain that they intend to entertain a contemporary audience, which presumably would expect to have its own values reinforced. If that is correct, then the evidence scattered throughout the *Iliad* and *Odyssey* that shows the existence of acknowledged rules of behavior between communities should be a fairly accurate reflection of prevailing attitudes of the eighth century. The fate of Troy and of Polyphemus and the

12. Note that even in the eighth-century imagination of the Heroic Age, armed conflict is not the automatic first recourse of injured parties but comes only after other nonviolent means of resolution have failed; for embassies seeking redress from an offending community, see, for example, *Il.* 3. 205–8; 11. 139–40 (Menelaus and Odysseus to Troy); *Od.* 21. 18–21 (Odysseus to Messenia); 21. 22–23 (Spartan Iphitos to Messenia). See the detailed discussion in Karavites, "Diplomatic Envoys in the Homeric World."

13. *Od.* 9. 105–545; see C. S. Brown, "Odysseus and Polyphemus," *Comp. Lit.* 18 (1966): 193–202. For other criticism of those who violate their obligations as hosts or guests, see *Il.* 13. 625 (Paris); *Od.* 21. 28 (Heracles). In the fifth century, Euripides' *Hecuba* focuses on the potentially disastrous results of violation of the duties of *xenia* (*dika xenōn*). Polymestor, *xenos* of Priam and Hecuba, received their son, Polydorus, who was sent during the Trojan War; but instead of caring for him Polymestor murdered the boy for the gold he carried. When Hecuba learns of the murder, she cries out for punishment of this crime against the duties of *xenia* and repeatedly (with the agreement of other characters and the chorus) condemns the deed as a sacrilege (*Hec.* 710–20; cf. 744, 781, 790–94, 852, 1085–87, 1234–37). On the obligations of *xenia*, see Herman, *Ritualised Friendship*, 118–28, who emphasizes: "Apart from the sanctions of public opinion and apart from an internalised sense of duty there was no agency outside the framework of the relationship capable of enforcing obligations. The partners themselves provided the sanctions. A man's whole moral personality was in this respect at stake" (125–26). The attitude toward Polymestor shows how true this remained in the late fifth century. Note also the respect for foreigners emphasized in the fourth century in Pl. *Laws* 5. 729E.

near death of Antinoos' father should therefore mean that respect for certain understood, but unwritten, rules regarding the relations between individuals and communities, whether they were related or not, was considered important and worth emphasizing already in the eighth century. This idea needs to be set against the common perception of Homeric figures as unrestrained predators who sought nothing more than the epithet "sacker of cities."[14]

Even in the epic image of battle certain rules of conduct are observed by the heroes of both sides as a feature of their respect for civilized behavior. Take the example of the aborted single combat between Trojan Glaucus and Achaean Diomedes. When these opponents discovered that their grandfathers had been linked through exchange of mutual hospitality (*xenia*), they could no longer fight one another.[15] In the heroic character, duty to the common goals of the army was outweighed by the greater obligations of *xenia*.[16] Such constraints were also recognized by entire communities. They involved a sense of mutual obligation, founded on the intermarriage and guest friendship of their members, which compensated for the lack of international law by promoting a more general, but strongly felt, consensus that relations between communities, even in war, should conform to commonly acknowledged, but unwritten, laws (*agraphoi nomoi*).[17] It was this that motivated the Ithacans' indignation against Antinoos' father and the Lacedaemonians' anger at the Trojans.

14. *Ptoliporthos*: e.g., *Il*. 15. 77 (Achilles); 2. 278 (Odysseus); 2. 728 (Oïleus); *ptoliporthios*: *Od*. 9. 504 (Odysseus).

15. *Il*. 6. 212–31; Herman, *Ritualised Friendship*, 1–2.

16. See M. I. Finley, *The World of Odysseus*, 2d ed. (New York, 1965), 103–9; A. W. H. Adkins, "'Friendship' and 'Self-Sufficiency' in Homer and Aristotle," *CQ* 13 (1963): 30–45; Herman, *Ritualised Friendship*, 5–6. Adkins concludes: "These two men [Diomedes and Glaucus] have never seen one another before, and yet, in virtue of a compact of guest-friendship made between their grandfathers, they will not fight against one another in a war in which they find themselves on opposite sides" (37).

17. See D. Woglasi, *Die Normen des altgriechischen Völkerrechts* (Νόμοι κοινοὶ τῶν Ἑλλήνων), (Diss., Freiberg in Breisgau, 1895); R. Hirzel, Ἄγραφος νόμος (Leipzig, 1900), 23–39; F. Flumene, *La 'legge non scritta' nella storia e nella dottrina etico-giuridica della Grecia classica* (Sassari, 1925); G. Ténékidès, *La notion juridique d'indépendence et la tradition hellénique: Autonomie de fédéralisme au Ve et IVe siècles av. J. C.*, Collection de l'Institut Français d'Athènes 83 (Athens, 1954), 17–24; P. Ducrey, "Aspects juridiques de la victoire et du traitement des vaincus," in *Problèmes de la guerre en Grèce ancienne*, ed. J.-P. Vernant (The Hague, 1968), 231–44; J. de Romilly, "Guerre et paix entre cités," *ibid.*, 207–20; id., *La loi dans la pensée grecque, des origines à Aristote* (Paris, 1971) 40–43; P. T. Manicas, "War, Stasis, and Greek Political Thought," *CSSH* 24 (1982): 673–88; H.-J. Gehrke, *Jenseits von Athen und Sparta* (Munich, 1986), 52–55.

These unwritten laws are nowhere exactly defined and are normally referred to simply as "laws of the Hellenes" (*nomima Hellēnōn*) or "laws of mankind" (*nomima anthrōpōn*). Nevertheless,
they were strongly felt when violated, as, for example, when heralds
were killed or when enemy dead were not returned for burial.[18]
They were a mixture of customs, behavioral norms, and notions
of justice, which Aristotle says included "all of those regulations
which seem to be agreed upon by all men" (*Rh.* 1.10. 1368b7–9).
In international affairs their strength arose from the familiarity of
common practice, respect for custom, and fear of shame (if not
reprisal—whether human or divine).[19]

The evolution of written agreements specifying friendship, alliance, and the like during the sixth and fifth centuries merely gave
specific form to these unwritten rules, and it would be wrong to
imagine that in the absence of a formal agreement states had no
obligations to one another. The difficulty today is that the exact
details of such obligations are almost never explicitly given in the
sources. Instead, authors assume (wrongly) that readers understand
the basic conventions that apply. A good illustration of this is
offered in an exceptional situation described by Thucydides. In
connection with the Spartan Brasidas' march north through Thessaly during the Archidamian War, Thucydides remarks that when
Brasidas' advance was blocked midway through Thessalian territory, he defended his lack of formal permission on the grounds
that he was unaware of any hostility that barred the two nations
(the Lacedaemonians and the Thessalians) from access to each
other's territory (4. 78.4). His appeal, significantly, was not to a

---

18. See, for instance, Hdt. 7. 136.3; cf. 9. 79; Thuc. 1. 3, 118; 4. 97 (quoted in
3.1 above); Eur. *Heracl.* 1010; *Supp.* 311, 526; cf. *Phoen.* 536–39; frag. 343 Nauck;
Arist. *Pol.* 3. 16.9. 1287b; Diod. 19. 37, 63. Hirzel, Ἄγραφος νόμος, 96, concludes:
"Das in den ἄγραφοι νόμοι ein Keim der griechischen Ethik liegt, ist längst bemerkt
worden. Und zwar gilt dies in einem weiteren Sinne als man sich bisher klar
gemacht hat, wenn man in dem ἄγραφος νόμος das ewige göttliche Naturgesetz
und damit vornehmlich ein die Gewissen der Menschen verflichtendes Gebot
erblickte."

19. The actual legal effect of the *agraphoi nomoi* could be deadly serious; take
the Thebans' insistence that the Plataeans had violated the unwritten "law of the
Hellenes" (*ton tōn Hellēnōn nomon*) at the outset of the Peloponnesian War and
should be condemned to death (Thuc. 3. 67.6; cf. 56.2, 58.3, 59.1 [Plataean
counterclaims in support of the *agraphoi nomoi*]). For how fifth-century belief in
unwritten laws served the literary, as well as the analytical, purposes of Thucydides, see Lateiner, "Heralds and Corpses in Thucydides," 97–106. On the role of
neutrality in the trial, see 6.4 below.

specific agreement existing between Thessaly and Sparta but to a generally recognized right. But as Thucydides explains, the Thessalians' opposition arose from a similar understood rule, for "among all the Hellenes alike to traverse the territory of a neighbor without permission was looked upon with suspicion" (78.2). Despite his defense, Brasidas knew he was in the wrong, and under cover of darkness he raced across the remainder of Thessaly before he could be prevented.[20]

The problem is that the *agraphoi nomoi* of interstate relations were neither clearly defined nor explicitly specified. This has led to scholarly debate about the nature and force of such "unwritten laws" and has even resulted in denial that any acknowledged rules akin to modern international laws existed in classical Greece.[21] G. E. M. de Ste. Croix, for instance, has argued from references in Thucydides and other fifth- and fourth-century authors that there is a distinction between behavior within the state, where all parties are equally constrained by legal strictures and ethical considerations apply, and interstate behavior, "where it is the strong who decide how they will treat the weak, and moral judgements are inapplicable." "For Thucydides," he concludes, "there was evidently no such thing as 'international law', in anything like the same sense as that in which there can be laws within the State."[22] Since de Ste. Croix makes his case with care and interprets much of fifth-century history accordingly, it is important to understand that the supposed evidence for this negative assessment will not stand up to close scrutiny.

To support the idea that relations between states were subject to no acknowledged rules de Ste. Croix cites Demosthenes, Isocra-

---

20. The right to prevent passage of foreign troops through one's territory was commonly recognized. For example, in the 460s, the Corinthian Lachartus challenged Cimon for failing to gain permission before bringing his army into the Corinthia (Plut. *Cim.* 17.2); during the Sicilian expedition neutral Acragas denied passage through its territory to belligerents (Thuc. 7. 32.1; discussed in 7.3 below). For a full examination of this issue, see D. J. Mosley, "Crossing Greek Frontiers under Arms," *RIDA* (1973): 161–69. For further discussion of the diplomatic situation of the Thessalian incident, see 6.3.B below.

21. E.g., M. Ostwald, "Was There a Concept ἄγραφος νόμος in Classical Greece?" in *Exegesis and Argument: Studies in Greek philosophy Presented to Gregory Vlastos*, ed. E. N. Lee, A. P. D. Mourelatos, R. M. Rorty (Assen, 1973), 70–104. See also the references in note 17 above.

22. G. E. M. de Ste. Croix, *The Origins of the Peloponnesian War* (London, 1972), 16 and 20; cf. K. J. Dover, *Greek Popular Morality in the Time of Plato and Aristotle* (Oxford, 1974), 310–16.

tes, and Aristotle, as well as Thucydides. Demosthenes, he says, offers a clear and dispassionate statement of the true situation in his speech *On the Liberty of the Rhodians* (15. 28–29): "What Demosthenes says (if I may give a close paraphrase) is that within States there are *nomoi* (laws and customs), which *put the weak on an equality with the strong* and enable them to deal with each other on equal terms, but that in international disputes (inter-State disputes, *en tois Hellēnikois dikaiois*) the strong simply coerce the weak."[23] Thus, de Ste. Croix continues, Demosthenes is saying that because there exist no effective sanctions outside of the state corresponding to those within, force is the only arbiter in international affairs. The flaw in this allegedly objective "evidence" is that even if we accept that Demosthenes believed the rhetoric he employs at this point, there are (as de Ste. Croix admits) several other places in the same speech where he assumes the existence of customary rules in interstate affairs (e.g., 3, 7–8, 13, 15, 25, 30) and even emphasizes the careful "legality" of past Athenian actions (9–10). Demosthenes is attempting (unsuccessfully) to convince his fellow citizens to disregard the lack of justifiable provocation and begin armed hostility against the current Rhodian government on behalf of certain exiled "democrats." But his advice, which he himself suggests is unjust (*ei mē dikaion* 28), was rejected in favor of the restraint proposed by other leaders, whom he accuses of being bribed (32); and this implies concern for and recognition of restraining rules in interstate affairs, not the opposite. Far from proving the Thrasymachian dogma that might determines right, Demosthenes' (hardly objective) pleading not only failed to convince the majority of Athenians but could not even be sustained throughout the entire speech.[24]

23. De Ste. Croix, *Origins of the Peloponnesian War*, 17.

24. There are other speeches in which Demosthenes confirms the existence and validity of rules akin to international laws, such as 16 (*Megalop.*) 6–10, 15, 24–25, where he argues that on the basis of justice no state should be oppressed by another; 51 (*Trierarch. Crown*). 13, where he complains that piratical acts of Athenian trierarchs rendered fellow citizens liable to reprisals (*sylai*) with the result that it was impossible for them to travel abroad without the safe-conduct immunity of a herald (*aneu kērukeiou*); 35 (*Lacr.*). 13, 26, where the legality of reprisals is admitted; 24 (*Timoc.*). 12, where prize courts for settling claims of foreigners alleging unlawful seizure of their property are described; and [Dem.] 7 (*Halon.*). 11–13, where legal settlements of interstate commercial disputes, even without specific treaty arrangements (*symbolai*), are claimed to have been traditionally recognized and respected. But despite these references, Demosthenes seems

De Ste. Croix's use of Isocratean rhetoric is similarly flawed. In his speech *On the Peace*, Isocrates contrasts the Athenians' current behavior in the Social War (357–355) with their attitude during the Corinthian War (395–386), when "we recognized the principle that it is not just for the stronger to rule over the weaker, even as now we recognize it in the nature of the polity which has been established amongst ourselves."[25] For de Ste. Croix this means that no rules comparable to the internal rule of law and justice were recognized when Isocrates made the comparison. But contrary to de Ste. Croix's interpretation, Isocrates is not denying the contemporary existence of rules of interstate conduct but only trying to convince his audience that Athens' current attempt to force the allegiance of its allies flies in the face of its own former insistence on the validity of restraints in foreign relations espoused in the Corinthian War. Elsewhere in the same speech Isocrates concludes from historical examples that "you will all impute extreme folly and madness to those who think that injustice is advantageous and who would hold in subjection by force cities of others, failing to reckon with the disasters which result from such a policy."[26] Isocrates' whole point in this speech is that standards of justice applicable to interstate affairs do exist, and, consequently, rules do too, and that the interests of Athens would be better served by paying closer attention to them.[27]

This is also the ironic meaning implied in de Ste. Croix's quotation of the following passage from Aristotle's *Politics*:

> When it comes to politics most people appear to believe that mastery is the true statemanship; and men are not ashamed of behaving to others in ways which they would refuse to acknowledge as just, or even expedient, among themselves. For their own affairs, and among

---

to me an unreliable source for international conventions, due to his unprincipled willingness to fabricate "facts" in the interest of proving his case; see 9.5.B below on his distorted characterization of neutrality.

25. Isoc. 8 (*On the peace*). 69, trans. Norlin.

26. Ibid., 17, trans. Norlin.

27. See also J. de Romilly, "Fairness and Kindness in Thucydides," *Phoenix* 28 (1974): 95–100; de Romilly observes: "But when Isocrates, after Athens' ultimate collapse, tried to find out a wise policy, the general lines of this policy could be derived from the lessons of the collapse. Isocrates saw that a wise policy could no longer be one that rested on force" (100). Isocrates' view may be reflected in the writings of other fourth-century intellectuals, such as Demetrius of Phalerum, who is credited with writing a treatise *Peri eirēnē* (see F. Wehrli, *Die Schule des Aristotles Texte und Kommentar* [Basel, 1944], 62–63).

themselves, they want an authority based on justice; but when other men are in question, their interest in justice stops.[28]

De Ste. Croix takes this at face value; but in context, it becomes clear that Aristotle equates such behavior with barbarism and suggests by his selection of examples that it was characteristic of non-Greek cultures (see especially 7.2. 1324b10–22, where he cites the Scythians, Persians, Thracians, Celts, Carthaginians, and Iberians). Aristotle's own conclusions about the proper conduct of foreign relations are that policies aimed at the acquisition of empire and the subjugation of others are neither statesmanlike nor useful, nor right, for "the Good (ta arista) is one and the same for individuals and communities; and it is the Good which the legislator ought to instil into the minds of his citizens." "Training for war," he continues,

> should not be pursued with a view to enslaving men who do not deserve such a fate [i.e., Greeks]. Its objects should be these—first, to prevent men from ever becoming enslaved themselves; secondly, to put men in a position to exercise leadership—but leadership directed to the interest of the led, and not to the establishment of a general system of slavery; and thirdly, to enable men to make themselves master of those who naturally deserve to be slaves [i.e., non-Greek barbarians]."[29]

In fact, Aristotle does not lament the absence (or nonexistence) of customary rules and standards of justice in interstate relations but only the problem that his fellow Greeks ignore them too often and thereby, contrary to their own best interests, reduce such relations to a state of barbarism. Like Isocrates, he offers advice based on his own best judgment about the existing situation and possible alternatives. Moreover, there can be no doubt at all that Aristotle himself believed in the existence of universally valid rules of interstate behavior; he says as much in the *Rhetoric*: "There is naturally a common idea of justice and injustice (koinon dikaion kai adikon) which all men intuitively understand in some way, even if they have neither communications nor treaty (synthēkē [i.e., a specific agreement]) with one another."[30]

---

28. Arist. *Pol.* 7.2.1324b32–36; trans. E. Barker, *The Politics of Aristotle* (Oxford, 1946).
29. Ibid., 7.13.1333b35–1334a2, trans. Barker.
30. Ibid., *Rh.* 1.3.1373b6–9; see W. von Leyden, *Aristotle on Equality and Justice: His Political Argument* (London, 1985), 84–90, 102–3.

De Ste. Croix also sees no evidence of anything like international laws in Thucydides. For him Diodotus' insistence on the policy of expediency in the Mytilenaean debate (3. 44.1–4); the anonymous Athenian proclamation at Melos about men "ruling wherever they can" (5. 105.2) and about the Spartans defining justice as whatever suited their country's interest (105.4); the undercutting of Brasidas' promises to Thracian cities with the comment that such cities were welcomed because they could be bargained away when the Spartans were ready to negotiate for peace (4. 81.2); the failure of appeals to traditional justice and practice by the Corinthians (1. 38.4–5, 39.2–3, 40.1–2, 42), the Plataeans (3. 71.4, 58, 59.2), and the Melians (5. 104, 112.2); and the many reports of willfully cruel treatment of noncombatants by the belligerents (e.g., 2. 67.4; 3. 32.1–2, 68.1– 4; 4. 57.3–4, 80.2–4; 5. 3.4, 32.1, 83.2, 116.4) provide "proof" that in Thucydides' judgment "all States ... always do what they believe, rightly or wrongly, to be in their own best interests, and in particular they rule wherever they can."[31] Thus de Ste. Croix concludes that "Thucydides refused to be drawn into passing moral judgement in matters of this kind, involving inter-State relations" and tried only "to state some of the basic and brutal facts about the position of imperial States and of those threatened by them, but to state those facts only, in the most general way possible, and not to pretend that he had any solution to problems that arise out of them."[32]

In this uncompromisingly negative assessment, de Ste. Croix unconsciously echoes the despairing assertion of Plato in the *Laws* that his imaginary lawgiver would condemn "the stupidity of the majority of mankind" for failing to perceive that all states are involved ceaselessly in a lifelong war against all others, "for what men in general term peace," he insists, "would be said by [the lawgiver] to be only a name; in reality every city is in a natural state of war with every other, not indeed proclaimed by heralds, but everlasting."[33]

Many examples from the text of Thucydides can be cited in support of this negative view. The fate of Melos is dramatically

31. De Ste. Croix, *Origins of the Peloponnesian War*, 22.
32. Ibid., 20 and 22.
33. Pl. *Laws* 626A, trans. B. Jowett, *The Works of Plato*, 3rd ed. (reprint, New York, 1956); compare the more hopeful view at *Rep.* 469B–71C, written earlier in his life.

emphasized, and there are also numerous instances of the failure of traditional justice and customary practice to restrain the actions of belligerents. Nevertheless, it must be understood that de Ste. Croix's assessment ignores what Plato so dismissively calls "the stupidity of the majority of mankind," for de Ste. Croix, like Plato, condescendingly remarks:

> I am sure Thucydides simply did not realise that most of his readers would be unable to forget the massacre [of the Melians] that was to come and would therefore feel strongly prejudiced against the Athenian speakers—any more than he realised that the speech he gave to the Athenians at Sparta [prior to the outbreak of the war], intended as an eirenicon, would seem anything but that to many people.[34]

We should be suspicious of dismissive claims like these.

What de Ste. Croix fails to see is just how the customary rules (the *agraphoi nomoi*) of interstate relations exerted their authority. It is not to deny the existence and force of such notions that Thucydides emphasizes paradigmatic cases of interstate injustice but to expose, in plain fact, devoid of self-serving apology or moralistic condemnation, the reality of such violations and their potentially negative effect. No one, not even the Athenians of the fourth century, wanted to be identified with the kind of injustice attributed to Athens (and Sparta) by Thucydides. This is why, for example, Isocrates tries to rewrite Thucydides' account of Melos, claiming that Athens could hardly be blamed if one of its "allies in revolt" was severely punished.[35] If justice did not matter, why apologize? If no customary rules were broken, why redefine the status of Melos? The reason is obviously that something had been violated, something recognizable and deeply felt by the majority of Greeks, who did blame Athens for overstepping an understood boundary and who were no less critical of Sparta for doing the same. But the point is that there was, in fact, no higher authority to enforce respect for customary restraints on an interstate level, particularly in warfare, that corresponded to the protection of all parties, whether weak or strong, guaranteed by the *nomoi* (laws and customs) within an individual state. For this reason, the authority of the *agraphoi nomoi* of interstate relations was, by necessity,

---

34. De Ste. Croix, *Origins of the Peloponnesian War*, 16.
35. Isoc. 4 (*Paneg.*). 100–102; 12 (*Panath.*). 63; cf. *Epist.* 2. 16; Lys. 25. 31; and Xen. *Hell.* 2. 3. See also Dover, *Greek Popular Morality*.

grounded in the moral consciousness of those involved. Thucydides does not reveal simply that rules based on self-restraint are especially vulnerable to willful—indeed flagrant—violation; he also shows that the revulsion of the community of states and its avowed repudiation of all disregard for justice and customarily accepted restraints both reaffirm their validity and demonstrate their advantage for the entire community, weak and strong alike.[36]

It should be remembered, however, that respect for general principles of interstate behavior embodied in the unwritten laws was no more or less perfect than modern respect for international law. Yet there should be no doubt that common belief in their validity influenced interstate relations generally and affected the issue of neutrality specifically. The Melians reportedly argue that their refusal to join the Athenian alliance is defensible on the grounds of justice (*to dikaion*), reasonableness (*to eikos*), and expedience (*to sympheron*). They make no appeal to a specific statute or international agreement but rather to an unwritten, but universally acknowledged (so they believe), right that every state, even a militarily weak and strategically insignificant one such as their own, has to the self-determination of its foreign policy.[37]

36. De Ste. Croix, *Origins of the Peloponnesian War*, 19, makes effective use of a rhetorical argument: "When [Thucydides] records appeals to 'justice' he usually makes them come—surely by design—from men on the losing side. ... As for appeals to the gods, they are apt to make us expect the very worst." By implication it is suggested that Thucydides constructs his reports of such appeals to point out their uselessness. But this is misleading. Following de Ste. Croix's reasoning, we should expect Thucydides to emphasize—implicitly, if not explicitly—the success of exponents of godless injustice. In fact, this does not happen at all. Exponents of policies that are obviously contrary to traditional rules of just behavior eventually meet with reversal and disaster, even if their disregard for justice appears successful in the short term. Athens easily suppresses Melos but fails in Sicily and loses the war; the Corcyraeans imagine they are better off for winning the support of Athens but soon lose virtually everything in the war they precipitate; the Spartans and Thebans eliminate Plataea but achieve no significant military advantage; Diodotus succeeds in preventing the wholesale slaughter of Mytilenaeans, but the loyalty of Mytilene is permanently lost, and the alliance is weakened, not strengthened. The truth is that Thucydides does not depict justice and piety in interstate relations as (to borrow from Plato) "the stupidity of the majority of mankind." His view is more complex, and, as Lateiner, "Heralds and Corpses in Thucydides," 99, argues, he recognizes that "norms of Hellenic behavior were seriously disturbed and damaged during the Peloponnesian War." It is wrong, however, to conclude that Thucydides intended to deny the existence of such norms or their potentially beneficial effect. See the insightful analysis of de Romilly, "Fairness and Kindness in Thucydides," 95–100.

37. For further discussion, see 7.1 below. The Melian argument was not isolated; compare Euripides' *Hecuba*; as W. Arrowsmith observes in *Euripides, The Complete Greek Tragedies*, vol. 3, ed. D. Grene and R. Lattimore (Chicago,

It may well be that the general willingness of the Greeks to acknowledge the dictates of unwritten, but understood, rules was one of the major reasons why international law never came to have the kind of juridical definition associated with its counterpart in the modern world. The archaic period witnessed some noteworthy attempts to regulate warfare through specific written agreements, but these agreements were never more than limited pacts among specific states. In the shadowy (late eighth-century?) Lelantine War, for example, the Chalcidians and Eretrians reportedly "agreed on the conditions under which they would engage in the struggle," which were "made evident by a stele in Amarysia which states that long-range missiles are not to be used."[38] Similarly, the city-states that belonged to the Delphic Amphictyony reportedly swore that "they would destroy no city of the Amphictyonic states nor shut any off from flowing water either in war or peace" and that "if anyone should violate the oath, they would march against that state and destroy its cities."[39] But on the whole, specific statutes are exceptional. Though warfare was endemic throughout the classical period, regulation of it remained primarily a matter of customary, rather than statutory, rules. Custom could, however, exert considerable moderating force, especially when, as Plato has Socrates imagine in the *Republic* (5. 471A), states restrained themselves out of a sense of obligation to the shared culture and extended community that existed despite the presence of conflict.[40]

III. ARBITRATION OF INTERSTATE DISPUTES AND MEDIATION IN WAR

The use of third parties for arbitration of interstate disputes evolved very early; and since arbitration cannot take place without the

---

1958), 6: "Confronted by the fact of power which makes her helpless, Hecuba, like the Melians, can only plead honor, decency, the gods, the moral law (*nomos*); when these appeals fail, what is civilized in her fails with them."

38. Strabo 10. 1.12 (448); Bengtson, *SVA*[2] no. 102.

39. Aeschin. 2 (*On the Embassy*). 115.

40. This, I believe, is the issue underlying the following passage from Euripides' lost play, the *Bellerophontes*, which is quoted by de Ste. Croix, *Origins of the Peloponnesian War*, 20, out of context (the context being lost): "I know small States which have honoured the gods and yet have to obey larger States that are ungodly, because they are overwhelmed by a greater number of spearmen" (Eur. frag. 286 Nauck, lines 10–12). The unknown speaker of these lines is surely objecting to a reality he or she does not accept—at least not any more than twentieth-century individuals of conscience willingly acquiesce to the immutability

presence and participation of assumedly neutral and unbiased parties concerned enough to act as arbitrators of a given conflict, acceptance of arbitration must have helped to promote restraint in interstate relations and encouraged the breakdown of the simple dichotomy of friends and enemies. Evidence of arbitration can be found as early as the eighth century, and mediation of ongoing wars from the beginning of the sixth.[41] Of critical importance here is the fact that arbitration and mediation are based on the premise that all states will not automatically take sides in a given interstate dispute and that therefore resolution of conflict can be achieved through the agency or adjudication of an impartial nondisputant. If arbitration is accepted, it also follows that juridical equality exists between the disputants regardless of their relative strength—military or otherwise.

Arbitration and mediation were primarily secular developments. Sanctuaries, although they often served as repositories of interstate agreements and through oracles constantly provided advice about interstate affairs, rarely acted as arbitrators.[42] Normally it was an individual or a select group of citizens from a state who the disputants agreed would render fair judgment.[43]

There is very little that distinguishes a state selected as an impartial arbitrator of a given dispute from a state that may be legitimately called a neutral. The difference, however, is that neu-

---

of what they see as the international injustice practiced by the superpowers. The norms exist despite violation. See Y. Garlan, *War in the Ancient World: A Social History*, trans. J. Lloyd (London, 1975), 57, quoted in the Summary below. Cf. Xenophon's description of the Athenians' fear of punishment for their treatment of the Melians and others (*Hell.* 2. 2.3).

41. There is one example of international arbitration from the eighth century, two from the seventh, and half a dozen fom the sixth (see Piccirilli, *Arbitrati*, vol. 1, nos. 1–10). There are fewer examples of mediation. The earliest recorded is the mediation by Bias of Priene of the settlement of a war fought over territory claimed by both Samos and Priene (ibid., no. 4). Ca. 492 the Corcyraeans and Corinthians mediated a peaceful resolution of the war between the Geloans and Syracusans on the condition that control of Camarina be transferred from Syracuse to Gela (ibid., no. 12).

42. See note 6 above.

43. Note that arbitration became so widely accepted that it entered into the mythological tradition (for example, legend made the giant Briareus act as arbitrator of the conflicting territorial claims of Poseidon and Helios to the Corinthia [Paus. 2. 1.6]). In the archaic period, arbitration typically involved territorial disputes arising from the rival claims of contiguous city-states; see now Piccirilli, *Arbitrati*, vol. 1, who includes an appendix on mythological examples. Mediation has received less attention, perhaps because it is mentioned less frequently and in less detail than arbitration.

trality is a legal position that depends on international recognition that such a right does in fact exist. An arbitrator may be any party so designated, and its impartiality need not extend beyond the immediate dispute being arbitrated. Corcyra, for example, asked Corinth in 435 to refer their dispute to any city-state in the Peloponnesus that both states could agree upon. This might (or might not) have been a state otherwise allied with Corinth. The only issue was that the state would act as an impartial arbitrator regarding the immediate dispute (Thuc. 1. 28.1–2). In contrast, a neutral state must be formally uncommitted, and its position respected in accordance with whatever rights and obligations are agreed upon by all parties. Of course, a neutral state may also serve as an arbitrator or mediator, but that is a separate issue.

Acceptance of arbitration and mediation as legitimate methods for conflict resolution could not help but promote recognition of the legitimacy of neutrality, not only because the use of arbitration and mediation as alternatives to armed conflict represented an important step in the evolution of juridical principles of international relations, but also because it presupposed the existence of impartial parties acknowledged to be such by the disputants.

IV. BILATERAL TREATIES AND THE EVOLUTION OF DIPLOMATIC FRIENDSHIP (PHILIA)

Despite their rarity, original texts of treaties from archaic Greece provide valuable information about how specific interstate agreements helped to promote the idea that refusal to take sides in a given conflict could not be taken automatically as a declaration of hostility toward one or the other of the belligerents. An important example of such a document is the sixth-century treaty between the city-state of Sybaris in Southern Italy and an otherwise unknown group, probably immediate neighbors of the Sybarites, named the Serdaioi.[44] The treaty reads as follows:

44. Meiggs and Lewis, no. 10 (550?–525); Bengtson, SVA² no. 120. The treaty must predate the destruction of Sybaris in 510 (Hdt. 6. 21; Diod. 11. 90.3; 12. 10.1–2; Strabo 6.1.13 (263); see T. J. Dunbabin, *The Western Greeks: The History of Sicily and South Italy from the Foundation of the Greek Colonies to 480 B.C.* [Oxford, 1948], 364–65); on the role of the *proxenoi*, see D. J. Mosley, "Bericht über die Forschung zur Diplomatie im klassischen Griechenland," in *Antike Diplomatie*, Wege der Forschung 462, ed. E. Olshausen and H. Biller (Darmstadt, 1979), 228.

ἀρμόχθεν οἱ Συβαρῖ|ται κ᾿ οἱ σύνμαχοι κ᾿ οἱ|Σερδαῖοι ἐπὶ φιλότατ|ι
πιστᾶι κ᾿ ἀδόλοι ἀε|ίδιον· πρόξενοι ὁ Ζε|ὺς κ᾿ ᾿Οπόλον κ᾿ ὄλλοι
θ|εοὶ καὶ πόλις Ποσειδα|νία.

The Sybarites and their allies and the Serdaioi united in friendship,
faithful, and without guile forever. Guarantors: Zeus and Apollo
and the other gods and the city Poseidonia.

A critical, but ignored, feature of this treaty is the way that it
clearly distinguishes between friendship (*philia*), that is, the designated relationship for the Sybarites and Serdaioi, and alliance
(*symmachia*), the relationship of other unnamed states to Sybaris.
Even though the exact details of *philia* are not specified, there can
be no doubt that whatever the exact obligations may be, they are
not the same as those required by the *symmachia* that exists
between other states and Sybaris.

This formal distinction between *symmachoi* and *philoi* also
appears in the reputed sixth-century treaty between the Carthaginians and Romans. According to Polybius, who gives a Greek translation of the original archaic Latin text, the treaty begins

εἰσὶ δ᾿ αἱ συνθῆκαι τοιαίδε τινές· "ἐπὶ τοῖσδε φιλίαν εἶναι ῾Ρωμαίοις
καὶ τοῖς ῾Ρωμαίων συμμάχοις καὶ Καρχηδονίοις καὶ τοῖς Καρχηδονίων
συμμάχοις."

On these terms there is to be friendship between the Romans and
their allies and the Carthaginians and their allies.[45]

In yet another sixth-century treaty, this time between the northwestern Greek states of Anaitos and Metapios, the text reads:

᾿Α Ϝράτρα τὸς ᾿Αναίτο[ς] καὶ τὸ[ς]|Μεταπίος· φιλίαν πεντάκον|τα
Ϝέτεα. κ᾿ ὁπόταροι μὲνπεδέοιαν,|ἀπὸ τὸ βομὸ ἀποϜελέοιάν κα τοὶ πρό|
ξενοι καὶ τοὶ μάντιερ. αἰ τὸ[ν] ὅρκον|παρβαίνοιαν, γνôμαν τὸρ ἰ[α]ρο-
μάορ|τ᾿ ᾿Ολυνπίαι.

This is the treaty between the Anaitoi and the Metapioi. Friendship
for fifty years; and whichever party fails to be steadfast, let the
proxenoi and manteis drag them from the altar. Should they break
the oath, let the priests at Olympia give judgment.[46]

45. Polyb. 3.22.4; Bengtson, *SVA*[2] no. 121; see F. Walbank, *Historical Commentary on Polybius*, vol. 1 (Oxford, 1957), 339–45.
46. Bengtson, *SVA*[2] no. 111; *gnōman* might also mean "be informed" or "know
of it" (cf. *Od.* 21. 36); but the idea of "give judgment" or "decide the matter"
seems preferable (cf. esp. Hdt. 1. 74.4, 157.3).

Once again, there are no details provided about exactly what *philia* represents in formal diplomatic terms. However, the *philia* negotiated between the Anaitoi and Metapioi should be contrasted with the *symmachia* designated in a roughly contemporary and otherwise very similar treaty between the Eleans and Heraeans:

ἁ Ϝράτρα τοῖρ Ϝαλείοις: καὶ τοῖς Ἐρ-
Ϝαοίοις: συνμαχία κ' ἔα ἑκατὸν Ϝέτεα:
ἄρχοι δέ κα τοῖ: αἰ δέ τι δέοι: αἴτε Ϝέπος αἴτε Ϝ-
άργον: συνέαν κ' ἀλάλοις: τά τ' ἄλ⟨α⟩ καὶ πὰ-
ρ πολέμο: αἰ δὲ μὰ συνέαν: τάλαντόν κ'
ἀργύρο: ἀποτίνοιαν: τôι Δὶ Ὀλυνπίοι: τοὶ κα-
δαλεμένοι: λατρειόμενον: αἰ δέ τιρ τὰ γ-
ράφεα: ταῖ καδαλέοιτο: αἴτε Ϝέτας αἴτε τ-
ελεστὰ: αἴτε δᾶμος: ἐν τἐπιάροι κ' ἐνεχ-
οιτο τôι 'νταῦτ' ἐγραμένοι.

The covenant between Elis and Heraia. There shall be an alliance for a hundred years, and this [year] shall be the first; and if anything is needed, either word or deed, they shall stand by each other in all matters and especially in war; and if they stand not by each other, those who do the wrong shall pay a talent of silver to Olympian Zeus to be used in his service. And if anyone injure this writing, whether private man or magistrate or community, he shall be liable to the sacred fine herein written.[47]

Given that copies of both treaties were recorded on bronze plaques deposited in the same Panhellenic sanctuary, there is no reason to doubt that if the Anaitoi and Metapioi had wanted to become full-fledged allies (*symmachoi*), they would have negotiated a *symmachia* instead of a treaty of *philia*.

Yet even if we recognize this distinction, the question remains whether *philia* between states meant something specific or perhaps represented nothing more than the intentionally vague diplomatic rhetoric all too familiar in modern diplomacy. Furthermore, even if *philia* proves to have special meaning for relations between states, it remains to be seen whether there existed any connection between the responsibilities of formal *philia* relationships and the status of states that remained uncommitted in times of conflict.

To begin with, we need to make a critical distinction between the friendship of individuals (also called *philia* and described by its

<hr />

47. Bengtson, *SVA*² no. 110; Meiggs and Lewis, no. 17; trans. M. Tod, *A Selection of Greek Historical Inscriptions to the End of the Fifth Century B.C.* (Oxford, 1933), no. 5.

cognates in Greek) and the formal interstate relationship of *philia* reflected in the language of treaties. On a private level, friendship was extremely important in both the social and the political life of any Greek *polis*;[48] but friendship between entire communities (i.e., between independent city-states) does not appear to have been initially identified with the same language as the personal relationship. In the Homeric poems, where the concept of state is still embryonic,[49] *symmachia* is not found, and there is only a single reference to friendly, but not necessarily allied, relations between communities (the Ithacans with the Thesprotians); and the term for this relationship is *arthmios* (*Od.* 16.427).

Arthmios is a rare word in extant Greek literature. There are only eight instances of *arthmios* in classical Greek, aside from the single example in Homer: two in Empedocles (frags. 17.23 and 22.1 Diehl), two in Theognis (326, 1312), and four in Herodotus (6. 83.2; 7. 101.2; 9. 9.2 and 37.4).[50] Neither Empedocles nor Theognis uses it to characterize relations between city-states, but both link it closely with *philia*.[51] Herodotus, on the other hand, uses it only to describe relations between states: Xerxes' belief that the Greeks

---

48. See, for instance, H. Hutter, *Politics as Friendship: The Origins of Classical Notions of Politics in the Theory and Practice of Friendship* (Waterloo, Ont., 1978); W. Jaeger, *Paedeia*, vol. 1, 2d ed. (New York, 1939), 199–201; Adkins, "'Friendship' and 'Self-Sufficiency' in Homer and Aristotle," 30–37; Herman, *Ritualised Friendship*, passim.

49. See V. Ehrenberg, "When Did the *Polis* Rise?" *JHS* 57 (1937): 147–59; C. Starr, "The Early Greek State," *PP* 12 (1957): 97–108 (also published in A. Ferrill and T. Kelly, eds., *Essays on Ancient History* [Leiden, 1979], 122–33); C. G. Thomas, "Homer and the *Polis*," *PP* 21 (1966): 5–14; F. Gschnitzer, "Stadt und Stamm bei Homer," *Chiron* 1 (1971): 1–17; J. V. Luce, "The *Polis* in Homer and Hesiod," *Proceedings of Royal Irish Academy* 78 (1978): 1–15.

50. This list, originally compiled from Stephanus (*Thesaurus Graecae Linguae*, 6th ed. [Paris, 1869], s.v. *arthmios*), has been checked on the Ibycus Scholarly Computer s.v. *arthmi-*. This produced one additional citation.

51.
  εἴ τις ἁμαρτωλῆισι φίλων ἐπὶ παντὶ χολῷτο,
    οὔποτ' ἂν ἀλλήλοισ' ἄρθμιοι οὐδὲ φίλοι
  εἶεν.
                                        (Theog. 335–37)

  Οὐκ ἔλαθες κλέψας, ὦ παῖ· καὶ γάρ σε διώμμαι·
    τούτοισ', οἷσπερ νῦν ἄρθμιος ἠδὲ φίλος
  ἔπλευ—ἐμὴν δὲ μεθῆκας ἀτίμητον φιλότητα—
    οὐ μὲν δὴ τούτοις γ' ἦσθα φίλος πρότερον.
                                        (Theog. 1311–14)

Cognates of *arthmios* are also associated with the idea of *philia* in the archaic period, e.g., the noun *arthmos* (*Homeric Hymn to Hermes* 526 ἐπ' ἀρθμῷ καὶ φιλότητι) and the verb *arthmeo* (*Il.* 7. 302 ἐν φιλότητι διέτμαγεν).

cannot withstand his attack if they are not *arthmioi* (7.102); Chileus of Tegea's warning to the Spartans that if the Athenians are not *arthmioi* with the other Greeks, no wall across the Isthmus will protect the Peloponnesus (9. 9.2); and relations between Argos and Tiryns (6.83) and Tegea and Sparta (9.37). All of these examples, like *Odyssey* 16.427, communicate the idea of a strong, unifying bond between states.

In the sphere of interstate diplomacy, however, there is no example of *arthmios* used in a formal treaty, such as *philia* is used; and even in literature, *arthmios* disappears altogether after Herodotus.[52] This consolidation suggests that whatever the original distinctions between the two words may have been, by the second half of the fifth century, *philia* was thought sufficient to communicate the ideas originally contained in both words.

The diplomatic meaning of *xenia* ("guest friendship") seems to have developed in a similar way. *Xenia* between individuals is fundamental to the conception of relations between different peoples in the Homeric poems. For example, Odysseus' bow and arrows were a gift from his Lacedaemonian *xenos* (*Od.* 21.13), and Athena bestirred Telemachus to action in the guise of Mentes, a Taphian *xenos* (*Od.* 1.105, 187). Moreover, so important were the obligations of *xenia* that they even overrode loyalty to the collective cause in warfare. Glaucus and Diomedes could not fight one another because their grandfathers were *xenoi* (*Il.* 6.215). In the Homeric conception, *xenia* connects individuals of different communities with ties of mutual amity and trust that are superior in importance to all other obligations.[53] What Herodotus reveals about the use of *xenia* in archaic diplomatic language is therefore extremely important.

Herodotus uses *xenia* twelve times in the sense of an interstate

---

52. Early citations of *arthmios* are distinctly East Greek, suggesting an Ionic dialect origin, which might account for the repeated (and seemingly redundant) connection of *arthmios* with the more common word *philia*.

53. A. W. H. Adkins, *Moral Values and Political Behaviour in Ancient Greece from Homer to the End of the Fifth Century* (London, 1972), 10–21; Finley, *World of Odysseus*, 103–9; and Herman, *Ritualised Friendship*, 10–40. The importance of *xenia* on a personal level continued well after the archaic period. Timocreon, the Rhodian poet, for example, bitterly criticizes Themistocles because he "did not bring Timocreon back from exile to his native Ialysus, although he was his *xenon*" (frag. 1). However, it is clear elsewhere (frag. 3) that Timocreon was kept in exile for his collaboration with the Persians; we can also see that in this case patriotism came to outweigh the older, "heroic" claims of guest friendship.

relationship between individuals or entire communities, and *xenos* sixteen times in the same way. The striking thing about these twenty-eight instances is that tyrants and monarchs are involved in all but one.[54] The repeated references to treaties of *xenia kai symmachia* between tyrants and other rulers, together with *xenia* between states ruled by tyrants, suggest strongly that this terminology was consciously borrowed from the language of heroic life by the practitioners of diplomacy in the age of tyranny and that Herodotus recognized this and used *xenia* and *xenos* accordingly.

It follows further that after the age of widespread tyrannical rule had passed and was in disrepute, diplomatic language especially favored by the tyrants also came to be considered tainted and therefore inappropriate to characterize relations between more democratically governed states. How else can we explain the complete absence of *xenia* and *xenos* from classical diplomatic documents or the fact that neither Thucydides nor Xenophon ever characterizes the relationship between states with these words? But if overtones of tyranny made *xenia* and *xenos* abhorrent, no such association existed for *philia,* and it is therefore no surprise that *philia* and *philos* completely supplanted *xenia* and *xenos* in the vocabulary of diplomacy and assumed their functions.[55]

If this reconstruction is correct, the diplomatic meaning of *philia* must have evolved in the archaic and classical periods to represent something of the sense of unity expressed in *arthmios* and something of the personal commitment of the heroic ethos contained in *xenia* but none of the military obligation basic to *symmachia.* The literary sources offer some clues to the resulting diplomatic idea. Herodotus, for example, mentions *philia* between states in nearly twenty different contexts.[56] In most instances there are no details, but we learn that Croesus made "friends" of those Greek cities he

54. *xenia*: Hdt. 1. 69.3, 27.5; 2. 182.1 and 2; 3. 39.2, 43.2; 4. 154.4; 5. 30.3; 7. 116, 165, 228.4; 8. 120; *xenos*: 1. 20, 22.4; 3. 21.1 and 2, 40.2, 43.2, 88.1; 5. 30.2, 33.3, [63.2 conjectured], 70.1, 91.2, 92.4; 7. 29.2, 237.3; 9. 76.3.

55. By the fourth century even relationships between individuals, which we would expect to be characterized as *xenia*, are called *philia*; consider, for instance, Cotys, king of the Paphlagonians, who sought *philia* with Agesilaus because of his *arete* and trustworthiness, i.e., his Homeric qualities (Plut. *Ages.* 11.1); see also Hdt. 1. 69 (Bengtson, *SVA*[2] no. 113) for a fifth-century author's intermingling of the terms.

56. Taking *philia, philios,* and *philos* into account, see Hdt. 1. 6, 53, 87.4, 172.2; 2. 152.5, 181.1 (twice); 3. 21, 39.2, 40, 49.1; 6. 89; 7. 130.3, 138.2, 151, 152.1 and 2, 163.2; 8. 140, 143.

could not subdue (1.6), that the Corinthians supplied ships to Athens because of "friendship" between the two states (6.89), and that Corinth joined Sparta in an expedition against Samos because the Corinthians were not on "friendly" terms with the Corcyraeans and held a grudge against the Samians for having once assisted the Corcyraeans to the embarrassment of Corinth (3.49).

This evidence suggests several things about diplomatic *philia*. First, negotiating *philia* could eliminate fears that either state might act in a hostile way toward the other or otherwise pose a military threat. Such appears to have been the basic intent, for example, in Lydian *philia* with the Greeks outside the limits of their empire, in Persian relations with Argos, and in the relationship between Carthage and Athens.[57] Indeed, the existence of *philia* could (and in some cases did) prevent one state from joining in hostility against another, as when, at the outset of the Peloponnesian War, the majority of Achaean cities refused to join either side due to their *philia* with both sides (Thuc. 2. 9.2). But perhaps the clearest example of *philia*'s potential for the prevention of military involvement appears in a *symmachia* between Amyntas and the Chalcideans, in which the terms of the treaty expressly forbid either party to conclude *philia* independently with Amphipolis, Acanthus, Mende, or the Bottiaeans, states against which the *symmachia* was intended.[58]

Second, *philia* was an official relationship, not a state of mind. Consider, for example, the Spartans' early offer to end the Peloponnesian War by making "peace, alliance, and friendship" (*eirēnē kai symmachia kai philia*) with Athens (Thuc. 4. 19.1). Neither party

---

57. For Lydia and the Greeks, see Hdt. 1. 6 (see 5.1 below); Persia and Argos, Hdt. 7. 151 (see 5.2 below); Carthage and Athens, Thuc. 6. 88.6; cf. Bengtson, *SVA*² no. 208; Meiggs and Lewis, no. 92 (see 7.4 below). This also may be the intent of the archaic treaties of *philia* (between the Metapioi and the Anaitoi and between the Romans and the Carthaginians) quoted above.

58.   Πρὸς Ἀμφιπολίτας, Βοττ[ι] | αίους, Ἀκανθίους, Μενδαίους μὴ π[οιεῖ] | [σθ]αι φιλίην Ἀμύνταμ μηδὲ Χαλκιδ[έας] | [χωρὶ]ς ἑκατέρους, ἀλλὰ μετὰ μιᾶ[ς γνώ] | [μης, ἐὰν ἀ]μφοτέροις δοκῆι, κοιν[ῆι] | [προσθέσθαι ἐκεί]νους. (Bengtson, *SVA*² no. 231, lines 18–23)

Neither Amyntas nor the Chalcidians may without the other enter into *philia* with the Amphipolitans, Bottiaeans, Acanthians, or Mendaeans, but if they agree and deem it beneficial, they may make an agreement with them in common.

J. Wickersham and G. Verbrugghe, *The Fourth Century B.C.: Greek Historical Documents* (Toronto, 1973), mistranslate *philia* as "alliance."

was envisioning cozy symposia of now devotedly amicable former enemies. *Philia* simply represents a diplomatic obligation, a commitment, that the citizens of the respective states will not injure one another or assist other states intending hostility.[59]

Finally, to distinguish *philia* from *symmachia* is not to deny that *philia* could be (and sometimes was) the basis for providing assistance to another state, such as when the Messapian chief Artas furnished the Athenians with javelin throwers (Thuc. 7. 33.4) after renewing his *philia* with Athens. The Athenian general Demosthenes likewise believed that the Phocians would, on account of their *philia* with Athens, join in attacking Doris and Boeotia; if not, he believed he could compel them (3. 95.1)—since their *philia* did not obligate them to do so, Demosthenes cannot be sure they will assist him voluntarily.

The language of diplomacy must be explicit enough to be understood but flexible enough to encompass the broadest possible range of different circumstances and requirements. This is, of course, why the specific terms of "alliance" have to be spelled out in detail. In formal use, the word "alliance," like "peace" or diplomatic "friendship," only acquires full meaning when defined by the terms of the agreement that has been negotiated. Indeed, without a detailed description of its content, the diplomatic term inevitably remains dangerously obscure. But this is not to say that diplomatic terms have no fundamental meaning. It would be wrong to think that *philia* and *symmachia* are synonymous or that *philia* and *eirēnē* (the diplomatic word for "peace") are interchangeable. Thus Demosthenes contrasts how easily two democracies may make peace (*ou chalepōs eirēnēn poiēsasthai*), while a democracy and an oligarchy cannot even safely maintain friendly relations (*ouk asphalē philian poiēsesthai*) with one another.[60] The Greeks were

59. It is this formal diplomatic *philia* that is envisioned, for instance, in the Corcyraeans' unsuccessful bid to extricate themselves from alignment with Athens in 427 and reestablish *philia* with the Peloponnesians (Thuc. 3. 70.2; cf. 1. 28.3 for reference to former *philia*; see Wilson, *Athens and Corcyra*, 28) or in the Plataeans' defense that, despite their alliance with Athens, they had been a friendly land (*philia chōra*) to the Spartans (3. 58.4) and therefore should not be judged as enemies.

60. Dem. 15 (*Rhod.*). 18. There have been many inaccurate statements about these terms: M. Amit, "A Peace Treaty between Sparta and Persia," *RivStorAnt* 4 (1974): 59–60, holds that *philia* means "alliance" on the basis of Thucydides' supposedly indifferent use of *symmachia* and *philia* in his account of the negotiations at Camarina (winter 415/414; see 7.3 below); W. M. Calder, *The Inscription*

not indifferent with regard to diplomatic language. The disappearance of *arthmios* and *xenia* as diplomatic terms shows this, as does the evolution of the comprehensive formula of *philia kai symmachia* ("friendship and alliance").[61] Such an agreement combines two different types of relationships into a single, all-encompassing agreement: as "friends" the parties will not cause injury to one another and as "allies" they commit themselves to mutual assistance in warfare.

For those who sought to remain neutral in a given conflict, the existence of *philia* as a specific relationship between states provided diplomatic means for retaining the goodwill and promoting the self-restraint of belligerents. The establishment of such agreements was not necessary for neutrality to exist, but there should be no doubt that having such an agreement increased a neutral state's security and enhanced its respectability.

V. ELECTIVE NONINVOLVEMENT IN MULTILATERAL ALLIANCES

The obligations imposed upon member states in multilateral alliances did not necessarily include compulsory involvement in any conflict entered into by members of the alliance. This may seem surprising; but evidence of the right to elective abstention can be gathered from the actions of states in (no less than) the Spartan alliance during conflicts of the archaic period onward. Despite a long-standing scholarly presumption that the Spartans wielded dictatorial power over their allies, what little we actually know about activities of the alliance suggests, on the contrary, that the right to decide whether to participate in a given conflict was not necessarily subordinated to the will of the hegemonial power of the alliance

---

from *Temple* G *at Selinus*, Greek, Roman, and Byzantine Monographs 4 (1963): 35–36 (echoed in Meiggs and Lewis, no. 38) maintains that the phrase including *philias de genomenas* (line 7) means that "hostilities have ceased" and *"friendship, that is peace*, has been restored." The distinction Calder should emphasize is that as a result of peace, *philia* has also been established. This is the sense of compound treaty formulas, such as during the Peloponnesian War (Thuc. 4. 19.2, 8. 37.1), in the Spartan treaty with the Erxadieis (W. Peek, "Ein neuer spartanischer Staatsvertrag," *AbhLeip* 65 [1974]: 3–15), and in Athenian negotiations with Persia (Andoc. 3 [*On the Peace*] 29; see 6.3.C below).

61. The earliest epigraphical evidence (restored) is the Athenian alliance with the Bottiaeans of 422 (Bengtson, *SVA*[2] no. 187).

unless a full assembly of alliance states was held and the majority voted for war.[62]

Take what we know specifically about Corinth. Herodotus suggests that even after the Corinthians entered the Peloponnesian League (the multilateral alliance referred to in antiquity as "the Lacedaemonians and their allies"), they continued to maintain considerable independence on the question of war or peace.[63] According to Herodotus, when Cleomenes called together the allies for an expedition against Athens about 506, he did not reveal the true purpose of the expedition, which was the installation of Isagoras as tyrant, but gave some other pretext.[64] At Eleusis, however,

62. Thuc. 5. 30.1. There has been much scholarly speculation about the "constitution" of the Peloponnesian League; see, for instance, U. Kahrstedt, *Griechische Staatsrecht*, vol. 1: *Sparta und seine Symmachie* (Göttingen, 1922); J. A. O. Larsen, "Sparta and the Ionian Revolt: A Study of Spartan Foreign Policy and the Genesis of the Peloponnesian League," *CP* 27 (1932): 136–50; id., "The Constitution of the Peloponnesian League I," *CP* 28 (1933): 257–76; id., "The Constitution of the Peloponnesian League II," *CP* 29 (1934): 1–19; V. Martin, *La vie internationale dans la Grèce des cités (VIe–IVe s. av. J.-C.)*, Publ. des l'Inst. Univ. des Hautes Études Internationales, Genèves, 21 (Paris, 1940), 186–242; K. Wickert, "Der peloponnesische Bunde von seiner Entstehung bis zum Ende des archidamischen Krieges" (Diss., Erlangen-Nürnberg, 1961); J. Huxley, *Early Sparta* (London, 1962), 64–86; W. G. Forrest, *History of Sparta, 950–192 B.C.* (London, 1968), 88–91; Jeffery, *Archaic Greece*, 120–23; R. Sealey, *A History of the Greek City-States, 700–338 B.C.* (Oxford, 1976), 83–86. However, there is virtually no discussion of possible abstention by states within the alliance, because most have assumed allied subordination from the beginning, such as de Ste. Croix, *Origins of the Peloponnesian War*, 108–10; R. Holladay, "Sparta's Role in the First Peloponnesian War," *JHS* 97 (1977): 55 n. 8; P. Cartledge, *Sparta and Laconia: A Regional History, 1300–362 B.C.* (London, 1979), 148. F. Gschnitzer, *Ein neuer spartanischer Staatsvertrag und die Verfassung des peloponnesischen Bundes*, Beiträge zur klassichen Philologie 93 (Meisenheim am Glan., 1978), 33–40, argues from the recently discovered Spartan-Erxadieis treaty (see Peek, "Ein neuer spartanischer Staatsvertrag") that the archaic alliances creating the league included the specific agreement that the allies would have "the same friends and the same enemies as the Lacedaemonians" and "follow wherever they led"; but the date of the Erxadieis inscription is far from certain (P. Cartledge, "A New 5th-Century Spartan Treaty," *LCM* 1 [1976]: 87–92; id., "The New 5th-Century Spartan Treaty Again," *LCM* 3 [1978]: 189–190; and D. H. Kelly, "The New Spartan Treaty," *LCM* 3 [1978]: 133–41, argue for a late fifth- or early fourth-century date) and does not *ipso facto* prove that all treaties from the beginning of the alliance were the same.

63. Although there is no direct evidence for when Corinth first allied itself with Sparta, the alliance must predate Corinthian participation in the expedition led by Cleomenes against Athens (ca. 506; Hdt. 5. 75–76) and postdate the fall of the tyranny at Corinth (ca. 580; Jeffery, *Archaic Greece*, 152–53; J. B. Salmon, *Wealthy Corinth: A History of the City to 338 B.C.* [Oxford, 1984], 240). On Corinthian freedom of action, ibid., 241–52.

64. Herodotus does not specify the public reason given for the expedition, but the charge may have been medism. Athens had just appealed to Persia, and an over-hasty surrender of earth and water had even been made by the Athenian ambassadors (Hdt. 5. 73). Sparta could therefore claim that intervention was a defensive precaution to forestall Persian ambitions in Greece.

the Corinthians declared that they considered the invasion unjust (perhaps they had discovered the real aim), and summarily withdrew (Hdt. 5.75).

This sequence of events implies several important things: First, Sparta could not automatically expect the aid of its allies in settling a private grudge or in intervening in the internal politics of another state; accordingly, a specious pretext was invented. Second, the Corinthians believed they had a right not to participate if the campaign did not comply with the terms of the alliance as they understood them.[65] Third, the rest of the allies, although they may have been more seriously intimidated by Sparta's power than Corinth was, also believed that their participation was unjustified and that their abandonment of the expedition was, therefore, legitimate and defensible.[66]

A second, related incident occurred soon afterwards. Smarting at the humiliating treatment they had received from Athens, the Spartans are said to have decided to restore Hippias and to have called together the states of the alliance in order to muster support (5.90–91). But again, with Corinth in the lead, the states strenuously opposed the proposal as unjustified (5.92–93); and significantly, the Spartans abandoned the entire project (5.94).

In these reports, Herodotus suggests that the other Peloponnesian states had a healthy respect for Spartan power yet did not consider themselves bound to support its foreign policy enterprises under any circumstances. Of course, Corinth might join Sparta in an expedition against Samos (ca. 525), but the reason given by Herodotus is not Corinth's treaty obligation to Sparta but the hope of revenge for a private insult suffered in the past (3.48). Furthermore, although the rejection or acceptance of a proposal by the majority of states came to be binding for all members in the fifth century,[67] there is still no evidence that the bilateral treaties of the archaic period, which stood at the foundation of the Peloponnesian League,

65. Herodotus says only that the departure of Corinth and then of King Demaratus caused the general breakup of the army; but if the rest of the allies had supported the real cause of the expedition, they could have stayed.

66. Note that a threat of reprisal against Corinth is not mentioned, either here or when the Corinthians convince the allies to reject Sparta's plan to restore Hippias (Hdt. 5. 92–93).

67. Cf. Thuc. 1. 125; 5. 30.1 (fifth cent.). The implication underlying the meeting of allies concerning Hippias is also that a majority consensus was being sought. However, nothing is said about a meeting before the earlier expedition against Athens.

denied the right of the allied parties to remain aloof from one another's private disputes. Neither the Spartans' involvement with Croesus nor their expedition against Polycrates of Samos nor their repeated military confrontations with the Argives nor their numerous attempts to impose their will on Athens through armed intervention—none of these belligerent actions is reported to have involved obligatory participation by the allies. Moreover, there can be no doubt at all that the Spartans themselves were under no obligation to support their allies in any given war, because they are clearly neutral in the Corinthian-Corcyraean War in 435–433 (Thuc. 1. 28.1) and have to be convinced to join Corinth in going to war with Athens in 432 (Thuc. 1. 68–86).[68] Sparta's military ascendancy at the end of the fifth century may have resulted in de facto elimination of the traditional freedom of elective nonparticipation for its allies, but that does not mean that understanding of it was lost or had never existed, only that the decisive military superiority of Sparta and the perceived danger of Athenian imperialism resulted in the submergence of the traditionally understood rights of autonomous states in the alliance.

SUMMARY

From the beginning, diplomatic relationships between Greek *poleis* were highly complex. The Greeks probably never had the simplistic notion that relationships were not possible outside of a dichotomy of friends and enemies.[69] With the evolution of independent communities, which conducted foreign policy through the negotiation of formal treaties that were often publicly displayed at Panhellenic sanctuaries, came shared expectations about what constituted proper diplomatic behavior and the responsibilities of states to one another. At the same time the exact details of every negotiated relationship varied in accordance with the specific circumstances

68. Note further the reservations that have been expressed as to just how involved Sparta was in the early years of the so-called First Peloponnesian War: Holladay, "Sparta's Role in the First Peloponnesian War," 54–63; D. M. Lewis, "The Origins of the First Peloponnesian War," in *Classical Contributions: Studies in Honour of Malcolm Francis McGregor*, ed. G. S. Shrimpton and D. J. McCargar (Locust Valley, N.Y., 1981), 71–78.

69. Let alone Plato's despairing assertion that all states were in fact in an eternal state of undeclared war with one another (*Laws* 626A; see 3.2 above); for recent discussion, see Manicas, "War, Stasis, and Greek Political Thought," 674–76, and Gehrke, *Athen und Sparta*, 52–55.

and interests of the parties when agreement was reached. This is reflected in the extraordinarily wide spectrum of responsibilities apparent in surviving documents and narrative accounts of diplomacy. Specific compacts could, as we have seen (in 3.3–4 above), provide formal justification for a state's abstention in the event of war. Universal alignment and compulsory involvement in every interstate conflict were never imagined as inevitable. On the contrary, what emerges from an overview of diplomatic conventions is a framework of limitations, which, at least in theory, restrained a belligerent's use of violence against parties that remained aloof from conflict.

The foundation of restraint in Greek warfare came from the acceptance of certain special categories of people and places as exempt from the violence of war. The respected status of heralds and the recognition of the inviolability of sanctuaries (*asylia*) provide obvious examples of customary restrictions; the compliance with the dictates of religious truces (*ekecheiriai*), however inconvenient, shows how strongly this commitment was felt.[70] Acknowledgement of the validity of certain unwritten rules of war (*agraphoi nomoi*) also contributed to the development of a sense of interstate responsibility that influenced the behavior of belligerents, whether or not specific interstate agreements existed. As Y. Garlan points out: "Even in the heat of battle or the intoxication of victory, men at war had to conform to a number of customs aimed, in a general way, at limiting the blind use of force. Though never codified, these customs were widely and correctly enough observed, even in relations with barbarians, for anyone contravening them to be blamed and to have sanctions imposed."[71] The use of arbitration as a means of resolving disputes was an especially positive development in this area because it involved formal recognition of the impartiality of the state chosen as arbitrator (*ekklētos polis*). Likewise, the mediating role played by concerned states promoted the idea that lack of positive commitment need not be automatically equated with hostility but could be reconciled with friendly attitude.

    70. See the discussion of Phlius and Mantinea's use of sacred truces (*ekecheiriai*) to avoid contributing forces to the allied Spartan army during the Corinthian War in 8.3.B below.
    71. Garlan, *War in the Ancient World*, 57; cf. P. Vinogradoff, *Outlines of Historical Jurisprudence*, vol. 2: *The Jurisprudence of the Greek City* (London, 1922), 162; see also Pritchett, *Greek State at War*, vol. 3, 315, quoted in note 75 below.

Even within the structure of alliances, states repeatedly acted as if the right to refrain from involvement in certain of the conflicts of their allies was assumed to exist. The behavior of Corinth in the late sixth century, of Corinth's own allies in the 430s, and of Thebes, Athens, and Corinth in the decade following the end of the Peloponnesian War all point to the reservation of this right even among allies.[72] Evidently the only way to prevent states from pursuing this diplomatic option was to forbid it specifically either by stating in the original treaty of alliance that the parties would "have the same friends and the same enemies"[73] or by prohibiting allies from entering into independent agreements that might prevent participation in an anticipated conflict. The latter is clearly specified in the alliance (*symmachia*) between King Amyntas of Macedon and the Chalcidians, which forbids either party to conclude *philia* separately with specified states.[74]

Scattered though the evidence may be, it nevertheless provides, in the aggregate, substantial support for the idea that something akin to the modern concept of neutrality might be a legitimate diplomatic option within the context of customarily respected rules of warfare. A state's neutral position could be founded on the relationship of *philia*, supported by the acknowledged legitimacy of the exemption of some parties from violence, and enforced by the consensus that even warfare should be conducted within bounds.[75] But this is all theoretical. We need to turn now to the realities that confronted would-be neutrals when they decided on abstention.

---

72. On sixth-century Corinth, see 3.5 above; on the Corinthian-Corcyraean War, ibid. and 5.3.C below; on Thebes, Athens, and Corinth, see 8.2 below.

73. E.g., the Athenian alliance of 478 (Arist. *Ath. Pol.* 23.5), on which, see J. A. O. Larsen, "The Constitution and Original Purpose of the Delian League," *HSCP* 51 (1940): 187–90. Compare also the Spartan-Erxadieis treaty (see note 62 above).

74. Bengtson, *SVA*[2] no. 231; see 3.4 above.

75. The effect of such intangible forces could be critical. Pritchett, *Greek State of War*, vol. 3, 315, notes: "It is an impressive fact for the modern scholar seeking to recover the religious convictions of the Greek soldiers that the entire Lakedaimonian army could be detained for several days in neutral territory, provisioning itself as best it could, while it awaited the decision of Zeus and his son." The incident is reported by Xenophon (*Hell.* 4. 7.2–7); see note 21 in chapter 8 below.

CHAPTER FOUR

The Realities of Remaining Uncommitted

The diplomatic developments outlined in the previous chapter encouraged the recognition of a wider range of formal policies than the simple dichotomy of ally or enemy. War did not extend to everyone. Rules applied. Some noncombatants and exempted places had to be honored. Alternative resolutions could be sought through the agency of impartial third parties. Even the conflicts of allies did not automatically extend to all members of a *symmachia*. Under the proper circumstances, abstention was possible. Diplomatic friendship could be preserved. Neutrality could be achieved. But how exactly did it happen? What were the circumstances that permitted adoption of a neutral position? Does the cumulative evidence point to any general preconditions or consistent requirements connected with abstention? What, in short, were the realities confronting would-be neutrals?

The first thing that one notices about states that stay out of wars in the classical period, especially when one compares them with modern neutral states, is the lack of connection between their policy and commercial interests. In this respect neutrality in the classical period differs distinctly from neutrality as it has evolved since the seventeenth century. Although neutral merchants are mentioned, and their rights are normally respected, there is nothing like the strong insistence on free trade and the absolute respect for the immunity of neutral commerce that has been a critical force behind the acceptance and legalization of neutrality in modern international law.[1] The only explicit association of neutral status and commercial advantage is found in contemporary references to Argos in the Archidamian War (431–421). In his *Peace* of March 421 Aristophanes has Hermes complain that the Argives are capitalizing on their neutral status by making money off of both sides.[2] Evidently there is more to this accusation than mere comic exaggeration, because Thucydides also emphasizes that the Argives profited from their neutrality. After the Peace of Nicias, he reports, the Argives decided to form their own alliance and challenge Sparta, seeing that their treaty with the Spartans was about to expire and Sparta's reputation was exceptionally bad (*malista kakōs*) due to the misfortunes they had suffered recently. The Argives themselves were in an excellent position, because they had taken no part in the Attic (i.e., Archidamian) War, being at peace with both sides (*amphoterois mallon enspondoi ontes*) and having reaped a harvest (*ekkarpōsamenoi*) from the war.[3] The exact source of the Argives' profit, however, is nowhere identified. All that we can say for certain is that traders from states that were not formally committed

1. On neutrality and commercial interests, see Jessup and Deák, *Neutrality*, vol. 1. For ancient respect of noncombatant commerce, see the examples cited below in 6.6 and 9.5.B (pp. 239–40). See also Xen. *Hell*. 4. 8.33 (safe passage of those who were not Athenian or allied with Athens is implied); [Dem.] 12 (*Philip's Letter*). 5 (illegal attack by Athens); note also Dem. 24 (*Timoc.*). 11–12. In addition, two later incidents of violence against neutral merchants emphasize the (at the time incorrect) expectation of immunity that existed among nonbelligerents; see Diodorus' account (19.4–5) of the Carthaginians' seizure and mutilation of Athenian traders at Syracuse in 312 (reported as an obviously criminal act and identified by Diodorus as the cause of divine retribution against Carthage) and Plutarch's description (*Demetr.* 33.3) of how Demetrius Poliorcetes seized a merchant ship bringing grain to Athens in 297 and executed its officers to prevent further commerce from reaching the city (an obviously extraordinary measure interpreted by Plutarch as evidence of Demetrius' unrestrained character).

2. Ar. *Peace*, 475–77; for the Greek, see note 22 in chapter 1. In the scholia to *Peace* 477 it is noted that the Argive policy was much satirized and the following example from Pherecrates' *Deserters* (*Hoi Automoloi*) is quoted: "For these wretched miscreants incline to both sides (*epamphoterizous*'), destroying us and sitting right in our way" (Edmonds, *FAC*, vol. 1, 217–19, frag. 19). Neutral commerce may also be satirized in a papyrus fragment of Old Comedy (Edmonds I 951–53) dating to the third century B.C. In it a Doric-speaking merchant, thrust forward to negotiate peace and revive trade, advises: "So then as you go around say that not Euarchidas ["Rulewell"] but Euempolos ["Tradewell"] offers the thing beloved by you (*to philion*) and has concern for you, just as someone castrated is anxious for his testicles" (Edmonds, *FAC*, vol. 1, 251–53, frag. 5E, a, lines 6–9).

3. Thuc. 5. 28. This is Thucydides' only use of the verb *ekkarpoomai*, which is otherwise rare in classical literature; cf. Eur. *Ion* 815 (in the sense "to have children by another woman"). Here, however, it clearly means "to enjoy the fruit of a thing" in the sense of "making a profit" (*LSJ*[9], s.v. *ekkarpoomai*).

must have expected to continue trading with impunity, since Thucydides reports Spartan ill-treatment of neutral traders in terms that indicate that this was an obvious violation of the conventional rules of war (the *nomoi Hellēnes*).[4]

A more complicated example that may have commercial interests as its basis appears in the policy adopted by reportedly pro-Spartan city-states in Southern Italy and Sicily from 431. According to Thucydides, the Spartans instructed their West Greek supporters to maintain an officially correct (i.e., neutral) stance in the conflict with Athens while they made preparations to enter the war openly on the Spartan side (2. 7.2). As far as we know, this policy was adopted and continued successfully until 427, when the Athenians decided to enter a regional conflict (separate from the ongoing Peloponnesian War) in West Greece and thereby, among other objectives, prevent further exportation of grain from Sicily to the Peloponnesus (3. 86.4). An important feature of this decision is that the Athenians did not move directly against Sicilian shipping but only indirectly and only when the right opportunity presented itself. In actual fact, therefore, the right of traders to move freely was never challenged or openly violated, even though traders were effectively prevented from supplying grain to the Peloponnesians just as surely as if the Athenians had instituted an embargo.[5]

What seems to be reflected in these and other rare instances where trade and neutral policy appear to be associated is the existence of a definite expectation that citizens of a state that remained uncommitted in a given conflict could pursue trade without interference from the belligerents. However, reality often conflicted with this expectation. The Spartans executed traders indiscriminately at the beginning of the Peloponnesian War, and— just as in modern wars—belligerents now and again either openly disregarded or found indirect ways to circumvent the customary

---

4. Thuc. 2. 67.4. See 6.6. below and B. R. MacDonald, "The Import of Attic Pottery to Corinth and the Question of Trade during the Peloponnesian War," *JHS* 102 (1982): 113–23. Phillipson, *International Law and Custom*, vol. 1, 133, interprets the *symbola* of Ar. *Birds* 1214 (see the scholia) as evidence that official labels were affixed to goods as a guarantee that they were not contraband. Noncombatant travelers may have carried official documents like passports; see Aen. Tac. 10.8; and Gauthier, *Symbola*, 75–76.

5. See 6.2 below.

respect for nonbelligerent trade if they believed their interests and military objectives were threatened.[6]

Neutrality of the classical period is more often directly involved with self-defense and the safety of the state than with protection of trade and profit. The various restrictions that neutrals imposed or attempted to impose on the activities of belligerents, such as prohibiting passage across neutral territory, limiting to a single ship the access of belligerents to a neutral harbor, refusing to allow belligerents within the city walls, and even denying water and withholding the sale of food, all represent distinctly self-defensive measures.[7] Collectively they tell us what a would-be neutral state perceived as its rights. When a state adopted a neutral position, it could declare restrictions on the belligerents that it deemed legitimate for protecting its policy. At the same time, the belligerents could—and did—insist that uncommitted states had reciprocal obligations, the foremost of which seems to have been impartiality. The Corcyraeans, for example, complained in 433 that if the Athenians intended to remain uncommitted in the Corinthian-Corcyraean War, they should either prevent recruitment of mercenaries by Corinth from within the Athenian empire or provide Corcyra with equal opportunity for recruiting.[8] In 429 Archidamus demanded, as proof of their impartiality, that the Plataeans receive both belligerents equally as friends.[9] Knowledge of these expectations could not help but influence the behavior of uncommitted states, especially since neutral states were often in no position to disregard the demands of the belligerents.[10]

---

6. On Spartan abuse of traders, see Thuc. 2. 67.4; cf. attacks on Southern Italian trade during the Athenian invasion of Sicily (in 7.2 below) and later attacks on traders contrary to customary practice (see note 1 above).

7. For a full list with references, see the Conclusion.

8. Thuc. 1. 35.3; discussed in 5.3C below. Note the interesting remark by H. B. Leech, "Ancient International Law," *Contemp. Rev.* 43 (1883): 264, that the Corcyraeans "commented on the injustice caused by the absence of a Foreign Enlistment Act at Athens, and criticized severely that benevolent neutrality which failed to find a footing in modern International Law." For the existence in the classical period of such legislation, however, see 8.4.B below and 9.3.B note 38 (quoting Aen. Tac. 10. 7).

9. Thuc. 2. 72.1 (*dechesthe amphoterous philous*); discussed in 6.4 below. At their trial the Plataeans claimed, despite everything, that they had maintained *philia* toward Sparta (3. 58.2 and 4) and fought on the Athenian side only from compulsion (*kat' anankēn* 58.2).

10. This really was the situation for Plataea; but unfortunately for the Plataeans, the Athenians insisted that neutrality be rejected even though they them-

The existence of neutral states complicated diplomacy and was a challenge to the authoritarian aims of the hegemonial powers. Clearly, weak states were always vulnerable to violation of their attempts to remain neutral, particularly when a powerful belligerent was strongly opposed to the policy. The fate of Melos makes this perfectly clear, as do the fate of Belgium in 1914 and the failure of numerous other "legal" attempts at neutral policy. No appeal to the legitimacy or the justice of the Melians' position, or even to the Athenians' self-interest, could prevail against Athens' refusal to accept and respect Melian neutrality.[11] It should be understood, however, that there is consistent evidence that throughout the classical period some instances of neutrality were admitted without regard to the absolute power of the state desiring to be neutral but in recognition that such a policy should (and could) be safely accepted by the belligerents. Fourth-century Megara is perhaps the best example of this phenomenon, but by the 360s a number of other states found ways to negotiate effective neutrality in the continued conflicts of that turbulent period.[12] The policy appears to have been more widespread during the struggle between Philip II and the Athenian alliance than has been recognized, despite Demosthenes' bitter condemnation of neutrals.[13]

But why do we find such an inconsistent mixture of acceptance of and resistance to the idea of abstention being legitimate? Certainly the right of a state to remain aloof from the conflicts of other states and to demand respect for that position is fundamental to achievement of at least limitation of, if not control over the

---

selves were in no position to provide support for Plataea. The behavior of the West Greek states from 431 suggests they knew exactly what was expected of neutral status, and the indirect response of Athens also suggests that the Athenians hesitated to attack shipping directly when unprovoked. Similar expectations and resulting demands between supposedly uninvolved and actively belligerent parties underlie the give-and-take of diplomacy between the Greeks and Persians during the fourth century (see 9.3.B below).

11. See 7.1 below.

12. See 8.3.C below (Megara) and 9.2.C (other states); cf. Salmon, *Wealthy Corinth*, 380–81: "The implication of the arrangements was that small states might remain neutral in the quarrels between the great powers. This was a principle which, if it could not eradicate the larger power struggles, at least might have helped restrict their effects to those states which insisted on taking part in them. The principle is well summarized by Xenophon (*Hell.* 7.4.7): 'so that they might make the peace with those who wanted it, and let those who wished to make war do so.'"

13. See 9.5 below.

chaos of unrestricted warfare. Since the right to neutrality could potentially benefit belligerents as much as nonbelligerents, why do we find such consistent hostility, whether it is in the actions of the states themselves or in the attitude of the sources? The answer, I believe, lies in the structure of archaic and classical Greek political thought. Basic to Greek culture was a competitive spirit that influenced every aspect of life, including interstate relations.[14] For this very reason, the evolution of numerous separate, independent, and, in theory, equal city-states brought with it countless interstate agreements that formally bound states to one another either individually or collectively. Security was the paramount aim of most formal agreements; and neutrality could be considered antithetical to this goal, since it left unresolved the question of commitment and thus denied the predictability of supportive involvement. This reality was recognized from very early on and deeply resented. Solon was notorious for having attempted to outlaw abstention in the event of the state being divided by internal conflict; and in interstate affairs the situation was the same. Many remained deeply hostile to those who refused to commit themselves; and the fact is that this tension was never resolved.

What we find on the belligerent side is a nearly constant antagonism characterized by reluctant acknowledgment of neutral rights, a determined insistence on obligations, and an ever-present readiness to punish the uncommitted when given the opportunity. This antagonism appears repeatedly in a variety of forms: in the vindictive proposal by one faction of the Greek alliance for the punishment of states that failed to support the Greek cause in 480; in Sparta's uncompromising refusal to accept neutrality as a diplomatic option for its allies at the end of the fifth and the beginning of the fourth century; and in Demosthenes' bitter denunciation of politicians who refused to attach their states to the anti-Macedonian coalition in 338.[15]

At the end of his celebrated analysis of the Corcyraean *stasis*, Thucydides summarizes this basic reality brilliantly: "Those citizens in the middle [i.e., aligned with neither faction] were destroyed by both sides, either because they would not share in the fight or

---

14. A point proven in detail by A. W. H. Adkins, *Merit and Responsibility: A Study in Greek Values* (Oxford, 1960); see also Carter, *Quiet Athenian*, 1–25.
15. On the Greek states in 480, see 5.2 below; on Sparta, 8.2–5 below; and on Demosthenes, 9.5.A–B.

out of jealousy that they should survive."[16] But this problem is hardly restricted to classical Greece. In *The Prince*, Machiavelli boldly advises:

> A prince is further esteemed when he is a true friend or a true enemy, when, that is, he declares himself without reserve in favour of some one or against another. This policy is always more useful than remaining neutral. ... And it will always happen that the one who is not your friend will want you to remain neutral, and the one who is your friend will require you to declare yourself by taking arms. Irresolute princes, to avoid present dangers, usually follow the way of neutrality and are mostly ruined by it.[17]

The dilemma identified by Machiavelli has a number of antecedents in fifth-and fourth-century diplomatic history,[18] but perhaps none more striking than the position of Athens dramatized in Euripides' *Suppliants*. On the one side, Creon, ruler of Thebes, menacingly pressures Theseus, king of Athens, to ignore appeals by the widowed wives of the Argive heroes slain—but not buried—at Thebes.[19] On the other, Aethra, Theseus' mother, angrily insists that he commit Athens to the side of the suppliants: "Do you see? Is your country so irresolute (*aboulos*), when, having been mocked, she fixes her gorgon stare on those who mock her? In strenuous labors she grows greater; but states which abstain from action (*hēsychoi poleis*), while moving in dark shadows, through excessive caution, have their very identity eclipsed."[20] Here is the Machiavel-

---

16. τὰ δὲ μέσα τῶν πολιτῶν ὑπ' ἀμφοτέρων ἢ ὅτι οὐ ξυνηγωνίζοντο ἢ φθόνῳ τοῦ περιεῖναι διεφθείροντο (Thuc. 3. 82.8).

17. Lerner, trans., *The Prince*, 83.

18. See in particular the parallel rhetoric used to describe the Syracusan demand that the Camarinaeans not remain neutral in 415 (7.3 below), the Carthaginian proposal that Acragas be neutral in 406 (8.1 below), and, as will be argued below (in 9.5), the encouragement of neutrality by Philip II of Macedon and the rejection of it as betrayal by the Demosthenic faction at Athens.

19. Eur. *Supp.* 467–75 (quoted above on pp. 17–18 with n. 20).

20.
> ὁρᾷς, ἄβουλος ὡς κεκερτομημένη
> τοῖς κερτομοῦσι γοργὸν ὄμμ' ἀναβλέπει
> σὴ πατρίς; ἐν γὰρ τοῖς πόνοισιν αὔξεται·
> αἱ δ' ἥσυχοι σκοτεινὰ πράσσουσαι πόλεις
> σκοτεινὰ καὶ βλέπουσιν εὐλαβούμεναι.
>   (Eur. *Supp.* 321–25)

My translation interprets lines 324–25 as I believe Euripides intended them to be understood; others have rendered them differently, e.g., Carter (*Quiet Athenian*, 12): "But dull and sluggish cities follow dull policies, Peering cautiously about them"; and Collard (Euripides, *Supplices*, vol. 2, 193): "Cities which are slow to act and deal in secret Keep secret too the ways their eyes are looking, so cautious

lian paradox and something more; for in the *Suppliants* the issue
of Athenian abstention involves not merely the political question
of alignment but also a deeper question about the extent to which
respect for religious custom, that is, the proper burial of the dead,
makes inaction morally offensive and in itself blamable. By juxta-
posing possible policy and impossible circumstances, Euripides thus
anticipates with uncanny accuracy one of the most intractable
obstacles to the modern acceptance of neutrality.

When Grotius published his landmark *De iure pacis ac belli* in
1624, he warned that those who abstained from involvement in a
war (his *medii*) must do nothing to hinder the "just" side; and to
this day, neutrals are often stigmatized as "passive supporters" of
injustice by one belligerent side or the other, each convinced that
its cause alone is "just." Despite all efforts to divorce neutral policy
from moral considerations, this remains a basic problem already
visible in the evidence from the late fifth century. During the
Peloponnesian War, in particular, the ideological propaganda of
the opposing belligerents severely undermined the position of neutrals. As M. Cogan puts it, "ideological oppositions are always
absolute: they are oppositions of right and wrong. Where material
powers, only, are opposed, there exists the status of neutrality for
those who provide support to neither side. But where philosophies
contend, nonparticipation is taken for acquiescence, and passivity
for passive support." Thus, in the increasingly ideological rhetoric

---

are they." Collard interprets σκοτεινὰ καὶ βλέπουσι as "their looks too are dark,"
i.e., their eyes avoid each other, in contrast to the Athenians' free and fearless
outlook; but even if this is literally accurate, I nevertheless believe that Euripides
intends Aethra to communicate the idea that εὐλάβεια leads not to civic distinction
and greatness but only to obscurity. In support, compare, for example, frag. 1052
Nauck:

> νεανίας γὰρ ὅστις ὢν Ἄρη στυγῇ,
> κόμη μόνον καὶ σάρκες, ἔργα δ' οὐδαμοῦ.
> ὁρᾷς τὸν εὐτράπεζον ὡς ἡδὺς βίος
> ὅ τ' ὄλβος ἔξωθέν τίς ἐστι πραγμάτων·
> 5 ἀλλ' οὐκ ἔνεστι στέφανος οὐδ' εὐανδρία,
> εἰ μή τι καὶ τολμῶσι κινδύνου μέτα·
> οἱ γὰρ πόνοι τίκτουσι τὴν εὐανδρίαν,
> ἡ δ' εὐλάβεια σκότον ἔχει καθ' Ἑλλάδα,
> τὸ διαβιῶναι μόνον ἀεὶ θηρωμένη.

> For strenuous labors give birth to manly prowess
> But excessive caution (*eulabeia*) holds obscure gloom over Hellas,
> A forsaken life spent forever hounded (lines 7–9).

of the war, Cogan argues, one of the recurrent political slogans involved the idea that "the city which could prevent the enslavement of others, but stands quietly by, is the true enslaver." "It is in this way, by characterizing the world as divided between those who oppose and those who support the aggressive Atticist ideology," reasons Cogan, "that the Spartans eliminated the notion of neutrality. ... And in the dissipation of opportunities for neutrality [the Spartans] helped to create conditions which would drive the Athenians to a state of fear in which they, too, would decide that neutrality was impossible and that the compulsions of war were total, unalterable, and irreconcilable."[21]

It is especially through his careful positioning of set speeches that Thucydides reveals how contemporary political rhetoric exerted an increasingly powerful influence on the issue of neutrality during the war.[22] Among the most striking examples are the Corinthians' bitter denunciation of Sparta's reluctance to oppose Athenian imperial domination as equivalent to willful enslavement of the subject states (1. 69.1; cf. 71.1), Brasidas' threat that Acanthus could no longer remain passively inactive but had to revolt openly from the Athenian alliance and declare itself for Sparta and for the cause of liberation (4.85–87); the Athenians' insistence that the safety of their empire could be guaranteed only by the subjugation of all islanders, including the neutral Melians (5.94–99); and Hermocrates' warning that the Camarinaeans could not safely consider neutrality an option because it meant supporting injustice and was therefore in itself equally unjust and deserving of punishment (6. 80.1–2). It is unlikely that Thucydides misrepresents this progression of ideologizing, especially since he obviously makes no effort to impose didactic uniformity in the History by suppressing contradictory evidence of the continued acceptability of neutrality. The two strands remain, unreconciled, true to the reality of the situation.

Despite his pessimistic assessment of abstention in the paradigmatic Corcyraean stasis ("those in the middle were destroyed by both sides, either because they would not share in the fight or out

21. M. Cogan, The Human Thing: The Speeches and Principles of Thucydides (Chicago and London, 1981), 84–85. On the political slogans of the period generally, see Grossmann, Politische Schlagwörter.

22. On the reasons for Thucydides' interest in neutrality, see pp. 22–28 in Chapter 2.

of jealousy that they should survive," 3. 82.8), Thucydides saw that in both domestic *stasis* and interstate warfare the policy persisted. The Corinthians urged it as most legitimate (*dikaios malista*) for Athens during the Corinthian-Corcyraean War (1. 40.4); Archidamus proposed it as acceptable for Plataea (2. 72.1), and subsequently, at the Plataeans' trial, when the Thebans pointed to the Plataeans' refusal as proof of their guilt (3. 64.3), the Spartan judges concurred (3. 68.1); the Athenians and the Spartans assigned neutral status to disputed Thracian cities in the Peace of Nicias (5. 18.5); and despite Melos, a number of South Italian and Sicilian city-states remained steadfastly neutral during the Athenian expedition against Syracuse.[23] These are just the examples about which Thucydides is specific. The diplomatic postures of Carthage, of the Persian king, of the cities of Crete, of Thessaly, are less clearly defined, but all may have involved recognized abstention.[24]

The plain fact is that although hostile ideological rhetoric exacerbated opposition to neutral policy, states continued to consider it a tenable option, preferable to alignment, as long as circumstances permitted. Surely it is correct to emphasize the potentially destructive effect of ideologizing on the possibility of neutrality; but equally, it is wrong to see this as a categorical denial and to conclude, as Cogan does, that "one of the general consequences of the ideologizing of the war was the virtual disappearance of this neutral ground even in the larger context of the Greek world as a whole."[25] The diplomatic realities of the Peloponnesian War were far more complex and (true to *to anthrōpinon*) less predictably consistent with ideological imperatives or traditional norms than might be expected. We can only appreciate this uneasy coexistence of contradictory concepts and practices by examining both the full range of Thucydidean information and other reflections of attitudes toward interstate politics wherever they occur (as in Euripides or Aristophanes, for instance).[26]

Faced with the combined obstacles of ideological opposition and willful disregard of traditional rules (which would-be neutrals were

23. On West Greek neutrality, see 7.2–3 below.
24. On Carthage, see 7.4 below; on Persia, Crete, and Thessaly, 6.3 below.
25. Cogan, *Human Thing*, 152.
26. Note the continued existence of neutral states, mentioned as late as the winter of 413/412 (Thuc. 8. 2.1). For gleanings from Euripides and Aristophanes, see, for example, the passages quoted above.

hardly in a position to punish), the states seeking to avoid involvement in a given conflict commonly sought to minimize the peril of steering a course between disputants by stressing their "friendship" (*philia*) toward the belligerents. The Serdaioi may be doing this as early as ca. 550, the Argives clearly do it in 480, the Achaeans in 431, the Corcyraeans in 427, the Melians in 416, the collective Greek states in ca. 362, and both the Athenians and the Spartans in 344/343.[27] In fact, this diplomatic stance became so commonly associated with neutral policy that belligerents could also use it as part of their negotiations with states whose neutrality they desired.[28]

The problem was that suspicion remained. In the highly complex balance of power that prevailed during the classical period, the existence of neutral states was especially troubling to the hegemonial powers, because the neutral states represented a model of independence potentially injurious to the interests of the dominant states. Resistance to recognized abstention was therefore always strong among the more powerful states, unless they happened to find it convenient for furthering their own aims.[29] There was, they argued, the possibility that a neutral state might be converted into an ally by an enemy or that alleged neutrality could serve as a cover for secret alignment.[30] But despite the existence of a few

27. On the Serdaioi, see 3.4 above; the Argives, 5.2 below; the Achaeans, 6.1 below; the Corcyraeans in 427, 6.5 below; the Melians, 7.1 below; the Greek states, 9.3.A below; the Athenians and the Spartans, 9.3.B.

28. E.g., Archidamus' proposal to the Plataeans (Thuc. 2. 72.1; see 6.4 below) and the Carthaginian proposal to Acragas in 406 (Diod. 13. 85.2; see 8.1 below).

29. Setting aside the Athenians' famous denial of Melian neutrality (see 7.1 below), we find Athens accepting the legality of neutral policy in the peace that ended the First Peloponnesian War (see 5.3.B–C below), in the Peace of Nicias, in which certain Thracian cities were designated as neutral (see 6.7 below), and in the first Common Peace of 371, which provided for the option of neutrality (Xen. *Hell.* 6. 3.18; see 8.5 below). Nor did the Spartans always oppose the legitimacy of neutral policy: they interpreted it as an obligation with legal force at the trial of the Plataeans (see 6.4 below), instructed sympathetic West Greek states to maintain an officially neutral posture at the outset of the Peloponnesian War (Thuc. 2. 7.2; see 6.2 below), and accepted along with Athens provisions for neutrality in the Peace of Nicias (see 6.7 below) and in the first Common Peace of 371 (see 8.5 below).

30. Consider Herodotus' accusation about Argive neutrality in 480 (see 5.2 below), Sparta's injunction to the West Greek states to imitate neutrality (6.2 below), Athenian opposition to the neutrality of Plataea (6.4 below) and Corcyra (6.5 below), the feigned neutrality of Camarina (7.2 below), Persian relations with Athens and Sparta (9.3.B below), and Demosthenes' accusation against neutral states of 338 (9.5 below).

notorious examples of abuse, misuse, and violation (problems paralleled in all periods), formal abstention came to be just as much a part of classical diplomacy—for better or worse—as any other policy option.

SUMMARY

The realities of remaining uncommitted were often far different from the abstract ideal of peaceful and friendly abstention from the conflicts of others. In reality, weak states were continually threatened by opposing forces they could hardly resist. This was so because the neutral position of states such as Thera, Melos, Megara, and Aegina was not the same as the unconditional inviolability accorded to sanctuaries. Instead, it depended on less reliable constraints, a combination of the voluntary self-restraint of more powerful states and the dogged determination of the would-be neutrals themselves to resist involuntary polarization. Since a neutral state was not *ipso facto* hostile and, in fact, normally claimed to be "friendly" toward the warring parties, acquiescence, if not formal acceptance, made more sense than open opposition.[31] In practice, however, this was always a precarious and unpredictable balance. The position of Corcyra prior to the Peloponnesian War may have once appeared advantageous and even wise; but freedom from alignment also meant isolation—the dilemma of Corcyra in 433—and could invite violation—the lesson of Melos in 416.[32]

To protect neutrality a state needed assurances and wherever possible formal guarantees that constrained the belligerents to respect its position. This could take the form of religious sanction, such as an injunction from the oracle of Apollo at Delphi,[33] or formal treaty arrangements imposing obligations to respect neutrality on both of the opposing belligerents[34] or even the undocu-

31. On neutrality and "friendship" (diplomatic *philia*), see 3.4 above.
32. On the contrasting linguistic characterizations of Corcyraean neutrality, see pp. 7–10 in Chapter 1. For the details of the situation of the Corcyraeans in 433, see 5.3.C below. For Melian neutrality, see 5.3.B below (Pentacontaetia), 6.1 (Archidamian War), and 7.1 (416).
33. In the case of Argos and the Cretan city-states in 480/479, for example (see 5.2 below).
34. E.g., the archaic treaties of Miletus with the Lydians and Persians (see 5.1 below), the Peace of Nicias (6.7 below), or the so-called neutrality clause of the first Common Peace of 371 (8.5 below).

mented, but formally expressed, assurances of belligerents that
neutrality was an acceptable policy.[35] In the absence of these specific
types of support states could nevertheless remain uncommitted and
could hope that their policy would succeed and be respected. Many
of the Peloponnesians believed this in 480, the Corcyraean government in 427, the Agrigentines in 415, the prevailing faction in
Corinth in 392, the Greek states sharing in the Common Peace ca.
362, and the Athenians and Spartans in the 340s.[36] In every instance,
as we will see, the position of abstention sought was founded on
the trust—whether justified or not—that the belligerents' ambitions were limited and would stop short of hostility toward those
who remained uncommitted.

But there is also truth in Machiavelli's contention that a genuinely friendly state will be more likely to demand support and that
a basically hostile one will urge (or accept) neutrality. This happens
repeatedly in the classical period, as the conflicting demands that
confronted Plataea in 429 and Camarina in 415 demonstrate vividly.[37] Hard choices had to be made, intentions calculated, risks
taken. Oddly enough, however, a steady succession of states
throughout the period adopted a neutral policy. No single reason
prompted the decision, and blatant disregard by belligerents was
too common to make automatic respect for any unilateral declaration a certainty. Perhaps more often than anything else it appeared
the lesser of evils when compared with the certainty of violence
that followed from formal commitment to one or the other of the
warring parties. Perhaps too, hope, despite the Athenians' scoffing
dismissal of it in the Melian Dialogue,[38] influenced policymakers,
hope that the inoffensiveness of maintaining "friendly relations"
(philia) with all parties would lead to acceptance of simple abstention. Such states, the "allies of neither side" or "those remaining
at peace," certainly knew that their policy involved calculated risk,
both because it lacked the more explicitly determined character of

35. E.g., the Spartan offer to Plataea in 429 (6.4 below), the Carthaginian offer
to Acragas in 406 (8.1 below), and the Phocian offer in the Third Sacred War (9.4
below).
36. On the Peloponnesians in 480, see 5.2 below; Corcyra in 427, 6.5 below;
Acragas in 415, 7.3 below; a Corinthian faction (?) in 392, 8.3.A below; the Greek
states sharing in the Common Peace ca. 362, 9.3.A below; Athens and Sparta in
the 340s, 9.3.B below.
37. On the eventual fate of Plataea in 427, see 6.4 below; on Camarina in 415,
7.3 below.
38. Thuc. 5. 102ff.; see 7.1 below.

an alliance and because it had an unencouraging record of failure, even when supported by formal agreement. But those states appear to have pursued the policy with full confidence that it was identifiable, legitimate, and possible within the realities of Greek warfare. Euripides could make Creon demand it, Aristophanes could make joking reference to it, Demosthenes could condemn it as loathsome treachery; but one thing no contemporary—in fact no one until the evolution of modern international laws of neutrality—seems to have done was deny that formal abstention from warfare was possible and had a recognized place in classical Greek diplomacy.

PART TWO

The History of Neutrality in Practice

From the Earliest Evidence to the Outbreak of the Peloponnesian War (ca. 600–431)

In most cases far too little information survives about archaic and early classical diplomacy to allow any confident reconstruction of exactly how uncommitted states obtained and conducted their policy during the wars of the period. Contemporary evidence is virtually nonexistent, and the historical narrative of Herodotus, our best source for virtually the entire period, contains unmistakable signs of bias, which exacerbate the difficulty of evaluating his testimony.[1] Nevertheless, a few valuable bits of information appear, and, taken together, they offer a picture of how states went about keeping out of conflicts they wanted no part of and of how the belligerents reacted to the existence of uncommitted states.

Although the archaic treaties of *philia* discussed above (see 3.4) provide for the possibility that states might refuse to offer military support for a "friend," even while guaranteeing that they would do the "friend" no injury, they do not actually specify what rights and obligations apply in the event of war. Nor can we supply the implied details of the existing treaties from what little is known of the archaic history of the states involved. All this remains conjectural. There is, however, at least one state whose diplomacy during the archaic period may explain how bilateral treaties could be the basis of successful abstention from warfare.

---

1. See chapter 2.

I. THE ARCHAIC DIPLOMACY OF MILETUS

The earliest diplomatic relationship that may have provided formally for a state to abstain from certain conflicts is reported by
Herodotus in his description of a late seventh-century settlement
of a conflict between the Milesians and the Lydians. The story is
not recorded elsewhere but cannot be discounted for that alone
and may belong to a reliable tradition in its basic details.[2] According
to the story, the Milesian tyrant Thrasybulus frustrated Alyattes'
aggression through a ruse that so demoralized the Lydian king that
he abandoned his efforts to subjugate Miletus. In summary, Herodotus comments: "And afterwards there was a reconciliation between
them in which they agreed to be guest friends and allies of one
another."[3] This is not an unexpected conclusion, but there is something odd and intriguing about the statement. The terminology
xenia kai symmachia is found only in Herodotus and only in his
description of archaic period treaties involving individual rulers,
especially tyrants.[4] We might assume that *xenia kai symmachia* is
an example of literary license in Herodotus, standing for *philia kai
symmachia*, the formal diplomatic language of comprehensive alliances attested in the late fifth century.[5] But we must then ask
whether such a comprehensive diplomatic formula, combining *philia* (let alone *xenia*) and *symmachia* (which are not found together
in any securely dated treaty prior to the eve of the Peloponnesian
War), could already have been in use before the end of the seventh
century.

2. Hdt. 1. 22.4; Bengtson, *SVA²* no. 105.
3. μετὰ δὲ ἥ τε διαλλαγή σφι ἐγένετο ἐπ' ᾧ τε ξείνους ἀλλήλοισι εἶναι καὶ
συμμάχους (Hdt. 1. 22.4).
4. On Herodotus' use of these terms, see chapter 2 and 3.5 above.
5. Aside from Herodotus' description (2. 181.1) of the sixth-century *philotēta
te kai symmachiēn* between Amasis and the people of Cyrene (which is not in
Bengtson, *SVA²*), the earliest extant record of the combined formula appears in
the Athenian-Bottiaean treaty of 422 (*IG* I², 90, line 25; Bengtson, *SVA²* no. 187
[*symmachia* is restored]). All other known treaties either have the comprehensive
formula entirely restored or specify only *philia* or *symmachia* (or something else);
cf. Bengtson, *SVA²* nos. 108 (alliance of Pisistratus and the Thessalians), 110 (Elis
and Heraea), 114 (Croesus with the Babylonian king Labynetus and the Egyptian
Amasis), 117 (Amasis and Polycrates). For examples of the combination in the
fifth century, see, for instance, Thuc. 4. 19.1; 6. 34.1; 8. 108.4; cf. Soph., *Aj.* 1053.
For a Spartan treaty with the otherwise unknown Aetolian Erxadieis of classical,
but disputed, date, which specifies [*philia*]*n* (?) *kai hiranan* ... *kai synma*[*chian*]
(lines 2–3), see Peek, "Ein neuer spartanischer Staatsvertrag," 3–15; Gschnitzer,
Ein neuer spartanischer Staatsvertrag; Cartledge, "The New 5th-Century Spartan
Treaty Again," 87–92; Kelly, "The New Spartan Treaty," 133–41.

One thing in favor of Herodotus' account is the appearance of *xenia* in the place of *philia*. We have already seen how Herodotus restricts the use of *xenia* as a diplomatic term to his description of relations during the age of tyrants.[6] Assuming, therefore, that Herodotus preserves a genuine tradition about the diplomatic language current in an earlier period but obsolete in his own day, the problem is to reconstruct what the combined relationship of *xenia* and *symmachia* involved in that earlier period.

To begin with, we need to take notice of the mid-sixth century treaty of *xenia kai symmachia* that reportedly existed between Croesus and the Spartans.[7] Since it involves the same formula, we might tentatively assume that this treaty would reflect the same understanding of *xenia kai symmachia* as the first treaty. However, all that we learn about the treaty is that when Cyrus invaded Lydia, Croesus summoned his Spartan allies (1. 77.3, 82.1, 83).

The Milesians' situation seems to have been quite different. At no time, either in the earlier Lydian wars against other Ionian city-states or even after the Milesians negotiated an agreement with Cyrus "on the same terms as their Lydian treaty," are the Milesians said to have been required (or asked) to supply military aid to the Lydians or Persians.[8] Other events muddy the waters still further. Some years later Histiaeus of Miletus convinced the other tyrants accompanying Darius' expedition against the Scythians to preserve the bridge over the Danube for the Persians' retreat (Hdt. 4. 137–42). Unfortunately, Herodotus does not say whether the presence of Histiaeus was formally required by the Milesians' treaty with Persia or was simply the result of personal ambition. Nor is there any mention of the treaty when Aristagoras conspired with Naxian exiles to obtain Persian assistance for an expedition against Naxos (5. 30–31). But the dependence of Aristagoras on the Persians is made plain when the expedition failed and Aristagoras

6. See 3.4 above.

7. Hdt. 1. 69.3; Bengtson, *SVA*[2] no. 113.

8. See Hdt. 1. 141.4, 143.1, 169.2. Herodotus specifically states at 1. 169.2 that because of their treaty with Cyrus, the Milesians remained neutral (ἡσυχίην ἄγειν) during Cyrus' campaign against Ionia. See G. M. A. Hanfmann, "Lydian Relations with Ionia and Persia," *Proc. Xth Int. Congr. Arch. Ankara-Izmir, 23–30 September 1973*, ed. E. Akurgal (Ankara, 1978), 25–35; V. La Bua, "Gli Ioni e il conflitto lidio-persiano," *Misc. gr. e rom.* 5 (1977): 1–64; id., "La prima conquista persiana della Ionia," *Misc. de st. class. in onore di Eugenio Manni* 4 (Rome, 1980): 1267–92; L. Boffo, "La conquista persiana delle città greche d'Asia Minore," *MemLinc* 26: 1 (1983); G. Walser, *Hellas und Iran: Studien zu den griechisch-persischen Beziehungen vor Alexander* (Darmstadt, 1984), 9–12.

reportedly began plotting revolt because he feared that the Persians would remove him as tyrant of Miletus (5. 35). By 500, then, the Milesian rulers had far less independence than they had enjoyed in the middle of the century.

But what had happened in the meantime to the treaty of *xenia kai symmachia*? The answer may be simply that the Milesians, despite their treaty, had become increasingly vulnerable to direct Persian interference. If so, then these events may not reflect, *de iure*, the terms of the Milesian-Persian treaty but only, de facto, the loss of independence caused by a distinct imbalance of power between Miletus and the Persian empire. It may also be that Herodotus' specific reference to *xenia kai symmachia* is in fact inaccurate. As we have seen, the sixth-century Sybarite-Serdaioi and Anaitoi-Metapioi treaties, as well as the Elis-Heraea treaty, specify either *philia* or *symmachia*, but not both.[9] Therefore, if the original Alyattes-Thrasybulus treaty involved both *xenia* and *symmachia*, they would more than likely have represented two quite distinct diplomatic ideas, different from either *philia* or *symmachia* as either stood alone or from the comprehensive *philia kai symmachia* of the fifth century.

In the first place, the establishment of personal "guest friendship" (*xenia*) between the respective heads of state looks suspiciously like a personal, rather than a public, relationship. And secondly, the alliance (*symmachia*) between the states themselves could not have been an unlimited commitment to joint military action, since the Milesians never assisted these "allies." Instead, the treaty (and this could apply to the Lydian-Spartan pact) must certainly have been restricted to defensive assistance only. How else can Herodotus say that the Milesians remained at peace (*hēsychiēn ēgon*) during the warfare of the sixth century *due to their sworn agreement* (*horkion* 1. 169.2)? This only makes sense if we remember that the earlier Lydian aggression against other Greek states of Western Asia Minor was hardly defensive and that later, just when Croesus might well have sought help against Cyrus, as he did from his Spartan *xenoi kai symmachoi*, the Milesians switched sides, negotiated a treaty with the Persians "on the same terms as their Lydian treaty," and remained at peace while the Persians took the offensive and invaded the region.

9. Bengtson, *SVA²* nos. 120, 111, 110; see 3.4 above.

Finally, among late sources, Diogenes Laertius reports in his *Life* of Thales that the Milesian philosopher Thales dissuaded the Milesians from allying themselves with the Lydians and thereby saved the state in the time of the Persian invasion of Cyrus the Great (1.25). He adds in the *Life* of Anaximander that the price of the Milesians' peace with Cyrus was payment of tribute (11.5). At the least, these reports agree in describing Miletus as remaining at peace in the midst of surrounding wars and in suggesting that this position was the result of bilateral agreements. It may be technically incorrect to claim that no Milesian-Lydian alliance existed, but since the Milesians, in fact, did not fight on the Lydian side, this error is understandable. It may also be true that the Milesians paid tribute to the Persians. If so, it could have been an obligation originally imposed in the Lydian-Milesian treaty and simply omitted by Herodotus. The underlying tradition, however, is consistent in attributing to Miletus a privileged exemption from the conflicts that engulfed the region during the sixth century; and, as we shall see, formal negotiations of a similar status appeared again during the Persian Wars.

II. THE PERSIAN WARS (490–479)

From their earliest agreements with Greek city-states, the Persians demonstrated a surprising readiness to respect and use Greek diplomatic institutions. Examples include the imposition of arbitration of interstate disputes in Ionia, respect for Panhellenic Greek sanctuaries, widespread use of Greek advisers (military and political), and even exploitation of Greek mythology as a propaganda weapon in interstate conflict.[10] During the diplomatic activity surrounding the

10. On arbitration, see Hdt. 6. 42.1; Piccirilli, *Arbitrati*, vol. 1, no. 11. On sanctuaries, see pp. 38–43 above and p. 94 below. On Persian respect for Delos in 490, see Hdt. 6. 97; see also Darius' letter to the satrap Gadates (Meiggs and Lewis, no. 12), though Darius was also brutal in the treatment of temples that belonged to offending states: Didyma was destroyed in revenge for the burning of the temple of Cybele at Sardis (Hdt. 5. 102.1; 6. 103.1; cf. Diod. 10. 25.1); Didyma was identified with Miletus and fell at the end of the Ionian revolt (6. 19; cf. 9.3, 25.2, 32). The destruction of temples at Naxos (6. 96) and Eretria (6. 101) and even at Athens (8. 53; but cf. 8. 54 and Paus. 1. 18.1, 20.2 [the temples of the Dioscuri and Dionysus are left standing]) could be justified the same way. In any case, these were exceptions, not the rule. On mythological propaganda, see Diodorus (10. 27.1–3), who reports that Datis alleged that the Athenian birth of Medus, the legendary founder of Media, justified Persian sovereignty over Athens; for mythology used for Xerxes in negotiations with Argos (Hdt. 7. 150.1–3), see 5.2 below.

Persian invasions of 490 and 480/479, this familiarity with Greek customs had an important influence on the course of diplomacy.

A more complex diplomatic picture than a strictly bipolar separation of slavish supporters (i.e., "medizers") and outright enemies lurks in the background of Darius' campaign against Athens and Eretria (492–490). The evidence is scanty and entirely from Herodotus, who unfortunately simplifies his account to the point of near obscurity. Nevertheless, it seems clear that at least one state actively sought to remain out of the conflict. The city-state involved is Carystus in Euboea.

When Datis reached Euboea in 490, he is said to have gone first to Carystus, because the inhabitants refused to comply with Persian demands. As Herodotus reports, "the Carystians did not give him hostages and said that they would not march against neighboring states, meaning Eretria and Athens."[11] Datis responded by attacking and forcing the Carystians to take the Persian side. Though skeletal, Herodotus' account plainly emphasizes the true nature of the Persians' aims: no position except complete acceptance of Persian authority was to be tolerated. Hence, even though the Carystians were obviously not attempting to oppose the Persians but only to avoid the shame (aidōs) of attacking their neighbors without provocation, Datis rejected their attempt to keep out of the conflict and sent a clear message to any other states that might have been ready to pursue a similar policy.

But if the Carystians knew that the Persians would reject their policy, why did they bother to attempt it and thereby expose their state to violence? Was it simple miscalculation? Or were they, perhaps, seeking a face-saving middle ground that they believed might be acceptable to the Persians? After all, the Milesians had won exemption from an earlier Persian-Greek conflict and would have provided a ready model for negotiation. If this is the correct reconstruction of the background to the confrontation at Carystus, then the real significance of Herodotus' report of the incident lies in its not-so-subtle message that the new Persian aggression could

---

11. ὡς δὲ περιπλέοντες τὰς νήσους προσέσχον καὶ ἐς Κάρυστον, οὐ γὰρ δή σφι οἱ Καρύστιοι οὔτε ὁμήρους ἐδίδοσαν οὔτε ἔφασαν ἐπὶ πόλις ἀστυγείτονας στρατεύεσθαι, λέγοντες Ἐρέτριάν τε καὶ Ἀθήνας, ἐνθαῦτα τούτους ἐπολιόρκεόν τε καὶ τὴν γῆν σφέων ἔκειρον, ἐς ὃ καὶ οἱ Καρύστιοι παρέστησαν ἐς τῶν Περσέων τὴν γνώμην (Hdt. 6. 99.2).

not be sidestepped through diplomacy but could be met only with force or capitulation.

A decade later, however, the diplomacy surrounding Persia's renewed aggression was far more sophisticated. While Xerxes undertook his historic military preparations for the full annexation of Greece, he also initiated a careful diplomatic offensive aimed at eroding the potential threat of collective Greek resistance.[12] Neutrality played a key role in this preliminary to the military confrontation, and its use as a legitimate policy by both the Persians and the Greeks is explicitly recorded in the sources.

The diplomatic maneuvering of Argos provides the most unequivocal example. Herodotus reports three versions of Argive policy in 480: (1) neutrality, based on a Delphic injunction and the Spartans' refusal to share the command (7. 148–49, attributed to the Argives themselves); (2) neutrality, from an agreement negotiated with Xerxes (7. 150, reported by other Greeks); and (3) pro-Persian alignment, due to a catastrophic defeat recently suffered at the hands of the Spartans (7. 152.3, uncredited gossip).

The third version is connected with Herodotus' later report (9. 12) that the Argives had promised to hinder the Spartan army's departure from the Peloponnesus in 479 and, having failed to do that, sent advance warning to Mardonius when the army was under way. This looks so obviously like an anti-Argive fiction that it can be dismissed.[13] The Argives' own account of their policy in 480, on the other hand, deserves serious attention, for it is attributed

12. One odious exception was the demand for earth and water, tokens of submission to Persian authority (Hdt. 4. 126, 127, 132.1; 5. 17.1, 18.1 and 2, 73.2; 6. 48.2, 49.1, 94.1; 7. 32, 131, 133, 138.2, 163.2, 233.1; 8. 46.4). While rendering them to Persia did not necessarily make the giver an active ally, it admitted such a possibility on demand (see, for example, 6. 99) and thus allowed Athens to accuse Aegina of planning to betray Greece (6. 49.2). Refusal was considered grounds for attack (e.g., 6. 94.1). After the Persian Wars there appears to be no further mention of "earth and water" in Persian diplomacy; perhaps it was necessary, at least in dealing with the Greeks, to abandon such offensive symbolism in favor of more specific diplomatic arrangements.

13. Herodotus prefaces his report of gossip that accused Argos of active medism with this warning: "For myself, though it be my business to set down that which is told me, to believe it is none at all of my business; let that saying hold good for the whole of my history" (Hdt. 7. 152.3, trans. A. D. Godley, *Herodotus*, vol. 3, Loeb Classical Library [Cambridge, Mass., and London, 1922]). In any case, warning Mardonius was not the same as providing active military support; and even though Herodotus says (9. 12.1) that the Argives "promised" to hinder the Spartan advance, this did not happen and makes the whole report highly suspicious.

directly to an injunction from Delphi and therefore could have been easily exposed if fictitious. By the time of Herodotus' investigation both the Delphic injunction and the Spartans' refusal to share the command were apparently given equal weight; but in 480 it seems more likely that the injunction from Delphi was the principal public defense. In the aftermath of the recent catastrophe suffered at Sepeia (ca. 494) the reluctance of Argos to commit itself to renewed military action would have been entirely understandable. A claim to shared command could have provided a reasonable pretext for abstention, but an injunction from Delphi was categorical and indisputable. Under the circumstances, the Argives' demand for shared leadership is therefore probably best understood as secondary reinforcement aimed at strengthening the Delphic justification with anti-Spartan propaganda, since the Spartans predictably refused the demand and could, on that account, be held responsible for the Argives' abstention.

The other account presented by Herodotus suggests that Xerxes may have exploited the old Milesian diplomatic model by offering the Argives special respect if they would remain aloof from the war. Herodotus reports Xerxes' proposal verbatim:

> We believe that Perses, from whom we have descended, was the son of Perseus, son of Danae, and Andromeda, daughter of Cepheus. If that be so, then we are descended from you. Therefore, neither should we march against the land of our forefathers nor should you, by aiding others, become our enemies; but simply reside among yourselves, remaining at peace. For if the outcome is according to my desire, I will esteem none more greatly than you.[14]

Incredible though this offer sounds, it may not be pure fiction. The Persians had apparently offered mythological ploys in the past (e.g., Diod. 10. 27.1–3); and Herodotus is able to cite independent corroboration that friendly relations with Persia did exist from the reign of Xerxes, for it happened that Athenian envoys, including Callias, the son of Hipponicus, were present at Susa when Argive envoys arrived to ask Artaxerxes, Xerxes' successor, "if the friend-

---

14. Ἄνδρες Ἀργεῖοι, βασιλεὺς Ξέρξης τάδε ὑμῖν λέγει· Ἡμεῖς νομίζομεν Πέρσην εἶναι ἀπ' οὗ ἡμεῖς γεγόναμεν, παῖδα Περσέος τοῦ Δανάης, γεγονότα ἐκ τῆς Κηφέος θυγατρὸς Ἀνδρομέδης. οὕτω ἂν ὦν εἴημεν ὑμέτεροι ἀπόγονοι. οὔτε ὦν ἡμέας οἰκὸς ἐπὶ τοὺς ἡμετέρους προγόνους στρατεύεσθαι, οὔτε ὑμέας ἄλλοισι τιμωρέοντας ἡμῖν ἀντιξόους γίνεσθαι, ἀλλὰ παρ' ὑμῖν αὐτοῖσι ἡσυχίην ἔχοντας κατῆσθαι. ἢν γὰρ ἐμοὶ γένηται κατὰ νόον, οὐδαμοὺς μέζονας ὑμέων ἄξω.   (Hdt. 7. 150.2)

ship (*philia*) which they had concluded with Xerxes still held good
with him as they wished or would they be considered by him to
be enemies."[15] Artaxerxes reportedly answered that the relationship
would indeed continue, since he considered no *polis* more friendly
(*philiōterēn*) than Argos.[16]

This story is also consistent with Herodotus' report of negotiations between Mardonius and the Athenians after Salamis
(8. 140–43). In that account, Alexander, king of Macedon, attempts
to mediate in the conflict by encouraging the Athenians to abandon
their futile attempts to resist Xerxes and come to terms (*homologe-
ein* 140.2). Mardonius, Herodotus relates, on orders from the king,
asks the Athenians to give up the war (*katalusasthai*). "Be free
(*eleutheroi*)," his message reads. "Make an agreement with us to
be comrades in arms (*homaichmiēn*) without fraud or deception"
(140.4). With a flourish of Panhellenic rhetoric the Athenians refuse
and warn Alexander never to return on such a mission or risk
suffering harm despite being a friend and proxenus (*proxeinon te
kai philon* 143.3).

The importance of this incident lies in its basic agreement with
other reports of the Persian use of diplomacy as a means to neutralize potentially hostile states. Miletus, we know, acquiesced, so
apparently did Argos, Athens did not. But as the case of Argos
most clearly shows, the intent was not to force these states to
become subordinate *allies*, but only to remove them as opponents,
and for this end, all that was required was an agreement providing
for their neutrality.

But why was the version attributing Argive neutrality to an
agreement with Xerxes suppressed by the Argives? The answer may
emerge from the connection of the second version with the demand
for a half share of the allied command (7. 150.3; cf. 7. 148.4).
Herodotus says bluntly that the Argives made the demand "in

15. Ἀργείους δὲ τὸν αὐτὸν τοῦτον χρόνον πέμψαντας καὶ τούτους ἐς Σοῦσα ἀγγέλ-
ους εἰρωτᾶν Ἀρτοξέρξην τὸν Ξέρξεω εἰ σφι ἔτι ἐμμένει τὴν πρὸς Ξέρξην φιλίην
συνεκεράσαντο, ἢ νομιζοίατο πρὸς αὐτοῦ εἶναι πολέμιοι (Hdt. 7. 151). The
Argives' fear of being considered *polemioi* may be connected with their recent
alliance with Persia's old enemies, the Athenians, in ca. 462 (Thuc. 1. 102.4; see
Gomme, *HCT*, vol. 1, 302–3). The passage should not be taken as support for
the belief that if the Argives were not *philoi*, they must automatically be *polemioi*.
16. Perhaps Artaxerxes considered Argos "most friendly" because it was the
most prominent Greek state aside from Thebes that had not opposed Xerxes, or
even because of their mythological relationship.

order to have a pretext for remaining neutral" (*hina epi prophasios hēsychiēn agōsi* 7. 150.3). What that suggests is that there were two wholly separate diplomatic requirements for Argive neutrality: (1) Persian acceptance of the policy and (2) Greek acceptance. Delphic sanction, together with Sparta's refusal to share leadership, provided a strong defense for Argive policy in the context of Greek international affairs. But after Xerxes' defeat, there was hardly any incentive for the Argives to trumpet diplomatic accord with the Persian king, especially given the tense postwar atmosphere in which one faction of the Greek allies was advocating the harsh punishment of all who failed to oppose the Persians.

Interestingly, the Delphic Oracle sanctioned abstention for the Cretans as well as for the Argives. When representatives inquired "whether it would be better for them to defend Greece" (7. 169.1–2), the Pythia made a seemingly desperate effort to put forth some credible justification and enjoined the Cretans not to forget the suffering of Minos! As in the response to Argos, the message was clear. Apollo approved, even ordered, the Cretans' abstention from the conflict. So, given the injunction of heaven, the Cretans quite naturally turned a deaf ear to Greek appeals and abandoned any intention of taking sides.[17]

Argos was actually not the only Peloponnesian state that adopted a neutral position during Xerxes' invasion. According to Herodotus, the list of the Peloponnesian forces mustered at the Isthmus in 480 included the Spartans, "all the Arcadians," the Eleans, Corinthians, Sicyonians, Epidaurians, Phliasians, Troezenians, and Hermionians (8. 72). The rest of the Peloponnesians are said to have ignored the situation, although such legitimate excuses for delay as the Olympian and Carnean festivals were now past (8. 72; cf. 8. 206). Herodotus digresses here in order to give a catalogue of the nations (*ethnea*) that inhabited the Peloponnesus (8. 73). In conclusion, he remarks that except for the states whose contingents were already at the Isthmus the remaining cities of the seven nations "adopted a neutral position" (*ek tou mesou kateato* 8. 73.3), adding, "And if it is permitted to speak freely, by taking a neutral position they were siding

17. No specific diplomatic negotiations with Persia are recorded, and none need be assumed; but it is perhaps noteworthy that by the middle of the fifth century, when our evidence is better, we find close political connections between some of the Cretan cities and Argos; see Meiggs and Lewis, no. 42 (= Bengtson, *SVA*² nos. 147–48); see 7.3 below on the Cretan states' continued abstention during the Peloponnesian War.

with the Persians."[18] But who is Herodotus talking about? The only obvious candidate, aside from Argos, is the group of Achaean cities in the northwestern Peloponnesus. At the time they were apparently not members of the Spartan alliance and are nowhere mentioned as participants in the war.

For their part, the Greek states committed to resisting Xerxes recognized that many states wanted no part of the war. As counter-measures, they voted to punish those states that voluntarily chose the Persian side and to send ambassadors to those that were holding aloof. Herodotus specifically lists embassies to Argos, Syracuse, Corcyra, and Crete (7. 145.2; cf. Diod. 11. 3.3). The outcome was allegedly a mixture of success and failure. As Diodorus reports, "some of them nobly chose alliance, but others delayed for a considerable time, holding on to their own safety alone and watching anxiously the outcome of the war."[19] Herodotus says nothing about threats against the neutrals, and he is followed in this by Diodorus. The appeal of the Greek allies, as we possess it, was to patriotism. Only those who medized of their own free will were threatened.

The Greeks' restraint was no doubt heavily influenced by the fact that the prestige of Apollo's oracle at Delphi stood behind the neutrals. Yet the Delphic sanction may have itself been motivated not by any commitment to diplomatic principle but by pragmatic concern for the safety of the sanctuary. The rumored greatness of Xerxes' military preparations had created consternation throughout Greece; prospects for successful resistance must have seemed remote. Accordingly, by following a cautious path of supporting a policy potentially acceptable to either side, the Delphians simultaneously maintained their influence and protected the sanctuary's privileged inviolability.[20] Irrespective of the outcome, Apollo's sanc-

---

18. τούτων ὦν τῶν ἑπτὰ ἐθνέων αἱ λοιπαὶ πόλιες, πάρεξ τῶν κατέλεξα, ἐκ τοῦ μέσου κατέατο· εἰ δὲ ἐλευθέρως ἔξεστι εἰπεῖν, ἐκ τοῦ μέσου κατήμενοι ἐμήδιζον (Hdt. 8. 73.3). This is one of only four times (3. 83.3; 4. 118.2; 8. 22.2, 73.3) that Herodotus uses this expression; all instances in Herodotus convey the idea of neutrality.

19. ὦν οἱ μὲν εἵλοντο γνησίως τὴν συμμαχίαν, οἱ δὲ παρῆγον ἐφ᾿ ἱκανὸν χρόνον, ἀντεχόμενοι τῆς ἰδίας μόνον ἀσφαλείας καὶ καραδοκοῦντες τὸ τοῦ πολέμου τέλος (Diod. 11. 3.4).

20. Despite the tale of miraculous salvation told by Herodotus (8. 36–39), Xerxes' attitude toward the oracle remains unclear. Parke and Wormell, Delphic Oracle, vol. 1, 167–79, doubt that Xerxes ever intended to violate the oracle, in spite of the historian's unequivocal account; see also the discussions in G. B. Grundy, The Great Persian War and Its Preliminaries (London, 1901), 232–35; C. Hignett, Xerxes' Invasion of Greece (Oxford, 1963), 439–47. Note furthermore the cautiously pessimistic oracles sent to Athens (7. 139.6–141).

tion of the right of the Argives and the Cretans to maintain a neutral posture in the conflict could easily be defended as wholly proper nonpartisan advice.

One further story reflects the accepting attitude of the belligerents toward states standing aside from the conflict. When the decision was reached to abandon Euboea after the naval battle at Artemisium, Themistocles reportedly sailed around to places along the shore where drinking water was available and at each place inscribed an appeal to the Ionians in Xerxes' fleet (8. 22; cf. 8. 19.1), begging them either to switch sides or at least to adopt a neutral position (8. 22.2).[21] Since this proposal is basically the same overture as Xerxes' offer to Argos, it could well be true; but even granting that it is fictitious, the fact that Herodotus presents it as unquestionably historical emphasizes the role he believed neutrality played in the diplomacy of the Persian Wars.

Xerxes' humiliating defeat naturally placed the neutrals in an embarrassing position. Their inaction, for whatever reason, could be portrayed as passive betrayal of the Greek cause (see, for example, Hdt. 8. 77.3). And indeed, in an apparent move to exploit potential resentment, the Spartans allegedly proposed at a meeting of the Delphic Amphictyony that any cities that had not shared in the fight against the Persians should be expelled from the amphictyony (Plut. *Them.* 20.3). If successful, this motion would have excluded not only the Argives but also such medizers as the Thessalians and the Thebans. According to Plutarch, Themistocles opposed the idea on the grounds that since only thirty-one states had participated (many of which were insignificant), most of Hellas would be excluded. In the end, the majority of the members of the amphictyony agreed with Themistocles, and the motion was rejected.

Thus died any thought of punishing the inaction of those who had not shared in the defense of Hellas. But there was a legacy. Xerxes' invasion had stretched the limits of legitimate diplomacy. And abstention from conflict, whether declared unilaterally or negotiated, even in a crisis of all-out war involving the majority of

---

21. τὰ δὲ γράμματα τάδε ἔλεγε. "Ἄνδρες Ἴωνες, οὐ ποιέετε δίκαια ἐπὶ τοὺς πατέρας στρατευόμενοι καὶ τὴν Ἑλλάδα καταδουλούμενοι. ἀλλὰ μάλιστα μὲν πρὸς ἡμέων γίνεσθε· εἰ δὲ ὑμῖν ἐστι τοῦτο μὴ δυνατὸν ποιῆσαι, ὑμεῖς δὲ ἔτι καὶ νῦν ἐκ τοῦ μέσου ἡμῖν ἔζεσθε καὶ αὐτοὶ καὶ τῶν Καρῶν δέεσθε τὰ αὐτὰ ὑμῖν ποιέειν (Hdt. 8. 22.2). W. W. How and J. Wells, *A Commentary on Herodotus,* vol. 2, 241: "It was more successful in causing suspicion of the Ionians (ch. 90) than in securing actual desertion (ch. 85)." On this, see Hdt. 7. 51–52.

Greek states, had to be accepted and reckoned with as an inevitable fact of Greek warfare.

III. THE PENTECONTAETIA (479–431)

During the Pentecontaetia there emerged a small group of states that sought to maintain a position of independent nonalignment and refused to become involved in the conflicts of the period. Three major conflicts dominated the international affairs of the Pentecontaetia: the continued war against Persia (actively between 478 and ca. 450), the so-called First Peloponnesian War (ca. 460–446/445), and the Corinthian-Corcyraean War (435–432).[22] The evidence concerning uncommitted states in each of these conflicts will be treated separately but should not be thought of as unrelated to the other conflicts.

A. THE CONTINUED WAR AGAINST PERSIA (478–ca. 450)

When the Athenians saw the grand anti-Persian alliance of 481 begin to disintegrate, they hastened to found a new organization of their own (Thuc. 1. 96.2). Most of the constitutional details of the new alliance, the so-called Delian League or First Athenian Confederacy, are unknown, but there is general agreement that the member states were bound by oath to support any military action taken by the alliance and that failure to meet the specified obligations constituted a violation of oaths. At least this is the modern conclusion drawn from the report that members swore "to have the same friends and enemies."[23] It follows that when the confederacy acted officially, abstention was *de iure* forbidden to any member.

There is evidence, however, that some kind of sanctioned neu-

22. For a detailed study of the period, see de Ste. Croix, *Origins of the Peloponnesian War*; R. Meiggs, *The Athenian Empire* (Oxford, 1972).

23. On the foundation and oaths, see Bengtson, *SVA²* no. 132; Arist. *Ath. Pol.* 23.5; Plut. *Arist.* 25.1; cf. Hdt. 9. 106.4 (oath of the islanders after Mycale). On the effect of the oaths, see, among others, G. Grote, *History of Greece*, vol. 4, new ed. (London, 1888), 352–53; G. Busolt, *Griechische Geschichte bis zur Schlacht bei Chaeronea*, vol. 3, part 1 (Gotha, 1893–1904), 72–79; K. J. Beloch, *Griechische Geschichte*, vol. 2, part 1, 2d ed. (Berlin, 1924–27), 63–65; E. M. Walker, "The Confederacy of Delos, 478–463 B.C.," *CAH*, vol. 5, 40–41; Meiggs, *Athenian Empire*, 45–46; de Ste. Croix, *Origins of the Peloponnesian War*, 298–307; D. Kagan, *The Outbreak of the Peloponnesian War* (Ithaca, N.Y., and London, 1969), 40–44.

trality was possible for confederacy members under certain circumstances. At least, this seems to be the best explanation of Thucydides' statement that when the Athenians went to war with Carystus in the 470s, they did so "without the rest of the Euboeans" (1. 98.3). Since the other major cities of Euboea belonged to the Delian League, this special qualification of the circumstances implies either that they refused willfully or that they were not required, perhaps because the dispute was not considered an alliance issue but strictly a private Athenian affair.[24] If so, the abstention of Euboean states may even reflect, *de iure*, certain restrictions on the extent of obligatory participation of league members. Something like this appears to have existed within the framework of the much older Peloponnesian League (see 3.5 above), and the same may have held true for members of the Athenian alliance.

Unfortunately the diplomatic status and rights of states that remained outside of the new alliance are even more obscure than those of the members. To assess the situation, we should remember that during the initial years of the Pentecontaetia the central concern continued to be the war against Persia. Hostility between Athens and Sparta and the divisive effect that it had on the Greek world were later developments.[25] Moreover, the withdrawal of Sparta and other former allies from active participation in the war does not seem to have meant that they were formally repudiating their membership in a defensive alliance aimed against Persia. Indeed, P. A. Brunt has argued convincingly that the original Hellenic alliance of 481 was still considered to be in effect when the Athenians were summoned to Sparta's aid during the Messenian revolt of ca. 462.[26] This continued relationship between the original

24. Eretria, Chalcis, and Styra were members of the Greek alliance during the war (Hdt. 8. 4; Meiggs and Lewis, no. 27) and presumably joined the Delian League immediately. Note that Thucydides calls their conflict with Athens in 446 a revolt (1. 114); see Meiggs, *Athenian Empire*, 69–70. Thucydides makes the Athenians the understood subject of 1. 98.3; but whether the Athenians *qua* leaders of the confederacy or *qua* Greek state acting independently is intended is left uncertain; for a view of the latter, see H. R. Rawlings, "Thucydides on the Purpose of the Delian League," *Phoenix* 31 (1977): 4. Against the latter is Thucydides' exclusion of the Euboeans specifically instead of the rest of the alliance as a whole.

25. This is Thucydides' view (1. 95.7, 102.1–4), although he is aware that an undercurrent of friction began almost immediately (1. 101.3). Herodotus (8. 3) and later sources (e.g., Arist. *Ath. Pol.* 23.4; Diod. 11. 50.1–8) suggest that the schism was more immediate.

26. P. A. Brunt, "The Hellenic League against Persia," *Historia* 2 (1953–54): 158, based primarily on Thuc. 1. 102.1–4; 3. 54.5.

participants in the Greek defense may have also influenced the diplomatic and military events of the period in ways that have never been properly appreciated.

We know that Aegina and Melos belonged to the Hellenic alliance. They did not, however, join the Athenian Confederacy in 478/477 and were not coerced into joining.[27] One reason for this may have been that they were protected by the pledges exchanged between the states of the earlier alliance (see Hdt. 7. 148). It may also simply be that their decision to remain aloof was respected, since Thera was also left unmolested, although the Therans had not been members of the Hellenic alliance. Carystus, on the other hand, was attacked by the Athenians and compelled to join the new alliance. But before we conclude that this was a naked act of Athenian imperialist aggression (especially since the Carystians controlled the port of Geraestus, which was critically important for any power seeking to dominate the Aegean), it is worthwhile to remember that the recent policy of the Carystians invited reprisal. In fact, the Carystians had medized. The very fact that they controlled a strategically vital port and had not been loyal to the Greek cause offered plenty of justification for hostility on the part of Athens, if not the league as a whole.

The island of Scyros also remained outside of the Delian League and was attacked, in this case by the full alliance.[28] We know nothing of the island's formal policy or even of its activities during the Persian Wars, and Thucydides provides no details about the motives for the league's attack. Plutarch, however, offers the explanation that international indignation over the islanders' predatory piracy was the chief cause of the Athenians' move against them (Cim. 8.3–4).

Here then are at least two states whose independent position outside of the Delian League was clearly violated. But despite Thucydides' silence, justification for the attacks can be found in the previous pro-Persian conduct of the Carystians and the piracy practiced by the Dolopians of Scyros. Since we have already seen that proposed reprisals against states that had remained neutral during Xerxes' invasion were rejected by the Delphic Amphictyony and that, furthermore, there existed states that had not belonged

27. Thuc. 2. 9.2; on 480, see Meiggs and Lewis, no. 27; Bengtson, SVA² no. 130.
28. Thuc. 1. 98.3; cf. Hdt. 9. 105; see Gomme, HCT, vol. 1, 281–82; M. B. Wallace, "Herodotus and Euboia," Phoenix 28 (1974): 36 n. 34; 44.

to the earlier Greek alliance and were not coerced into joining the
Delian League (e.g., Thera), there is no compelling reason to believe
that the attacks on Scyros and Carystus represented blatant imperialistic disregard for the independence and nonalignment of these
states. Where no such justification existed, it appears that restraint
continued to be observed and the position of uncommitted states
tolerated. This situation becomes clearer, however, when we examine the evidence (scant though it is) concerning diplomacy surrounding the First Peloponnesian War (ca. 460–446/445).

B. THE FIRST PELOPONNESIAN WAR (ca. 460–446/445)

For about fourteen years in the middle of the fifth century the
Athenian alliance was at war with a loose coalition of Peloponnesian states (including the island of Aegina). This conflict, known
as the First Peloponnesian War, ended about 446/445 with the
ratification of a peace treaty effective for thirty years.[29]

While the war as a whole is one of the most obscure in Greek
history, several details point to the existence of successfully neutral
states. It should be emphasized immediately that when Athens
repudiated the Hellenic alliance of 481 just prior to the outbreak
of this war, whatever protection that old pact may have afforded
states like Aegina and Melos against Athenian aggression came to
an end. For Aegina, in any case, the old guarantees were meaningless, since the Aeginetans sided with the Peloponnesians in the war
and were ultimately defeated. Yet the terms of peace provided for
Aegina's continued autonomy despite the imposition of tribute
payments to Athens.[30] Unfortunately, it remains unclear whether
the specified autonomy included the right to maintain an independent foreign policy. Other evidence suggests, however, that this
seemingly inconsistent arrangement was possible.[31] So, even in
defeat, Aegina seems to have maintained what amounted to nonaligned status.

For the Cycladic islands of Melos and Thera the situation was
quite different. There is no evidence that these ethnically Doric
states either took sides or were in any way affected by the war or

29. Thuc. 1. 98.2; cf. Plut. *Cim.* 8.3–6; *Thes.* 36.1–2.
30. Bengtson, *SVA²* no. 144; de Ste. Croix, *Origins of the Peloponnesian War*,
293–94.
31. Thuc. 1. 67.2, 108.4, 139.1, 140.3; Diod. 11. 78.4.

its outcome.[32] Whether their position involved a declared policy of neutrality has not been recorded, but their status was clearly recognized in the terms of the Thirty Years' Peace of 446/445. According to Thucydides, the Corcyraeans later argued (1. 35.1–2) and the Corinthians acknowledged (1. 40.2) that "it is stated in the treaty [of 446/445] that if any Hellenic state is allied with neither side, it is permitted to enter whichever alliance it pleases."[33] This stipulation not only formally recognized the existence of nonaligned states but also acknowledged that they possessed certain rights. It must be admitted, however, that the exact intention of the belligerents was clearly not the defense of neutral status but the assurance that they would have the right to convert neutrals to allies without violating the peace. Therefore, just how much protection the treaty provided to states seeking to avoid commitment to either alliance in the event of aggression by one or the other depended entirely on the willingness of the opposing alliance to defend the neutral as a matter of self-interest. A test of this reality was not long in coming.

C. THE CORINTHIAN-CORCYRAEAN WAR (435–432)

Near the end of the Pentecontaetia, neutrality became a debated issue. After two years of defending themselves in a bitter war against Corinth and its allies, the Corcyraeans decided to seek help from Athens. At the same time the Corinthians sent a counter-embassy to prevent the Athenians from taking any action. Thucydides gives an account of the debate that occurred at Athens when the issue of an alliance with Corcyra came before the Assembly (1. 32–36, the Corcyraean speech; 37–43, the Corinthian). We have examined how the language of these two speeches subtly reflects the respective speakers' attitudes toward the former uncommitted policy of Corcyra and the proposed change to alignment with Athens (see chapter 1, pp. 7–9). At present, we will consider what the speeches say about neutral policy.

In their speech, the Corcyraeans insist that it is not right (*ou dikaion*) that the Athenians allow the recruitment of sailors within

32. On Miletus, see 5.1 above; on stipulations for renegade Thracian cities in the Peace of Nicias, see 6.7 below (Thuc. 5. 18.5).

33. εἴρηται γὰρ ἐν αὐταῖς τῶν Ἑλληνίδων πόλεων ἥτις μηδαμοῦ ξυμμαχεῖ ἐξεῖναι παρ' ὁποτέρους ἂν ἀρέσκηται ἐλθεῖν (Thuc. 1. 35.2).

their empire by the Corinthians. The Corcyraean ambassador says
bluntly: "Either you should prevent them from recruiting mercenaries from your dominions or also send aid to us on whatever terms
you may be induced to accept" (1. 35.4). The point of this statement
seems to be that the current laissez-faire policy of the Athenians is
unfair because it benefits the Corinthians. But behind the complaint
lies the implication that nonbelligerents could allow their citizens
to serve foreign states and could even send military supplies to the
belligerents without necessarily being considered to have committed
a hostile act as long as both belligerents were provided equal
assistance or access.[34] The issue, then, is not the freedom of recruitment but the alleged lack of impartiality.

For their part, the Corinthians argue that strict neutrality is the
only proper policy for Athens. While acknowledging the right of
nonaligned states to ally themselves with the parties of the treaty
(1. 40.2–3), the Corinthians nevertheless warn the Athenians that
in this case they must either remain completely aloof from the
conflict or be considered to have taken sides. "The right course for
you," the Corinthians advise, "is to stand aloof from both sides."[35]
The problem is that since a state of war already existed between
the Corinthians and Corcyraeans, Athens could not accept Corcyra
as an ally without almost certainly being forced into a state of war
with Corinth (1. 40.3). The Corinthians therefore argue that the
"right thing" for the Athenians to do is to remain strictly neutral
(40.4). Significantly, they urge this as a superior option even to any
obligation that might be attached to the terms of the Thirty Years'
Peace. In effect, they say that given the circumstances, neutrality is
the most proper policy (over alliance with either party at war), and
they add that by choosing this, the Athenians will act in accordance
with the institutions of the Hellenes (*kata tous Hellēnōn nomous*
41.1).[36]

In addition, the Corinthians ask the Athenians to show the same
self-restraint that Corinth had championed during the recent con-

34. See 6.2 and 7.2 below for discussion of this behavior among states in
Magna Graecia.
35. καίτοι δίκαιοί γ' ἐστὲ μάλιστα μὲν ἐκποδὼν στῆναι ἀμφοτέροις (Thuc. 1.
40.4).
36. On the force of *nomos* at the time, see, M. Ostwald, Nomos *and the
Beginnings of Athenian Democracy* (Oxford, 1969), 33; Gomme, HCT, vol. 1,
172–73 (1. 37.3). The influence of the "unwritten laws" (*agraphoi nomoi*) on
interstate relations is discussed in 3.2 above.

flict between Samos and Athens. When that war broke out, they claim, other members of the Peloponnesian alliance favored sending aid to Samos but were persuaded to remain neutral by the Corinthians, who argued that neither alliance should interfere in disputes between hegemonial states and their subordinate allies (1. 41.2, 43.1). Even though the Corinthian-Corcyraean conflict is obviously not parallel, the Corinthians nevertheless speak as if it is and insist that an Athenian-Corcyraean alliance will violate this beneficial understanding.

When (at a reconsideration held after the alliance was rejected in a first vote) the Athenians resolved to ignore the warnings of the Corinthians and accept an alliance (albeit a defensive one [*epimachia* 1. 44.1]), it was surely not in contempt of the principles involved but rather, as seems more likely, out of concern for the damaging effect they could have on Athenian hegemony.[37] Athens had already lost Argos as an ally in the middle of the century, when the Argives made a separate peace with Sparta and ceased thenceforth to support either alliance.[38] Samos had recently attempted to secede from the Athenian Confederacy, and there had been, as the Corinthians emphasize, widespread support of the Samians' struggle for self-determination. These developments meant that the Corcyraean appeal represented a tempting opportunity for Athens to strengthen its position while preventing an important, previously neutral power from aligning itself with the Peloponnesian alliance. This was simply realpolitik; and even though it did not, in fact, violate the terms of the existing peace, there was serious indecision at Athens, which allowed only a strictly

37. Note the Athenians' care to make only a defensive alliance with Corcyra (1. 44.1). Their concern for legal correctness—they would remain at peace unless Corinth attacked—may also be detected in the pretexts which I believe were used by the Athenians as quasi-legal justifications for their aggressive treatment of Carystus (medism) and Scyros (piracy). On Athens' motivation for allying with Corcyra, see also Gomme, *HCT*, vol. 1, 177, who argues that the Athenians were anxious not to be technically the aggressors if a general conflict resulted from the alliance. Again they are concerned with legality. De Ste. Croix, *Origins of the Peloponnesian War*, 78, also concludes that the Athenian-Corcyraean treaty did not breach the peace and argues that the Corinthian claim that it did was "groundless."

38. Despite its existing alliance with Athens (Thuc. 1. 102.4; Paus. 1. 29.9; 4. 24.7), Argos abandoned the Athenians in 451/450 and negotiated a separate thirty years' peace with Sparta (Thuc. 5. 14.4, 22.2, 28.2, 40.3; Paus. 5. 23.4). Thereafter Argos remained strictly neutral until 421 (Thuc. 2. 9.2; Diod. 12. 42.4; Ar. *Peace* 475–77; see 6.1 below with note 2).

defensive alliance to be (just barely) accepted (Thuc. 1. 44.1). But legal or not, even an *epimachia* was a dangerous development that left only two alternatives: either the Corinthians would have to suffer the humiliation of abandoning their war with Corcyra or the Athenians, if Corinth persisted in attacking, would be forced to enter the war in defense of Corcyra. When the latter occurred, the practical wisdom of continued toleration of the existence of neutral states must have seemed questionable in light of the potentially serious impact on the balance of power that Corcyra's new alignment was likely to have.

SUMMARY

The Persian invasions of Greece and the Pentecontaetia provide us with our first broad view of the Greek world coping with the existence and consequences of neutral policy. Neither during the Persian conflict nor afterwards, when the evolution of opposing hegemonial alliances resulted in a new bipolarity, was the diplomatic situation so restricted that all states took sides. Some refused to align themselves (e.g., Corcyra, Thera, Melos, Aegina, and after 451/450, Argos); and though meager, the available evidence suggests that there was international acceptance of this nonalignment. Careful neutrality must have been a key element in the policy of these states, although we have only indirect references to that policy. The leading states clearly had the power to eliminate this status; but just as the belligerents of the Persian Wars for the most part refrained from carrying out reprisals against the states that abstained, so too during the Pentecontaetia the leading states appear to have acted with restraint. How else can we explain, for example, the respect of Thera, which never had any special protection of its nonalignment and yet was not compelled to enter either the Delian or the Peloponnesian alliance?

Bilateral agreements had long served to protect certain states from unwanted involvement in the conflicts of others. Even among collective alliances there is no certain evidence that the individual member states automatically surrendered their right to abstain from given conflicts under certain circumstances. But the Pentecontaetia appears to have witnessed something new in Greek diplomacy— something we can just barely see today through the obscurity of our very limited sources. For the first time, it seems, some states unilaterally declared themselves to be uncommitted and remained neutral on a permanent basis. This was certainly the policy of Corcyra, Thera, and Melos, and, doubtlessly, of other states about which no evidence happens to survive.

Formal acknowledgment of these uncommitted states in the Thirty Years' Peace of ca. 446/445 might have proven to be an important step toward international legalization of nonalignment, even though the mutual suspicion and hostility between the two major alliances remained unresolved. But in 433 the inherent danger present in the existence of uncommitted states was exposed. Alignment of an important naval power such as Corcyra meant that the rough balance of power between the Athenian and Spartan alliances was seriously threatened. The same terms and understanding that protected militarily insignificant states like Thera and Melos also applied to Corcyra. When the Corinthians urged the Athenians to reject the Corcyraeans' appeal for alliance, they were all too painfully aware of this. Since they could not argue that the provisions of the Thirty Years' Peace were being violated, they claimed that the Corcyraeans had lawlessly misused their position and deserved punishment, not protection. This was rhetoric, not condemnation of either general principle or specific legality, for in practically the same breath the Corinthians exhorted the Athenians to remain neutral in accord with justice and the *nomoi* of the Hellenes.[39]

But whether the unwritten *nomoi Hellēnes* could protect the position of a would-be neutral state in the face of an all-out war between the major alliances remained to be seen. The Corinthians insisted that no such protection was warranted in the case of Corcyra and warned the Athenians that any aid supplied to the Corcyraeans would be interpreted as an act of war against Corinth. So much for the *nomoi* of the Hellenes. But the Athenians' response is revealing. If we consider the diplomatic principles involved in the situation confronting Athens, we can see that the Athenians did not ignore the Corinthians' warning in contempt of the principle of respect for the rights of nonaligned states but, on the contrary, acted in accordance with the conviction that these rights were valid and enforceable. Recent history no doubt influenced their thinking, for already in the middle of the century the Athenians had lost a critically important ally when Argos made a separate peace with

39. Thuc. 1. 40.4, quoted above in note 35.

Sparta and ceased thenceforth to support either alliance.[40] More recently, Samos had attempted to withdraw from the Athenian alliance. According to the Corinthians, there was widespread support for the Samian cause and deep resentment at Athens' use of force to restore Samian loyalty.[41]

Public opinion clearly approved self-determination and the freedom of individual states to make their own foreign policy decisions. But this meant that the Corcyraean appeal represented an unexpected opportunity for the Athenians to benefit from the diplomatic conventions that had seemed to work against them recently. Corcyra's position was undeniably legal, and alliance with Athens did not violate the terms of the Thirty Years' Peace. Accepting the Corcyraeans as allies was, however, extremely risky for Athens. The Corinthians' professed determination to prosecute the war with the Corcyraeans meant that even a strictly defensive alliance could very possibly lead to Athenian involvement. If a general war between the Athenian alliance and Corinth and its allies was to be avoided, it would happen only because Corinth's allies exercised their right to refuse to participate in a conflict in which Corinth was judged to have acted unjustly in violation of the *nomoi* of the Hellenes. Whether the Athenians truly expected this to happen is uncertain, but their concern for legality, reflected in the carefully restrictive defensive agreement concluded with Corcyra (*epimachia* Thuc. 1. 44.1), shows that respect for diplomatic rules remained strong during these years and influenced the majority of Athenians to insist that their policy conform to the dictates of the existing conventions.[42]

40. See note 38 above.
41. Thuc. 1. 40.5, 41.2–3.
42. In fact, Athenian assistance for Corcyra was not claimed as a breach of the peace, precipitating Sparta's agreement to join the Corinthians in a war against Athens (see Thuc. 1. 88, 139). The Spartans knew full well that legally the Athenians were in the right (7. 18.2–3).

CHAPTER SIX

The Peloponnesian War to the Peace of Nicias (431–421)

In 431 some states clearly wanted no part of the Peloponnesian War and openly refused to take sides. Thucydides' self-promoting statement that the entire Greek world was involved in the war, some joining in immediately and others intending to do so (1. 1.1), should not be taken as a pronouncement of definitive fact. The truth is that Thucydides knew full well that the situation was far more complicated, and he did not hesitate to acknowledge the existence of neutrals at the outset of the war. In his catalogue of the opposing alliances (2.9), he mentions four such states by name—Argos, Achaea (except Pellene), Thera, and Melos—and hedges about the Acarnanians by saying that "most" of them (*hoi pleious*) sided with Athens. All named neutrals are designated by simple exclusion from the list of committed states except the Achaeans, who required this parenthetical explanation: "They had *philia* with both sides: and the Pellenians alone of the Achaeans sided [with the Peloponnesians] at the outset, though later they all did."[1]

In addition to this group, there are a number of other states that Thucydides does not mention specifically in his initial list of allies and neutrals but that figure in our assessment of the diplomatic

---

1. Λακεδαιμονίων μὲν οἵδε ξύμμαχοι· Πελοποννήσιοι μὲν οἱ ἐντὸς Ἰσθμοῦ πάντες πλὴν Ἀργείων καὶ Ἀχαιῶν (τούτοις δὲ ἐς ἀμφοτέρους φιλία ἦν· Πελληνῆς δὲ Ἀχαιῶν μόνοι ξυνεπολέμουν τὸ πρῶτον, ἔπειτα δὲ ὕστερον καὶ ἅπαντες) (Thuc. 2. 9.2).

details and role of neutrality in the war. Since the evidence is often widely scattered and differs considerably from state to state, it will be necessary to discuss each case separately. The cumulative effect of the evidence is, however, quite coherent and revealing.

I. STATES IDENTIFIED AS NEUTRAL AT THE OUTSET OF THE WAR

A. ARGOS

The Argives were safely protected from involvement in the war by a combination of a thirty years' peace treaty negotiated with Sparta in 451/450 and their long-standing goodwill toward Athens.[2] Unfortunately, the exact nature and details of the latter relationship are unclear. All we know for sure is that a *symmachia* was negotiated immediately after the Athenian dismissal from Ithome ca. 462 (Thuc. 1. 102.4). However, the subsequent peace treaty with Sparta (451/450) and the reported exclusion of Argos from the Thirty Years' Peace between Athens and Sparta in 446/445 suggests that the *symmachia* of ca. 462 had expired or been repudiated prior to 446/445, perhaps in connection with the separate peace of 451/450.[3]

During the Archidamian War (431–421), Argos remained steadfastly neutral.[4] In 421, however, the situation changed. When their peace treaty with Sparta expired, the Argives abandoned their passive policy and attempted to wrest political leadership of the

2. Thuc. 5. 14.4, 22.2, 28.2, 40.3; Bengtson, *SVA*² no. 144.
3. According to Pausanias (5. 23.4), who claims to have seen the text of the treaty on a bronze stele at Olympia, Argos was specifically excluded from the Spartan-Athenian treaty of 446/445. However, Argos and Athens could, if they wished, have friendly relations (ἐπιτηδείως ἔχειν πρὸς ἀλλήλους); de Ste. Croix, *Origins of the Peloponnesian War*, 293, presumes that this meant Athens "was not to receive Argos into military alliance." Still, an alliance with the Thessalian Confederacy, concluded at the same time as the Argive alliance (ca. 462) and on the same terms (Thuc. 1. 102.4), was used by some of the Thessalian cities as grounds for supplying cavalry to Athens in 431 (Thuc. 2. 22.3; see 6.3.B below); so presumably the Argive treaty could also have been considered valid if it had not been expressly canceled.
4. See Thuc. 5. 28.2 and Ar. *Peace* 475–77, the latter quoted in note 22 in chapter 1. Unfortunately, Thucydides provides no details after his initial notice (2. 9.2); however, the steadfastness of the policy can be seen in Aristophanes' joke (in February 424) about Cleon's efforts to win Argive support, since if Cleon is supposedly working for it, the whole idea must be unthinkable for a rational politician (*Knights* 865–66; see Meiggs, *Athenian Empire*, 319; Tomlinson, *Argos and the Argolid*, 116–17). On the limited protection of the status, see Thucydides' remark about the execution of the Argive citizen Pollis (Thuc. 2. 67.1; discussed in 6.6 below).

Peloponnesus from Sparta.[5] By 416 the dream of ascendancy had been shattered, and a hard-pressed democratic government entered into a formal alliance with Athens.[6] Subsequently, the Argives joined in the Sicilian expedition in 415 (6. 29.3, 43; 7. 57.5) and sent a contingent to Ionia in 412 (8. 25, 27.6). But strangely, there is no further record of Argive participation, either in Thucydides or Xenophon, though the latter mentions that two Argive ambassadors accompanied an Athenian embassy to Persia in 408 (*Hell.* 1. 3.13). Later Xenophon adds without explanation that Argos was the only Peloponnesian city that did not join in the final siege of Athens in 405 (*Hell.* 2. 2.7). Whether the withdrawal from active participation was the result of a formal policy change or represents a simple lack of nerve is uncertain. Whatever the details, it seems to have worked, for no punitive measures by the Peloponnesian alliance are recorded.

B. ACHAEA

Very little is known about the Achaeans' foreign policy prior to 431.[7] They seem to have done nothing during Xerxes' invasion (Hdt. 8. 73.3; see 5.2 above), but in the First Peloponnesian War (ca. 460–446/445) they aligned themselves with Athens and joined Pericles' expedition against Oeniadae in Acarnania (Thuc. 1. 111.3; Plut. *Per.* 10.3). In the terms of the Thirty Years' Peace (446/445) Athens agreed to give up control;[8] and nothing further is recorded about the Achaeans until Thucydides comments on their neutrality in 431.

During the Archidamian War there is only one incident involving the Achaeans. In 429, Brasidas allegedly encouraged his troops to consider the Achaean coast "friendly" (*oikeia*) because of a Peloponnesian hoplite force present there (2. 87.6); and indeed, when

---

5. Thuc. 5. 27–81; Bengtson, *SVA*[2] nos. 190, 193, 196; Tomlinson, *Argos and the Argolid*, 118–25.

6. Bengtson, *SVA*[2] no. 196. See Andrews, *HCT*, vol. 4, 151.

7. See J. K. Anderson, "A Topographical and Historical Study of Achaea," *BSA* 49 (1954): 80–85; J. A. O. Larsen, *Greek Federal States: Their Institutions and History* (Oxford, 1968), 126–28; on the identification of the Achaean cities, see Hdt. 1. 145.

8. Thuc. 1. 115.1; see Gomme, *HCT*, vol. 1, 348; de Ste. Croix, *Origins of the Peloponnesian War*, 293; Bengtson, *SVA*[2] no. 156. The exact nature of the relationship is unclear. Thucydides equates Achaea with Nisaea, Pagae, and Troezen, which Athens held (note the verb εἶχον in 1. 115.1); see also 4. 21.3.

disaster struck, the remnants of his expedition retreated initially to Achaean Panormus (92.1) and then, after splitting up, to Leucas and Corinth (92.6). But despite Brasidas' rhetoric, it seems certain that the Spartans did not consider the Achaeans themselves to be genuinely sympathetic, for in 426 they specifically excluded Achaeans from participation in the foundation of Heraclea Trachinia (Thuc. 3. 92.5).

The Achaean stance remained unchanged until 419, when Alcibiades persuaded the inhabitants of Patrae to extend their walls to the sea in conjunction with the building of an Athenian fort at Achaean Rhium (Thuc. 5. 52.2; cf. Isoc. 20 [Loch.]. 15). Protests from Corinth and Sicyon halted the project, which may have been connected with Athenian efforts to gain the support of these cities. A glimpse of Athens' intentions can be seen in the Athenian demand of 425 that Achaea be returned as a condition for peace (Thuc. 4. 21.3). In 419, however, the Spartans reacted quickly by intervening and "arranged matters in Achaea, which previously had not been favorable to their interests" (5. 82.1).[9] Ironically, therefore, Athenian meddling resulted not in Achaean alignment with Athens but in the subordination of the Achaeans to the Peloponnesians, who subsequently established a permanent naval base in Achaea (see 7. 34.1).

C. THERA

Thera and Melos are the only Aegean islands Thucydides specifically names as uncommitted in 431 (2. 9.4). Their apparently anomalous status may be the result of their traditionally close ties with Sparta. According to legend, both islands were colonized by the Lacedaemonians (Hdt. 4.147 [Thera]; Thuc. 5. 84.2 [Melos]), and both retained a strong Doric identity. Still, it seems that neither state had taken sides (in contrast to Aegina) during the First Peloponnesian War. Such states were acknowledged in the treaty ending that war. The treaty granted uncommitted states the right to join either alliance (see 5.3.B–C above); but under the circumstances, it is no surprise to find these islands continuing to hold aloof in 431.

9. Larsen, *Greek Federal States*, 87, suggests that the growth of democratic government in Achaea was also a threat that the Spartans were anxious to stifle.

Thucydides does not mention Thera again, but the island appears in the Athenian tribute quota list for 429/428 and can be restored in the list of 430/429.[10] R. Meiggs suggests that Thera "probably was persuaded to enter the Athenian empire at the time of the assessment of 430."[11] In regard to this "persuasion," two opinions have been expressed. K. J. Beloch argued that Thera's entrance into the Delian League was probably voluntary and for that reason Thucydides made no further mention of it. Other scholars have hypothesized that an unrecorded Athenian campaign was required to compel Thera's incorporation.[12] Proponents of the latter view point to the mention of Thera together with Samos in an Athenian decree of 426 dealing with the procedure for collecting tribute.[13] Although the context in which the Therans are mentioned cannot be recovered and despite the fact that the Therans were otherwise paying tribute (unlike Samos, which paid only an indemnity), this fragmentary document has nevertheless been used to support the idea that a combination of indemnity and annual tribute was connected with Thera's entrance into the alliance.

An obvious weakness in this hypothetically violent incorporation of Thera into the Athenian alliance is that the more serious the incident, the more difficult it becomes to explain Thucydides' silence. Since Thera and Samos might need special mention in a decree for any number of reasons unrelated to Thera's entrance into the Athenian alliance, there are really no grounds for believing that military force was required to compel the Therans to abandon their neutrality.

D. MELOS

Unlike Thera, Melos refused to bow to Athenian pressure. In view of the rapidity of Thera's alignment, it seems likely that the Athenians also pressured Melos from the beginning of the war, although

10. *ATL*, vol. 1, 150, list 26 (429/428); vol. 1, 149, list 25 (430/429).
11. Meiggs, *Athenian Empire*, 321.
12. Beloch, *Griechische Geschichte*, vol. 2, part 1, 353 n. 3; among "other scholars" are B. D. Meritt, *Documents on Athenian Tribute* (Cambridge, Mass., 1937), 36–37; *ATL*, vol. 1, 285; vol. 2, 52; vol. 3, 336; Gomme, *HCT*, vol. 2, 12; Meiggs and Lewis, 187 (to no. 68); D. Kagan, *The Archidamian War* (Ithaca, N.Y., and London, 1974), 198.
13. Meiggs and Lewis, no. 68, lines 20–21.

the sources say nothing.[14] However, in 426 diplomatic persuasion changed to military confrontation. According to a brief notice in Thucydides, "the Athenians ... sent ... sixty ships and two thousand hoplites to Melos under the command of Nicias, son of Niceratus. For the Athenians, since the Melians were islanders yet were unwilling to yield and would not enter Athens' alliance, wished to induce them. But when, though their land was ravaged, they did not come over, the Athenians left."[15] This is the only mention of Melos during the Archidamian War.

A second Athenian expedition did not come against the island until 416. Thucydides introduces it with this explanation: "The Melians are colonists of the Lacedaemonians, and were not willing to submit like the other islanders. However, at first, being on neither side, they remained at peace. Then when the Athenians attempted to compel them by ravaging their land, they entered into a state of open warfare."[16] Many modern historians, despite Thucydides' testimony, have pointed to a Spartan inscription as evidence that Melos had openly supported the Peloponnesian alliance prior to 426.[17] The inscription records donations "for the war" (lines 4–5, 11–12, 16, 23) from a combination of individuals and states, including "the friends [of Sparta] among the Chians" (line 9), the Ephesians (line 23), and the Melians (lines 1, 14). Since there is insufficient comparative material for dating the inscription more

14. Note the diplomatic missions in 431 to the strategically crucial islands lying off the west coast of mainland Greece (Thuc. 2. 7.3). A small island situated on the western edge of the Cyclades, Melos was of neither strategic nor military consequence. In 480 it had no triremes to contribute to the Greek fleet at Salamis (Hdt. 8. 48); its neutral stance during the Pentecontaetia (see 5.3.B above) makes it unlikely that any warships were built after 480.

15. οἱ Ἀθηναῖοι ... μὲν ναῦς ... ἔστειλαν ... ἐξήκοντα δὲ ἐς Μῆλον καὶ δισχιλίους ὁπλίτας· ἐστρατήγει δὲ αὐτῶν Νικίας ὁ Νικηράτου. τοὺς γὰρ Μηλίους ὄντας νησιώτας καὶ οὐκ ἐθέλοντας ὑπακούειν οὐδὲ ἐς τὸ αὐτῶν ξυμμαχικὸν ἰέναι ἐβούλοντο προσαγαγέσθαι. ὡς δὲ αὐτοῖς δῃουμένης τῆς γῆς οὐ προσεχώρουν, ἄραντες ἐκ τῆς Μήλου αὐτοὶ μὲν ἔπλευσαν (Thuc. 3. 91.1–3).

16. Μήλιοι Λακεδαιμονίων μέν εἰσιν ἄποικοι, τῶν δ' Ἀθηναίων οὐκ ἤθελον ὑπακούειν ὥσπερ οἱ ἄλλοι νησιῶται, ἀλλὰ τὸ μὲν πρῶτον οὐδετέρων ὄντες ἡσύχαζον, ἔπειτα ὡς αὐτοὺς ἠνάγκαζον οἱ Ἀθηναῖοι δῃοῦντες τὴν γῆν, ἐς πόλεμον φανερὸν κατέστησαν (Thuc. 5. 84.2).

17. Andrewes (HCT, vol. 4, 156–58), provides a summary of the search for some justification of Athens' hostility aside from outright imperialism (to Andrewes's list add Grote, History of Greece, vol. 5, 534: Melos enjoying the benefits of empire without paying). For whatever reason, Thucydides disregards all such apologetic pretexts in favor of presenting the incident as a case of Athenian imperialism in its most blatant manifestation (on this attitude, see de Romilly, Thucydides and Athenian Imperialism, 273–74, 284–86). The inscription in question is IG V[1], 1; Meiggs and Lewis, no. 67.

closely than the late fifth or early fourth century on the basis of letter forms, the contents of the document have supplied the primary evidence for determining its probable date. Due to the likely restoration of triremes in line 7, a date in the Archidamian War, prior to Sparta's surrender of its fleet at Pylos in 424 (Thuc. 4. 23.1), or a date after the commencement of the Ionian War in 412 (8.3) has been proposed; but the year 427, when Alcidas took a Peloponnesian fleet across the Aegean and visited Ephesus (3. 32.2), has become the most widely preferred historical context.[18]

There are several problems with the existing consensus. In the first place, we have to ask why the Spartans, who (if the paucity of evidence is any indication) rarely set up documents of any kind for public display, would publish a list of contributors including states and individuals liable to Athenian retaliation. It seems, on the contrary, very unlikely that the Spartans would have gone to abnormal lengths to reveal the identity of supporters within the Athenian empire or to expose hostile behavior on the part of a supposedly neutral state like Melos. Furthermore, from the language of the document, it appears that the Chians mentioned in the inscription made an unofficial contribution while the Ephesians and Melians acted officially. Thucydides' account of Alcidas' expedition has been cited as a possible occasion for this unusual combination of public and private contributions. However, it should be noted that Alcidas treated any Chians he encountered as enemies until the Samians convinced him to act otherwise (3. 32.3) and that although he anchored at Ephesus, the official attitude of that city— an Athenian ally—is unknown.[19] But above all, there remains the

18. This early date is far from certain and has been vigorously challenged; D. Lewis in Meiggs and Lewis, 184 (to no. 67) has proposed 395/394 on the grounds that (1) in that year Agesilaus used Ephesus as a base (Xen. *Hell.* 3. 4), (2) the appearance in the inscription of Persian darics is easier to accept after 404 than during the Archidamian War (note, for example, the necessity for imitation of Athenian coinage by Tissaphernes ca. 412, presumably because Persian coinage was unacceptable), and (3) publication of donations is entirely understandable during the early years of Sparta's undisputed hegemony. However, C. J. Tuplin notes the existence of a new (unpublished) fragment of Meiggs and Lewis, no. 67, in a review of the second edition of Meiggs and Lewis (Oxford, 1988) (see *LCM* 14.1 [January 1989] 12). The new fragment apparently contains a reference to Aeginetan exiles, and since these exiles were restored at the end of the war, the new fragment may provide important evidence for dating the inscription prior to the end of the Peloponnesian War.

19. Thucydides (3. 31.1) reports hearsay, attributed to the Lesbians, that Ionia was ripe for revolt; but Alcidas' initial hostility suggests, at least, gross misunderstanding of Ionian sympathies by the Spartans.

basic problem that the implication of Melian wrongdoing that results from a pre-426 date for the inscription is hard to reconcile with Thucydides' preface to the Athenian attack, especially in light of one further piece of evidence.

The Athenian tribute reassessment of 425/424 includes an annual assessment of fifteen talents for Melos.[20] As Meiggs points out, Thucydides generally chooses to ignore the details of Athens' financial history despite his awareness that money was a crucial factor in the war.[21] But the reassessment of 425/424 is certainly a significant omission, because it so clearly reflects Athens' unrealistically high expectations, not only of the allies' ability to increase their payments (some assessments jumped to as much as five times their previous level) but also of its own ability to extend financial obligation to states that had not been previously tributary, such as additional Cycladic islands, including Melos, and cities in the Euxine.[22]

The inclusion of Melos is not surprising after the Athenian military demonstration of the previous year. But what the assessment reveals is an obviously important, yet unreported, motivation for the attack, namely the desperate search for more revenue. No one would have denied that the assessment amounted to extortion. Still, the unfortunate truth was that Athens had the power to fulfill its threats. Indeed, a reflection of how effective this intimidation could be appears in the subsequent payments, which are known from two neighboring islands assessed with Melos at the time.[23]

The message of the tribute reassessment was that financial necessity had driven Athens to abandon its respect for the unsupportive abstention of states like Melos. By attacking Melos, the Athenians drove this message home and pressured other states into compliance with demands for contributions toward the expenses of the war. If this reconstruction is correct, it means that Athens was not attacking Melos because the Melians were failing to remain strictly neutral but because their refusal to contribute to the cost of the war hindered Athenian efforts to procure revenue from every pos-

20. Meiggs and Lewis, no. 69, col. 1, line 65.
21. Meiggs, *Athenian Empire*, 327.
22. Ibid., 327–31, with Appendix 14, 538–61.
23. The Cycladic islands Anaphae, Ceria, Pholegandros, Belbina, Cimolos, and Sicinos are all apparently assessed tribute for the first time (Meiggs and Lewis, no. 69, col. 1, lines 85–90). Sicinos and Pholegandros, at least, began paying (see Meiggs, *Athenian Empire*, 328 n. 4).

sible source. Thus it seems unnecessary to conclude that the Melians were guilty of any specific diplomatic wrongdoing that provoked the Athenians into retaliation. But whether guilty or innocent the Melians did undeniably fall victim to the escalating necessities of war and to the war's increasingly injurious impact on respect for customary diplomatic restraints.

E. SUMMATION OF NEUTRALS LISTED BY THUCYDIDES

Argos, Achaea (except Pellene), Thera, and Melos are the only states that Thucydides specifically identifies as neutral at the outset of the Peloponnesian War. For a variety of reasons none maintained its neutrality throughout the twenty-seven years of the war; but there is no indication that the policy was particularly extraordinary or unrealistic. Since Thucydides is chiefly concerned with reporting the details of the war, he tends to neglect the neutrals until such time as they become involved in some noteworthy way. For example, Argos and the Achaean cities are hardly mentioned until they become active participants after the Peace of Nicias; and the apparently uneventful incorporation of Thera into the Athenian alliance receives no notice at all. Melos, however, receives a great deal of attention, due to the circumstances surrounding the eventual failure of its policy. It seems clear that Thucydides is especially interested in presenting a more dramatic account of the issues underlying the Athenian conquest of the island, evidently because they provide an instructive illustration of the changing attitude of Athens toward militarily weak, but independent, states such as Melos, which existed within Athens' imperial reach.

One common feature of the policy of the named neutrals should be emphasized. Adoption of a neutral position was not directly related to the real military power of states pursuing it but appears rather to have been an option that they expected the belligerents to accept as a matter of convention. Although Argos was a potentially dangerous foe to either belligerent, the Achaean cities were relatively weak, and Melos and Thera completely vulnerable. That all of these states eventually became involved in the war only emphasizes how terribly difficult it was to remain uncommitted in a time of general conflict between powerful hegemonial alliances. Failure did not mean that no abstention was possible, only that it was difficult to maintain.

II. THE WEST GREEKS DURING THE ARCHIDAMIAN WAR

Despite his omission of all West Greek states from the catalogue of allies (2.9), Thucydides remarks of the last-minute preparations of the belligerents that

> in addition to their existing fleet, the Lacedaemonians also gave orders to those in Italy and Sicily who had taken their side to build ships in proportion to the size of each city, so that a total number of five hundred ships might be reached, and to get ready a specified sum of money, but in other respects to remain at peace and to receive the Athenians, if they came with no more than a single ship, until these preparations were completed.[24]

Without Thucydides' explanation, the subsequent failure of these "allies" to provide any known aid to the Peloponnesians prior to 412 (see Thuc. 3. 86.2; 6. 10.4, 11.2–4, 84.1) would be very difficult to understand. If, however, we set aside Diodorus' skeletal and obviously prejudiced view and subtract from Thucydides' statement the Spartans' unrealized hope of ships being supplied from West Greece, the obvious conclusion is that the Dorian city-states of Sicily and Italy, despite their sympathies, adopted an outwardly neutral stance at the outset of the war.

There was nothing surprising about this. In spite of their traditional kinship with the Dorians of the Peloponnesus, the Dorian states of Sicily and Italy were surely no more anxious than Melos or Thera to expose themselves to retaliation by the Athenians (or by pro-Athenian West Greeks; see 4. 61.4; 6. 18.1). The corresponding inaction of the Chalcidian states of West Greece, at least two of which (Rhegium and Leontini) are known to have been allied with Athens before 431, is probably explicable on similar grounds.[25] In Greek diplomacy even the existence of an alliance did not always preclude the adoption of neutrality.[26] Assistance

24. Λακεδαιμονίοις μὲν πρὸς ταῖς αὐτοῦ ὑπαρχούσαις ἐξ Ἰταλίας καὶ Σικελίας τοῖς τἀκείνων ἑλομένοις ναῦς ἐπετάχθη ποιεῖσθαι κατὰ μέγεθος τῶν πόλεων, ὡς ἐς τὸν πάντα ἀριθμὸν πεντακοσίων νεῶν ἐσομένων, καὶ ἀργύριον ῥητὸν ἑτοιμάζειν, τά τε ἄλλα ἡσυχάζοντας καὶ Ἀθηναίους δεχομένους μιᾷ νηὶ ἕως ἂν ταῦτα παρασκευασθῇ (Thuc. 2. 7.2).
25. Rhegium (433/432): IG I², 51 (I³, 53); Meiggs and Lewis, no. 63; Leontini (433/432): IG I², 52 (I³, 54); Meiggs and Lewis, no. 64.
26. As a diplomatic label symmachia was ambiguous with regard to offensive and defensive cooperation (cf. the strictly defensive epimachia; Thuc. 1. 44; 5. 48.2). The introduction of a formula specifying that the allies would have "the same friends and enemies" (τοὺς αὐτοὺς ἐχθροὺς καὶ φίλους) was aimed at eliminating this uncertainty (e.g., Thuc. 3. 75.1). Occasional examples of states refusing

was a matter for negotiation. For Athens' allies in the West (and for Sparta's too for that matter), this requirement for aid provided especially useful flexibility. If Athens made no specific request for aid, allied states were under no obligation to become involved; and even if Athens did appeal, its allies, being independent, might refuse to comply on the grounds that the conflict did not conform to the specified obligations of the alliance. It is clear both from the reported appeal of the Rhegians and Leontines to Athens in 427 (3. 86.3) and the Egestaean's in 416 (6. 6.2, 13.2) that mutual support was not unconditional but had to be justified and negotiated. Accordingly, in 431, Athens' supposed allies in the West—like Sparta's—remained on the sidelines of the conflict.

By 427 Athens was no longer willing to accept this situation. Thucydides says that the Athenians wanted to prevent further exportation of grain from Sicily to the Peloponnesus (3. 86.4). The problem was, however, that since Athens loudly championed the right of neutrals to use the sea without interference (see 6.6 below) and since the Dorian states of Sicily, in spite of their rumored preparations, had—so far as we know—done nothing hostile, there was no legitimate cause for interfering with their nonmilitary commerce, even when it involved the Peloponnesus. Though Thucydides does not say so explicitly, it seems likely that concern over possible negative consequences of direct interference influenced the Athenians to employ indirect means to hinder Sicilian shipping. By going to the aid of Leontini in its war with Syracuse, the Athenians fomented an all-out intra-island conflict in Sicily. The beauty of this move was that it allowed the Athenians to continue supporting publicly the principle of unrestricted trade while simultaneously preventing it from being practiced by their opponents due to the outbreak of a crippling war.

III. UNNAMED NEUTRALS OF THE ARCHIDAMIAN WAR

A. THE CRETAN STATES

The cities of Crete provide typical examples of states that may have been neutral during the Archidamian War but are nowhere

---

to participate in allied conflicts suggest that support was not automatic unless the defensive situation was indisputable. For allied refusal to support offensive campaigns, see, among other instances, Corinth (3.5 above); Corinth, Thebes, and Athens (8.2 below); the Phocians (9.2.D below); the Eleans (9.5.A below).

specifically identified as such. What is certain is that the Cretans played virtually no role in the events of the first ten years of the war. Even as mercenaries, they are not mentioned before the Athenian expedition to Sicily in 415 (Thuc. 6. 25.2, 43; 7. 57.9). But the question is, Was this noticeable absence the result of a formal decision (as in the Persian Wars; see 5.2 above) or simply the de facto outcome of geographic isolation?

The evidence is mixed. We know that in the summer of 429, the Athenians dispatched twenty triremes to reinforce Phormio at Naupactus but instructed them first to sail with Nicias (either the little-known Gortynian proxenus of Athens or the famous general, who was Athenian proxenus of Gortyn) against Cydonia, a city-state in northwestern Crete.[27] According to Thucydides, Nicias accused the Cydonians of being hostile (*polemian*) to Athens and promised to bring them over to the Athenian side. These were the stated reasons for the expedition, but Thucydides denies that they were true and explains that Nicias' real intention was to bring assistance to Polichne, a neighboring state then in conflict with Cydonia. So, if we believe Thucydides, the alleged hostility of Cydonia was nothing more than a fictitious pretext. Cydonia is not known to have supported the Peloponnesian alliance either before or after this incident; and indeed, none of the states mentioned—Gortyn, Cydonia, Polichne—appears to have had any official connection with either Athens or Sparta. On the contrary, Thucydides emphasizes the haphazardness of the expedition which seeks to capitalize on an unexpected opportunity to win over Cretan cities but, in the end, accomplishes nothing.

If the Cretan cities had any formal policy, the basis of it may have been the policy of Argos. Treaties from the middle of the fifth century closely linked Argos to the Cretan cities of Cnossus and Tylissus. According to the terms that survive from one of the treaties, these states were to act jointly in matters of foreign policy.[28] Perhaps, then, the neutral policy of Argos was also adopted by its Cretan allies and, following their lead, by other Cretan city-states anxious to avoid the conflict and possibly to enjoy the relative safety and advantages of nonalignment.

27. On Nicias, see W. R. Connor, "Nicias the Cretan?" *AJAH* 1 (1976): 61–64; G. Herman, "Nikias, Epimenides and Omissions in Thucydides," *CQ* 39 (1989): 83–93.

28. See Meiggs and Lewis, no. 42, A, ll. 6–20. Cretan neutrality might carry the economic advantages enjoyed by Argos (See 6.1); but not without risks (see 6.6).

B. THE THESSALIANS

The policy of the Thessalian Confederacy may be another case of formal abstention. Although the Thessalians had had alliances with Athens in the past,[29] their desertion during the battle at Tanagra (Thuc. 1. 107.7; Diod. 11. 80.1–6) and the Athenians' subsequent military intervention on behalf of an exiled leader, Orestes (Thuc. 1. 111.1; Diod. 11. 83.3) show that there was serious instability in relations between the two states. At the outset of the Peloponnesian War, the Thessalians are not mentioned in Thucydides' catalogue of allies and neutrals (2.9) but appear almost immediately in support of Athens during the first Peloponnesian invasion of Attica in the summer of 431 (2.22–23). No explanation of their presence is given, but it would hardly be surprising if the Thessalians had come in the expectation of participating in a great and perhaps decisive contest. As it turned out, however, they found the Athenians vexed by the invasion, yet resolved to concede control of their territory to the Peloponnesian alliance rather than risk a decisive land battle. Indeed, in their single token engagement, the Thessalian cavalry proved, at considerable risk, that cavalry without supporting infantry can do little beyond harassing a powerful land army (2. 22.2).

After 431 the Thessalians sent no further military aid to Athens. The little information we have about the Thessalians suggests that no formal obligation existed. For example, Thucydides mentions that in 429 a threatened invasion by the Thracian dynast Sitalces, an ally of Athens (2.95, 101.4), caused "the Thessalians, Magnesians, and other subjects of the Thessalians, and the Hellenes as far south as Thermopylae" to mobilize in alarm (2. 101.2; cf. Diod. 12. 51.1). On the other hand, in 426, when the Spartans founded Heraclea as an anti-Athenian outpost in Trachinia (3.92), the Thessalians are said to have felt menaced and therefore made war on the colonists until they eventually exhausted them (3. 93.2; cf. 5. 51.1). Significantly, alliance with the Athenians is nowhere suggested as a reason for hostility.

Between 424 and 422, first a Peloponnesian expedition under Brasidas and subsequently a reinforcement army attempted to

---

29. There had been a Peisistratid alliance (Hdt. 5. 63) and a joint alliance with Athens and Argos ca. 462 (Thuc. 1. 102.4, 107.7); see Larsen, *Greek Federal States*, 112–13, 122–26.

march through Thessaly en route to Macedonia and Thrace (4. 78–79.1, 132.2; 5. 13.1). Thucydides describes these expeditions in detail but nowhere specifies the official relationship, if any existed, between the Thessalian Confederacy and either of the belligerents. The closest he comes is in the following note about Brasidas' passage through Thessaly in 424:

> For Thessaly was in any case not easy to traverse without an escort and especially with an armed force, seeing that among all the Hellenes alike to traverse the territory of a neighbor without permission was looked upon with suspicion; and besides, the majority of Thessalians had always been well-disposed to the Athenians. As a result, if the Thessalians had not been dominated by a narrow clique rather than their native form of constitutional government, he [Brasidas] would never have advanced, and indeed at that time, while he was proceeding, other Thessalians of the opposition party confronted him at the Enipeus River and attempted to prevent him from going further; and they stated that he was doing wrong in proceeding without the common consent of all [i.e., without the official permission of the confederacy].[30]

If the Thessalians were Athenian allies at this time, as A. W. Gomme assumes, Thucydides certainly has gone out of his way to obfuscate that fact.[31] Not only does Thucydides not mention any alliance between Athens and the Thessalian Confederacy, but he attributes to Brasidas the claim that he had entered Thessaly as a friend, bearing arms not against the Thessalians but against Athens, and was unaware of any hostility that barred the Spartans or the Thessalian nations from access to each other's territory (4. 78.4). Surely Thucydides could not attribute this claim to Brasidas if the Thessalian Confederacy was allied with Athens. Taken at face value (and we have no grounds for suspicion), Thucydides' account rules out this possibility.

---

30. τὴν γὰρ Θεσσαλίαν ἄλλως τε οὐκ εὔπορον ἦν διιέναι ἄνευ ἀγωγοῦ καὶ μετὰ ὅπλων γε δή, καὶ τοῖς πᾶσί γε ὁμοίως Ἕλλησιν ὕποπτον καθειστήκει τὴν τῶν πέλας μὴ πείσαντας διιέναι· τοῖς τε Ἀθηναίοις αἰεί ποτε τὸ πλῆθος τῶν Θεσσαλῶν εὔνουν ὑπῆρχεν. ὥστε εἰ μὴ δυναστείᾳ μᾶλλον ἢ ἰσονομίᾳ ἐχρῶντο τὸ ἐγχώριον οἱ Θεσσαλοί, οὐκ ἄν ποτε προῆλθεν, ἐπεὶ καὶ τότε πορευομένῳ αὐτῷ ἀπαντήσαντες ἄλλοι τῶν τἀναντία τούτοις βουλομένων ἐπὶ τῷ Ἐνιπεῖ ποταμῷ ἐκώλυον καὶ ἀδικεῖν ἔφασαν ἄνευ τοῦ πάντων κοινοῦ πορευόμενον.   (Thuc. 4. 78.2–3)

On the textual problems here, see Gomme, HCT, vol. 3, 542–43, and vol. 2, 347 (to 3. 62.3). I accept Gomme's interpretation that the adverbial construction at the beginning of 78.3 goes with isonomia and has the sense "according to the customs of the country" (Gomme).

31. Gomme, HCT, vol. 3, 541.

We are also told that in 423 the Spartan Ischagoras prepared to cross Thessaly with reinforcements for Brasidas but was prevented when King Perdiccas of Macedon, at the insistence of Nicias, aroused opposition among his personal friends in Thessaly (4. 132.2). If the Thessalians were Athenian allies, why would Nicias appeal to the king of Macedon instead of directly to the Thessalians? Moreover, the Athenians are said to have been particularly anxious about the loss of Amphipolis in the previous winter (424/423), because they were not certain they could prevent the Peloponnesians from crossing Thessaly (4. 108.1). It was for this reason that Nicias appealed to an ally, Perdiccas, for help in forestalling the Peloponnesians (4. 130.2; 5. 13.1).[32]

One further incident should be considered. During the winter of 413/412, Agis made an expedition against the Oetaeans on the Maliac Gulf and also "compelled the Phthiotic Achaeans and other Thessalian subjects in that region—over the complaints and unwillingness of the Thessalians—to give some hostages and money ... and tried to bring them over into alliance" (8. 3.1). Once again there is no evidence of an existing alliance with Athens. The Thessalians are not urged to revolt; instead, Agis nibbles at their dependencies and pressures them to accept an alliance with Sparta by means just short of war.

In addition to the evidence found in Thucydides, there exists a fourth-century dedication at Delphi, erected in honor of a prominent Pharsalian family, which fits exactly with the contention that the Thessalians remained neutral during the war. The critical epigram reads: "Daochus son of Agias am I, of the land of Pharsalus, who ruled all Thessaly, not by force but by law, for twenty-seven years; and Thessaly was filled with long and fruitful peace and wealth."[33] Aside from reservations expressed by Gomme and an earlier chronology (ca. 455–425) once proposed by E. Meyer, no

---

32. This roundabout appeal is interpreted differently (in line with the belief that the Thessalians were Athenian allies) as a reflection of the poor state of relations between the states, which is hypothesized from jokes about Athenian intrigue with the oppressed Penestai of Thessaly in Ar. *Wasps* 1271–74 (produced in 422), and in Eupolis, frag. 209 (produced about the same time); for sensible reservations, see Gomme, *HCT*, vol. 3, 622–33.

33.   Δάοχος Ἀγία εἰμί, πατρὶς Φάρσαλος, ἀπάσης
         Θεσσαλίας ἄρξας, οὐ βίαι ἀλλὰ νόμωι,
         ἑπτὰ καὶ εἴκοσι ἔτη· πολλῆι δὲ καὶ ἀγλαοκάρπωι
         εἰρήνηι πλούτωι τε ἔβρυε Θεσσαλία.
                  (Dittenberger, *SIG*³, 274 vi)

one has hesitated to connect the rule of Daochus I with the twenty-seven years of the Peloponnesian War.[34] The cumulative evidence is strong: (1) the Thessalian Confederacy had a constitutional office, the *tageia*, which placed the confederacy under the legal rule of an individual during extraordinary circumstances; (2) Daochus I, the man of the epigram and grandfather of Daochus II, who erected the Delphic monument, should have been a mature adult during the latter half of the fifth century; and (3) twenty-seven years is precisely the length of the Peloponnesian War (431–404). Furthermore (4), the presence of Menon of Pharsalus as commander of a Pharsalian contingent in Attica during the first year of the war proves only that Menon championed pro-Athenian involvement (a suggestive contrast to the pacific policy associated with Daochus I) and does not pose a chronological problem. And, finally (5), the report that immediately after the Athenian defeat in 404 Lycophron of Pherae attempted to establish himself as *tagos* (Xen. *Hell.* 2. 3.4) also fits the twenty-seven year chronology of Daochus I in the Peloponnesian War and indicates only that beginning in 404 there was a new era of violent usurpation of the *tageia*.

Taken together, the evidence in Thucydides and the Daochus monument make a strong case for connecting the *tageia* of Daochus I with the disappearance of the Thessalians as Athenian supporters after 431 and their subsequent inactivity during the remainder of the war. Thessaly may not be specifically referred to as a neutral state, but there seems to be little doubt that the confederacy was not formally allied with either side and viewed itself as officially neutral.[35]

C. PERSIA

Amazingly, the exact diplomatic position of the Persians at the outset of the Peloponnesian War is nowhere stated in the sources.

---

34. See most recently T. Martin, *Sovereignty and Coinage in Classical Greece* (Princeton, 1985), 106, 109–15.

35. It would still be legitimate to ask, Why is Thucydides so vague? He obviously knew what the Thessalians were doing. Why then does he avoid being specific? While no truly satisfactory explanation for this—and numerous other omissions in Thucydides—can be found, it is possible that the lack of any broad characterization of Thessalian policy stemmed from Thucydides' exclusive concentration on individual incidents that involved the confederacy in the war. Since the nonparticipation of the Thessalians was accepted without challenge, the details of their policy and normal activities were of no interest to his narrative.

This may seem a surprising omission, but it becomes understandable when we remember how little attention the sources pay to states that are not actively involved in the main events of a given conflict, regardless of the importance of such states or even of their later involvement.[36] On the policy of Persia, Thucydides only digresses long enough to comment that both the Athenians and the Spartans were initially uncertain about what stance the Persians would adopt.[37] Later he adds that the Spartans continued actively to seek Persian support after the outbreak of the war. One group of envoys journeying to Artaxerxes in 430 "to see if they might persuade him to supply money and become an ally" receives special notice because they were captured by the Athenians.[38]

By the winter of 425/424, so many Peloponnesians had gone to Susa and appealed to the king that he reportedly sent Artaphernes to tell the Spartans that he had been receiving numerous conflicting proposals and therefore invited them to entrust something definite to envoys who would accompany Artaphernes to Susa.[39] If this statement is accurate, it can only mean that Artaxerxes had remained uncommitted prior to 425/424. Despite occasional incidents of satrapal aid to disaffected Athenian allies,[40] the king was still holding aloof from the war. However, the capture of Artaphernes revealed that the king's position might change. Although the motive for change is nowhere reported, it may be significant that contemporary plays of Aristophanes and other comic playwrights contain prominent jokes about Persian intrigue.[41] Athens may have seemed vulnerable, the successes of Brasidas impressive, the opportunity to regain old Asiatic dependencies tempting. In any case, the Athenians took the situation seriously but reacted with cautious diplomacy. An embassy was sent to escort Artaphernes back to Susa. Unfortunately, its instructions are unknown; and when they

36. See the discussion above in chapter 2.

37. See 1. 82.1; 2. 7.1; cf. Diod. 12. 41.1.

38. Καὶ τοῦ αὐτοῦ θέρους τελευτῶντος Ἀριστεὺς Κορίνθιος καὶ Λακεδαιμονίων πρέσβεις Ἀνήριστος καὶ Νικόλαος καὶ Πρατόδαμος καὶ Τεγεάτης Τιμαγόρας καὶ Ἀργεῖος ἰδίᾳ Πόλλις, πορευόμενοι ἐς τὴν Ἀσίαν ὡς βασιλέα, εἴ πως πείσειαν αὐτὸν χρήματά τε παρασχεῖν καὶ ξυμπολεμεῖν (Thuc. 2. 67.1).

39. Thuc. 4. 50.1–2; for earlier embassies, see notes 37 and 38 above.

40. On Pissuthnes' aid to the Samians, for example, see Thuc. 3. 34, 42.2; A. T. Olmstead, History of the Persian Empire (Chicago, 1948), 343; D. M. Lewis, Sparta and Persia (Leiden, 1977), 59–62; J. M. Cook, The Persian Empire (London, 1983), 130.

41. See Ar. Ach. 91–125 (produced 425); Knights 478 (produced 424); cf. Wasps 1137 (produced 422); Leucon Presbeis (frag. 703 Kock).

reached Ephesus, the ambassadors learned that Artaxerxes had died, and so abandoned their mission and returned home.[42]

While Thucydides says nothing else about Persia until after the Athenian disaster in Sicily, Andocides provides a tantalizing (and much discussed) story about Athenian-Persian diplomacy connected with the years immediately following Artaxerxes' death (424). In a speech delivered about a dozen years after the end of the war, Andocides claims that his uncle Epilycus once negotiated a "treaty" (spondai) and "friendship for ever" (philia eis hapanta chronon) with King Darius II.[43] When combined with separate, but apparently associated, epigraphical and prosopographical evidence, the treaty—usually referred to as the Peace of Epilycus—can be dated to roughly the middle of the Peloponnesian War.[44] Although the exact year of the treaty is uncertain, there is general agreement that the treaty is authentic and was negotiated with Darius II before the Athenians' Sicilian expedition of 415–413. Few specific details are known, but both Andocides and a fragmentary Attic inscription connected with the Epilycus treaty speak of spondai (i.e., presumably, a peace treaty).[45] As quoted above, Andocides also claims that the treaty involved friendship (philia). Andocides emphasizes this feature in order to make the point that Athens' subsequent aid to rebel satrap Amorges violated the treaty and thus justified the king's alliance with Sparta in 413/412.[46]

42. Thuc. 4. 50.3; see Gomme, HCT, vol. 3, ad loc.
43. Andoc. 3 (On the Peace). 29.
44. Bengtson, SVA² no. 183; A. E. Raubitschek, "Treaties between Persia and Athens," GRBS 5 (1964): 151–59. Dates proposed include 424/423 (H. T. Wade-Gery, Essays in Greek History [Oxford, 1958], 207–11; Meiggs and Lewis, no. 70; Meiggs, Athenian Empire, 134–35; Lewis, Sparta and Persia, 76–77; Bengtson, SVA² no. 138); 422/421 (A. Blamire, "Epilycus' Negotiations with Persia," Phoenix 29 [1975]: 24–25); 424–418 (W. E. Thompson, "The Athenian Treaties with Haliai and Dareios the Bastard," Klio 53 [1971]: 119–24); and ca. 415 (Raubitschek, 156–57).

45. 15   ἐπ[ειδὴ δὲ οἱ πρέσβες]
    [οἱ π]αρ⟨ὰ⟩ βασιλέως ἥκ[οντες ἀγγελλῶσι Ἡ]-
    [ρακ]λείδην συμπράτ[τεν ἑαυτοῖς προθύ]-
    [μως] ἔς τε τὰσπονδὰς [...............]
    [...] ἄλλο ὅτι ἐπαγγέλ[ειαν, ἔναι Ἡρακλε]-
20 [ίδηι] γῆς ἔγκτησιν κα[ὶ οἰκίας Ἀθήνησι]-
    [ν καὶ ἀ]τέλειαν καθάπε[ρ τοῖς ἄλλοις πρ]-
    [οξένο]ις   (IG II², 8, lines 15–22)

See now M. B. Walbank, Athenian Proxenies of the Fifth Century B.C. (Toronto and Sarasota, Fla., 1978), no. 47, pp. 258–68.

46. On the revolt of Amorges (414 or earlier to 412), see Cook, Persian Empire, 208–9.

More than one attempt has been made to interpret the Epilycus treaty as a renewal of the controversial Peace of Callias.[47] The objections to this convenient identification are, however, over-whelming. According to the unanimous testimony of the sources, the alleged terms of the Peace of Callias were unfavorable to the Persians. Why then would Darius II be willing to reaffirm an ignominious agreement at a time when Persia's entry into the war in opposition to Athens was under serious consideration? And even if Darius had been willing to reaffirm formally a humiliatingly disadvantageous treaty, why would Andocides choose to be so vague about it, and why would Thucydides ignore it altogether?

Perhaps the most critical, though widely misunderstood, feature of the Epilycus treaty is its specification of *philia*. This detail has been noticed in the past but has never been properly explained, for the fact is that as far as we know the establishment of diplomatic "friendship" (*philia*) between Persia and Athens was new and represented an important formalization of the relations between the two powers. If it is right, as it must be, to reject the idea that the Epilycus treaty was nothing more than a renewal of an existing agreement negotiated by his predecessor, then the *spondai kai philia* accepted by Darius II must represent the formal cessation of Per-sian-Athenian hostility, which went back to the time of the Persian invasions of Greece. But achieving a formal end of their old hostility was almost certainly not the aim of the *spondai*. What mattered most of all was the treaty of *philia*. As A. Blamire succinctly puts it, *philia* involved "a formal guarantee that neither party would in any way assist the other's enemies."[48] Hence the treaty that Epilycus negotiated for Athens with the new Persian king, Darius II, pro-vided confirmation through a formal agreement that he would continue to refrain from active participation in the ongoing Greek conflict.

Given the Athenians' acute concern about Persian intentions after Artaphernes was intercepted, not to mention their extremely careful and respectful handling of him, it is not at all surprising to learn (from Andocides) that they subsequently sent another embassy to Darius II to obtain his *philia*. Thucydides had no special reason to be interested, since the outcome was maintenance of the

47. E.g., Wade-Gery, *Essays in Greek History*; Meiggs, *Athenian Empire*.
48. Blamire, "Epilycus' Negotiations with Persia," 23.

status quo. After all, the Epilycus treaty was nothing more than a traditional *philia* agreement, which had no impact on the war, aside from relieving the minds of the Athenians and postponing Persia's entry into the conflict by as much as ten years. Yet for the study of classical neutrality, this flurry of diplomatic activity provides an especially valuable glimpse of the kind of interaction that went on between the belligerents and states that continued to abstain from involvement in the war.

IV. THE PROPOSED NEUTRALITY OF PLATAEA (429)

Plataea's ill-fated role in the war (431–427) also involved the issue of neutrality, in 429 and again in 427.[49] In 429, when Archidamus brought a Peloponnesian army into their territory, the Plataeans boldly demanded that he withdraw, because the invasion violated the sworn guarantee against attack granted to Plataea by the Greek allies in 479 (Thuc. 2. 71.2–4).[50] According to Thucydides, however, Archidamus replied that the Plataeans' appeal to the oath of 479 could only be justified if their action corresponded to their rhetoric (2. 72.1). As it was, Archidamus claimed, Plataea's continued alliance with Athens (2. 2.1) violated the spirit of the old covenant; so

49. The full account is given in Thuc. 2. 2–6, 71–78; 3. 20–24, 52–68; neutrality is treated in 2. 72–74; 3. 64.3, 68.1.

50. The exact nature of the status granted in Plataea in 479 is described in two ways in our sources, as *autonomia* (Thuc. 2. 71.2–4, 72.1; cf. 3. 59.2) and as *asylia* (Plut. *Arist*. 21.1). According to the account attributed by Thucydides to the Plataeans themselves, Pausanias had made the Greek allies swear in 479 to defend Plataea's *autonomia* against any unjust violation (2. 71.2–4). They imply (3. 55) that this covenant did not preclude their keeping an existing alliance with Athens (Hdt. 6. 108; Thuc. 3. 55, 68.5; Bengtson, *SVA*² no. 119). The Spartans, however, reject the idea that the Plataeans could continue to be guaranteed against attack while taking the Athenian side in the present war (2. 72.1); and, in the end, Sparta declares that the Plataeans' refusal to renounce their alliance with Athens cancels the obligations of the covenant (2. 74.3).

Plutarch (*Arist*. 21.1) introduces the completely different idea that the grant of 479 involved *asylia* (Πλαταιεῖς δ' ἀσύλους καὶ ἱερους ἀφεῖσθαι τῷ θεῷ θύοντας ὑπὲρ τῆς Ἑλλάδος). In classical usage *asylia* means "inviolability," that is, immunity from attack or plunder, and applies to sanctuaries. If Plataea was granted *asylia* in 479, it seems very strange that Thucydides nowhere mentions it. The temptation for later sources, however, to distort the nature of the covenant into a grant of *asylia* is understandable, since recognition of that status would imply that the Spartan-Theban destruction of Plataea was impious as well as unduly harsh. Thucydides' account is, therefore, preferable, but see the doubts about his accuracy in M. Ostwald, *Autonomia: Its Genesis and Early History*, American Classical Studies 11 (1982), 16–22.

he offered the Plataeans two choices: (1) alliance with the Peloponnesians against Athens or (2) adoption of neutrality. The exact words of the second proposal run as follows: "And if not [alliance], then remain at peace, as we have previously proposed, enjoying your own possessions; and be not with either side; but receive both as friends, while neither for hostile purpose; and this will satisfy us."[51] In response, the Plataeans raised two objections: (1) the Athenians, who held their women and children, would have to approve the proposal and were unlikely to do so and (2) if the Thebans were included in the stipulation about receiving both sides, they would surely try again to seize the city (2. 72.2).[52]

Archidamus countered with an offer to hold the city-state in trust until the conclusion of the war while the Plataeans themselves evacuated to wherever they wished (2. 72.3). But the Plataeans, after they had consulted the Athenians and had received guarantees of support (73.1–3), resolved to maintain their alliance with Athens regardless of the consequences (74.1). When Archidamus learned this, he called upon the gods to witness that the Plataeans had first broken the oath of 479 by refusing all of the "reasonable" (eikota) proposals that he had made (74.3), and he immediately began hostilities (75.1).

The ensuing siege is reported in considerable detail by Thucydides (2. 75–78; 3. 20–24). It dragged on until 427, when the exhausted remnant of the garrison finally surrendered to the Spartans, having been promised that no one would be punished contrary to justice (3. 52.1–3). But when five Spartan judges arrived, they asked only whether or not the prisoners had rendered any good service to the Spartans and their allies in the present war (52.4). At this point Thucydides reports opposing speeches delivered by

51. εἰ δὲ μή, ἅπερ καὶ τὸ πρότερον ἤδη προυκαλεσάμεθα, ἡσυχίαν ἄγετε νεμόμενοι τὰ ὑμέτερα αὐτῶν, καὶ ἔστε μηδὲ μεθ᾽ ἑτέρων, δέχεσθε δὲ ἀμφοτέρους φίλους, ἐπὶ πολέμῳ δὲ μηδ᾽ ἑτέρους. καὶ τάδε ἡμῖν ἀρκέσει (Thuc. 2. 72.1).

52. The Plataeans specifically fear further internal subversion if Thebans are allowed to come and go—a major factor in the abortive attack of 431 (Thuc. 2. 2.1–3; Diod. 12. 41.2–4). Even the second of the Plataeans' professed objections (quoted above) may disguise this underlying internal uncertainty. There is, however, plenty of evidence that neutrals could refuse to admit belligerents within their walls without forfeiting neutral status; see Thuc. 6. 44.2–3 (South Italian city-states); 50.1 (Messene); 50.3, 51.1 (Catana); 51.1 (Camarina); 62.2 (Himera); all discussed below in 7.2–3. This suggests that Archidamus' proposal contained nothing more than normal diplomatic language, which the Plataeans unexpectedly take issue with in their extreme state of insecurity about Theban intentions.

the Plataeans (53–59) and the Thebans (61–67); and the issue of Plataea's neutrality returns.[53]

The Plataeans are defensive about their failure to accept the offer of neutral status, the Thebans indignant. The Plataeans take the position that they should not be blamed for maintaining their alliance with Athens, because (1) they were bound to honor a debt of benefaction to Athens for defense against Thebes (3. 55.3) and (2) as mere followers, they should not be held responsible for policies mandated by their superiors (55.4). In response, the Thebans argue that (1) dependence on Athens as a defense against Thebes was unnecessary, because of the protection afforded by the oaths sworn by the Greeks in 479 (63.2); (2) in the balance, honoring the debt to Athens was less important than opposing Athenian aggression against other Greek states (63.3–4); and (3) if following orders released a subordinate from responsibility, then Plataea's refusal to medize in 480/479 could be considered as nothing more than blind obedience to Athens and, therefore, no just cause for protection (64.1–2).

But the Thebans remind the judges especially of the Plataeans' refusal to remain neutral:

> For you have abandoned [the oath sworn with Pausanias] and in violation of its principles have instead aided the enslavement of the Aeginetans and certain others of the sworn parties, rather than trying to prevent it, and have done these things not unwillingly but while enjoying the laws under which you have always lived up until now and were not, like us,[54] under violent compulsion. Moreover, you would not accept the final proposal of neutrality—so that you support neither side—made by us before the siege.[55]

Thucydides himself believed that this was the decisive argument made against the Plataeans. In summary, he reports that the judges defended their harsh verdict on the grounds that they had urged the Plataeans to remain outside of the conflict as impartial (koinoi)

---

53. See the recent discussion of W. R. Connor, *Thucydides* (Princeton, 1984), 91–95; also C. W. MacLeod, "Thucydides' Plataean Debate," *GRBS* 18 (1977): 227–46; neither, however, focuses his attention on the issue of neutrality.

54. This is an allusion to the earlier argument that the Thebans had unwillingly medized because of the unlawful influence of a ruling clique (3. 62.3–6).

55. ἀπελίπετε γὰρ αὐτὴν καὶ παραβάντες ξυγκατεδουλοῦσθε μᾶλλον Αἰγινήτας καὶ ἄλλους τινὰς τῶν ξυνομοσάντων ἢ διεκωλύετε, καὶ ταῦτα οὔτε ἄκοντες ἔχοντές τε τοὺς νόμους οὕσπερ μέχρι τοῦ δεῦρο καὶ οὐδενὸς ὑμᾶς βιασα-μένου, ὥσπερ ἡμᾶς. τὴν τελευταίαν τε πρὶν περιτειχίζεσθαι πρόκλησιν ἐς ἡσυχίαν ἡμῶν, ὥστε μηδετέροις ἀμύνειν, οὐκ ἐδέχεσθε. (Thuc. 3. 64.3)

observers. But since the Plataeans had refused these proposals, the judges concluded that the Plataeans themselves had freed the Spartans from any previous obligations and were responsible for the resulting hostilities.[56] Thus, in the end, the Plataeans were legally condemned in an interstate court of law for their refusal to accept what could be claimed, in the context of contemporary diplomatic thinking, to be a legitimate and reasonable offer—neutrality.

If we examine the collective evidence of the original proposal and subsequent speeches, there are several important conclusions that can be drawn about the Spartan, Theban, Athenian, and Plataean attitudes toward neutrality. The Spartans were willing to attack Plataea in deference to Thebes (3. 68.4) but were also very much concerned about religious scruples. Since the Spartans had once sworn not to invade Plataea unjustly (2. 71.2–4), it was important to Archidamus to shift responsibility for the attack in 429 onto the Plataeans. His offer of neutrality served this purpose admirably because it allowed the Spartans to maintain the appearance of acting justly (2. 74.3). Moreover, Plataea's refusal to accept could be (and was) later given as the legal justification for condemning the Plataeans (3. 68.1). Neutrality had thus served a useful propaganda purpose, although observers like Thucydides recognized that in truth it revealed the cynical and self-serving attitude of the Spartans.

For the Thebans, Plataea's rejection of neutrality provided the key argument in favor of the imposition of a harsh punishment (3. 64.3). However, neutrality was not the real issue. Plataea's stubborn independence hindered Thebes' ambition to dominate Boeotia; worse still, as an ally of Athens, Plataea was a serious strategic threat to Thebes. What the Thebans wanted was the elimination of Plataea. Everyone knew this; and the Plataeans' rejection of neutrality was in no small part influenced by their fear that the Thebans would not honor neutrality but continue to work for the city's destruction (2. 72.2). In other words, Plataean neutrality was almost certainly not what the Thebans were seeking (or probably even willing to accept), but as it turned out, Plataea's rejection of the policy helped the Thebans achieve their real goal.

56. διότι τόν τε ἄλλον χρόνον ἠξίουν δῆθεν αὐτοὺς κατὰ τὰς παλαιὰς Παυσανίου μετὰ τὸν Μῆδον σπονδὰς ἡσυχάζειν καὶ ὅτε ὕστερον ἃ πρὸ τοῦ περιτειχίζεσθαι προείχοντο αὐτοῖς, κοινοὺς εἶναι κατ' ἐκείνας, ὡς οὐκ ἐδέξαντο, ἡγούμενοι τῇ ἑαυτῶν δικαίᾳ βουλήσει ἔκσπονδοι ἤδη ὑπ' αὐτῶν κακῶς πεπονθέναι (Thuc. 3. 68.1). For translation, see above, p. xxv.

Athens' opposition to Plataean neutrality was adamant. Aside from the fact that the Athenians held the civilian population more or less hostage (2. 6.4, 72.2), the Athenians seemed determined to convince the Plataeans that rescue was possible if Plataea trusted its alliance with Athens (2.73). This was, of course, utterly false; and it creates the suspicion that the Athenians considered neutrality dangerous to their interests not only, I think, because it meant the loss of an existing ally, but also because of the precedent it might set for other allies.

Belligerent pressure aside, the Plataeans themselves may have truly wanted to be neutral. Once their original appeal to the oaths of 479 was countered by Archidamus' offer to accept their neutrality, it was clear that if the offer were rejected, hostilities would be inevitable. The fact that the Plataeans consulted Athens (2.73) in spite of their expressed mistrust of Thebes suggests that they retained some confidence in Sparta's promises, considered the offer serious, and even hoped to convince the Athenians to accept the Spartans' assurances. The Athenians promised aid and sent none. At their trial in 427, the Plataeans did not argue that neutrality was an unreasonable offer but that their fear of Thebes and obligations to Athens made the offer impossible to accept (3.55). Under the circumstances, there was little else they could have said. In 429, their attitude toward the option of neutrality was mistrustful, because they knew that it depended on the acceptance and self-restraint of all parties involved. So, they decided not to accept the offer but to run the risk of siege rather than expose themselves to the double jeopardy of defying and thereby alienating the Athenians without in any way diminishing the Thebans' hatred and thirst for revenge. But as the outcome proved, neutrality was a double-edged sword, for in refusing it, the Plataeans gave their enemies a perfect legal pretext for annihilating them.

V. THE FAILURE OF CORCYRAEAN NEUTRALITY (427)

At the outset of his celebrated description of the Corcyraean revolution, Thucydides mentions that among the preliminary developments that exacerbated internal tensions were two abortive attempts to shift Corcyra into a position of neutrality. The first reportedly occurred when envoys from both Athens and Corinth arrived in Corcyra during the summer of 427. Thucydides explains:

"On the arrival of Attic and Corinthian ships bringing envoys and after the envoys had stated their cases, the Corcyraeans voted to remain allies of Athens according to the terms of their existing agreement, but also to remain friends with the Peloponnesians as before."[57] This may sound like an impossible policy, but it actually fits well with what we are learning about the complex diplomacy of the time.

In the first place, the existing alliance with Athens was a mutual defense agreement (*epimachia*).[58] If strictly interpreted, this meant that Corcyra was required only to help defend the Athenians and their allies in the event of attack by the Peloponnesians. Indeed, the Corcyraeans had been conspicuously absent from Athenian expeditions in the four years since the war had begun (2. 25.1). Evidently they had, in spite of their inclusion in the list of normal allies (2. 9.4), adhered to this diplomatic distinction (the single exception occurring when Athens brought a large fleet of its own into the area). Secondly, by offering to maintain *philia* with the Peloponnesians, the Corcyraeans were giving formal assurance that henceforth they would not join in any future aggression against Athens' enemies if they were willing to reciprocate. Had this compromise policy won acceptance, it could have allowed the Corcyraeans to maintain their *epimachia* with Athens while simultaneously defusing the hostility of the Peloponnesian alliance—the very position Plataea found it could not achieve!

In a short time the new policy received clearer definition. As *stasis* between pro- and anti-Athenian factions progressed, the leaders of what Thucydides describes as the anti-Athenian faction gained the upper hand and immediately published a more unequivocal declaration of neutrality. "In the future," they announced, "[the Corcyraeans] would remain at peace and receive neither side if they came with more than a single ship, but regard any larger number as hostile."[59] The populace was compelled to ratify this proclamation, and an embassy was dispatched to Athens in the hope of

---

57. καὶ ἀφικομένης Ἀττικῆς τε νεὼς καὶ Κορινθίας πρέσβεις ἀγουσῶν καὶ ἐς λόγους καταστάντων, ἐψηφίσαντο Κερκυραῖοι Ἀθηναίοις μὲν ξύμμαχοι εἶναι κατὰ τὰ ξυγκείμενα, Πελοποννησίοις δὲ φίλοι ὥσπερ καὶ πρότερον (Thuc. 3. 70.2).

58. Thuc. 1. 44.1; Bengtson, *SVA²* no. 161.

59. τό τε λοιπὸν μηδετέρους δέχεσθαι ἀλλ' ἢ μιᾷ νηΐ ἡσυχάζοντας, τὸ δὲ πλέον πολέμιον ἡγεῖσθαι (Thuc. 3. 71.1). In support of the translation above, which takes ἡσυχάζοντας with Κερκυραίους, the implied subject of δέχεσθαι, see Gomme, *HCT*, vol. 2, 361.

justifying the policy and mitigating any hostile reaction (3. 71.2). This attempt failed, however, and at the same time, further *stasis* led to the ascendancy of the opposing faction, which immediately ratified a combined offensive and defensive alliance with Athens.[60]

Despite their rapid failure, the Corcyraean declarations tell us something about how a state might establish itself as a neutral. Initially, the Corcyraeans attempted, on the one hand, to retain their existing treaty commitment with Athens and, on the other, to protect themselves against attack from the Peloponnesians through the promise to maintain *philia*. This rather clumsy union of diplomatic elements was, however, quickly superseded by a clearer declaration that sought, in effect, to return to the familiar nonalignment of the past and made the island's determination to be impartial in the ongoing conflict perfectly clear by stating that neither belligerent would henceforth be allowed to visit Corcyra with more than a single ship.

Limitation of belligerent presence to a single ship was a recognized practice of neutral states.[61] But the problem with Corcyra's shift to neutrality was that internal dissension destroyed the effectiveness of the declarations. In spite of its diplomatic correctness, the neutral policy faced even greater internal opposition, because it had not resulted from a peaceful agreement but from murder and coercion. Still, the faction responsible must have believed that the policy would be accepted, since they actually sent an embassy to Athens in order to justify the new stance to Corcyraeans who had taken refuge there (3. 71.2). Surely if the leaders of the controlling faction had had no hope of winning respect for the policy, they would not have exposed any of their number to risk of reprisal

60. Some scholars, including Kagan, *Archidamian War*, and I. A. F. Bruce, "The Corcyraean Civil War," *Phoenix* 25 (1971): 109, characterize Corcyra's initial resolution as "a naive and unrealistic decision" (Bruce, 109), but this judgment seems unfairly influenced by hindsight. At the time, Corcyra had the examples of numerous other states (e.g., the Argives, the Achaeans, the Cretans, the West Greeks, the Thessalians, even the Plataeans) as models of the possibility of such a policy. The fact that this and the succeeding proclamation quickly fell victim to the extremism of the moment does not mean that those who sought to declare the policy lost touch with reality, only that they misjudged the extent to which the pressures of the war had nullified the traditional restraints of customary practices. Wilson, *Athens and Corcyra*, 88, simply remarks that "in making these moves, the *oligoi* seem to have grossly overplayed their hand." He sees only pro-Spartan alignment as the goal.

61. See the parallel limitation imposed by the West Greeks, discussed in 6.2 above and in 7.2–3 below.

by the Athenians. On the contrary, they must have expected to be able to persuade the expatriate Corcyraeans at Athens to support the island's shift to neutrality. Had factional opposition not been so closely associated with one or the other of the belligerent alliances, the declaration might possibly have succeeded. But as it was, compromise swiftly yielded to open hostility between the opposing groups, and all hope that neutrality would be maintained vanished in the wake of mounting extremism.

Failure of the proposed neutral policy must have come as a bitter surprise. Nonalignment had been a long-standing diplomatic posture for Corcyra (see 1. 35.1, 37.2–5). Only the dire necessity of war with the Corinthians forced its abandonment; and a return seems to have been considered a natural compromise when the restoration of a large number of pro-Peloponnesian citizens created a dangerous escalation of internal tensions (3. 70.1). Neutrality was the policy that both sides needed in order to restrain the increasing identification of private animosities with the hostilities of the belligerents. But if the proponents of neutrality expected that it would be accepted without serious opposition, they deceived themselves. Not only was the strength of the pro-Athenian faction far greater than that of the opposition, but the Athenians themselves also exploited the internal unrest to their own advantage and ultimately manipulated their supporters into committing Corcyra to even closer alignment with Athens than had existed prior to the abortive attempt to secure neutrality.[62]

VI. THE TREATMENT OF NEUTRALS AT THE OUTSET OF THE ARCHIDAMIAN WAR

In his narrative of 430, Thucydides recounts the capture of six Peloponnesian ambassadors and their summary execution by the Athenians as justifiable retaliation for the Spartans' slaughter of Athenian and allied traders caught aboard merchant vessels sailing around the Peloponnesus (2. 67.1–4). After describing the incident, he adds the following comment as a kind of footnote: "For at the beginning of the war the Lacedaemonians destroyed as enemies everyone whom they captured at sea, not only those fighting on

---

62. "Having the same friends and enemies" (i.e., an offensive and defensive alliance; Thuc. 3. 75.1; Bengtson, *SVA*[2] no. 172); cf. also 8.3. E below.

the side of the Athenians but also those on neither side."[63] Thucydides' accusation is leveled against Sparta alone and leaves no doubt that such action violated the conventional rules of warfare.[64] Just how long the indiscriminate slaughter at "the beginning of the war" continued is unclear, but it may be significant that there are later reports of Peloponnesian privateers allegedly threatening sea trade routes (2. 69.1: from Caria and Lycia to Phaselis and Phoenicia in the winter of 430/429; 3. 51.2: in the Saronic Gulf in 427). However, given the vagueness of Thucydides' statement and the lack of follow-up, neither the nationality (or nationalities) of the neutrals nor the nature of their activity when seized can be determined.

Among those captured and executed in 430 was an Argive citizen named Pollis. His execution with the others is justified with the same comment about retaliation for the Spartans' execution of Athenian and allied merchants, but Thucydides adds the important clarification that Pollis was acting "in a private capacity" (idia 2. 67.1). Since Argos was officially neutral (2. 9.2; 5. 28.2; see 6.1 above), the presence of Pollis was clearly unauthorized and did not represent an intentional violation of the Argives' neutral impartiality.[65] Nevertheless, when taken together with the report of Sparta's harsh treatment of neutrals, the implication remains that belligerents were at least inconsistent about respecting citizens of uncommitted states.

---

63. πάντας γὰρ δὴ κατ' ἀρχὰς τοῦ πολέμου οἱ Λακεδαιμόνιοι ὅσους λάβοιεν ἐν τῇ θαλάσσῃ ὡς πολεμίους διέφθειρον, καὶ τοὺς μετὰ Ἀθηναίων ξυμπολεμοῦντας καὶ τοὺς μηδὲ μεθ' ἑτέρων (Thuc. 2. 67.4).

64. Compare the outcry against Alcidas' similar treatment of captives in 427 (3. 32). Execution of ambassadors was abnormally harsh treatment, as Thucydides' special explanation indicates; but, in fact, ambassadors were not protected by international custom in the way heralds were; see Kienast, RE Suppl. 13 (1973), 544–46; Mosley, Envoys and Diplomacy, 81–89; Adcock and Mosley, Diplomacy in Ancient Greece, 154.

65. Thucydides is remarkably careful about making these kinds of accurate distinctions when the actions of individuals conflict with the formal diplomatic position of their state; compare, for instance, his clarification of the circumstances that allowed Brasidas to cross Thessaly (2. 78.2–3, quoted above in 6.3.B); of the status of the Cretans who joined in Athens' Sicilian expedition (7. 57.9); or of the Acarnanians' role in the same expedition (7. 57.10). Other examples of clarification of status appear often in Thucydides, such as when he remarks that Argives serving in Sicily did not participate specifically because of the Argive-Athenian alliances of 420 and 416 (5. 47.1–12, 82.5; Bengtson, SVA² nos. 193, 196), but for private reasons. The point here is that the treaty itself did not obligate them to assist Athens in an offensive war (7. 57.9).

VII. NEUTRALITY SPECIFIED IN THE PEACE OF NICIAS (421)

The exact terms of the fifty-year Spartan-Athenian Peace of Nicias are quoted by Thucydides (5. 18–19), who dates the negotiation and ratification of the treaty to the winter and early spring of 422/421 (5. 14–17, 19.1, 20.1). For the study of neutrality, the fifth provision, which follows, holds considerable importance.

> The Lacedaemonians and their allies are to restore Amphipolis to the Athenians; and in as many cities as the Lacedaemonians have handed over to the Athenians, the inhabitants who wish are to be allowed to depart together with their possessions. The cities are to be autonomous so long as they pay the tribute set in the time of Aristides; and it is prohibited, after the time when the treaty took effect,[66] for the Athenians and their allies to bear arms [against them] for the purpose of doing harm so long as they pay the tribute. These cities are Argilus, Stagirus, Acanthus, Stolus, Olynthus, and Spartolus. They are to be allies of neither side, neither Lacedaemonians nor Athenians; but if the Athenians persuade the cities, it is allowed for the Athenians to make such cities as are willing their allies.[67]

This passage has caused difficulty for both textual critics and historians due to its highly compressed language.[68] In particular, scholars have questioned the present syntax of the passage, which seems to make the same cities that either have been or are to be handed over to Athens subsequently designated as autonomous and neutral providing they pay the tribute assessed by Aristides. Various emendations aimed at separating the clauses and thereby establish-

66. My translation here reflects the aorist tense (ἐγένοντο), which I take to cover the possibility that an attack could occur before news of the treaty reached the region. If so, its effect was to be nullified; Gomme, HCT, vol. 3, 672.

67. Ἀποδόντων δὲ Ἀθηναίοις Λακεδαιμόνιοι καὶ οἱ ξύμμαχοι Ἀμφίπολιν. ὅσας δὲ πόλεις παρέδοσαν Λακεδαιμόνιοι Ἀθηναίοις ἐξέστω ἀπιέναι ὅποι ἂν βούλωνται αὐτοὺς καὶ τὰ ἑαυτῶν ἔχοντας. τὰς δὲ πόλεις φερούσας τὸν φόρον τὸν ἐπ' Ἀριστείδου αὐτονόμους εἶναι. ὅπλα δὲ μὴ ἐξέστω ἐπιφέρειν Ἀθηναίους μηδὲ τοὺς ξυμμάχους ἐπὶ κακῷ, ἀποδιδόντων τὸν φόρον, ἐπειδὴ αἱ σπονδαὶ ἐγένοντο. εἰσὶ δὲ Ἄργιλος, Στάγιρος, Ἄκανθος, Στῶλος, Ὄλυνθος, Σπάρτωλος. ξυμμάχους δ' εἶναι μηδετέρων, μήτε Λακεδαιμονίων μήτε Ἀθηναίων· ἢν δὲ Ἀθηναῖοι πείθωσι τὰς πόλεις, βουλομένας ταύτας ἐξέστω ξυμμάχους ποιεῖσθαι αὐτοῖς Ἀθηναίους.   (Thuc. 5. 18.5)

Gomme's first note ad. loc. (HCT, vol. 3, 668) summarizes the context of the fifth provision as follows: "This begins the third part of the treaty—part 1, access to common shrines (Sec. 2); 2, duration and general terms (Sec. 3–4); 3, particular claims and concessions (Sec. 5–8); 4, arrangements for the oath, publication, future amendments, and date of coming into force (Sec. 9–19.1)."

68. See especially Gomme's discussion in HCT, vol. 3, 668—71.

ing clearly differentiated classes of cities have been proposed and are discussed by Gomme.[69] Gomme personally preferred Steup's emendation, which divides the cities into three groups: (1) Amphipolis, (2) cities that had already been surrendered by the Peloponnesians, and (3) six cities that were to be tributary to Athens but with certain privileges and guarantees.

Gomme's reconstruction may be sensible from a modern legalistic standpoint, but it remains doubtful that such strict distinctions were originally intended. As Gomme admits, the whole treaty, at least in Thucydides' version, falls well short of the standards of completeness applied in modern international agreements.[70] His suggestion, however, that there are "signs of haste," especially in sections 5 and 11, is vitiated by his otherwise determined effort to blame all obscurity on textual corruptions. Certainly a more sensible approach is to accept the document as it exists and admit that, whether intentionally or not, the authors of the treaty left this section surprisingly vague by modern standards, though, as Gomme and others have shown, it is by no means incomprehensible.

Very little is known about the six states designated as neutrals, aside from the fact that they were located in Thrace and were all in revolt from the Athenians, to whom they had previously been tributary.[71] Their proposed neutrality in the Peace of Nicias has generally been interpreted as an ad hoc compromise intended to be a protection against Athenian reprisal following Spartan withdrawal from Thrace. Following this interpretation, the agreement was Sparta's price for the return of Amphipolis, though the true weakness of the Spartan position is revealed by the concession that the designated states would be required to pay tribute to Athens.[72]

But were these terms merely an ad hoc response unique to the circumstances confronting the belligerents in 421? In fact, the Peace of Nicias was almost certainly not the first treaty to combine some form of independence and autonomy with the payment of tribute. We have already seen the combination suggested in the treaty between the Milesians and Cyrus, which dates to the mid-sixth century (see 6.1 above); and something along the same lines must

69. Gomme, HCT, vol. 3, 670–72.
70. Ibid., 668.
71. Ibid., 664.
72. See, among others, Beloch, Griechische Geschichte, vol. 1, part 1, 341–43; Gomme, HCT, vol. 3, 670; Kagan, Archidamian War, 342–43.

have been accepted in connection with the status of Aegina in the Thirty Years' Peace of 447/446. In 432 the Aeginetans charged that the Athenians had not left them autonomous, as specified in the peace (Thuc. 1. 67.2; cf. 139.1, 140.3). They did not, however, make a similar claim about their payment of tribute (Thuc. 1. 108.4; Diod. 11. 78.4). If the Aeginetans' annual payment of 30 talents violated the terms of the treaty, it would hardly have escaped comment.[73] However, the simultaneous concession of "autonomy" granted to Aegina as special status and exemption apparently not shared by other states in the Athenian empire, together with the payment of tribute imposed on all members, suggests that there was a precedent for the arrangements provided in the Peace of Nicias.

What may have been innovative and unprecedented about the Peace of Nicias was the combination of autonomy and liability to tribute with insistence on neutrality. It is no surprise that the belligerents selected neutrality as the best compromise under the circumstances. For the Spartans, proposing that these renegade states be recognized as neutrals was a way to guarantee their freedom without providing continued military support and without giving the appearance of having abandoned them if they refused to accept the proposals and were thereafter compelled to return to the status of subject allies. For the Athenians, accepting the neutrality of these states, despite the fact that they had revolted, was tolerable, because there seemed to be no other way to regain the far more important city of Amphipolis. The stipulation that the cities could be fully regained by peaceful means but for the present would be required to pay tribute also reflects the experience of Corcyra, where pro-Athenian partisans eventually brought the state into full alliance with Athens.

The motives of the belligerents seem clear enough, but their acceptance of the compromise was not shared by the six states involved. Thucydides relates that the Spartans could not convince the Chalcidians to ratify the peace during the summer of 421 (5.35.2), and Olynthus is reported to have attacked and recaptured its port, Mecyberna, from the Athenians in the winter of 421/420

73. On the amount, see Meiggs, *Athenian Empire*, 183; on the island's position in the treaty generally, see D. M. Leahy, "Aegina and the Peloponnesian League," *CP* 49 (1954): 232–43; de Ste. Croix, *Origins of the Peloponnesian War*, 293–94; Ostwald, *Autonomia*, 26–30, 39–41.

(5.39.1). In addition, in several other references to the continued hostility of the Chalcidians, Thucydides makes it clear that the terms of 5. 18.5 were never implemented (5. 21.2, 26.2; 6. 7.2, 10.5).[74]

Once again, neutrality had been used by the major powers as a convenient vehicle for preserving the appearance of justice and restraint. Not surprisingly, the small powers that were the recipients of these "reasonable" proposals were suspicious and unwilling to entrust themselves to a policy that depended entirely upon the voluntary self-restraint of the parties involved. And indeed, when the situation was reversed, as happened when Corcyra declared itself neutral, the Athenians took immediate action to subvert the declaration.

SUMMARY

The incidents involving neutrality during the Archidamian War provide a great deal of evidence about classical diplomatic practices during a general conflict. We see distinctions made between private and official actions taken by citizens of neutral states when they overstepped the limits of accepted neutral behavior (e.g., the execution of Pollis of Argos). We see something of both belligerent and nonbelligerent expectations about the rights and obligations of states that adopt a neutral position (as in the cases of Plataea, the West Greek states, and Corcyra). We see neutrality succeed (in, for example Argos) and fail (in Corcyra). Fortunately we are able to gather far more information than we might otherwise because Thucydides provides detailed analyses of several incidents involving neutrality. Neutrality is used, abused, declared, rejected, subverted, and in the end required as an obligation for the future, which amounted to a tacit acknowledgment that further conflict was likely, if not inevitable.

During this first, ten-year phase of the war, Athens showed itself rhetorically supportive of, but in actual fact consistently hostile to, neutrality. There was no hesitation about executing Pollis, a citizen of a neutral state, along with the rest of the ambassadors captured in 430. Plataea was forced to reject the offer of neutrality. The

---

74. Instead, a renewable ten-day truce was eventually established (prior to the winter of 416/415 [6. 7.2]).

commerce of the West Greek states was hindered, the neutral ambitions of Corcyra thwarted, the neutrality of Thera suppressed, the position of Melos challenged with armed intervention. Nowhere do we see respect and restraint until 421. But then, like a deus ex machina in a Euripidean tragedy, both the Athenians and the Spartans suddenly insist that certain Chalcidian states would henceforth be neutral!

To the weak and vulnerable states, such as the Thracian cities, neutrality must have looked increasingly dangerous and futile. We need only review the Plataeans' response to Archidamus (Thuc. 2. 72.2) or the Athenians' reaction to Corcyra's declaration (3.72.1) to understand how deeply hostile the hegemonial states had become to the existence of neutral states and to recognize how experience of that hostility reduced the number of states able—and willing—to remain neutral.

CHAPTER SEVEN

From the Peace of Nicias to the End of the Peloponnesian War (421–404)

The Peace of Nicias was a failure. It was never fully accepted or implemented and brought not real peace but only a brief pause in the armed hostilities, which soon broke out again, beginning with scattered incidents of fighting and culminating in a renewal of full-scale warfare that drew an ever-increasing number of previously uncommitted states into the conflict.

I. THE ISSUE OF MELIAN NEUTRALITY (416)

The fate of Melos provides a bleak example of the belligerents' hostile refusal to recognize neutral status when it conflicted with their military or security goals. Melos was not a party to the Peace of Nicias. The island's unresolved dispute with Athens (see 6.1 above) was a separate conflict from the war between the major alliances, to which Melos had remained uncommitted prior to the outbreak of the Peloponnesian War and thereafter. Following their attack in 426, the Athenians made no further move against the island, although, according to Thucydides, a state of war existed from that time (5. 84.2). In 416, however, the Athenians returned with a large force drawn from their alliance (84.1) and starved the Melians into unconditional surrender (116). Such were the bald facts. Yet the Athenian subjugation of Melos obviously represented much more to Thucydides.

A critical issue in the confrontation between Athens and Melos was the island's disputed status. To emphasize this Thucydides goes to the extraordinary length of recreating the diplomatic negotiations that preceded the final Athenian siege. Just how accurately the resulting Melian Dialogue represents the original words of the speakers cannot be determined. Yet there is no reason to doubt that neutrality figured prominently in these diplomatic preliminaries, since neutrality was the Melians' long-standing policy and the position of their final offer, as the following excerpts show.

(431) αὕτη μὲν Λακεδαιμονίων ξυμμαχία· Ἀθηναίων δὲ ... νῆσοι ὅσαι ἐντὸς Πελοποννήσου καὶ Κρήτης πρὸς ἥλιον ἀνίσχοντα, πᾶσαι αἱ Κυκλάδες πλὴν Μήλου καὶ Θήρας. (Thuc. 2. 9.4.)

This was the Lacedaemonian alliance; and [the allies] of the Athenians were ... all of the Cycladic islands between the Peloponnesus and Crete lying East except Melos and Thera.

(426) τοὺς γὰρ Μηλίους ὄντας νησιώτας καὶ οὐκ ἐθέλοντας ὑπακούειν οὐδὲ ἐς τὸ αὐτῶν ξυμμαχικὸν ἰέναι ἐβούλοντο προσαγαγέσθαι. (3. 91.2)

[The Athenians] wanted to bring over the Melians, for they were islanders but were unwilling to be subject and enter the [Athenians'] alliance.

(416) Ὥστε [δὲ] ἡσυχίαν ἄγοντας ἡμᾶς φίλους μὲν εἶναι ἀντὶ πολεμίων, ξυμμάχους δὲ μηδετέρων, οὐκ ἂν δέξαισθε; (5. 94)

[Melians:] So then you would not accept that we, remaining neutral, be friends instead of enemies, and allies of neither side?

Ἐν δ᾿ ἐκείνῳ οὐ νομίζετε ἀσφάλειαν; δεῖ γὰρ αὖ καὶ ἐνταῦθα, ὥσπερ ὑμεῖς τῶν δικαίων λόγων ἡμᾶς ἐκβιβάσαντες τῷ ὑμετέρῳ ξυμφόρῳ ὑπακούειν πείθετε, καὶ ἡμᾶς τὸ ἡμῖν χρήσιμον διδάσκοντας, εἰ τυγχάνει καὶ ὑμῖν τὸ αὐτὸ ξυμβαῖνον, πειρᾶσθαι πείθειν. ὅσοι γὰρ νῦν μηδετέροις ξυμμαχοῦσι, πῶς οὐ πολεμώσεσθε αὐτούς, ὅταν ἐς τάδε βλέψαντες ἡγήσωνταί ποτε ὑμᾶς καὶ ἐπὶ σφᾶς ἥξειν; (5. 98)

[Melians:] But do you not think there is safety in that other policy of ours [i.e., remaining aloof]? For here again it is necessary, seeing that you have forced us to abandon pleas of justice and seek to persuade us to obey your interests, that we too educate you as to what is best for us and try to persuade you to accept it, if it happens also to be to your advantage. For how will you not make enemies of as many states as are now allies of neither side, when they have seen our case and conclude that someday you will also come against them?

προκαλούμεθα δὲ ὑμᾶς φίλοι μὲν εἶναι, πολέμιοι δὲ μηδετέροις. (5. 112.3)

[Melians:] We propose to you that we be your friends, but enemies of neither side.[1]

In the dialogue of 416, the Melians base their resistance to Athens on three principles: conventional justice (to dikaion), expedience (to sympheron), and reasonableness (to eikos). The justice of their position is stressed repeatedly (5.86, 90, 98, 104) and provides the basis of their expressed hope (100–113) for both divine and human assistance if Athens persists in attacking. In their responses, the Athenians offer no direct denial of these arguments and even admit that no one would believe that they had been injured by Melos (89). What they argue instead is that the cause of the Melians' refusal to join Athens in the war has no relevance under the circumstances, because the Melians do not have the power to sustain their policy against Athens' refusal to accept it, regardless of its merit. In their response the Athenians tell the Melians, "We presume that you aim at accomplishing what is possible in accordance with the real thoughts of both of us, since you know as well as we know that what is just is arrived at in human arguments only when the necessity of both sides is equal, and that the powerful exact what they can, while the weak yield what they must."[2] In short, not conventional justice and fair phrases but power and self-interest are, in the Athenians' view, the real forces that dictate the actual behavior of states (89, 97, 105).

Given the Athenians' rejection of the constraints of what they hold to be conventional justice, the Melians argue that Athenian acceptance of their neutrality would in fact be both expedient and in full accord with Athens' own narrow self-interest. Two reasons are given: (1) if the Athenians refuse to act with restraint, they cannot expect to be treated with moderation should they ever be defeated (90) and (2) by acting unjustly, they constantly increase the ranks of their enemies (98). The Athenians counter that they do not fear being defeated by the Spartans but by their own subjects (91.1) and insist that, in any case, the Melians must allow them to take the risk (91.2), for independent states on the mainland would not be aroused by the subjugation of Melos, while islanders who

---

1. For pre-416 discussion, see 5.3.A–B and 6.1 above.
2. Trans. Smith; ἐπισταμένους πρὸς εἰδότας ὅτι δίκαια μὲν ἐν τῷ ἀνθρωπείῳ λόγῳ ἀπὸ τῆς ἴσης ἀνάγκης κρίνεται, δυνατὰ δὲ οἱ προύχοντες πράσσουσι καὶ οἱ ἀσθενεῖς ξυγχωροῦσιν (Thuc. 5. 89).

saw Melos succeed in defying the Athenians' demand for submission might act recklessly and thus endanger Athens (99).

The Melians respond that the Athenians' fear is groundless, because it would be unreasonable for Athens' subjects not to distinguish between the status allowed an independent state and their own subject position (96). But the Athenians brush this argument aside with the statement that their subjects believe that states that preserve their freedom do so only because of their power (97).

With chapter 100, the focus of the dialogue shifts to the reasons why the Melians may (or may not) hope to resist the Athenians successfully. While the issue of neutrality is temporarily superseded, it returns in the end when the Melians make this final offer: "We propose to you that we be your friends, but enemies of neither side, and that you withdraw from our territory, having made a truce on whatever terms seem best to both parties."[3]

The contents of the Melian Dialogue have been so often discussed and analyzed that it is amazing how rarely the issue of neutrality has received any comment at all.[4] Yet a considerable measure of the dialogue's force arises from the confrontation between the Melians' insistence on the validity of their neutral status within the framework of recognized diplomatic customs and the Athenians' equally forceful insistence that such rules without the power of enforcement are nothing more than meaningless illusions seductively creating false hopes among the weak but incapable of engendering restraint on the part of the strong.

It is important to remember that Melos was not a subject state in revolt but a nonaligned neutral whose position, as far as we know, had not been challenged by the Athenians prior to the Peloponnesian War (see 5. 3.B above). Unfortunately for Melos, the outbreak of war in 431 brought a change in the Athenian attitude; and it is the evolution in the Athenian position that Thucydides illuminates by focusing on the suppression of this

---

3. προκαλούμεθα δὲ ὑμᾶς φίλοι μὲν εἶναι, πολέμιοι δὲ μηδετέροις, καὶ ἐκ τῆς γῆς ἡμῶν ἀναχωρῆσαι σπονδὰς ποιησαμένους αἵτινες δοκοῦσιν ἐπιτήδειοι εἶναι ἀμφοτέροις (Thuc. 5. 112.3).

4. For example, it received no comment in the recent discussions of P. Pouncey, *The Necessities of War: A Study of Thucydides' Pessimism* (New York, 1980), 83–104, and Connor, *Thucydides*, 147–57; others, like Andrewes, *HCT*, vol. 3, 157, sidestep the issue. Andrewes remarks "On balance it seems unlikely that the attack of 416 was due solely to an Athenian whim, without any antecedent quarrel."

stubborn, but harmless, neutral state. The echoes of the earlier extensive treatment of the issue of Plataean neutrality are obvious and no doubt intentional, as is the easily recognizable foreshadowing of the important role of neutrality during the subsequent expedition to Sicily.[5]

But for Thucydides it was surely neither the Melians themselves nor their hoped-for status that were of critical interest but rather the implications and meaning of Athens' subjugation of Melos; for in the rhetoric that the Athenians use to justify their actions there emerges a new language of diplomacy and a new conception of interstate relations. The dialogue provides a nearly natural context in which this can largely be accomplished by comparison of the speakers' words. Thucydides thus sets in juxtaposition traditional, customary rules of interstate behavior, which balanced rights and obligations to the benefit of weak and powerful alike, and the newly evolved ethos of hegemonial, imperial Greek states that refused to accept any restraints on the pursuit of self-interest. It is only with the perfect vision of hindsight that we see in Athens' disastrous defeat in Sicily and final loss of the war how the dramatized confrontation over Melian neutrality reveals a tragic and fatal flaw in the Athenian position. In the end, it becomes clear that with the determined suppression of Melos the once intelligent and confident imperial state has begun to lose control of itself and can no longer differentiate between necessary precautions for security and destructive misuses of power.

II. THE CITY-STATES OF SOUTHERN ITALY (415–413)

Athens' great military campaign in Sicily once again brings the posture and activities of uncommitted states to the attention of our sources. Despite traditional ties of ethnic kinship and existing economic, political, and diplomatic connections that encouraged active participation, the West Greeks proved to be surprisingly cautious about taking sides.[6] When Athens sent an unprecedented

5. See 6.4 above and 7.2–3 below. Connor, *Thucydides*, 147–57, provides an insightful analysis of these echoes and foreshadowing but fails to comment on the underlying importance of the issue of neutrality to all these passages.

6. On the racial alignment, see Thuc. 3. 86.2–4; 4. 61.4; 6. 6.2, 44.3, 76.2, 80.3; 7. 57–58; on economic ties, 3. 86.4; 6. 88.9; on political commitments before the war, 3. 86.3 (the Leontine-Athenian treaty of 433/432 [*IG* I², 50 = Meiggs and Lewis, no. 64; Bengtson, *SVA*² no. 163]); see also the Rhegian-Athenian treaty of

armada to Magna Graecia in 415, the majority of the Greek city-states of Italy, regardless of past alignment, kinship, or any other pressure, remained strictly neutral. According to Thucydides' catalogue of allies (7.57–58), only Thurii and Metapontum formally aligned themselves, both with Athens and both because of internal dissension that made it impossible for them to do otherwise (57.11).[7]

Much information about the policy of the Italian states can be gleaned from the narratives of Thucydides and Diodorus. For example, when the Athenian fleet reached Italy and proceeded along the coast, some states, while refusing the fleet admittance to their cities and providing no market, nevertheless furnished water and anchorage, although Tarentum and Locri refused to supply even these (Thuc. 6. 44.2). At Rhegium, Athens' former ally (see note 6 above), the Athenians were also denied entrance to the city, though a market was provided (44.3). A conference was also held to discuss the question of alliance. Thucydides reports that "[the Athenians] addressed speeches to the Rhegians, claiming that since they were Chalcidians, they should help the Leontines who were also Chalcidians. But [the Rhegians] replied that they would not support either side but would do whatever the rest of the Italians decided in common."[8] Despite minor differences in what each of the Italian states provided to the Athenian fleet, the position adopted by the majority was a carefully noncommittal balance that was neither hostile to nor supportive of the expedition.

Several general principles that underlie the position of the Italians

---

433/432 (IG I², 51 = Meiggs and Lewis, no. 63; Bengtson, SVA² no. 162) and the Egestaean-Athenian treaty of disputed date (ranging from 458/457 to 418/417; IG I², 19–20.1.2 = Meiggs and Lewis, no. 37; Bengtson, SVA² no. 139). On Athenian policy toward the West prior to the Peloponnesian War (an interest reflected in Thuc. 1. 36.2), see T. E. Wick, "Athens' Alliance with Rhegion and Leontinoi," Historia 25 (1976): 288–304.

7. On the meaning of 7. 57.11, see Dover, HCT, vol. 4, 439, who translates: "Thurioi and Metapontion took part on the Athenian side, as was inevitably imposed upon them by the state which their internal conflicts had at that time reached." Thucydides adds this footnote to explain their exceptional action. Also supporting Athens in Italy but omitted from the catalogue was Artas, an Iapygian chieftain (7. 33.4). Etruscans (6. 88.6, 103.2; 7. 53.2) are also mentioned (7. 57.11). Diodorus (13. 3.4–5) gives essentially the same account but adds that Thurii accorded the fleet every courtesy—a detail omitted by Thucydides. Thurii was not allied with Athens at the time; see Thuc. 7. 33.5–6.

8. καὶ πρός [τε] τοὺς Ῥηγίνους λόγους ἐποιήσαντο, ἀξιοῦντες Χαλκιδέας ὄντας Χαλκιδεῦσιν οὖσι Λεοντίνοις βοηθεῖν· οἱ δὲ οὐδὲ μεθ᾿ ἑτέρων ἔφασαν ἔσεσθαι, ἀλλ᾿ ὅτι ἂν καὶ τοῖς ἄλλοις Ἰταλιώταις ξυνδοκῇ, τοῦτο ποιήσειν (Thuc. 6. 44.3).

emerge from Thucydides' account. In the first place, commerce with the belligerents, whether the sale of supplies on the spot (6. 44) or shipment to the war zone in Sicily (6. 103.23; 7. 14.3, 25.1), evidently was not considered inconsistent with neutral status. However, supplies destined for either belligerent were liable to seizure or destruction. One reported incident occurred during 413 when the Syracusans destroyed a number of ships laden with supplies en route from Italy to the Athenian army in Sicily and burned a shipment of timber stockpiled for the Athenians in Caulonia (7. 25.2).[9]

Another principle involved the neutral states' right to demand respect for territorial integrity. It was clearly no violation of neutrality for wary nonbelligerents to prohibit the armed forces of the warring parties from entering their cities[10] or to deny water and anchorage to a belligerent fleet[11] or to refuse passage of armed forces through their territory. The last was upheld in 413 when Croton prevented an Athenian army under Demosthenes and Eurymedon from traversing its territory, and thus forced an unexpected detour.[12]

Finally, there is a controversial piece of evidence involving the Rhegians that might, depending on its interpretation, have bearing on the question of whether an otherwise neutral state could make contributions to a belligerent without forfeiting its claim of neutrality. At issue are three badly mutilated fragments of an Athenian

9. On neutral commerce, see also Thuc. 5. 28.2; Ar. *Peace* 475–77 (Argos; see 6.1 above); Thuc. 2. 67.4 (unidentified neutrals; see 6.4 above); and for later evidence, see Diod. 19. 103.4–5 (312); Plut. *Demetr.* 33.3 (297). The Corinthian decision reported by Thucydides (7. 34.1) to stand guard opposite Naupactus to protect merchants bound for Sicily seems to be a recent necessity resulting from the Peloponnesians' emergency decision to use merchant ships as troop transports (7. 7.3, 18.4, 19.1).

10. See Thuc. 6. 44.2–4; cf. 34.1; for other fifth-century examples, see 6. 50.1 (Messene; discussed below); 6. 62.2 (Himera and Camarina; also discussed below). Admission of belligerents was also reportedly raised as an issue by the Plataeans; see 2. 72.2 (in 6.4 above).

11. See Thuc. 6. 44.2. This is connected with the limitation of belligerent presence to a single ship (Thuc. 2. 7.2; 3. 71.1; 6. 52.1 and 50.1). The combined evidence indicates that in practice neutrals could permit or prohibit belligerents' fleets from using their coastline and harbors. The Spartans exploited this principle in 429 when their fleet used neutral Achaean territory as a base for attacking the Athenian fleet stationed at Naupactus (Thuc. 2. 86–92; see 6.1 above).

12. See Thuc. 7. 35.2. See also Thuc. 7. 32.1 (Acragas; discussed below); 4. 78.2–3, 108.1; 5. 13.1 (the Thessalian Confederacy; see 6.3 above); cf. Hdt. 9. 12 (Argos; see 5.2 above). For possible inscriptional evidence, see *IG* I², 57 (= Meiggs and Lewis, no. 65); cf. the parody of the convention in Ar. *Birds* 188–89.

inscription recording contributions by at least four West Greek states, including Rhegium.[13] No one has doubted that the document belongs to the Peloponnesian War,[14] but the extant portions of the inscription show payments in excess of 290 talents from Naxos, Catania, the Sicels, and Rhegium—sums that must represent contributions made by these states to the Athenian field commanders during either the expedition of 427–424 or 415–413.

The argument for connecting the document with the later expedition assumes that although the Rhegians provided no active military support, they nevertheless contributed more than 50 talents to the Athenian campaign. If this assumption is correct, it must mean that Thucydides either was unaware of the Rhegians' contribution or did not regard it as a noteworthy compromise of their declared neutrality. But both alternatives seem to be excluded by Thucydides' own account. It is virtually impossible to believe that Thucydides could have known about such a substantial contribution and could still have written about the despair of the Athenian generals when Egesta produced only 30 talents and Rhegium refused to support them at all. Thucydides' emphasis of the inadequacy of Egesta's 30-talent contribution is actually only one example of the considerable concern he took to report the Athenians' financial situation (see 6. 62.4, 71.2, 88.4, 93.4, 94.4; 7. 14.2, 15.1, 16.2, 31.3). Hence it seems highly unlikely that he would not have learned about a minimum of some 300 talents of contributions from a number of other states that had been officially recorded at Athens.[15]

On the other hand, the evidence for identifying the payments with the Athenian expedition of 427–424 is entirely consistent with Thucydides' account. Rhegium was an ally in that conflict and served as the headquarters for the Athenian fleet (3. 86.2–5), Naxos (4. 25.7–9) and a number of the Sicels (3. 103.1–2, 115.1; 4. 25.9) fought on the Athenian side, and Catana was apparently friendly (5. 4.6). Furthermore, allied appeals for greater Athenian interven-

13. *SEG XVII*, 7; the reference to Rhegium (lines 11–12) is Ρεγῖ[νοι ---] 𐊀ΧΧΠ [---].
14. See B. D. Meritt, "Greek Inscriptions," *Hesperia* 26 (1957): 198–200, no. 49.
15. Cf. 6. 94.4, for example. Note that the Athenian generals were compelled to send to Athens for money at the beginning of the winter of 415/414 (6. 71.2, 74.2; cf. 93.4, 94.4 [300 talents sent from Athens]) and again in the winter of 414/413 (6. 14.2; cf. 16.2 [120 talents sent]). A single Sicel contribution is recorded for the winter of 415/414 (6. 88.4), though a wider collection was intended (6. 71.2).

tion during the winter of 427/426 (3. 115.3–4) undoubtedly carried with them the promise of substantial contributions for the upkeep of the enlarged fleet. To disregard this positive evidence in preference for a context that contradicts Thucydides' account of the situation in 415 simply makes no sense and is an approach that should be rejected once and for all.

The possibility that a state that refrained from committing itself and professed to be impartial could nevertheless make contributions to a belligerent without violating its impartiality cannot, however, be dismissed out of hand. In the Peace of Nicias, several Thracian cities were designated as neutrals but were required to pay tribute to Athens.[16] This seems to suggest that, at least in theory, contribution of money might be reconciled with a diplomatic position otherwise recognized as neutral. However, since the only other possible example, that of Melos' contributions to the Spartans during the period of its neutrality, cannot be substantiated and from the evidence is highly unlikely,[17] it seems best to conclude that unless support was mandated by an international agreement, voluntary contributions to either belligerent or blatantly preferential treatment of any kind would have been perceived as an offense violating the obligations of neutral status.

The confidence of the majority of Italian Greek city-states in the legitimacy of their neutrality is impressive. Even though Thucydides consistently portrays Athens' imperialistic aims as restricted to Sicily, rumors that the Athenians secretly had wider imperialistic ambitions must have created serious concern about the wisdom of abstention.[18] Thucydides may assert that it was only after Alcibiades reached Sparta that there was any talk of Athens' intention to subjugate Italy (6. 90.2, 91.3; cf. Plut. *Alc.* 17.3), but, interestingly, the Spartans are credited with fully accepting this view (6. 93.1), and Gylippus is said to have hastened to Tarentum, thinking that there was no longer any hope for Sicily but wishing to save Italy (6. 104.1; cf. Plut. *Nic.* 18.5). However, the Italians evidently shared none of Sparta's alarm, for with the exception of

---

16. Thuc. 5. 18.5; see 6.7 above.
17. See 6.1 above (Meiggs and Lewis, no. 67).
18. Thucydides limits the Athenians' original aim to conquest of Sicily in both 427 (3. 86.4; 4. 65.3–4) and 415 (6. 1.1, 6.1, 8.4, 15.2, 23.1); but see the claims of Alcibiades (6. 15.2, 90.2) and accusations of Hermocrates (6. 34.1–2); cf. Plut. *Nic.* 12.1–2.

Thurii and Metapontum (which joined Athens!) they never became involved. Unlike the Sicilians, who had good reason to mistrust Athenian motives (see 6. 88.1, for example), the Italians appear to have seen no lurking treachery in the Athenians' apparent willingness to accept their neutrality, and concluded with confidence that their position would be unaffected by the outcome in Sicily.

III. NEUTRAL STATES IN SICILY (415–413)

The diplomatic situation in Sicily became exceedingly complicated as a result of the Athenian intervention of 415. The true motive behind Athens' decision to join with Egesta and Leontini in a war with Selinus and its allies, foremost of which was Syracuse, was widely believed to be the subjugation of the entire island (see, for instance, Thuc. 6. 33.2). But there were also some important holdouts who believed, like the Greek states of Southern Italy, that the customary diplomatic rules would remain unaffected and that abstention from any involvement, at least at the beginning, would be the wisest policy. Fortunately, some valuable details about their neutrality are preserved in the sources.

A. ACRAGAS

Thucydides makes it perfectly clear that Acragas remained neutral throughout the Athenian invasion[19] and reports two incidents that help to define the expected rights and obligations of Acragas' neutrality. The first occurred in the early summer of 413, when Nicias learned that a large body of reinforcements from northwestern Sicily was heading for Syracuse, and sent word to the Centoripes, Alcyaeans, and other Sicel allies of Athens in the interior of Sicily to prevent the force from passing through their territory (7. 32.1). Nicias was certain that they would take that route, "for the Agrigentines refused to give them passage along the road through their territory."[20] Nicias was right; and the Sicels ambushed the reinforcements, killing over one-third of them (7. 32.2). Nicias'

19. 7. 32.1, 33.2, 46, 50.1, 58.1; cf. Diodorus' wrong account (13. 4.2), condemned by Dover, HCT, vol. 4, 412. On Acragas at the time, see J. A. de Waele, *Die historische Topographie der griechischen Akragas auf Sizilien*, vol. 1, Archeol. Studien van het Nederlands Hist. Inst. te Rome 3 ('s Gravenhage, 1971), 123–24.
20. Ἀκραγαντῖνοι γὰρ οὐκ ἐδίδοσαν διὰ τῆς ἑαυτῶν ὁδόν (Thuc. 7. 32.1).

confident expectation, based on Agrigentine policy, demonstrates quite clearly the principle, already observed in regard to Croton, that belligerents had no right to enter the territory of neutral states without permission.

Secondly, when *stasis* broke out at Acragas later in 413, and there seemed to be a possibility of the pro-Syracusan faction getting the upper hand, Syracuse dispatched fifteen ships under the command of a certain Sicanus with orders to bring the city over if he could (7. 46). But while Sicanus was still at Gela, the pro-Syracusans were expelled; and since the opportunity for intervention was lost, he returned to Syracuse without accomplishing anything (7. 50.1). However, the implication of this report is that Syracuse limited its attempt to intervene at Acragas to a time when internal dissension offered a combination of opportunity and justification (i.e., support of the pro-Syracusan faction). If so, then absolute respect for Agrigentine neutrality was necessarily secondary to opportunity and self-interest.

B. MESSENE

Sicilian Messene lay in a strategic location on the narrow strait that separated northeastern Sicily from the territory of Rhegium at the extreme southwest corner of Italy (see 4. 1.4, 24.4; 6. 48). During the Leontine-Syracusan War (427–424), the Messenians had actively supported Syracuse (3. 90; 4.1, 24–25); but when the Athenians arrived in 415, they refused to commit themselves.

According to Thucydides, the Athenians initially sought to win the Messenians over through peaceful persuasion. "Alcibiades," he reports, "having sailed in his own ship to Messene and made proposals to them for an alliance, when he did not persuade them but received the answer that they would not allow [the Athenians] in the city but would furnish a market outside, sailed back to Rhegium."[21] The details of this incident are especially valuable, for they clearly express what a neutral state considered its obligation to be in a given circumstance. Moreover, when Thucydides later reports that Camarina reluctantly (and clandestinely) joined Syra-

---

21. μετὰ δὲ τοῦτο Ἀλκιβιάδης τῇ αὑτοῦ νηὶ διαπλεύσας ἐς Μεσσήνην καὶ λόγους ποιησάμενος περὶ ξυμμαχίας πρὸς αὐτούς, ὡς οὐκ ἔπειθεν, ἀλλ᾿ ἀπεκρίναντο πόλει μὲν ἂν οὐ δέξασθαι, ἀγορὰν δ᾿ ἔξω παρέξειν, ἀπέπλει ἐς τὸ Ῥήγιον (Thuc. 6. 50.1).

cuse during the winter of 415–414 (see below), he says nothing about Messene committing itself and is likewise silent about any change in policy after the failure of the pro-Athenian plot during the late summer or early fall of 415 (6. 74).

As we should expect, Messene is absent from Thucydides' catalogue of allies (7. 57–58). Admittedly, there is a chance that the omission might be unintentional, since Thucydides dismisses the northern regions of Sicily with the offhand remark that "the Himeraeans came from the region that faces the Tyrrhenian Sea, where they were the only Hellenic inhabitants; and they alone from that region supported [the Syracusans]."[22] Furthermore, unlike Acragas, which interrupted the series of pro-Syracusan cities along the southwest coast and was therefore of special interest, Messene had a policy that required no special explanation. Even the further omission of Messene from Thucydides' generalization that virtually all Sicily except Acragas sided with Syracuse by 413 (7. 33.2) cannot be used as evidence of anything, since Naxos and Catana, both allies of Athens, are also not excepted. Given that there is agreement in the positive testimony of Thucydides and Diodorus (13. 4.2), it seems virtually certain that Messene remained formally neutral, not just at the beginning of the conflict, but throughout.

C. CATANA

Catana was a Chalcidian state (6. 3.3) that had sided with Leontini and Athens in the previous war (427–424).[23] In 415, however, Thucydides says that the Catanaeans initially refused to receive the Athenian army, because of opposition from a pro-Syracusan faction (6. 50.3) elsewhere described as small (6. 51.2).[24] Subsequently, they allowed only the generals to enter and address their assembly (51.1). But while Alcibiades spoke, some soldiers broke through a postern

22. καὶ οἵδε μὲν τῆς Σικελίας τὸ πρὸς Λιβύην μέρος τετραμμένον νεμόμενοι, Ἱμεραῖοι δὲ ἀπὸ τοῦ πρὸς τὸν Τυρσηνικὸν πόντον μορίου, ἐν ᾧ καὶ μόνοι Ἕλληνες οἰκοῦσιν· οὗτοι δὲ καὶ ἐξ αὐτοῦ μόνοι ἐβοήθησαν (Thuc. 7. 58.2).

23. In the late fall of 415 the Athenians attempted to bring over Messene by treachery from within. This effort failed when Alcibiades warned the pro-Syracusan faction, which succeeded in eliminating the conspirators and preventing the admittance of any Athenians (Thuc. 6. 74). However, Thucydides' account indicates that the opposing factions within Messene were about equally balanced; this may help to explain why the state remained on the sidelines. On the text and translation of 6. 74, see Dover, HCT, vol. 4, 349 (ad loc.).

24. On its racial identity, see Thuc. 6. 3.3; on an earlier alliance, 3. 86.2; 5. 4.6.

gate and began walking around in the agora. The moment supporters of the Syracusan cause noticed the soldiers, they slipped away;
and the remaining citizens voted for alliance with Athens (51.2).
Whether the pro-Syracusan minority could have continued to prevent Catana from siding with Athens is doubtful, but the fact that
they were initially able to keep Catana from committing itself
indicates that the option of neutrality was seriously considered,
even if quickly abandoned.[25]

D. HIMERA

Like Catana, Himera was only temporarily neutral. However, Thucydides' account makes it clear that the Athenians did not immediately consider Himera hostile. When they sailed there in 415, they
were not received and departed without incident (6. 62.2). This did
not mean that the Himeraeans were already opposed to Athens,
because Gylippus and Pythen are said to have arrived in the
following year and to have persuaded the inhabitants to fight on
the Syracusan side (7. 1.2). On the contrary, the implication is that
Himera remained neutral at the outset of the conflict and only
abandoned that policy when the prospects of Syracusan victory
improved.

E. THE SICELS

The non-Greek Sicels of Sicily also took seriously the option of
remaining neutral. This was especially important because the Sicels
were numerous and militarily capable. Their potential to be decisive
in the conflict of 415–413 may be estimated from the eagerness
with which the belligerents solicited their support. But appeals
notwithstanding, a certain number of the Sicels, at least initially,
followed the example set by Acragas and other Greek city-states

25. Diodorus claims that in the summer of 415 Catana, Himera, Gela, and
Selinus promised to support Syracuse (13. 4.2). Obviously, this information is not
derived from Thucydides, but from another source (13. 4.4–5). Thucydides'
version of Catana's compulsory alliance with Athens is given. The same contradiction occurs in the account of Himera's diplomacy (compare Diod. 13. 4.2 and
7.6–7 with Thuc. 7. 1.4). Thucydides says plainly that Himera allied itself with
Syracuse only after Gylippus arrived. Unless we assume that the initial promise
of support alleged by Diodorus (13. 4.2) was made informally (and perhaps
secretly), Thucydides' version of events must be preferred.

and remained aloof from the war.[26] Diodorus is explicit about this in his brief list of Sicilian responses to the appeals of Syracuse during the summer of 415:

> The cities of the Sicels, while they were inclined by goodwill toward the Syracusans, nevertheless remained neutral, awaiting the outcome.[27]

Thucydides records only Hermocrates' general uncertainty about the Sicels prior to the arrival of the Athenians:

> And let us, sending envoys to the Sicels, confirm the allegiance of some and endeavor to make friendship and alliance with others.[28]

But subsequently, Thucydides clarifies that as the conflict progressed an increasingly larger number of the Sicels took sides, whether under the compulsion of Athenian aggression (e.g., 6. 88.3–5) or out of a self-interested desire to support the side whose prospects for victory seemed better (e.g., 6. 103.2 [Athens]; 7. 1.4 [Syracuse]). In this context, the Sicels are described as "previously spectators" (*hoi proteron perieōrōnto* 6. 103.2) or "now far more eager to take sides" (*hoi polu prothumoteron proschōrein hetoimoi* 7. 1.4). Elsewhere they are grouped with cities that Nicias anxiously (and more accurately) refers to as "however many are now neutral" (*hosai nun hēsychazousin* 7. 12.1) in his dispatch to Athens of the winter of 414/413.

The Athenians' willingness to attack Sicel cities that refused to join their side (6. 88.5) may have been influenced by a sense of racial distinction. The Sicels were *barbaroi* (6. 2.6, 11.7, 17.6, 20.4; 7. 57.11, 58.3), and that appears to have offered a ready excuse for unrestrained aggression. This distinction is especially noticeable, for in dealing with the Greek city-states, the Athenians carefully refrained from attacking states that remained neutral (intrigue

---

26. Together with the Sicani, the Sicels inhabited most of the interior of Sicily (6. 2.4–5); see Dover, *HCT*, vol. 4, 213–14. Thucydides distinguishes between pro-Syracusan (6. 34.1, 88.4–5; 7. 1.4–5, 58.3) and pro-Athenian (6. 62.5, 88.3–6, 103.2; 7. 32.1, 57.11) Sicels but only rarely identifies them further (e.g., 7. 1.4, 32.1). By 415 a number of Sicel cities had fallen under Syracusan control (6. 34.1, 45, 88.5; cf. 3. 103.1 and Diod. 12. 29), but apparently the majority of cities remained autonomous (6. 88.4), whether individually (7. 32.1) or under regional chieftains (6. 62.3; 7. 1.4).

27. αἱ δὲ τῶν Σικελῶν πόλεις τῇ μὲν εὐνοίᾳ πρὸς Συρακοσίους ἔρρεπον, ὅμως δ᾽ ἐν ἡσυχίᾳ μένουσαι τὸ συμβησόμενον ἐκαραδόκουν (Diod. 13. 4.2).

28. καὶ ἐς τοὺς Σικελοὺς πέμποντες τοὺς μὲν μᾶλλον βεβαιωσώμεθα, τοῖς δὲ φιλίαν καὶ ξυμμαχίαν πειρώμεθα ποιεῖσθαι (Thuc. 6. 34.1).

notwithstanding, as in 6. 74.1 [Messene]), as did the Syracusans
(intrigue notwithstanding, see, for example, 7. 46, 50.1 [Acragas]).
All of this seems to reflect more than merely random activity. The
consistency of the sources seems to indicate that the hegemonial
states believed that by limiting their aggression against neutrals to
non-Greeks, they would not adversely affect the attitude of uncommitted Greek states or jeopardize respect for customary rules of
war among Hellenes.

F. CAMARINA

The duplicitous policy of Camarina represents a clear case of self-
interested exploitation of neutrality. A comparatively weak and
traditionally hostile neighbor of Syracuse (Thuc. 6. 6.3, 78.2–4,
88.1), Camarina had broken ranks with the other Dorian states in
the previous war (427–424) and sided with Leontini (3. 86.2; 4. 25.7,
58, 65.1). An alliance with Athens was also concluded (427–425)
while Laches was the Athenian general (6. 75.3); and as recently as
422, an Athenian embassy under Phaeax was promised Camarinaean support for a renewed war against Syracuse (5. 4.6). But in
415, Camarina initially declared that it would remain neutral
(6. 52.1; Diod. 13. 4.2). Soon after, there was dissension in the city;
and when the Athenians heard that Camarina would come over to
their side if they went there, they sailed down the coast and sent
a herald to the city; "but [the Camarinaeans] would not admit
them, stating that their oaths were to receive the Athenians only
when they put in with a single ship, unless they themselves sent
for more."[29] Thus rebuffed, the Athenians withdrew to Catana.

As K. J. Dover has noted, the importance of this incident lies in
the details of the Camarinaeans' response. However, having considered but rejected that the oaths (horkia 6. 52.2) refer either to the
treaty sworn at Gela in 424 (4. 65.1–2) or to Sparta's injunctions
to its West Greek friends in 431 (2. 7.2), Dover concludes that the
oaths must refer to the Athenian alliance made with Laches
(427–424) and that, according to the terms of that alliance, Camarina "must have sworn ... that she would always receive a single
Athenian ship, while the Athenians for their part swore that they

29. οἱ δ' οὐκ ἐδέχοντο, λέγοντες σφίσι τὰ ὅρκια εἶναι μιᾷ νηὶ καταπλεόντων
Ἀθηναίων δέχεσθαι, ἢν μὴ αὐτοὶ πλείους μεταπέμπωσιν (Thuc. 6. 52.1).

would not attempt to bring in more than one ship except at Kamarina's own request."[30] The problem with this explanation is that there are not only no parallels for such terms among known alliances but the very idea of the explicit definition of safeguards against treachery in a treaty of alliance is difficult to accept.

There is a simpler and more convincing explanation of the Camarinaeans' *horkia*. If we accept that Diodorus has correctly reported neutrality as the initial policy of Camarina in 415,[31] Thucydides' seemingly enigmatic remarks actually make perfect sense. The dispatch of a herald in advance (6. 52.1) reflects Athenian concern for proper diplomatic form in order to learn the Camarinaeans' intentions and to avoid violation of their territorial integrity if permission to proceed is denied.[32] The Camarinaeans' refusal to receive the Athenians if they came with more than a single ship is perfectly normal neutral behavior. And the qualification "unless they themselves sent for more [than a single ship]" also agrees with the idea that the Camarinaeans are at the time uncommitted, though nevertheless willing (so they say) to consider bringing in the Athenians in the future. All these points are consistent with the neutral policy that Diodorus attributes to Camarina and, importantly, neither require nor deny the possible existence of alliances with either Athens or Syracuse or both states.

The evidence that has misled previous commentators is Thucydides' reference to existing alliances in the context of the winter of 415/414. On the one hand, the Syacusans are said to have learned that "the Athenians were sending ambassadors to Camarina in

---

30. Dover, *HCT*, vol. 4, 317.
31. Diodorus' use of *homologeō* may be significant. In a diplomatic context *homologeō* is often used for the making of a specific agreement with terms (*LSJ*[9], s.v. *homologeō* II: 3). Take, for example, Bengtson, *SVA*[2] no. 135 (=Thuc. 1. 103.3 [defeat of Naxos]); *SVA*[2] no. 152 (=Ael. Arist. *Panath.* 153 [Peace of Callias]); *SVA*[2] no. 165 (=Thuc. 2. 95.2 [Athenian alliance with Sitalces]); *SVA*[2] no. 180 (=Thuc. 4. 69.4 [surrender of the Peloponnesian garrison at Nisaea]); *SVA*[2] no. 211 (=Andoc. 3 [*On the Peace*]. 11 [defeat of Athens]); see also Thuc. 1. 101.3, 108.4; 4. 118.11. Evidence for the noun *homologia* is the same; see *SVA*[2] nos. 159, 160, 170, 178, 180, 182, and so on. More importantly, *homologeō* is explicitly associated with agreements involving the swearing of an oath; see *SVA*[2] no. 159 (=*IG* I[2], 50 [*IG* I[3], 48]), where it is a likely restoration (line 24) in the treaty between Athens and Samos and *SVA*[2] no. 206 (=Plut. *Alc.* 31.2), where Alcibiades is also called upon to swear to what the Athenian generals have agreed with Pharnabazus.
32. Cf. the Athenians' later respect for Croton's territory (7. 35.2), which differs only in the omission of the details of diplomatic protocol reported here, and all belligerents' respect for Agrigentine territory (7. 32.1).

accordance with the alliance concluded in the time of Laches
[427–424] to see if they might somehow win them over."[33] Even
though the phrasing of this statement reveals nothing about the
terms of the alliance and clearly suggests that the Camarinaeans
no longer consider themselves bound by it, it is on the basis of this
statement that Dover, for example, interpreted the *horkia* of 6. 52.1
as a reflection of the terms of the Laches alliance.[34]

To complicate matters, Thucydides also indicates that the token
support that the Camarinaeans provided to Syracuse during 415
(6. 67.2) was sent on the basis of an alliance (80.1; cf. 75.3). When
this alliance was concluded is nowhere stated, but if Diodorus
(13. 4.2) is right about Camarina's initial policy, it is most likely
to have been made between the Athenians' arrival in Italy, when
Camarina was still undecided, and the winter of 415/414, when
Camarina aided Syracuse. But even if the alliance was concluded
prior to the incident reported by Thucydides at 6. 52.1, he could
hardly have had in mind any alliance of Camarina with Syracuse
(which some believe the *horkia* imply), for an alliance between
Camarina and Syracuse could not have included a stipulation allowing for Camarina to call in the Athenians!

What, then, do the *horkia* refer to? And how can the incident
in 6. 52.1 be explained? Given the existence of both an older
Athenian alliance and a recent pact with Syracuse, it seems safe to
assume that the Camarinaeans, like other states (e.g., Acragas and
Catana), were experiencing serious internal conflict between pro-
Athenian and pro-Syracusan factions and that neutrality represented a compromise, in which the opposing factions swore oaths
to maintain neutrality unless after proper deliberation the majority
resolved to bring in one side or the other (though naturally only
the Athenians are mentioned at 6. 52.1). In the meantime, to forestall Syracusan hostility, and perhaps because the Athenians were
indisputably the aggressors, a minimal amount of assistance was
furnished to the Syracusan defense.[35]

---

33. καὶ πυνθανόμενοι τοὺς Ἀθηναίους ἐς τὴν Καμάριναν κατὰ τὴν ἐΗπὶ Λάχητος
γενομένην ξυμμαχίαν πρεσβεύεσθαι, εἴ πως προσαγάγοιντο αὐτούς (Thuc. 6. 75.3).

34. Dover, *HCT*, vol. 4, 316f.; see also note 31 above.

35. In the same section, Thucydides refers to the alliance as *proteron philian*,
and Hermocrates later calls it *tēn ekeinou philian* (78.1). Amit, "A Peace Treaty
between Sparta and Persia," 59–60, takes this to mean that *philia* and *symmachia*
"frequently" mean the same thing; but this overlooks the complexity of the
diplomatic situation. Camarina's old alliance with Athens may well have been a

But despite the Camarinaeans' token aid to Syracuse, neither the Syracusans nor the Athenians were certain what policy Camarina intended to pursue. This resulted in an extraordinary diplomatic confrontation between the belligerents, both of which sent embassies to Camarina during the winter of 415/414. In the opposing speeches, which Thucydides attributes to the Syracusan leader Hermocrates (6. 76–80) and the otherwise unknown Athenian Euphemus (82–87), the option of neutrality is specifically attacked by Hermocrates:

> Nor should that precaution—to assist neither side on the excuse of being allies of both—be considered by anyone to be either fair to us or safe for you; for it is not fair in fact as the plea of right represents it. For if by not taking sides, the one who is suffering shall be defeated and the conqueror prevail, what else have you done but failed to aid one party to be saved and not prevented the other from doing wrong?[36]

This is a timeless, fundamental statement of opposition to the concept of neutrality: if war is defined to be a violent confrontation between a right or just party and a wrong or unjust party, then neutrality can be interpreted as a kind of passive support of the party in the wrong (see chapter 4, pp. 77–79). One expects it to be followed by a specific threat of retaliation; and indeed, Hermocrates warns of possible punishment (80.4) before concluding that the only choices for Camarina are alignment with Athens or Syracuse. Thus is neutrality eliminated.

Euphemus, on the other hand, sidesteps the issue of neutrality entirely and focuses instead on Athens' desire to renew the former alliance (*tēs proteron symmachias* 82.1). He seeks to dispel apprehension that the Athenians aim at the subjugation of all Sicily,

---

comprehensive *philia kai symmachia*. In the first stages of their negotiation for Camarinaean assistance, the Athenians learned that this old alliance was no longer honored but that Camarina had declared itself neutral. This meant, in effect, that *philia* still existed (i.e., Camarina would not do harm to Athens) and could serve as the basis of an appeal for renewed alliance (78.1). The *philia* and the *symmachia* represent different relationships, the former merely providing grounds for seeking the latter. See further the discussion of *philia* in 3.4 above.

36. καὶ μὴ ἐκείνην τὴν προμηθίαν δοκεῖν τῳ ἡμῖν μὲν ἴσην εἶναι, ὑμῖν δὲ ἀσφαλῆ, τὸ μηδετέροις δὴ ὡς καὶ ἀμφοτέρων ὄντας ξυμμάχους βοηθεῖν. οὐ γὰρ ἔργῳ ἴσον ὥσπερ τῷ δικαιώματί ἐστιν. εἰ γὰρ δι' ὑμᾶς μὴ ξυμμαχήσαντας ὅ τε παθὼν σφαλήσεται καὶ ὁ κρατῶν περιέσται, τί ἄλλο ἢ τῇ αὐτῇ ἀπουσίᾳ τοῖς μὲν οὐκ ἠμύνατε σωθῆναι, τοὺς δὲ οὐκ ἐκωλύσατε κακοὺς γενέσθαι; (Thuc. 6. 88.2)

including Camarina, once Syracuse is defeated; but his argument is disturbingly ambiguous (especially 85.1), and despite his insistence that a more powerful and ambitious neighbor like Syracuse can only be considered an enemy, the attitude of Athens toward respect for weak states is suspiciously unclear.

Subsequently, after deliberating about their situation, the Camarinaeans reportedly answered that "since they are allies of both sides that were at war, it seemed to them to be true to their oath to support neither for the present."[37] According to Thucydides, this declaration concealed Camarina's decision to continue supporting Syracuse (88.1). Despite traditional hostility toward their powerful neighbor, the Camarinaeans were in the present crisis more fearful that if Syracuse won without their help, punitive action would follow. Yet because they also wished to preserve the Athenians' goodwill for as long as possible, they continued to declare themselves neutral. The declaration was, in fact, nothing more than a *dikaios logos*, that is, empty rhetoric that thinly disguised the self-interested exploitation of a legitimate policy.[38] Machiavellian to the core, it revealed (as Thucydides saw) that neutrality was truly no more or less respected than any other principle of international behavior battered by the relentless forces of the war.

IV. THE DIPLOMATIC POSITION OF CARTHAGE (415–413)

The Carthaginians were very much involved in the diplomacy of the Athenian invasion of Sicily. At the time of the invasion Carthage was extremely prosperous, militarily strong, and involved enough in affairs of the Greek world to recognize that the ascendant naval power of Athens was potentially threatening to its interests.[39] But

37. ἐπειδὴ τυγχάνει ἀμφοτέροις οὖσι ξυμμάχοις σφῶν πρὸς ἀλλήλους πόλεμος ὢν, εὔορκον δοκεῖν εἶναι σφίσιν ἐν τῷ παρόντι μηδετέροις ἀμύνειν (Thuc. 6. 88.2). Or *euorkon dokein einai sphisin* may be translated as "it seemed to them that they were acting in good faith." The allusion, in my opinion, is to the *horkia* in 6. 51.1, not to oaths that they had sworn with the belligerents when they had concluded alliances.

38. The Achaeans in 431 offered a legitimate precedent for abstaining due to restrictive treaties with both belligerents (based on conflicting *philia*; Thuc. 2. 9.2; discussed in 6.1 above), which is paralleled by the diplomatic position unsuccessfully proposed by the Melians in 416 (5. 112.3; see 7.1 above) and the combined *epimachia* and *philia* sought by the Corcyraeans as a pretext for withdrawing into neutrality (3. 70.2; see 6.5 above).

39. For this characterization, see the speech of Hermocrates (Thuc. 6. 34.2). Athenian interest in Carthage at the time of the earlier involvement in Sicily

the Carthaginians were also cautious. It was their refusal to assist Egesta in 416 that led to the Egestaean appeal to Athens (Diod. 12. 82.7). Hermocrates also proposed that Syracuse seek Carthaginian support, whether secret or open (Thuc. 6. 34.2), but nothing further is heard of this, and Thucydides reports that during the winter of 415/414, the Athenians "in the hope of obtaining assistance ... sent a trireme to Carthage with a proposal of friendship."[40] The outcome of this appeal, however, is unknown; and we hear nothing of Carthaginian involvement, although Thucydides does mention subsequent Etruscan aid following a similar overture made about the same time (6. 88.6; 7. 57.11). Here then we have both belligerents seeking Carthaginian support but neither receiving any.

Our sources do not say whether the offer of *philia* made by Athens was accepted, but there is one further and tantalizing bit of information. In a badly mutilated Athenian decree, Hannibal and Himilkon, the very generals who commanded the Carthaginian invasion of Sicily in 406, are named in connection with the details of some form of diplomatic agreement.[41] Whether this decree is related to the contact mentioned by Thucydides we simply do not know, but if *philia* was negotiated in 415/414, it might well have

---

(425/424) is suggested by references in Ar. *Knights* 1303–4 (a joke about Hyperbolus taking a hundred triremes to Carthage; for what reason is ambiguous) and 173–74 (an allusion to Carthage as the western limit of the Athenian *archē*; cf. *Wasps* 700). The hope of subjugating Carthage (after Sicily and Italy) expressed by Alcibiades (Thuc. 6. 15.2, 90.2) reveals something of his character but nothing about official Athenian policy, especially considering the silence about such schemes in reports of the public debate at Athens prior to the Sicilian invasion.

40. Trans. B. Jowett, *Thucydides* (Oxford, 1881) καὶ ἔπεμψαν μὲν ἐς Καρχηδόνα τριήρη περὶ φιλίας, εἰ δύναιντό τι ὠφελεῖσθαι (Thuc. 6. 88.6). The phrase *peri philias* is accurately rendered by Jowett but distorted by Smith who translates, "they sent also to Carthage *on a mission of friendship*" (my italics). From its use in 5.5.1 concerning the negotiations of Phaeax with South Italian cities *peri philias* and from the parallel usage of the phrase *peri symmachias* (5. 30.4, 32.6), it is clear that Thucydides means "in regard to" or "in respect to" *philia* in 6. 88.6. The relationship did not exist at the time the embassy was sent; if it had, the phrase would include *kata* (e.g., 2. 82; 3. 86.3; 6. 75.3), *dia* (e.g., 1. 137.4; 2. 100.3), or *es* (e.g., 8. 88), *inter alia*; cf. the use of *pempein*, "to send in regard to" (e.g., 3. 13; 6. 34.2). The contrast with the following phrase (ἔπεμψαν δὲ καὶ ἐς Τυρσηνίαν, etc.) recounting the dispatch of a second trireme to the Etruscans, who have offered aid but who cannot be characterized as having any particular diplomatic relationship with the Athenians, is also striking.

41. *IG* I², 47 + (*IG* I³, 123); B. D. Meritt, "Athens and Carthage," *Athenian Studies Presented to William Scott Ferguson*, Harvard Studies in Classical Philology, *Suppl.* 1 (Cambridge, Mass., 1940), 247–53; Meiggs and Lewis, no. 92; Bengtson, *SVA²* no. 208.

been modeled on the recent *philia* treaty between the Athenians and King Darius II of Persia (see 6.2 above). This formal *philia* encompassed more than mere "friendship," for it also entailed understood responsibilities and communicated mutual assurances of restraint, which made it tantamount to a modern nonaggression pact.[42] Nor was *philia* an unprecedented diplomatic relationship for Carthage. Polybius preserves the alleged details of just such an earlier *philia* treaty between Carthage and the rising Italian city-state of Rome.[43] The Carthaginians knew exactly how to use diplomacy to avoid confrontation and to neutralize potential adversaries (see especially 8.1 below). But during the Sicilian conflict of 415–413, even if the Carthaginians negotiated diplomatic *philia* with Athens (or perhaps because of it), there is nothing to indicate that they were in any way actively involved. Entanglement in the struggle between Greek states was plainly not what the Carthaginians wanted. They remained on the sidelines, peacefully biding their time, awaiting the outcome and the opportunity not to assist the Athenians but to intervene decisively for themselves.

V. UNIDENTIFIED NEUTRAL STATES (413/412)

In 416 the Melians reportedly warned the Athenians that if Melian neutrality was not respected, all existing neutrals would be converted into enemies (Thuc. 5. 98). At the time, Athens confidently disregarded the warning (5. 99), but Athens' catastrophic defeat in Sicily produced dramatic confirmation that the fate of Melos had not passed unnoticed:

> During the following winter [413/412], all the Hellenes were immediately stirred up over the great Athenian disaster in Sicily. Those who were allies of neither side thought that even if they were not called upon, they ought not to remain aloof from the war any longer but should voluntarily go against the Athenians, for everyone believed that had the Athenians prevailed in Sicily, they would have

42. See 3.4 above. Note also the Carthaginian offer to recognize the Agrigentines as *philoi* if they will remain neutral in 406 (Diod. 13. 85.2). For fourth-century examples, see 9.3.A–B below.

43. Bengtson, *SVA*[2] no. 121 (Polyb. 3. 22.4: ἐπὶ τοῖσδε φιλίαν εἶναι Ῥωμαίοις καὶ Ῥωμαίων συμμάχοιςꞌ καὶ Καρχηδονίοις καὶ Καρχηδονίων συμμάχοις), dated to ca. 508/507, with which the roughly contemporary *philia* agreement between the Sybarites and Serdaioi (*SVA*[2] no. 120 [before 510]; Meiggs and Lewis, no. 10 [550–525?]) should be compared.

come against them; and besides, they believed the remaining war would be brief and to have a share in it would be glorious.[44]

Unfortunately, Thucydides does not specify the states to which he refers in this remark. This must be partly due to the incomplete condition of the *History*. As it is, Book 8 covers only the events of the winter of 413/412 through the summer of 411 or roughly one and a half years of the more than eight years remaining in the war. Who, then, are these unidentified neutrals? At present, the only candidates that appear to qualify definitely are certain Greek city-states of Magna Graecia and the king of Persia.

The neutral stance adopted by the West Greek city-states during the earlier years of the war has already been discussed (in 6.2 above). But in the continuation of the war after 413, Thucydides first mentions triremes from Tarentum and Italian Locri (8. 91.2), as well as from Syracuse (8. 26.1), in the Peloponnesian fleet. None of these states had openly aided the Peloponnesian war effort previously (see 6. 10.4), and their timely appearance suggests that they are at least one group that Thucydides had in mind when he made the statement at 8. 2.1.

The king of Persia also joined forces with the Peloponnesians after the Athenian disaster. Neither side had previously been able to secure Persian support (see 6.3 above), but from 412 Darius II allied himself with Sparta and decisively influenced the remainder of the war.[45] Hence Thucydides could also have been thinking of the Persians, although it must be admitted that he speaks specifically in terms of Hellenic involvement.

SUMMARY

There is abundant evidence that neutrality played an important role in the politics of West Greece during the Peloponnesian War. The Dorian supporters of the Peloponnesian alliance appear to

---

44. Τοῦ δ' ἐπιγιγνομένου χειμῶνος πρὸς τὴν ἐκ τῆς Σικελίας τῶν Ἀθηναίων μεγάλην κακοπραγίαν εὐθὺς οἱ Ἕλληνες πάντες ἐπηρμένοι ἦσαν, οἱ μὲν μηδετέρων ὄντες ξύμμαχοι, ὡς, ἤν τις καὶ μὴ παρακαλῇ σφᾶς, οὐκ ἀποστατέον ἔτι τοῦ πολέμου εἴη, ἀλλ' ἐθελοντὶ ἰτέον ἐπὶ τοὺς Ἀθηναίους, νομίσαντες κἂν ἐπὶ σφᾶς ἕκαστοι ἐλθεῖν αὐτούς, εἰ τὰ ἐν τῇ Σικελίᾳ κατώρθωσαν, καὶ ἅμα βραχὺν ἔσεσθαι τὸν λοιπὸν πόλεμον, οὗ μετασχεῖν καλὸν εἶναι. (Thuc. 8. 2.1)

45. Thuc. 8. 18, 27, 58; Bengtson SVA² nos. 200, 201, 202; Amit, "A Peace Treaty between Sparta and Persia," 55–64.

have had recourse to a formally neutral stance at the outbreak of the war; both the Dorian and Chalcidian states of Italy, with the eventual exceptions of Thurii and Metapontum, remained neutral during the Athenian expedition to Sicily, and the option of neutrality was, at one time or another, considered, adopted, defended, used, and abused by one or another of the West Greek states and even by the Carthaginians between 415 and 413.

Thucydides is, without question, the most important source of information, but his preoccupation with the details of the military conflict results in the omission of many details that might clarify the activities and official policies of those states that either initially or permanently maintained neutrality. This is particularly noticeable in the case of Acragas and Messene, which Thucydides hardly mentions, the Italian states, which are summarily treated at best, and, finally, states like Catana, Himera, Camarina, and the Sicels, which are basically neglected until they become involved in the conflict. A few additional bits of information are provided by Diodorus, some valuable but all of questionable reliability. Diodorus' confirmation of the initial neutrality of Camarina is perhaps the most significant bonus.

Nevertheless, a consistent picture of the rights and obligations associated with neutrality emerges. Neutrals could restrict belligerent presence to a single ship, could refuse to permit a belligerent fleet to land on their coastline even to take water, and had the option of admitting or prohibiting belligerent forces not only from entering their cities but also from traversing their territory. They could also provide a market whether in or outside of their cities but had no immunity when sending provisions to one or the other of the belligerents. Neutral status was not without clearly recognizable advantages, both political and economic. Occasionally, these factors are revealed as the motivations for the adoption, rejection, and even exploitation of neutrality. Naturally, neutrality was resisted by the belligerents. Thucydides attributes to Hermocrates a sharp attack on the acceptability of neutrality as an option for Camarina, which includes the often-repeated argument that neutrality equaled passive support of the "unjust" cause.

Finally, the evidence available for the West Greeks provides some information about what political and military conditions were necessary to ensure that neutrality was respected. Magna Graecia was a diverse conglomeration of relatively powerful city-states that were in close contact with a far greater and often hostile non-Greek population. Seemingly because of this, there appears to have been noticeably less inclination on the part of the Greek states to accept the idea that conflict between Greeks of different ethnic origins (i.e., Dorians and Chalcidians) was inevitable. Ethnic identity and the resulting alignment did exist, as the war of 427–424 demonstrates, but it must also be remembered that that war ended in a general reconciliation and that in both 422 and 415, Athens found it difficult to win any adherents with its racial propaganda.

In 415, therefore, Athens was confronted by a situation in which the West Greek states, because they were too powerful to coerce openly, had to be accepted on their own terms. This meant that while Syracuse remained the primary objective, the neutrality of states unwilling to join the Athenian side had to be viewed as at least temporarily advantageous in that it deprived the enemy of many potential allies. As in so many wars, ancient and modern, when the Athenians eventually faltered, a number of the neutrals closest to the conflict quickly committed themselves to the "just" cause. But not all. Acragas, Messene, and the majority of the Italian city-states, and even the Carthaginians, remained neutral throughout the conflict.

CHAPTER EIGHT

From the Carthaginian Invasion of Sicily to the Spartan Defeat at Leuctra (406–371)

The end of the fifth century brought radical adjustments in the diplomatic realities confronting the Greek city-states. In mainland Greece the hegemony of Sparta, in Sicily the ascendancy of Syracuse, and in Asia Minor the restored rule of the Persian king all profoundly affected the way that states of every rank conducted diplomacy and decided which policy to pursue when conflict erupted. The negative impact of the Peloponnesian War on respect for traditionally accepted rules of war was great and led many states to abandon virtually all trust in restraint on the part of belligerents.

I. NEUTRALITY DURING THE CARTHAGINIAN INVASION OF SICILY (406)

In Sicily, a complex series of events following the Athenian disaster led to a crisis that provides an immediate glimpse of the new reluctance of even staunchly neutral states to continue trusting in the policy.[1] After Athens' defeat Egesta was hard pressed by Selinus and feared that Syracuse, a *symmachos* of Selinus, might enter the conflict to punish Egesta for bringing the Athenians to Sicily. In

---

1. A detailed account of events in Sicily after the Athenian defeat is given by Diodorus (13. 43–44, 54–59, 63, 79.8–114 [based on Timaeus; see L. Pearson, "Ephorus and Timaeus in Diodorus, Laqueur's Thesis Rejected," *Historia* 33 (1984): 1–20]). See also [Xen]. *Hell.* 1. 1.37, 5.21; 2. 2.24.

desperation, the Egestaeans offered to hand over their city to Carthage in return for military support. The Carthaginians accepted the offer and sent an embassy to Syracuse, ostensibly to submit the dispute to Syracusan arbitration but actually hoping that if the Selinuntines refused arbitration, Syracuse would decline to aid them in the war. But the Syracusans ignored the demand for arbitration and declared that they intended to maintain both their alliance with Selinus and peace with Carthage (Diod. 13. 43).

In 409/408, however, the Carthaginians invaded, capturing Selinus and Himera (Diod. 13. 54–62). Encouraged by this initial victory, they sent a second invasionary force in 406 (13. 79–114). But before the Carthaginian generals began hostilities, they sent ambassadors to the Agrigentines, "asking them preferably to become allies but otherwise to stay neutral and be friends of the Carthaginians and thereby remain in peace."[2] This was sensible diplomacy. Acragas was powerful and at the time extraordinarily prosperous, the result, in no small measure, of the city's long-standing policy of abstention from war.[3] The Carthaginians must have been well aware of this; and indeed, their proposal cleverly sought to reassure the Agrigentines that Carthage would honor their neutrality if formal alliance was rejected. The similarity to the Persian proposal to Argos in 480 and to Sparta's proposal to Plataea in 429 is striking.[4] Together these examples surely reflect a common diplomatic strategy employed by belligerents to strengthen their own position either by gaining an ally or at least by reducing the number of opponents.[5]

The Agrigentines flatly refused both the Carthaginian alliance and complete abstention.[6] Once again neutrality could not be sustained. Nevertheless, we learn several things about the contempo-

---

2. καὶ πρῶτον μὲν ἀπέστειλαν πρέσβεις πρὸς τοὺς Ἀκραγαντίνους ἀξιοῦντες μάλιστα μὲν συμμαχεῖν αὐτοῖς, εἰ δὲ μή γε, ἡσυχίαν ἔχειν καὶ φίλους εἶναι Καρχηδονίοις ἐν εἰρήνῃ μένοντας (Diod. 13. 85.2); cf. 94.2, where Dionysius of Syracuse claims similar overtures were made to him at this time.

3. On their earlier policy, see 7.2 above. For a description of the resulting prosperity, see Diodorus (13. 81.4–84.6, 89–90.4), who concludes that Acragas was "virtually the wealthiest of the Greek cities of that time" (90.3).

4. See 5.2 above (Argos) and 6.4 above (Plataea); cf. also 9.3.A–B below (fourth-century examples of similar diplomatic overtures).

5. Machiavelli comments on the same phenomenon in sixteenth-century Italian diplomacy; see p. xiii, note 12 in the Preface.

6. Already during the previous invasion of 409/408 Acragas had joined the Greek alliance led by Syracuse (Diod. 13. 56.1–2, 58.3) and given refuge to the survivors from Selinus (58.3).

rary conception of the policy. First, the incident of 406 plainly shows that neutrality could be negotiated and that it was certainly not limited to Greek diplomacy but could—and did—play a part in the wider, truly international diplomacy of classical warfare. Secondly, we see once again the special rhetorical connection between *philia* and neutrality. There is, however, a reversal of normal roles, with the belligerent rather than the neutral introducing the linkage, for in this case the Carthaginians are promising in advance to accept *philia* if Acragas remains neutral. Finally, the outcome, while no surprise, emphasizes a reality in Greek international life: policies are not permanent. Acragas could not continue in its role as a neutral state under any circumstances. Whatever they may have suspected about the Athenians' true ambitions in Sicily, the Agrigentines never wavered from their neutrality. Yet from the first arrival of the Carthaginians to attack Selinus, despite seemingly generous diplomatic assurances allowing for continuation of their former (and very successful) policy, the Agrigentines immediately joined the Greek resistance. As much as anything this decision reflects a failure of trust, and a resulting lack of confidence, that declared or negotiated exemption would be secure and respected by the belligerents.[7]

II. THE EVIDENCE FROM CONFLICTS BETWEEN 404 AND 396

The Spartans resented that the Eleans had entered into a hostile alliance during the Peace of Nicias, had failed to pay their portion of the costs of the war, and had used their sacred office as administrators of the Panhellenic sanctuary at Olympia to humiliate Spartans by banning them from the sanctuary. After their victory in 404, the Spartans were ready to punish the Eleans for these offenses and engineered a provocation for moving against them

---

7. It would be wrong to associate fear of "Punic perfidy" with this decision. The image of treachery and untrustworthiness associated with Carthage arose only later in the context of the third-century Roman-Carthaginian struggle for supremacy in the western Mediterranean and was almost certainly the self-serving creation of the Romans, employed as propaganda in defense of their implacable hostility to the Carthaginians. By comparison, earlier diplomatic evidence suggests nothing unusual about the relations between Carthage and other states; see the treaty with the Etruscans (Bengtson, *SVA²* no. 116), Persia (*SVA²* no. 129), Syracuse (*SVA²* nos. 131, 210, 233, 261), Athens (*SVA²* no. 208), the rulers of Catana and Leontini (*SVA²* no. 341), the Corinthian general Timoleon (*SVA²* no. 344), and Rome itself (*SVA²* nos. 121, 326).

with military force.[8] For our purposes the key issue in the Spartan-Elean conflict is how other states reacted to it. Did the *de iure* obligations of their alliances with Sparta or the de facto ascendant military superiority of the Spartans compel states to take the Lacedaemonian side in the war? Or was formal abstention possible?

It seems that all of these alternatives existed simultaneously. Athens, for example, had recently accepted an alliance requiring the Athenians "to have the same friends and enemies" as the Spartans; and they supported the Spartan side, however reluctantly.[9] Indeed, no one opposed Sparta directly. The Corinthians and Boeotians, however, although they belonged to the Spartan alliance, refused to side with Sparta; yet neither, as far as we know, provided any aid to the Eleans. Apparently, both states believed that the best they could do to express their opposition to Sparta's aggression was simply to remain neutral and thereby remind the Spartans that they, in any case, were independent allies and not obedient subjects.[10] And it should be remembered that their abstention may well have had a kind of quasi-legal (if not truly *de iure*) foundation in the customary right of individual states not to participate in wars that the full alliance had not approved and that were not strictly defensive (see 3.5 above).

The issue arose again in 396, when the Spartans dispatched Agesilaus to campaign against the Persians on behalf of the Asiatic Greek city-states. This time Corinth, Thebes, and Athens all reportedly declined to participate. Provocative though this decision has seemed to modern commentators, it attracted scant attention in

8. Taking up the complaints of outlying villages that had been forcibly annexed to the city-state of Elis, the Spartans demanded that their independence be restored (Xen. *Hell.* 3. 2.25).

9. Λακεδαιμόνιοι ... ἐποιοῦντο εἰρήνην ἐφ' ᾧ τά τε μακρὰ τείχη καὶ τὸν Πειραιᾶ καθελόντας καὶ τὰς ναῦς πλὴν δώδεκα παραδόντας καὶ τοὺς φυγάδας καθέντας τὸν αὐτὸν ἐχθρὸν καὶ φίλον νομίζοντας Λακεδαιμονίοις ἕπεσθαι καὶ κατὰ γῆν καὶ κατὰ θάλαττον ὅποι ἂν ἡγῶνται (Xen. *Hell.* 2. 2.20). On Athenian participation, see *Hell.* 3. 5.8; cf. Diod. 14. 17.7 (Athens is not named specifically).

10. Note also that in 403 Corinth and Thebes likewise refused to join the Spartan expedition against the Athenian democrats occupying the Piraeus. Again the formal (i.e., legal) justification for refusing would have been that intervention in the internal affairs of an alliance state was not a legitimate cause for summoning allied support; see Xenophon (*Hell.* 2. 4.30), who relates the Corinthian and Theban official reason as follows: "They did not think they would be true to their oaths if they took the field against the Athenians when the latter were doing nothing in violation of the treaty" (trans. C. L. Brownson, Xenophon, *Hellenica*, Loeb Classical Library [Cambridge, Mass., and London, 1918]); cf. *Hell.* 3. 5.5, 8, 16; 5. 2.33.

the ancient sources. Xenophon mentions only Thebes and offers no explanation (*Hell*. 3. 5.5), while Diodorus and Plutarch are altogether silent. Only Pausanias, in the historical sketch that precedes the guide to Laconia, provides a detailed list of boycotting states (3. 9.2–3). According to his account, the Corinthians were eager to join the campaign but were prevented by a dire omen, which occurred when the temple of Olympian Zeus at Corinth burned down just at that time (9.2). "The Athenian excuse", he explains, "was that the city was [still] coming back from the Peloponnesian War and the sickness of the plague to the prosperity it once had; but really they knew from reports that Conon had gone up to see the King; and for this reason most of all, they kept quiet" (9.2). Pausanias then adds the cryptic remark about Thebes' refusal that "they gave the same excuse as the Athenians" (9.3).

Since Xenophon provides no explanation, the information from Pausanias, the historical reliability of whose sources is always difficult to assess, should be approached with considerable caution. Nevertheless, in this case Pausanias appears to be supplying reliable information about contemporary diplomacy.

In the first place, his statement that the Corinthians' refusal was based on a religious obstruction is perfectly in keeping with accepted custom.[11] The situation with Athens is more remarkable. A recent treaty with the Spartans obligated the Athenians, in Xenophon's words, "to have the same friends and enemies as the Lacedaemonians and follow wherever they led on land and sea" (*Hell*. 2. 2.20). Since the Athenians had done just this both in the Spartan war with Elis and the subsequent Asiatic campaign of Thibron (399), it seems especially hard to believe that suddenly in 396 they could seriously claim that the injuries of the Peloponnesian War made it impossible for them to join in Agesilaus' expedition. But as Pausanias himself notes, the prospect of Conon leading Persian opposition against Sparta created a difficult diplomatic situation.

For the Athenians to unilaterally defy the terms of their alliance with Sparta must have remained unthinkable; yet participation in

---

11. See, for instance, the proviso cited in Thuc. 5. 30.1 that the Peloponnesian alliance would submit to majority rule "unless there were some hindrance on the part of the gods or heroes" (cf. 30.3). Compare 5.2 above (Argos and the Cretans claiming divine injunction) and 8.3.B below (religious claims of Phlius and Mantinea). For further discussion of the concept, see de Ste. Croix, *Origins of the Peloponnesian War*, 118–22.

the campaign might mean that the Athenians would contribute to a decisive Spartan victory over the Persians and thus place themselves in deepened subservience to the new masters of Greece. The diplomatic solution—claiming that they had to abstain on the grounds of continued weakness—thus sought effectively to avoid participation (and thereby avert potential injury to their interests) without formally violating in any way the terms of the alliance (and thereby definitely exposing the state to injury).

Pausanias' statement about Theban policy is the most enigmatic. How could the Thebans possibly offer the same excuse as Athens? Thebes had neither suffered as badly as Athens from the Peloponnesian War generally nor from the plague specifically. It would be tempting to ignore Pausanias if it were not for the context. This statement comes within a larger description of Theban-Spartan relations that contains both considerable specific detail and analysis. For example, the name of the Spartan ambassador to Thebes, Aristomelidas, is given along with an explanation of why he was sent, and the subsequent incident at Aulis is reported together with an explanation of why it occurred. Evidently then Pausanias is following a good historical source at this point. For this reason, the explanation of what the Thebans said in order to avoid participation in the proposed expedition may be reliable.

Possibly the twenty-seven years of the Peloponnesian War had taken a great enough toll for the excuse to be credible. Whatever the case, the credibility of the excuse is not as important as the alleged fact that it was given at all. For whatever the excuse, it remains true that at the time the Thebans still believed that diplomacy could serve to avoid participation and confrontation with Sparta. Obviously, if accurately reported, the excuse they offered was weaker in their case than for the Athenians, but it was something, and it shows that even though they soon after went to war with Sparta, at this point all three states (Corinth, Athens, and Thebes) were still looking for some way to maintain peaceful relations and yet to abstain from supporting Sparta's aggressive foreign policy ventures.

The single, insurmountable problem during this period of diplomatic maneuvering was the hostility of Sparta. Simply put, superiority had bred contempt for the traditional rules of interstate behavior. The defeat of Athens had not resulted in the reestablishment of respect for international rules guaranteed by the power of

the victorious Spartans. Instead, the Spartans proved to be dictatorial and self-serving. In assessments of the origins of the Corinthian
War, both ancient and modern, too little attention has been paid
to the idea that frustration over unfulfilled promises lay at the
bottom of the growing opposition to Sparta during these years. Yet
it seems quite clear from the little evidence that survives that
Sparta's disregard for traditionally respected principles of lawful
and just conduct in its dealings with other states was an important
factor in the move from passive to active opposition. On the eve
of the Corinthian War, Xenophon represents the Thebans as com-
plaining bitterly about Sparta's treatment of Elis, its failure to share
the rewards of the Peloponnesian War with its allies, and its installation of harmosts and decarchies (*Hell.* 3. 5.8–15). At the same time,
according to the Oxyrhynchus historian, the Athenians displayed
remarkable concern for strict legality in their own behavior in
order to avoid bringing discredit to the city (*Hell. Oxy.* 1. 1–3).[12]

Although individual politicians and their factions agitating for
war with Sparta may have been more influenced by their own
identification with competing political ideologies or by personal
ambition (or even by secret motives like bribery) than by anger
over Sparta's disrespect for the traditionally recognized rights and
obligations of states in the area of international affairs, their public
rhetoric was nevertheless legalistic and moral in its tone. In the
arena of public debate, Sparta was portrayed as the aggressor, the
lawbreaker, the tyrant state that could only be restrained by force.
And as the indisputable evidence of Spartan behavior accumulated,

---

12. Note also Paus. 3. 9.11. With I. A. F. Bruce, *A Historical Commentary on
the* Hellenica Oxyrhynchia (Cambridge, 1967), 51–52, and Hamilton, *Sparta's
Bitter Victories,* 181 n. 48, I prefer the restoration of B. P. Grenfell and A. S. Hunt,
The Oxyrhynchus Papyri, part 5 (London, 1908): [*dia*]*ba*[*lou*]*si* ("give a bad name
to or bring to discredit") to that of V. Bartoletti, ed., *Hellenika Oxyrhynchia*
(Leipzig, 1959): [*kata*]*ba*[*lou*]*si* ("injure or harm"). The former has close linguistic
parallels in Thuc. 3. 109.2 and 8. 109 and fits better with the sense of indignation
among the *gnōrimoi* and *charientes* over the escalation from private opposition
to Sparta to public violation of Athens' oaths. These citizens insisted that the city
remain legally blameless in its dealings with Sparta, even if it meant surrendering
Demaenetus to the Spartan harmost on Aegina (*Hell. Oxy.* 1.3; 3.1–2). Diodorus
(15. 19.4) also describes internal opposition to Agesilaus' aggressive foreign policy
during this period in terms of disrepute (*adoxein*); see R. E. Smith, "The Opposition to Agesilaus' Foreign Policy, 394–371 B.C.," *Historia* 2 (1953–54): 274–88.
See also Diod. 14. 2.1; Isoc. 4 (*Paneg.*). 122; 8 (*On the Peace*). 96–97, 100; Plut.
Lys. 13.5; *Ages.* 6.1.

the influence of pro-Spartan politicians within their respective states correspondingly declined, until it reached the point where those politicians could no longer restrain their states from military confrontation with Sparta.[13]

These developments are important to our study of formal abstention from warfare, because the Corinthians, the Thebans, and even the Athenians attempted to express their opposition to Sparta's foreign policy by adopting a middle position that they held to be diplomatically correct. This policy quickly failed, however, in the face of Sparta's increasingly belligerent behavior. Whatever the rationale of Sparta's actions, the fact remains that instead of treating other states as theoretical equals and honoring their right at least to abstain from Sparta's offensive conflicts, the Spartans became increasingly dictatorial during this period and repeatedly showed nothing but cynical concern for the outward form of legality in their conduct. The result was that the opportunity for constructive progress toward greater respect for the rights of individual states was lost, and even for states that had been among Sparta's staunchest allies in the previous war, no alternative to military confrontation remained.

13. Reflections of contemporary concern about Sparta's behavior appear in Xen. *Hell.* 2. 4.30; 3. 5.12–13 and Diod. 14. 2.1; cf. the prophetic words in Thuc. 1. 77.6. Sparta's behavior was also the subject of contemporary comedy; see Theopompus frag. 65 (Edmonds, *FAC*, vol. 1, 870–73 [= Plut. *Lys.* 13.5]): "Even the comic poet Theopompus was thought absurd in likening the Lacedaemonians to tavern-women, because they gave the Greeks a very pleasant sip of freedom, and then dashed the wine with vinegar; for from the very first the taste was harsh and bitter" (trans. B. Perrin, *Plutarch's Lives*, vol. 4, Loeb Classical Library [Cambridge, Mass., and London, 1916]). On the ancient accusation that certain politicians at Thebes manipulated Sparta into a declaration of war, see Hamilton, *Sparta's Bitter Victories*, 182–208. But note how Sparta initiated the decisive confrontation when Agesilaus attempted to sacrifice at Aulis (in Boeotia) without permission. All three accounts of the incident (Xen. *Hell.* 3. 4.3–4; Plut. *Ages.* 6.6; Paus. 9. 9.3–5), despite superficial differences, agree that the Boeotian authorities were reacting to the unexpected action of Agesilaus. Xenophon in particular, since he is elsewhere clearly apologetic for Spartan behavior, would hardly have passed up this opportunity to condemn the Boeotians if it had not been common knowledge among his audience that the sacrifice was performed without permission and was therefore in some sense illegal (note Plutarch's explanation in terms of violated procedure). The truth is that we know next to nothing about an individual's right to sacrifice in foreign territory; it seems wiser to interpret the unexpected violence of the Boeotian reaction as a manifestation of their resentment that the Spartans were constantly disregarding "the laws and customs" of other Greeks (Plut. *Ages.* 6.6) than to impute to the Boeotians premeditation not attested in the sources.

III. THE CORINTHIAN WAR (395–386)

A. THE ISSUE OF NEUTRALITY AT CORINTH

The outbreak of hostilities between Sparta and Thebes put Corinth in an extremely difficult position. If the Corinthians supported Thebes, Corinth itself would be put in greater jeopardy than Thebes because of its location directly in the line of march between the Peloponnesus and Boeotia. On the other hand, continuation of the recent policy of "passive resistance" to Spartan aggression must also have seemed extremely dangerous, given Sparta's willingness, if not eagerness, to go to war with Corinth's partner in this policy. But, worst of all, if Corinth took the safest course and slavishly supported Sparta, it could only be understood as a defeat for the principle that Sparta's allies were under no automatic obligation to join in the hegemonial power's offensive conflicts unless they were bound to do so by the specific terms of their treaty. The Corinthians were thus faced with a very difficult decision, which they resolved initially by refusing to take sides. Although this policy succeeded for the moment, when the Spartan invasion of Boeotia proved to be a fiasco, the Corinthians decided that the time had come to join with the open opposition.[14]

The Corinthians soon regretted their involvement, as Xenophon

14. On the unexpectedly poor outcome of the Spartan campaign in 395, including the death of Lysander and the Spartans' ignominious retreat from Boeotia under truce, all of which led to the condemnation and exile of King Pausanias, see Xen. *Hell.* 2. 5.17–25; for the chronological sequence, see Diod. 14. 81.2–3 (battle at Haliartus) and 82.1 (alliances). Resentment at Sparta's unrestrained behavior was an important factor in Corinth's decision and one that has been strangely underrated by ancient and modern commentators alike. The main causes that have been proposed are Persian bribery (*Hell. Oxy.* 2; Xen. *Hell.* 3. 5.1–2; 5. 2.35; Plut. *Lys.* 27.1; *Ages.* 15.6; Paus. 3. 9.8; Justin 6. 2), internal factional rivalry (*Hell. Oxy.* 2.2), resentment at Sparta for failing to share the spoils of the Peloponnesian War (Xen. *Hell.* 3. 5.5; Justin 5. 10; Plut. *Lys.* 27.2; see Hamilton, *Sparta's Bitter Victories,* 199, 260–61) and damaging Corinth's commercial interests (D. Kagan, "The Economic Origins of the Corinthian War [395–387 B.C.]," *PP* 16 [1961]: 321–41; Larsen, *Greek Federal States,* 157; Hamilton, 199, 260–61). All of these factors must have had some influence on individual politicians and factions within Corinth during this period; but the evidence of the timing of Corinth's change in policy together with the tremendous risk that open opposition to Sparta represented must surely reflect at least the majority's belief that given the circumstances of the crisis, all the less radical alternatives, including continued neutrality, had become untenable. This argument is paralleled in Diod. 14. 82.2–4. Diodorus connects the alliance with "hatred of Sparta's harsh rule" but at the same time emphasizes the fear of Sparta among city-states in the Peloponnesus. Further evidence is offered by Xenophon (*Hell.* 4. 4.15), who observes that the Phliasians were so mistrustful of the Spartans during this period

relates: "As the Corinthians, however, saw that their own land was being laid waste and that many of them were being killed because they were continually near the enemy, while the rest of the allies were living in peace themselves and their lands were under cultivation, the most and best of them came to desire peace, and uniting together urged this course upon one another."[15] Next, Xenophon describes how this movement precipitated a bloody internal struggle in which the principal accusation brought against the citizens who sought to extricate Corinth from the war was that they wanted to hand the city over to the Spartans.[16] But this was obviously not true in the beginning, for the hope of this faction was clearly not that Corinth change sides and become an active ally of Sparta but only that Corinth recover its original neutral position in the conflict.

The disastrous failure of the secession movement emphasizes just how dangerous this kind of policy change could be. The moment it became clear that there was serious agitation in favor of taking Corinth out of the war, Corinth's own allies made every effort—even to the point of allowing Argos to annex Corinth—to prevent it from happening.[17] This was nothing new. Corcyra's attempt to withdraw from the war in 427 met with a similar reaction (see 6.4 above). Apparently no one at Corinth remembered.

B. THE SACRED TRUCES OF PHLIUS AND MANTINEA

Corinth was not the only state that wanted no part of the war. Phlius and Mantinea had the same desire, but both states were so

---

that they would not allow any Spartan to enter their city; see also below on the Phliasians' policy during the war.

15. Xen. *Hell.* 4. 4.1, trans. Brownson.

16. Xen. *Hell.* 4. 4.2. For a detailed study of the *stasis*, see now Salmon, *Wealthy Corinth*, 362–70.

17. The Corinthians did not seem to realize just how vital their city-state was to the interests of the belligerents: to Athens, as the only defensible obstruction in the land route from the Peloponnesus to the city, whose walls were still in ruins; to Thebes, as a barrier against the Spartan invasion of Boeotia; to Argos, as the focus of hostility, which kept the Spartans occupied and therefore away from Argos; and to Sparta, as the only land bridge to Central Greece. For the allies, Corinthian neutrality was just as damaging as an alliance with Sparta because it effectively removed the barrier to Spartan troop movement (see Hamilton, *Sparta's Bitter Victories*, 217). The Corinthians themselves apparently assumed that when they joined the anti-Spartan alliance, the allies would carry the war into the Peloponnesus with an offensive campaign against Sparta in Laconia (see the speech of Timolaus of Corinth reported in Xen. *Hell.* 4. 2.11–12); and perhaps that was the strategy that led to the battle near Nemea.

weak militarily that open defiance of Sparta was out of the question. For that reason, they resorted to an extraordinary pretense in order to pursue the policy of passive nonbelligerency that they desired while avoiding confrontation with, and inevitable reprisal from, the Spartans, who would not, they knew, voluntarily accept their abstention.

Phlius had a decidedly anti-Spartan government that must have been very reluctant to contribute troops to the Spartan invasion of Boeotia and was doubtless one of the allied contingents whose spiritless support caused the Spartans' ignominious retreat from Haliartus.[18] In the following year, the Phliasians refused altogether to join the Spartan campaign on the grounds that a "sacred truce" (*ekecheiria*) was in force (*Hell.* 4. 2.16). None, least of all the religiously scrupulous Spartans, could object to this appeal to piety. Whether the plea of sacred truce was legitimate or merely a clever manipulation of religious duty, it could not be resisted without unacceptable consequences. So the Spartans acquiesced at the time and even sent troops to the Phliasians' rescue when they suffered a serious defeat at the hands of Iphicrates (Xen. *Hell.* 4. 4.15). After the war, however, on reviewing the conduct of their allies, the Spartans became suspicious after Phliasian exiles accused the government of having intentionally withheld military support and having banished citizens purely for their pro-Spartan leanings (*Hell.* 5. 2.8–10).

Mantinea followed a course remarkably similar to that taken by Phlius. In the beginning of the war, the Mantineans also contributed troops to the Spartan army, but like the Phliasians, they proved to be spiritless and unreliable.[19] In fact, the Mantineans' resentment of Sparta was very strong and in no way secret.[20] It probably should be no surprise, therefore, that the Mantineans soon claimed that a sacred truce prevented them from participating

18. Xen. *Hell.* 3. 5.23; cf. Justin 6. 4. Furthermore, the Phliasians initially refused to allow Spartan soldiers to enter the city (*Hell.* 4. 4.15; 5. 3.12). However, even between allies this was not in itself a hostile act; Athens' allies appear to have regularly banned its forces from entering their cities; see Plut. *Phoc.* 7.1; Isoc. 15 (*Antid.*). 123–26; for the reason, see, among others, Dem. 8 (*On the Chersonese*). 24–25.

19. Mantinea is listed among the Spartan allies that fought at the battle of Corinth in 394 and is mentioned among the garrison troops skirmishing in the Corinthia after the battle; see Xen. *Hell.* 4. 2.13, 4.17; on their unreliability, see *Hell.* 3. 5.23; 5. 2.2.

20. Xen. *Hell.* 4. 5.18; 5. 2.2; Plut. *Ages.* 22.4.

in the war (*Hell.* 5. 2.2). It also happened that after the peace settlement of 387, the Mantineans found their actions questioned by the Spartans, who were, in retrospect, incensed at the Mantineans both for their avoidance of military service and their continued grain trade with the enemy state of Argos.[21]

C. THE POLICY OF MEGARA

We know that like the other members of the Peloponnesian alliance studied thus far, Megara showed signs of discontent with Spartan leadership in the years following the end of the Peloponnesian War.[22] Still, the Megarians were understandably cautious. Megara is not mentioned as one of the states boycotting the Spartan campaign against Elis in 402 or against the Persians in 396. And although they are not mentioned either way, there is no reason to think that the Megarians joined the Corinthians in refusing to participate in the invasion of Boeotia in 395. The situation changed radically, however, when Corinth joined the anti-Spartan alliance. With the Isthmus blocked, Megara was in an impossible position. It was now surrounded on all sides by belligerent states hostile to Sparta and cut off from any support from the Peloponnesus unless aid was sent by sea; and even this would have been easy to prevent,

21. Xen. *Hell.* 5. 2.1–7. The connection with Argos has an unexpected twist. During the war the Argives also attempted to use the proclamation of a sacred truce to prevent Spartan invasion of their territory (*Hell.* 4. 7.2–3); but after consulting both Olympia and Delphi, Agesipolis disregarded the Argive declaration of the truce in 388 and invaded anyway (7.3–7). For what it is worth, Xenophon adds that during the invasion an earthquake occurred, the army was struck by lightning, and sacrifices were ill omened. These details support Xenophon's none-too-subtle message that the gods opposed this violation of *nomos*, despite the support of the oracles consulted.

22. Two incidents reflect this. First, Athenians exiled by the Spartan-backed oligarchy of the Thirty were for some time given refuge despite the Spartans' decree that they were to be expelled from all cities (Xen. *Hell.* 2. 4.1; Lys. 7. 4; 12. 17; Plut. *Lys.* 2.7; cf. Diod. 14. 6); eventual compliance with the Spartan demand can only have increased resentment. Second, when Lysander attempted to gain Megarian citizenship for his pilot, Hermon, he is said to have been rebuffed (Dem. 23 [*Aristocr.*]. 212; although Pausanias [10. 9.4] says that the grant was made; see R. P. Legon, *Megara: The Political History of a Greek City-State to 336 B.C.* [Ithaca, N.Y., and London, 1981], 261–62, who suggests that the Megarians may have later backed down; Xenophon [*Hell.* 1. 6.32] adds to the uncertainty by referring to Hermon as a Megarian in a context that is earlier than the request; despite these uncertainties, a valid tradition of resistance to Spartan high-handedness seems to emerge immediately after 404). Further evidence of ill will between Lysander and the Megarians is found in Lysander's famous retort to a Megarian's criticism that the man's words lacked a city (Plut. *Lys.* 22.1; *Mor.* 71E, 190E, 229C [wrongly attributed to Agesilaus in 213A]; Them. *Or.* 27.344C).

since the Megarians had not rebuilt the ruined long walls from the city to the eastern port at Nisaea, and the western port of Pagai was several kilometers away. Under the circumstances, the Megarians had no choice but to adopt whatever policy would save them from disaster.

Given the weakness of the Megarians' position and the traditional view that there existed only a rigid dichotomy of friends and enemies in classical Greek warfare, we might expect the Megarians to have switched sides and joined the anti-Spartan alliance. This should have been the only option possible, aside from self-destructive loyalty to the Spartan alliance; and indeed, it seems to have been the basis of K. J. Beloch's conclusion that Megara remained faithful to the Spartan alliance throughout this period.[23] Other historians, however, including S. Accame, C. D. Hamilton, and R. P. Legon, have interpreted the situation differently and offered the tentative suggestion that the reason for the absence of Megara is that the Megarians adopted a policy of neutrality.[24]

Admittedly, the evidence for Megarian neutrality is exclusively negative. There is no mention whatsoever of Megarian involvement during the Corinthian War. Nevertheless, there is really no other convincing explanation for the status of Megara during the war. It seems clear that anti-Spartan forces moved freely through the Megarid; but under the circumstances, troop movements may prove nothing, since the Megarians never were able during any period to prevent hostile forces from traversing their territory.[25] More sig-

23. Beloch, *Griechische Geschichte*, vol. 3, part 1, 70 n. 3; cf., for example, E. Meyer, *RE* 15 (1932), 192, s.v. Megara.

24. S. Accame, *Ricerche intorno alla guerra corinzia* (Naples, 1951), 61–62; Hamilton, *Sparta's Bitter Victories*, 218; Legon, *Megara*, 265; cf. N. G. L. Hammond, *A History of Greece to 322 B.C.*, 2d ed. (Oxford, 1967), 522. Legon concludes: "Another solution to the puzzle of Megarian survival in the Corinthian War is possible and, I believe, more likely to be correct: Megara may simply have sat out the war—not formally severing her ties with Sparta, but incapable of honoring them either. Her policy, in other words, might have been *de facto* or even *de iure* neutrality." Hammond characterizes Megara as "proverbial for her prosperity because she remained neutral."

25. Legon, *Megara*, 264 n. 25, claims that the narrative of Xenophon implies "frequent passage of anti-Spartan forces through the Megarid," but Xenophon is actually very vague on this point, unless we make inferences on the basis of his remark that Spartan troops were forced to sail rather than march back from Boeotia after the battle at Coronea (*Hell.* 4. 3.15, 4.1, where the word is *apepleuse*). The evidence offered in Plato's *Theaetetus*, the dramatic setting of which is Megara during the Corinthian War, is better. In *Tht.* 142C Euclides laments that his Athenian friend, Theaetetus, who has been wounded in the fighting at Corinth, has not stopped to visit him in Megara instead of proceeding directly to Athens.

nificant is the lack of evidence for Spartan retaliation after the war. Megara is nowhere mentioned as coming under the punitive scrutiny focused on other allies. Given Sparta's angry attitude, the silence about Megara is probably best understood as an admission that the Megarians had no other choice—that is, the Spartans accepted their neutral policy on the grounds that it was absolutely necessary, just as they had accepted West Greek, Plataean, and Thracian neutrality in the Peloponnesian War.[26]

D. THE POLICY OF AEGINA

Xenophon does not mention the Aeginetans in his narrative of the early years of the war, so when he suddenly focuses on Aegina as a critical site of military activity beginning in 389, he offers a few words of explanation in the way of background. It is unfortunate that he says so little, especially since information about the foreign policy of less powerful Greek states is so frustratingly scarce. Xenophon obviously knows much more about Aegina than he relates, but his interest is limited to what is absolutely essential to the narrative of the major events of the war. So, when he comes to the point where Aegina is the focus of action, he only remarks: "Eteonicus, being again in Aegina, *although the Aeginetans had previously been maintaining normal relations with the Athenians*, since the war was now being fought openly at sea and *since it was approved by the ephors*, urged anyone wishing to do so to carry off plunder from Attica" (my italics).[27] With this statement Xeno-

---

26. For parallels in the diplomacy of the West Greek states, Plataea, and the Thracian cities, see 6.2, 4, and 7 above. During the 380s, Megara continued to be considered impartial in regard to Sparta (see Plut. *Mor.* 215C for the proposal of Megara as arbitrator between Athens and Sparta, datable to 386–380 [Legon, *Megara*, 268; cf. Meyer, *RE* 15 (1932), 192]). All of this is reflected in the famous remark of Isoc. 8 (*On the Peace*). 117–18, which praises Megara's successful policy of maintaining peaceful relations with all other states.

27. ὧν δὲ πάλιν ὁ Ἐτεόνικος ἐν τῇ Αἰγίνῃ, καὶ ἐπιμειξίᾳ χρωμένων τὸν πρόσθεν χρόνον τῶν Αἰγινητῶν πρὸς τοὺς Ἀθηναίους, ἐπεὶ φανερῶς κατὰ θάλατταν [ὁ πόλεμος] ἐπολεμεῖτο, συνδόξαν καὶ τοῖς ἐφόροις ἐφίησι λῄζεσθαι τὸν βουλόμενον ἐκ τῆς Ἀττικῆς (Xen. *Hell.* 5. 1.1). Others, such as Brownson, translate "although previously the Aeginetans had been maintaining commercial intercourse with the Athenians." Rendering *epimeixia* as "commercial intercourse" is wrong in this context, since it is clear from other usage that the term refers broadly to the entire spectrum of peaceful relations between states and not simply to trade; see *LSJ*⁹, s.v. *epimeixia*, with reference to Hdt. 1. 68, Thuc. 5. 78, and Pl. *Laws* 949E. Amit, *Great and Small Poleis*, 55 n. 157, also takes *epimeixia* to mean "relations" generally but argues that its use with the dative makes the expression causal. Hence he translates,

phon attempts as briefly as possible to answer the reader's most immediate questions: What had Aegina been doing previously in the war, and why did Eteonicus happen to return to the island at this time?[28] His answers appear to be that Aegina had remained neutral during the early years of the war and that Sparta had for some time accepted this policy, but when Sparta became hard pressed by the changing necessities of the war, the ephors revoked Sparta's acceptance of Aegina's neutrality.

The remark that Aegina maintained "normal relations" with Athens after the outbreak of the war is not as surprising as might be expected, even in light of the long history of hostility between the two states. The explanation almost certainly lies in the paradoxical fact that during the Peloponnesian War the Aeginetans had suffered terribly at the hands of the Athenians: the entire population of Aegina was expelled by the Athenians in 431, the exiled citizens were bitterly attacked during the subsequent conflict, and the scattered survivors were not resettled on the island until the end of the war (after twenty-seven years of absence).[29] Recovery from such devastation must have come slowly; and since Aegina had always

---

"and because of the former relations of the Aeginetans towards the Athenians," by which he maintains that Xenophon means "their mutual animosity and hatred." But this is wrong. There is no need to force Xenophon into agreement with such preconceived beliefs about the immutability of interstate relations. The concessive use of *kai* understood by other translators in this context is in no way "erroneously rendered," as Amit claims. Later in the statement, on the meaning "approved" for *syndoxan* with the dative, see *LSJ*[9], s.v. *syndokeō*, I:3, citing Xen. *Cyr.* 8. 5.28.

28. Since this is Xenophon's first reference to Eteonicus in Aegina, the remark that he was "again in Aegina" is cryptic. Possibly his "return" is in the capacity of harmost. Eteonicus held this office at Thasos in 410 (*Hell.* 1. 1.32) and subsequently served under Lysander (Diod. 13. 106.4), who delegated to him the important task of bringing the cities of Thrace under Spartan control in 405 (*Hell.* 2. 2.5). He probably served again as a harmost during the general installation at the end of the war (Diod. 14. 10.1, 13.1; Plut. *Lys.* 13.3–4); and his previous presence at Aegina, cited here by Xenophon, could have been during that period. The harmost in 396 was Milon according to *Hell. Oxy.* 6.3, 8.1–2; but see Bruce, *Commentary on the* Hellenica Oxyrhynchia, 54, for doubts about the name.

29. For animosity between Aegina and Athens in the archaic period, see, for instance, Hdt. 5. 81–89; 6. 88–92; 7. 145 (480); during the Pentecontaetia, Thuc. 1. 105.2, 108.4. For the expulsion in 431, see Thuc. 2. 27; the Athenian vendetta against the exiles, Thuc. 4. 56.2–57.4, 67.1, 4; the restoration of surviving citizens by Lysander, Xen. *Hell.* 2. 2.9; Plut. *Lys.* 13.3–4. On the central role played by the Piraeus in international trade during this period, see Isoc. 4 (*Paneg.*). 42; on Aegina's poverty, Dem. 23 (*Aristocr.*). 211.

been a rather poor agricultural state that depended heavily on trade, much of which must have been conducted through the principal commercial center of Athens, the outbreak of the Corinthian War, if it disrupted Aegina's ability to continue its commercial relations with Athens, might well have meant economic ruin for the island. That the Aeginetans adopted a policy that permitted normal relations with Athens to continue despite the war is therefore quite understandable in terms of economic survival, old hatreds notwithstanding.

Xenophon's allusion to "the approval of the ephors" for Eteonicus' action in 389 implies that the decision to involve Aegina in the war was official and originated with the Spartans rather than the Aeginetans. It furthermore follows that the Spartans must have been aware of the existing position of Aegina and decided to pressure the Aeginetans to become involved only when the war expanded into a naval conflict. Once again this policy has a clear parallel in the Peloponnesian War. At the outset the Spartans themselves urged friendly West Greek states to maintain an officially neutral position until circumstances permitted their open assistance.[30]

E. THE EVIDENCE OF BELLIGERENT ACTIVITY

Even the actions of the principal belligerent states during the Corinthian War reflect an awareness that neutrality had advantages and could be a desirable policy. We have already argued that the aim of the peace movement at Corinth in 393/392 was to secure neutral status; and it is possible that the benefits of abstention enjoyed by the Megarians and Aeginetans provided some of the impetus for this movement. Phlius and Mantinea pleaded religious obstructions to stay out of the war. Other states were affected. In 389, for example, the Achaeans threatened to withdraw their support for Sparta and negotiate a separate peace with the anti-Spartan alliance if the Spartans failed to send immediate military aid to the fighting

---

30. On the West Greeks, see 6.2 above. Admittedly, Aeginetan gratitude to Sparta for the restoration of 405/404 must have been great and created strong feelings of obligation, but there is no exact information about what the formal relationship between Aegina and Sparta was during this period aside from the comment of Xenophon quoted here.

in Acarnania.[31] At the same time the situation in the anti-Spartan alliance was worse. By 392 each of the major allies seemed more interested in achieving a separate peace for itself than in continuing unified opposition to Sparta or even in maintaining unanimity in negotiations for peace. The Argives, in particular, appear to have entered into independent talks with the Spartans in complete disregard of the interest of their allies. Andocides makes this clear in his speech *On the Peace* when he complains bitterly that the Argives were claiming the right to a "traditional peace" with the Spartans, which they alone would enjoy.[32]

If they had succeeded, the result of all of these cases of individual negotiations for separate peace treaties would have been de facto neutrality for the states making peace, unless the other belligerents followed suit and ceased fighting. The assumption prevailing in these states must have been that, on the one hand, their former allies would tolerate their withdrawal without hostility or reprisal and, on the other, that their separately negotiated peace treaty would subsequently prevent injury by their former enemies. Interestingly, these were exactly the assumptions that underlay the abortive diplomatic initiative of Corcyra in 427 (see 6.5 above).

F. NEUTRALITY AMONG AEGEAN AND ASIATIC GREEK STATES

During the Corinthian War the diplomacy of the Greek city-states of Asia Minor and the Aegean was in no way collective and uniform.[33] Of course, this does not mean that the individual diplo-

31. See Xen. *Hell.* 4. 6.1–3, where the Achaean ambassadors at Sparta are quoted as saying: "But now that we are besieged by the Acarnanians and their allies, the Athenians and Boeotians, you take no thought for us. Now we cannot hold out if these things go on in this way, but either we shall abandon the war in Peloponnesus and all of us cross over and make war against the Acarnanians and their allies, or else we shall make peace on whatever terms we can" (trans. Brownson).

32. Andoc. 3 (*On the Peace*). 26–28 ("traditional peace," *patrian eirēnēn* 27); on the speech generally, see K. J. Maidment, trans., *Minor Attic Orators*, vol. 1, Loeb Classical Library (Cambridge, Mass., and London, 1953), 484–95; Hamilton, *Sparta's Bitter Victories*, 249–59; but the best treatment is that of R. J. Seager, "Thrasybulus, Conon, and Athenian Imperialism, 396–386 B.C.," *JHS* 87 (1967): 105–7, who concludes that Andocides' aim was to prove that empire and peace could be compatible; see also Ryder, Koine Eirene, 36–38.

33. The foreign policy of these states has too often been lumped together under the label "the Greek cities of Asia," with the islands ignored altogether. An important exception to scholarly habits of generalization in regard to these states is R. J. Seager and C. J. Tuplin's careful examination of the evolution of propaganda focused on the issue of "the freedom of the Greeks of Asia" ("The

matic history of each of these states (or of even very many of them) can be fully reconstructed. The evidence is just too thin for that. There are, however, scattered indications that some East Greek states sought to remain neutral during the warfare of the period.

Diodorus reports that after the Persian fleet had won a decisive victory near Cnidus in 394,

> Pharnabazus and Conon put to sea with all their ships against the allies of the Lacedaemonians. First of all they induced the people of Cos to secede, and then those of Nisyros and of Teos. After this the Chians expelled their garrison and joined Conon, and similarly the Mytilenians and Ephesians and Erythraeans changed sides. Something like the same eagerness for change infected all the cities, of which *some expelled their Lacedaemonian garrisons and maintained their freedom*, while others attached themselves to Conon (my italics).[34]

The assertion here in italics represents Diodorus' (or his source's) attempt to clarify, without going into the specific details, the diplomatic complexity of the situation created by the Persian victory. It should hardly be surprising that some states did not attach themselves to Conon but instead "maintained their freedom (*eleutheria*)"; but what did this mean in effect? Obviously, not all of the liberated city-states were anxious to exchange their formal obligation to Sparta for a similar relationship with either the Athenians (Conon) or the Persians (Pharnabazus), but that does not mean that they could have refused to join any party, unless they felt virtually certain that they could successfully maintain a nonaligned position. Their refusal to align themselves was, therefore, another important step in the dissolution of a strict "allied or enemy" mentality.[35]

Freedom of the Greeks of Asia: On the Origins of a Concept and the Creation of a Slogan," *JHS* 100 [1980]: 141–54).

34. Trans. C. H. Oldfather, *Diodorus Siculus*, vol. 6, Loeb Classical Library (Cambridge, Mass., and London, 1954).

Φαρνάβαζος δὲ καὶ Κόνων μετὰ τὴν ναυμαχίαν ἀνήχθησαν ἁπάσαις ταῖς ναυσὶν ἐπὶ τοὺς τῶν Λακεδαιμονίων συμμάχους. καὶ πρῶτον μὲν Κῴους ἀπέστησαν, εἶτα Νισυρίους καὶ Τηίους. μετὰ δὲ ταῦτα Χῖοι τὴν φρουρὰν ἐκβαλόντες προσέθεντο τοῖς περὶ Κόνωνα· παραπλησίως δὲ μετέβαλον καὶ Μιτυληναῖοι καὶ Ἐφέσιοι καὶ Ἐρυθραῖοι. τοιαύτη δὲ τῆς μεταστάσεως σπουδή τις εἰς τὰς πόλεις ἐνέπεσεν, ὧν αἱ μὲν ἐκβάλλουσαι τὰς φρουρὰς τῶν Λακεδαιμονίων τὴν ἐλευθερίαν διεφύλαττον, αἱ δὲ τοῖς περὶ Κόνωνα προσετίθεντο.   (Diod. 14. 84.3–4)

35. Lewis, *Sparta and Persia*, 143, argues that the rapidity of the Spartan collapse was due to a combination of the unpopularity of Sparta's past behavior

Two Asiatic cities are mentioned by name. Summarizing a speech attributed to the Spartan commander Dercylidas upon leaving the surviving military governors (*harmostai*) at Sestus, Xenophon relates that the harmosts "ought not to be discouraged, either, when they reflected that even in Asia, which had belonged from all time to the king, there was Temnus—not a large city—and Aegae and other places in which people were able to dwell without being subject to the king" (*Hell.* 4. 8.5).[36] This is the only specific reference to Temnus and Aegae in Xenophon's *Hellenica*, but the Oxyrhynchus historian supports the reliability of Xenophon's assertion with his own statement that the cities of Mysia were independent (*autonomous*) from Persia at the time of Agesilaus' invasion in 396.[37] But what can we say about the foreign policy of these "independent" cities? Surely those mentioned by Diodorus as freed from Persian domination but not attached to Conon would seem likely to have assumed a neutral position in the ongoing war. Why not? They must have been initially encouraged in this policy by the moderate and undemanding behavior of Conon and Pharnabazus. But unfortunately, the continued success of the position was soon jeopardized when the Athenians instituted an aggressive and wholly uncompromising campaign to reclaim their lost naval empire.[38] As a result, for those Aegean and Asiatic city-states that had adopted

---

and the moderate assurances of Conon and Pharnabazus that cities would be free and ungarrisoned (Xen. *Hell.* 4. 8.1–2, where "free" is *autonomous*), and interprets Diodorus' statement as evidence that the cities were "not pushed too hard" (n. 55). I agree with Lewis here but think that something needs to be said about the subtle, yet significant, differences between the accounts of Xenophon and Diodorus. Since Xenophon makes no distinction between categories of states, it might be thought that his account, if not contradictory to Diodorus', at least offers no specific support. However, Xenophon's vagueness on the overall diplomatic situation is interesting. He avoids saying that the cities rushed to join (i.e., ally themselves) with Persia; rather, this account suggests that the cities were grateful but uncertain about what course to follow and therefore sought first simply to ingratiate themselves with Pharnabazus by offering gifts of *xenia*. As argued above in 3.4, *xenia* should not be confused with *symmachia*. We can therefore conclude that although Xenophon is less specific than Diodorus, he says in effect the same thing.

36. Trans. Brownson.

37. *Hell. Oxy.* 21(16). 1–2; cf. Xen. *An.* 1. 6.7, 9.14; *Hell.* 3. 1.13. Note too the characteristically aggressive behavior of Agesilaus and his refusal to respect the independence and nonalignment of the Mysians (*Hell. Oxy.* 21[16]. 2).

38. For the claim that Athens desired to rebuild its fifth-century maritime empire, see Xen. *Hell.* 3. 5.10; Andoc. 3 (*On the Peace*). 15; Nep. *Conon* 5; cf., among others, K. J. Beloch, *Die attische Politik seit Perikles* (reprint, Stuttgart, 1967), 344–46; F. H. Marshall, *The Second Athenian Confederacy* (Cambridge,

a neutral attitude toward the ongoing conflict, it became increasingly difficult (for some even impossible) to maintain this position, as we can see, for example, from the evidence for Aegina.

IV. DEVELOPMENTS BETWEEN THE KING'S PEACE (386) AND THE FIRST COMMON PEACE OF 371

A. AGITATION IN THE PELOPONNESIAN LEAGUE

The harshly punitive treatment of Mantinea and Phlius after the King's Peace illustrates how determined the Spartans were to eliminate the idea that anything resembling neutral policy would be tolerated among their Peloponnesian allies. No one could (or did) accuse either Phlius or Mantinea of open opposition to Sparta or even rebellion from the Peloponnesian alliance. Their only real fault was their questionable use of a religious pretext to escape from active participation in the war. Nonetheless, through their punitive intervention, the Spartans attempted to eliminate any thought of abstention among their allies and coerce them into faithful obedience.[39]

The result of Sparta's hard line with its allies was not, however, what might have been expected, for the allied states did not fall back neatly into line. The year after the Spartans punished Phlius, the allies made a bold proposal. When the Spartans decided to supply Acanthus with military aid in its resistance to the expansion of the Chalcidian League, the Peloponnesian allies proposed that Sparta allow the substitution of monetary contributions for actual participation (Xen. *Hell.* 5. 2.21, 3.10; cf. 6. 4.2). There was, of course, a fifth-century precedent for this proposal in the conversion

---

1905), 1–11; P. Cloché, "La politique thébaine de 404 à 396 av. J.-C.," *REG* 31 (1918): 315–43; Seager, "Thrasybulus, Conon, and Athenian Imperialism, 396–386 B.C.," 95–115; Larsen, *Greek Federal States*, 170 with n. 1; Hamilton, *Sparta's Bitter Victories*, 289–98. For the actual steps taken, see especially the expedition of Thrasybulus in 389 (Xen. *Hell.* 4. 8.25–30; Diod. 14. 94, 99.4–5) and reflection of past imperial policy in a decree of 387 honoring Clazomenae (Tod no. 114). G. T. Griffith, "Athens in the Fourth Century," in *Imperialism in the Ancient World*, ed. P. D. A. Garnsey and C. R. Wittaker (Cambridge, 1979), 127–33, objects to this scholarly consensus but is unconvincing about the public policy of Athens during the Corinthian War.

39. This is even the conclusion of Xenophon (*Hell.* 5. 2.1; cf. Diod. 15. 5.1), who is otherwise carefully apologetic about Spartan behavior.

from contributions of ships and men to cash payments that occurred during the early years of the Athenian empire (Thuc. 1. 99.1–3). But there was an important difference. In 383, Sparta's acceptance of the cash substitution was not part of the early evolution of the alliance but a fundamental change that ended an obligation some allied states had borne for more than a century. War-wearied from participation in Sparta's endlessly aggressive foreign policy, the allies were looking for a way out. As subsequent events revealed (see 8.5 and 9.2.C below and 5.A–B above), the substitution of money for men was the first step toward complete neutralization of several members of the Peloponnesian alliance.

B. THEBAN NEUTRALITY (383)

Outside of the Peloponnesus there is some evidence of states using neutral policy during this period. Take the complex events of 383. In that year one of the factional leaders at Thebes secretly approached the Spartan commander of a relief column marching through Boeotia on the way to Olynthus and persuaded him to seize the Theban acropolis. The injustice and illegality of the seizure were admitted from the beginning; but the Spartans nevertheless decided to keep control of the acropolis both to support a pro-Spartan government in Thebes and to guarantee Theban subservience.[40]

A critical issue in this incident, which has been totally ignored in modern scholarship, is Thebes' exact diplomatic position at the time of the seizure. We know from Xenophon that the faction that urged the seizure claimed in its defense that its opponents wanted Thebes to ally itself with Olynthus, Sparta's enemy in the current

---

40. Note that Agesilaus and others who defended the seizure did not argue, as Thrasymachus does in the *Republic*, that their self-interest *was* justice. Instead they attempted to bypass the problem of their obvious violation of the rules of international conduct by alleging that they were in fact saving Thebes from the danger of medizing (Xen. *Hell*. 5. 2.35–36). It seems clear that Xenophon did not really believe this excuse; see *Hell*. 5. 4.1. Other versions of contemporary reaction include Isoc. 4 (Paneg.). 126; Plut. *Pel*. 6.1; *Mor*. 576A. It should be noted that not all Spartans supported the seizure; see, for example, Xen. *Hell*. 5. 2.32; Diod. 15. 19.4; Plut. *Ages*. 23.4. When disaster later befell Sparta, Xenophon (*Hell*. 5. 4.1) suggests that this was divine retribution for the seizure—doubtless a widely held belief at the time.

conflict between Acanthus, Sparta's new ally, and the Chalcidian League, led by Olynthus. In addition, the pro-Spartan faction reportedly reminded the Spartans of several odious examples of former Theban opposition to Spartan foreign policy and promised that there would be no further lack of cooperation and that they would henceforth abandon efforts (opposed by Sparta) to dominate Boeotia.[41] What then does all of this tell us about the official position of Thebes in 383? First, it is not at all surprising that the Olynthians were seeking Theban support, in light of the Spartan alliance with Acanthus, but it is also clear that no such alliance existed at the time when Phoebidas seized the Theban acropolis. The only official act that we know the Thebans carried out at this time was a prohibition against citizens enrolling among the mercenary troops of the Spartan force marching through Boeotia.[42]

Secondly, we know that Thebes was preoccupied with intense factional disputes in which no single party had won control and that two Spartan armies passed through Boeotia on the way to Thrace with neither protest nor opposition. On the other hand, a resolution was adopted forbidding citizens to enroll in the army as mercenaries. Taken together, these bits of information are consistent with the conclusion that the Thebans were remaining carefully neutral in 383 and that this policy represented a compromise resulting from their unresolved internal conflict, which prevented the adoption of any active policy at the time. The unexpected intervention of Phoebidas subverted this policy, but no one could (or did) attempt to argue that the Thebans' policy made the seizure legally justified. On the contrary, even the supporters of the seizure at Sparta argued privately, as they had often in the past, that the illegality of the act could be ignored on the grounds that the state's self-interest should take priority over justice.[43] But publicly, since this was a truth that the Spartans felt they could not proclaim to other states as the justification of the seizure, they fabricated the

41. The only detailed account of the seizure is provided by Xenophon (*Hell.* 5. 2.25–36), who recreates the speech of Leontidas (33–34), the Theban instigator of the incident; cf. Polyb. 4. 27.4; Diod. 15. 20.1–2; Nep., *Epam.* 10; *Pel.* 6; Plut. *Pel.* 5.1–6.3; *Ages.* 23.3–4; Paus. 9. 1.3.

42. Xen. *Hell.* 5. 2.27; for a fifth-century precedent for this, see Thuc. 1. 35.4 (requested of Athens during the Corinthian-Corcyraean conflict), discussed in 5.3.C above.

43. Compare the private with the public rhetoric in Xen. *Hell.* 5. 2.32 and 35; cf. Plut. *Ages.* 23.4.

excuse that they had intervened in order to save the city from medism.[44]

C. ATHENIAN NEUTRALITY (379)

During the years after the King's Peace, Athens followed a quite different diplomatic path from Sparta, and neutrality played a part in Athenian diplomacy. For Athens, the King's Peace provided much-needed relief from the costly military activity of the Corinthian War, and between 386 and 379 the Athenians refrained from warfare and maintained a public posture of scrupulous adherence to the terms of the King's Peace.[45]

This pacific policy was put to the test in 379, when a small band of Theban exiles set out from the frontier of Attica and overthrew the pro-Spartan government at Thebes. News of the conspirators' success brought immediate support from two Athenian generals, who rushed to Thebes with reinforcements and assisted in the expulsion of the Spartan garrison from the Theban acropolis. This was not, however, an authorized venture on the part of the two generals. They knew it but must have expected nothing but praise for their action. If so, it was a fatal miscalculation. The ruling majority at Athens was not about to abandon the pacific policy of the previous seven years. Nevertheless, it was obvious that Athens' position had been seriously jeopardized, and the Athenians therefore defended the passes into Attica as a precaution against Spartan retaliation. No attack came, but ambassadors arrived in Athens to demand an explanation. To prove their official innocence, the Athenians thereupon arrested the two generals, charged them with illegally aiding the Theban conspirators, executed one, and exiled

44. Two popular leaders, Ismenias and Androcleidas, who had been hostile to Sparta, were accused of receiving bribes from Persia to the injury of Greece and were condemned in an obvious (and sorry) propaganda spectacle in which judges drawn from the various states of the Peloponnesian alliance presided over a show trial (Xen. *Hell.* 5. 2.35–36).

45. For a good summary, see R. J. Seager, "The King's Peace and the Balance of Power in Greece, 386–362 B.C.," *Athenaeum* 52 (1974): 44–47. Perhaps the most significant indication of how committed the Athenians were to this policy is the fact that when Sphodrias, the Spartan harmost at Thespiae, made his abortive raid against the Piraeus in 379, the port was still without gates (Xen. *Hell.* 5. 4.20); note also that Xenophon places the beginning of serious military preparations after the acquittal of Sphodrias (5. 4.34). Until then, Athens continued to trust in its existing policy (see Seager, 46–47). On Athens' application of this policy in its relations with Persia during this period, see 9.3.B below.

the other.[46] In all of this, the Athenians acted with extreme concern in order to demonstrate that they had not conspired with the Thebans and had no intention of joining in an alliance with them. Indeed, the occupation of Attic passes was not meant to be hostile to Sparta or to deter the Spartans from entering Boeotia but was merely a self-defensive precaution against the uncertainty of the moment.[47] But the irrefutable proof of innocence was supplied by the trial and punishment of the generals.

Diodorus unintentionally confirms this reconstruction, for in his account of these events he offers the contrary claim that the Athenians immediately allied themselves with Thebes and went in full force to the defense of the Thebans. This is obviously false, but it nevertheless reveals how ashamed of their true actions the Athenians were at a later date and how the record could be altered to provide a more noble lie. The less dramatic (and for some unacceptable) truth of the situation was that the Athenians sought to preserve the existing peace by demonstrating that they had intended to be and would definitely remain officially neutral in any conflict that arose between Sparta and Thebes.

V. THE NEUTRALITY CLAUSE IN THE FIRST COMMON PEACE OF 371

According to Xenophon, the peace treaty negotiated at Sparta in 371 included the following stipulation: "If any state should act in violation of this agreement, it was provided that any which so desired might aid the injured cities, *but that any which did not so desire was not under oath to be the ally of those who were injured*" (my italics).[48] This provision is the first official recognition of neutrality in the multilateral peace treaties of the fourth century and thus represents a landmark in the evolution of the role played by

46. The most detailed and trustworthy account is found in Xen. *Hell.* 5. 4.1–19; cf. Diod. 15. 25–27; Plut. *Pel.* 14.1.

47. This is an important point, the connection of which with the issue of neutrality was recognized by Marshall, *Second Athenian Confederacy*, 12, who commented: "Chabrias had indeed barred the road through Eleutherae against the army of Kleombrotos, but it was one thing to refuse a belligerent passage through neutral territory, another to recognize officially help given to Thebes by unauthorized generals."

48. Trans. Brownson: εἰ δέ τις παρὰ ταῦτα ποιοίη, τὸν μὲν βουλόμενον βοηθεῖν ταῖς ἀδικουμέναις πόλεσι, τῷ δὲ μὴ βουλομένῳ μὴ εἶναι ἔνορκον συμμαχεῖν τοῖς ἀδικουμένοις (Xen. *Hell.* 6. 3.18); see also Diod. 15. 50; Plut. *Ages.* 28; Aeschin. 2 (*On the Embassy*). 32; Dem. 9 (*Third Phil.*). 16.

neutrality in the diplomacy of that century. But why was it suddenly necessary to specify the right of neutrality in 371? What were the intentions of the participating states in their acceptance of such a provision? And what effect did the provision actually have on subsequent events? To answer these questions we need to examine the diplomatic and military situation that faced not simply the major Greek powers but also, wherever possible, the weaker states that existed in their shadows.

It has long been recognized that Athens was the state behind the inclusion of a neutrality clause in the peace treaty sworn at Sparta.[49] Athens' situation had become increasingly difficult during the 370s due on the one hand to Athens' failure to achieve a significant military victory over the Spartan alliance and on the other to its steadily deteriorating relations with Thebes, which raised the specter of war on a second front. For these reasons, the Athenians sought to gain through negotiation what they had been unable to achieve militarily. The problem was that the Athenians had to find a way to avoid giving the appearance either of surrendering the freedom of the Boeotian cities to Thebes by omission of them in the treaty or of betraying the interests of their own allies (and other states), who looked to Athens for leadership in the struggle against Spartan domination.[50] Accordingly, in the peace negotiations of 371, the Athenians used an adroit mixture of veiled promises and implied threats, which won acceptance of a treaty that permitted the signatory states to remain neutral during any conflicts arising from enforcement of the specific terms of the Common Peace.

The reality was that the Athenians proposed the neutrality clause to escape being obligated to enter a conflict with Thebes while there remained strong anti-Spartan feeling among their allies. This feeling made formal ratification of any agreement that even had the appearance of accommodation of the Spartans diplomatically dangerous, if not impossible, and made the neutrality clause a

49. Xen. *Hell.* 6. 3.1–3; see G. E. Underhill and E. C. Marchant, *Commentary on Xenophon's* Hellenika (Oxford, 1906), 236–37, to be preferred to Diod. 15. 50. See, among others, F. Hampl, *Die Griechische Staatsverträge des 4. Jahrhunderts v. Christ Geb.* (Leipzig, 1938; reprint, Rome, 1966), 105; Underhill and Marchant, 240; T. T. B. Ryder, "Athenian Foreign Policy and the Peace Conference at Sparta in 371 B.C.," *CQ* 13 (1963): 237–41; id., *Koine Eirene,* 64–69; Buckler, *Theban Hegemony,* 49–51; Seager, "The King's Peace and the Balance of Power in Greece, 386–362 B.C.," 50–53.

50. So Seager, "The King's Peace and the Balance of Power in Greece, 386–362 B.C."

necessary and defensible solution. The Spartans accepted the clause because they were confident that the Athenians would use this legal pretext to avoid any involvement if the Spartans themselves accused Thebes of wrongdoing and attacked. As for the Thebans, they accepted the clause because they saw in it the potential for greater freedom to pursue an aggressive foreign policy in Boeotia without necessarily facing a coalition of opposing states, since they fully expected Athens to invoke the clause and remain neutral in any subsequent conflict.[51]

As we have seen before (in 5.3.B and 6.7 above, for example), interstate agreements acknowledging a formal right of neutrality repeatedly prove to be connected with the self-interests of the major powers, who obviously viewed neutrality as a convenient face-saving device, permitting them to pursue their own foreign policy goals under the aegis of agreed diplomatic rules. This is especially clear in 371, for the neutrality clause arises directly from the politics of the powerful states and not from the aspirations of weaker would-be bystanders. But while this may be true, once accepted, the neutrality clause nevertheless provided, by extension, a new legal foundation for the international relations of all the participating states in succeeding conflicts. T. T. B. Ryder rightly emphasizes that the clause represents a crucial advance from the two previous Common Peace treaties (of 386 and 375/374) because the earlier treaties contained no reference to the role of all participating states in the guarantee of peace and therefore provided no clear definition of the obligation of a state in the event of a conflict between other states.[52] In contrast, the first Common Peace of 371 not only specified exactly how enforcement would be carried out but also protected the right of any state to remain aloof from the process of enforcement. By guaranteeing this freedom of choice, the treaty thus formally legalized and institutionalized the neutrality of any state that formally accepted the peace.

Nor is this merely modern speculation, for there is perfectly clear contemporary evidence that the potential impact of the neutrality clause was immediately recognized. In his narrative of the

---

51. For an excellent interpretation of the diplomacy behind the speeches of the Athenian ambassadors at Sparta (Xen. *Hell.* 6. 3.3–17), followed here, see Ryder, "Athenian Foreign Policy and the Peace Conference at Sparta in 371 B.C.," 237–41 (summarized in id., Koine Eirene, 65).

52. Ryder, Koine Eirene, 68.

immediate aftermath of the peace, Xenophon states that when
Cleombrotus sent from Phocis to ask the authorities at Sparta what
to do about the army that he had with him, a Spartan named
Prothous made the following proposal:

> They ought first to disband the army in accordance with their oaths
> and send round word to the various cities to make contributions,
> as large as each city chose to make, to the temple of Apollo, and
> afterwards, in case anyone tried to prevent the cities from being
> independent, *to call together again at that time all who wished to
> support the cause of independence* and lead them against those who
> opposed it; for ... in this way the gods would be most favourably
> inclined toward them and the cities would be least annoyed (my
> italics).[53]

The Spartan *ekklesia*, which Xenophon characterizes as driven by
fate (*to daimonion*), rejected this advice as utter nonsense and
ordered Cleombrotus instead to lead his army immediately against
the Thebans. And so Cleombrotus marched to Leuctra.[54] But what
about the advice of Prothous? Surely it indicates that the neutrality
clause was taken seriously in more states than just Athens. The
less powerful states, which had labored so long under the yoke of
Sparta's hegemony, especially must have welcomed the stipulated
option of neutrality as tantamount to confirmation of their right
to determine for themselves whether or not they would contribute
to Sparta's continued foreign policy ventures.

Equally clear, however, was the Spartans' determination to resist
any interpretation of the neutrality clause that interfered with their
continued dictation of the foreign policy of their allies. For Sparta,

---

53. Trans. Brownson.

Προθόου λέξαντος ὅτι αὐτῷ δοκοίη διαλύσαντας τὸ στράτευμα κατὰ τοὺς
ὅρκους καὶ περιαγγείλαντας ταῖς πόλεσι συμβαλέσθαι εἰς τὸν ναὸν τοῦ
Ἀπόλλωνος ὁπόσον βούλοιτο ἑκάστη πόλις, ἔπειτα εἰ μή τις ἐῴη αὐτονόμους
τὰς πόλεις εἶναι, τότε πάλιν παρακαλέσαντας ὅσοι τῇ αὐτονομίᾳ βού-
λοιντο βοηθεῖν, ἄγειν ἐπὶ τοὺς ἐναντιουμένους· οὕτω γὰρ ἂν ἔφη οἴεσθαι
τούς τε θεοὺς εὐμενεστάτους εἶναι καὶ τὰς πόλεις ἥκιστ' ἂν
ἄχθεσθαι·   (Xen. Hell. 6. 4.2)

54. Xen. *Hell.* 6. 4.3. Prothous was a Laconian whom Plutarch also mentions
as opposing the expedition against Thebes (*Ages.* 28.4). Prothous may not have
been the only Spartan willing to accept the idea that the treaty placed new
limitations on Sparta's hegemony. King Cleombrotus had no enthusiasm for a
policy (continuously urged by Agesilaus) of aggression against Thebes and
attempted up until the eve of the battle at Leuctra to achieve a negotiated
settlement—efforts reportedly scorned by the Spartans who accompanied him in
the field (*Hell.* 5. 4.16, 25; 6. 4.2–3, 5; cf. Polyb. 9. 23; Diod. 15. 51; Nep. *Epam.*
6; Plut. *Ages.* 26).

the role of leader had fossilized. No true flexibility could be realized, since even recognition of the need for reorganization and reform of Sparta's foreign policy was unthinkable for the vainglorious Spartan majority. Instead, the Spartan leadership continued to allow self-interest to dictate policy and flatly denied that there could be any question of rights as long as the power existed to coerce obedience from their allies. Anything else, they believed, was simpleminded nonsense. Yet the fact remains that the international situation *was* evolving. Neutrality looked increasingly attractive to weaker states, and they wanted the hegemonial powers to accept it. For their part, the leading states seem to have been surprisingly slow to recognize that once they approved neutrality in an interstate agreement as all-encompassing as a Common Peace, this right could not easily be restricted to the major powers alone. Instead, the concept of neutrality as legitimate for all states, regardless of military power, was strengthened and, as events proved, was becoming increasingly difficult for the greater powers to deny and dismiss.

SUMMARY

During the thirty-five years from 406 to 371 diplomacy was in turmoil, and the position of states attempting to remain uncommitted during the conflicts of the period was shaken by uncertainty. At the beginning there was, it appeared, virtually no remaining trust in the reliability of traditional diplomatic assurances. In 406 Acragas abandoned its long-standing neutrality, despite Carthaginian pledges to respect the policy. Between ca. 403 and 399 Thebes, Corinth, and even Athens attempted to resist Spartan military adventurism by refusing to participate, but they soon discovered that the policy was unworkable in the face of Sparta's increasingly hostile attitude. Still, during the resulting Corinthian War (395–386), Corinth itself, Aegina, Megara, Phlius, and Mantinea all sought to sidestep the conflict through a variety of methods, ranging from traditional to highly unorthodox.

In 383 Thebes adopted a carefully noncommittal stance when Sparta embarked on a war with the Thracian Chalcidians, only to have the Theban acropolis treacherously seized by a passing Spartan commander. In 379 the Athenians categorically denied that there had been any official involvement in the insurrection against Spar-

tan occupation of Thebes and even tried the two generals accused
of providing assistance to the Theban exiles. Rhetoric and demon-
strations of innocence aside, the Athenians also immediately occupied the passes on the Attic frontier against any Spartan aggression.

Throughout all of these incidents the absence of a predictable
pattern of diplomatic behavior among both the belligerents and the
would-be neutrals is striking. On the surface it looks as if, diplomatically speaking, the states were suffering from a breakdown in
confidence, which resulted in a confused succession of ad hoc
responses to specific circumstances that did not adhere in any
consistent way to customary rules and restraints of interstate behavior. As Plato despaired in the *Laws*, the international situation
appeared to have degenerated to the sorry point where all men
were continuously hostile to one another and every city was in a
permanent state of war with every other.[55] This is indeed a grim
characterization; but is it accurate?

Discouraging though much of it is, the evidence provided by
incidents involving efforts to secure a neutral position does not in
fact prove that there had been a complete collapse of the traditional
authority of diplomatic rules. The Hobbesian state of nature
described by Plato is largely imaginary. At the same time that
customary diplomatic rules were being ignored and broken in a
succession of well-documented (and notorious) cases, pressure for
the restoration of their authority was also building steadily in the
background and can be glimpsed in the historical record. To begin
with, in virtually every instance of failed neutrality discussed in
this chapter there exists an implicit contrast between the expectation that abstention would be a legitimate and acceptable policy
and the failure of that expectation to be realized. Take the incident
in 406. We do not actually know whether the Carthaginian offer
to respect Agrigentine neutrality was merely a specious ploy to
divide opposition or was made in good faith. On the other hand,
we do know that throughout the period states sought to abstain

55. Pl. *Laws* 626A, quoted above in 3.2, with note 33. This statement by Plato,
written near the end of his life, reflects Plato's personal reaction to the nearly
ceaseless warfare of his lifetime and its detrimental consequences for diplomatic
alternatives to the dichotomy of friend or enemy. Unfortunately, some scholars,
such as Martin, *La vie internationale*, 577–94, have mistakenly taken this to be
literally true as a description of interstate relations throughout the classical period;
see 3.2 above for discussion of the presence and force of *agraphoi nomoi* in
classical diplomacy.

from conflicts and must have hoped, with some degree of confidence, that the policy would succeed; the examples of the Asiatic states freed in 394, the Theban government in 383, the framers of the first Common Peace in 371 support this.[56] These repeated incidents of stubborn insistence that remaining uncommitted was not an act of hostility or betrayal but only a reasonable course, defensible within the traditional rules of interstate diplomacy, have to be set against the list of failures. Moreover, at least in the case of the Megarians, a neutral policy seems to have been the formal and successful diplomatic attitude assumed throughout the conflicts of the period.

Much of the distortion that obscures our understanding of the true diplomatic situation in the early fourth century can be traced to the combination of inadequate treatment and negative attitude in the sources. Xenophon, in particular, presents a highly subjective account of the period that is narrowly focused on the mainland Greek adventures of Sparta, whose uncompromisingly aggressive foreign policy he rarely questions, let alone criticizes, even when Sparta is blatantly guilty of violating basic rules of interstate behavior.[57] In his narrative the policies of Megara, the Asiatic Greek states, Corinth, Thebes, and Athens are all treated with virtually no interest in the underlying diplomatic rights and obligations or in the relationship between the policies that were customarily accepted and those that had to be created specifically to meet the realities of the period. Worse still, in places where objective reporting of the facts would reveal much about the dynamics of interstate diplomacy at the time, Xenophon manipulates the evidence, especially through selective omission, in a transparent effort to provide a version of events that supports Spartan policy.[58]

56. On Carthage, see 8.1 above; the Asiatic Greeks, 8.3.F; Thebes, 8.4.B; the first Common Peace of 371, 8.5.
57. See the discussion of sources in chapter 2.
58. Take, for instance, the biased version of Phoebidas' seizure of the Theban acropolis in 383 and its aftermath (see 8.4.B above). The recent attempt by V. Gray, *The Character of Xenophon's* Hellenica (London, 1989), to defend Xenophon (including such comments as "Negative characterisations of the work, based on the expectation that he should be writing like Thucydides but is not, are all too easy" [2] and "My own approach is not to criticise Xenophon for failing to do what he never intended" [63 n. 7]) totally ignores the fact of Xenophon's willful distortion of historical events. Even if Xenophon's purpose is to demonstrate the working of moral principles in human history (Gray, 180), the criticism remains valid, and the problems created for serious historical investigation of the period cannot be simply brushed aside and ignored.

Unfortunately, the other sources, most notably Diodorus, provide very little independent information about diplomacy. Only the short fragment of the Oxyrhynchus historian contains serious diplomatic analysis (see 8.2 above), which is all the more valuable because it contrasts sharply with—and thus highlights vividly—the other sources' comparative lack of interest in or disregard for the details of diplomacy.

Despite these serious problems and the difficulties they create for reconstructing the diplomacy of the early fourth century, it would be wrong to accept Plato's despairing characterization of international life—universal hostility subject to no rules—as a permanent condition. The guaranteed right of neutrality included in the first Common Peace of 371 was neither an unprecedented diplomatic mirage nor an intentional sham. Currents of support for the recognition of and respect for abstaining parties can be detected throughout these years. Far from giving up in Platonic despair, a number of states continued to pursue alternative postures to the strict dichotomy of friends or enemies. It was indeed a difficult period, but it was not devoid of successful neutral policy and ended with the issue of abstention from interstate conflict squarely at the center of diplomatic reality.

CHAPTER NINE

From the Battle at Leuctra to the Victory of Philip II at Chaeronea (371–338)

The Spartan defeat at Leuctra brought the question of neutrality to the forefront of interstate politics. From the moment that the true extent of Sparta's losses became known, a new order of interstate allegiances began to emerge in which neutrality was a more frequently sought-after option, despite vigorous efforts by the leading states to suppress it. Between 371 and 338 there is a sharp increase in the number of states withdrawing from alliances and refusing to participate further in the continued warfare between the hegemonial states.

I. THE SECOND COMMON PEACE OF 371 AND ITS AFTERMATH

As expected, Athens took advantage of the neutrality clause in the Common Peace of 371 and held aloof during the Spartan invasion of Boeotia, which ended in a disastrous defeat at Leuctra. But the unexpected Theban victory caused an immediate change in Athenian policy. Neutrality was abandoned and, in a stunning reversal of diplomatic principle, the newly recognized right of neutrality was specifically repealed from the terms of a revised Common Peace sworn soon after the battle.[1] With the exception of Elis, the states present accepted the following oath: "I will abide by the

---

1. Xen. *Hell.* 6. 5.1; Bengtson, *SVA²* no. 270. On the absence of the Thebans and Jason, see Ryder, Koine Eirene, 131–33; Buckler, *Theban Hegemony*, 68.

terms of peace that the king sent down and the decrees of the Athenians and their allies; and *if anyone marches against any city of those having sworn this oath, I will bring aid with all my strength*" (my italics).[2] Here then, within a few months of swearing a Common Peace at Sparta (i.e., the first Common Peace of 371) that expressly freed the participating states from any obligation to aid one another if the peace were violated, virtually all of the same states accepted a new treaty whose oath explicitly precluded the right to remain neutral. But why? Why did the participating states reverse the landmark position they had adopted just a short time before?

Recent explanations of the reversal have differed more in emphasis than in concept. Ryder, for example, calls the repeal of the right of neutrality a "natural development" from an optional to a compulsory guarantee of peace, in which the participants committed themselves to be the guarantors but did not consider this commitment to be in any sense the formation of an alliance (*symmachia*) between signatories. In his view, the reason for the prohibition was that the Peloponnesian states needed security and the Athenians hoped to exact concessions from Sparta that would win prestige for their own state and at the same time strengthen the Peloponnesian alliance's ability to withstand an attack by Thebes.[3]

J. Buckler, on the other hand, contends that the compulsory assistance clause in fact "turned the peace into a virtual defensive alliance, with the Thebans as the unspoken enemies."[4] In his view the clause was the result of the Athenians' unwillingness to defend

---

2. Ἐμμενῶ ταῖς σπονδαῖς ἃς βασιλεὺς κατέπεμψε καὶ τοῖς ψηφίσμασι τοῖς Ἀθηναίων καὶ τῶν συμμάχων. ἐὰν δέ τις στρατεύῃ ἐπί τινα πόλιν τῶν ὀμοσασῶν τόνδε τὸν ὅρκον, βοηθήσω παντὶ σθένει (Xen. *Hell.* 6. 5.1). For a detailed discussion, see Ryder, Koine Eirene, 71–74, 131–33, who follows M. Sordi, "La pace di Atene de 371–370 a.c.," *RivFil* 29 (1951): 53, in explaining "the decrees of the Athenians and their allies" as those adopted at the foundation of the Second Athenian League and recorded on the decree of Aristoteles (Tod, no. 123; Bengtson *SVA²* no. 257), which defined and guaranteed the freedom and autonomy of the members. Xenophon (*Hell.* 6. 5.2) says that the Eleans refused to swear to the peace because they claimed the right to recover Margane, Scillus, and Triphylia. These border communities had been separated from Elis by the Spartans after the war of ca. 402–400 (*Hell.* 3. 2.30–31), but the Eleans had never renounced their claim to them.

3. Ryder, Koine Eirene, 72–73; Ryder rightly rejects the older view of Marshall, *Second Athenian Confederacy*, 78–81, that the oath of compulsory defense proves Athens was attempting to secure Peloponnesian states as new members of the confederacy.

4. Buckler, *Theban Hegemony*, 68–69.

the peace alone, together with their concern that its integrity be guaranteed by all participating states.

The differences between these interpretations are not as great as they might seem. In fact, their basic assumptions are identical. In both versions, the basic premise is that the major powers were primarily responsible for determining the specific form of the post-Leuctra peace. However, if the terms are viewed from the perspective of the central issue, that is, whether the option of neutrality would be legitimate, the terms of the second Common Peace of 371 appear, on the contrary, to be the result of forces that originated with the subordinate allies rather than with the hegemonial states.

There is considerable evidence that Xenophon seriously distorts the truth of the situation when he implies that it was out of loyalty to Sparta that the members of the Peloponnesian alliance eagerly rushed to join the relief army that Archidamus mustered immediately after the defeat at Leuctra (*Hell.* 6.4.18). In the first place, Xenophon's own narrative contradicts such a view. In his description of the aftermath of the defeat at Leuctra, he explains, somewhat apologetically, that the surviving Spartan officers decided not to risk further engagement with the Thebans in part because of the poor morale of their allies. All are said to be without heart, and some not even displeased by the disaster (*Hell.* 6.4.15). Plutarch emphasizes this view of the allies in his remark that when they were called upon to continue the war just prior to Leuctra, they were reluctant and felt heavily burdened, although they did not yet have the courage to oppose or disobey the Spartans (*Ages.* 28.3; cf. the speech of Prothous quoted above in 8.5 with note 53).

Worse still for Sparta, in Xenophon's own account, Jason of Pherae revealed that following the defeat at Leuctra certain of the allies had begun negotiations regarding friendship (*peri philias*) with the Thebans (*Hell.* 6.4.24). This is an especially important revelation, because, as we have found, in Greek diplomacy *philia* is often linked with neutral policy.[5] Thus, if Sparta's allies entered into a *philia* with Thebes, they might use this relationship both to protect themselves from Theban retaliation and to refuse to fight against Thebes. What is misleading here is Xenophon's later asser-

5. On the connection between *philia* and neutrality, see 3.4 above (generally) and 9.4.B below (the fourth-century Persian-Greek relationship). On the specific term *peri philias* in a diplomatic sense, see 7.4 above, especially note 40 (on Thuc. 6.88.6).

tion that Sparta's allies rushed zealously to join the relief army. But since there are clear indications that resistance to Sparta's leadership was building, surely the correct story, distorted by Xenophon, must have been that the allies rushed (if they did so) not to bolster the Spartans but to protect surviving contingents of their own fellow citizens. It follows that Xenophon's assertion really says nothing reliable about the attitude of the allies toward Sparta or toward their responsibility to the Peloponnesian alliance. And once this distortion is revealed for what it is, Xenophon's credibility collapses, and there remains no evidence for refuting the idea that the Athenians were actually responding to unrest among the allied states when the neutrality clause was inserted in the first Common Peace and reacting in the second Common Peace to allied agitation (now plainly visible in their negotiations with Thebes) by guaranteeing military assistance if the subordinate states remained loyal to their former alliance.[6]

The foremost concern of the states that ratified the peace treaty at Athens was, obviously, fear of Thebes.[7] For the Athenians

6. See Ryder, Koine Eirene, 74. The argument here could be further strengthened if we accepted the interpretation of Sordi, "La pace di Atene de 371–370 a.c.," 56–58, who takes akoulouthein in Hell. 6. 5.1 absolutely ("[the allies] were in need of a leader") and accepts the emendation of houtō for oupō (see the critical note in E. C. Marchant's Oxford Classical Text, doubted by Grote, History of Greece, vol. 8, 191 n. 2, and rejected by Marshall, Second Athenian Confederacy, 78 n. 2). These changes produce an important shift in the meaning from "the Athenians calculated that the Peloponnesians still felt obliged to follow Sparta, and that Sparta was not yet in the same sort of position as she had put Athens in [in 404 B.C.]" (trans. Wickersham and Verbrugghe, Greek Historical Documents, 58) to "the Athenians calculated that the Peloponnesians still felt in need of a leader and that the Spartans were in such a position as they had put the Athenians in [in 404]" (my translation). The latter fits neatly with the argument made here that Sparta's allies were increasingly unwilling to follow wherever the Spartans might lead. However, it cannot be pushed too far, because the resulting statement is inconsistent with Xenophon's attempts elsewhere (as in his remarks concerning the allies' strong support of the relief army) to minimize the decline in Sparta's authority and to disguise in ambiguity the true nature of Sparta's relationship with its allies. Regardless of what the truth may have been, Xenophon was almost certainly not ready to go as far as Sordi's interpretation takes him. On Xenophon's attitude toward neutrality specifically, see chapter 2.

7. Buckler, Theban Hegemony, 68–69; cf. Ryder, Koine Eirene, 76; Bengtson, SVA² no. 270, all of whom emphasize this point. Beloch, Griechische Geschichte, vol. 3A, 173, saw the new treaty primarily as Athens' attempt to supplant Sparta as the leader of the Peloponnesian states. Marshall, Second Athenian Confederacy, 79, equivocates. It is, however, hard to believe that an aggressive foreign policy offensive aimed at further humiliation of Sparta and expanded hegemony were behind the Athenians' push for a new treaty. Basic protection of the autonomy and freedom of member states was the foundation of the Athenian Confederacy, not Athenian hegemonial ambition (J. Cargill, The Second Athenian League: Empire or Free Alliance? [Berkeley, Los Angeles, and London, 1981], 1–3).

especially, the Theban victory at Leuctra was the cause of immediate consternation. The Theban messenger who was sent to announce the victory and to call upon the Athenians to join with Thebes in taking revenge on Sparta caused such distress that the *Boulē* failed even to offer him the usual hospitality (*Hell.* 6. 4.19–20). Thebes was the real danger to Athens, and the Athenians knew it. They also seem to have realized, contrary to what is generally believed by modern scholars, that Sparta's defeat offered greater risk than opportunity to Athens.[8] An important reason for this was that the very policy that appeared to serve Athens' diplomatic aims perfectly in the first peace treaty of 371—the recognized right to neutrality—had now, in the wake of Sparta's unexpected defeat, become potentially catastrophic for Athens in the event of a land war with the Boeotians. The Athenians knew that they were no match for the Thebans, especially since Thebes was supported by a powerful ally, Jason of Pherae;[9] and yet the neutrality clause meant that none of the land powers capable of bringing critical aid to Athens in the event of a land-based attack were under any obligation to do so.

The Spartans, on the other hand, faced potentially catastrophic consequences if the terms of the first Common Peace were left standing.[10] Their control over the Peloponnesian alliance, and possibly even their own security, would clearly be endangered. If the allies appealed to the neutrality clause and refused to participate in further campaigns, the hegemonial position of Sparta could be destroyed. As recently as the first Common Peace of 371, Sparta swore on behalf of its allies and clearly expected their continued obedience. But by the time of the second conference, Leuctra had

8. Modern accounts (see note 7 above) tend to discuss only the perceived opportunity for Athens and fail entirely to consider the very dangerous situation that Athens' weakness as a land power created. Representative of the prevailing consensus is Hammond, *History of Greece*, 495, who observes: "Athens, hoping to make political capital out of Sparta's defeat, summoned a conference of all states which wished to maintain the King's Peace of 371."

9. For Jason's formal alignment with Thebes at this time, see Buckler, *Theban Hegemony*, 65–69; for the more complicated evidence surrounding his nominally hostile relations with Athens, see Cargill, *Second Athenian League*, 83–87.

10. Unfortunately, Xenophon is the only source for this conference and peace, and he fails to mention Sparta. For this reason some have doubted Spartan participation (e.g., Marshall, *Second Athenian Confederacy*, 80). However, Xenophon's narrative of later events clearly assumes that Sparta accepted this peace and felt bound by its terms; see *Hell.* 6. 5.5, 10, 36–37, defended by, among others, Hampl, *Griechische Staatsverträge*, 20 n. 1; Sordi, "La pace di Atene de 371–370 a.c.," 34; and Ryder, Koine Eirene, 71–72.

intervened, and the situation was radically different. There are some indications that the loyalty of Sicyon and Pellene had already deteriorated;[11] and Elis did not hesitate not only to renew its claims to territory taken away by the Spartans at the beginning of the century but also to remain outside of the peace in order to prosecute those claims in defiance of Sparta. For Xenophon, who was always reluctant to draw attention to Sparta's failings, the situation surrounding the conference at Athens seems to have presented such intolerable difficulties that he simply omitted any mention at all of Spartan presence or participation in either the conference or the resulting Common Peace.

Concerning states other than Sparta and Athens, Xenophon says that with the exception of the Eleans all of those represented at Athens "were delighted" with the new peace terms (echairon tō horkō, Hell. 6. 5.2). If there was any reason for the mainland Greek states and particularly the members of the Peloponnesian alliance to rejoice in the new agreement, it surely arose not from the elimination of the neutrality clause of the earlier treaty but from the formal acceptance by Sparta of the principles of autonomy and independence characterized by the new treaty's reference to the "decrees of the Athenians and their allies." From the beginning of the new confederacy in 378, Athens had been at pains to erase the bitter memory of fifth-century imperial policies by emphasizing its commitment to the terms of the King's Peace and by reassuring both member and prospective member states that it would not interfere in their internal affairs or impose upon them garrisons, governors, or tribute.[12] For the Spartans to accept these limitations

---

11. Sicyon's loyalty may have crumbled during the 370s. The state was rocked by an abortive democratic revolution in 375/374 (Diod. 15. 40.4), is absent from the list of Spartan allies in 374 (Xen. Hell. 6. 2.3), was present during the fighting in 370 (Hell. 7. 2.2; cf. 6. 5.29), appears to have formally renounced its alliance with Sparta in 369 (see Underhill and Marchant, Commentary on Xenophon's Hellenika, 272, on Hell. 7. 1.18), is attacked by Sicilian forces sent to aid Sparta in 369 (Hell. 7. 1.22), and is counted among hostile states in 367/366 (Hell. 7. 1.44, 2.2, 2.11; cf. Paus. 6. 3.3). Xenophon's claim that the Peloponnesian states (including Sicyon) participated enthusiastically in the relief force that hurried north after Leuctra has been questioned already (see 8.5 above; cf. A. Griffin, Sikyon [Oxford, 1982]; C. H. Skalet, Ancient Sicyon with a Prosopographia Sicyonia [Baltimore, 1928], 72). Note too that Pellene abandoned the Spartan alliance during the course of 369 (Hell. 7. 2.2, 11; cf. 6. 5.29).
12. See the clear statement of this pledge in the confederacy charter (Bengtson, SVA² no. 377; Tod, no. 123, lines 15–23: "If anyone wishes, of the Greeks or of the barbarians living on the mainland, or of the islanders, whoever do not belong to the King, to be an ally of the Athenians and of their allies, it shall be permitted

formally must have been viewed as more than full compensation for the loss of what was, after all, a hollow right to neutrality, given the unresolved threat of hostility from Thebes and the hegemonial states' long-standing refusal to accept and abide by any limitations to their aggressive foreign policy ambitions.

The Peloponnesian states' increased confidence is reflected in such contemporary events as the Mantineans' immediate reoccupation and restoration of the city destroyed by Sparta in 385, the antioligarchic revolution at Argos that occurred at this time, and, of course, the independent and confrontational policies of the Eleans and Arcadians.[13] Neutrality in future conflicts may have been sacrificed under certain circumstances, but the right of any state to pursue even this policy could not help but be strengthened by the leading states' formal acceptance of wide-ranging limitations on their freedom to coerce the weak. If Xenophon's claim about the high spirits of the participants is reliable, it was not the repeal of the neutrality clause but the formal recognition of rights previously withheld from Sparta's allies that inspired enthusiasm.

II. NEUTRALITY DURING THE THEBAN HEGEMONY (370/369–362)

A. DEBATE AT ATHENS (WINTER 370/369)

When the Athenians abstained from involving themselves during the Theban invasion of the Peloponnesus in the late fall of 370, the

---

to him, being free and autonomous, governing himself according to the constitution which he prefers, neither receiving a garrison nor accepting a governor nor paying tribute" [trans. Cargill, *Second Athenian League*, 19]). For a detailed reassessment of the evidence for Athens' compliance with its rhetoric, see Cargill, 131–60, who concludes: "In fact, this entire ... survey of Athenian performance on the promises of the decree of Aristoteles ... shows that those promises were kept. The Athenians swore to abandon the imperialist policies of the fifth century, and they adhered to their word" (160).

13. Xenophon (*Hell.* 6. 5.3–5) says specifically that the Mantineans were reacting to the terms of the peace. Diodorus, who does not mention the peace conference at Athens, is the only source on the *stasis* at Argos, which he places in 370 (15. 57.3–58.4) and attributes to the democratic government's desire to eliminate wealthy opponents (i.e., the political force that would typically have used fear of Sparta to moderate the more radical policies of the democracy). It is noteworthy that Argive refugees are said to be serving in the Spartan army during the following year (15. 62.1). On Elean and Arcadian policies at this time, see Xen. *Hell.* 6. 5.3, 5–9; Diod. 15. 59.1–3. Notice that the Spartans staunchly defended their eventual military intervention at Tegea as justified within the letter of the peace treaty (*Hell.* 6. 5.36).

question of whether this policy was justified in light of the recent peace treaty's obligatory assistance clause became a matter of public debate reported in detail by Xenophon (*Hell.* 6. 5.33–48). According to Xenophon, an embassy from Sparta and its remaining allies appealed to Athens for help against the Theban invasion and included prominently among their supporting arguments that the Athenians were required by the oath of the peace treaty to come to their aid (5.36). This, together with the Corinthians' appeal, is said to have convinced the Athenians to commit themselves and send aid to Sparta (5.49).

Left unmentioned in Xenophon's reconstruction is the likely influence of fear that any further aggrandizement of Thebes could lead to disaster for Athens, especially if increased Theban strength were combined with the inevitable isolation of Athens that would result from further abstention. Also, the Athenians' duty to uphold the terms of the treaty that they themselves had accepted the previous year could not easily be disavowed, despite charges of Spartan misbehavior, without promoting even further erosion of faith in international agreements. Athens could not remain neutral; and it is extraordinary to learn that they seriously debated the issue.

B. ACHAEAN NEUTRALITY PRIOR TO 367/366

In a close study of Achaean policy after Leuctra, M. Cary argues that support of Sparta was short-lived (the Achaeans supplied no aid during the campaign of 370/369, for example) and that "in the early sixties [the Achaeans] remained consistently neutral."[14] In 367, however, the Theban general Epaminondas reportedly decided that if the Achaeans could be compelled to accept an alliance, the consequential threat of military support from Achaea could be used to exert greater control over Thebes' other Peloponnesian allies. This plan brought about a dramatic change in Achaean policy.

14. M. Cary, "The Alleged Achaean Arbitration after Leuctra," *CQ* 19 (1925): 165–66. Cary answers the criticisms put forth by Grote, *History of Greece*, vol. 8, 189, and E. von Stern, "Geschichte der spartanischen und thebanischen Hegemonie" (Diss., Dorpat, 1884), 154–55. On Achaean foreign policy during the period, see Xen. *Hell.* 4. 6.1–5.1.1; Diod. 15. 75.2; Plut. *Ages.* 22.5 on activities in northwestern Greece; *Hell.* 4. 2.18; Diod. 15. 31.2 on Achaea as an ally of Sparta; *Hell.* 6. 4.18 on the relief force in 371; Polyb. 2. 39.9 on Achaean arbitration after Leuctra; cf. Strabo 8. 7.1 (384); Piccirilli, *Arbitrati*, vol. 1, no. 42; Walbank, *Commentary on Polybius*, vol. 1, 226–27.

Our understanding of these events is based on Xenophon's un-
usually detailed account of the accompanying diplomacy. He
reports that when Epaminondas followed up on his strategy to
coerce Achaean allegiance and marched into the northwestern Peloponnesus, the ruling aristocrats in Achaea agreed to an alliance in
which they pledged to "follow wherever the Thebans led" on the
conditions that the Thebans not interfere in the internal politics of
the cities or banish any of the leading citizens. These terms were
allegedly accepted by Epaminondas but immediately criticized by
certain Arcadians and exiled Achaeans who complained that the
arrangement favored Sparta, since it left the Achaean aristocrats in
control (the aristocrats, presumably, being pro-Spartan). The
Theban government is said to have been convinced by these arguments. It disregarded the agreement made by Epaminondas, installed harmosts and garrisons in the Achaean cities, and supported
democratic revolutions that banished the aristocratic leadership.
The whole Theban intervention subsequently failed, however,
because the exiled aristocrats organized themselves, attacked the
cities individually, and expelled the Theban garrisons. In conclusion
Xenophon adds that "after their restoration, the Achaean aristocrats no longer pursued a neutral course, but fought eagerly in
support of the Spartans."[15] This is one place where Xenophon has
been truly helpful and supplied an especially valuable glimpse of
the complex workings of contemporary policy making. Nevertheless, even if Xenophon did not specifically say that the Achaeans
were neutral up to the time of the Theban intervention, we might
otherwise have identified their policy not only from their selection

15. ἐπεὶ δὲ κατελθόντες οὐκέτι ἐμέσευον, ἀλλὰ προθύμως συνεμάχουν τοῖς Λακεδαιμονίοις (Xen. Hell. 7.1.43). On the invasion, see Xen. Hell. 7. 1.41–43; Diod.
15. 75.2; on the resulting alliance; Bengtson, SVA[2] no. 283; for the date, Beloch,
Griechische Geschichte, vol. 3, part 2, 241–42; Ryder, Koine Eirene, 170–72,
followed here. Diodorus' account differs in two important points from that of
Xenophon: (1) Epaminondas is said to have won over (MSS prosēgageto; Wesseling
prosēgagen) the Achaeans and (2) liberated (ēleutherōsen) Dyme, Naupactus, and
Calydon, which were garrisoned by the Achaeans. The second point adds valuable
information (which Xenophon omits) suggesting that Thebes also had territorial
ambitions: Dyme is in Achaea, but Naupactus and Calydon are in Aetolia (Jacoby,
FGH 65, Daemachus frag. 1). However, the first point is misleading since Diodorus
says nothing of the nearly immediate repudiation of the alliance by the Achaeans
(but cf. 15. 85.2, where they are hostile). On the invasion, see Buckler, Theban
Hegemony 185–93. However, his assertion that the Achaeans were Spartan allies
at the time of the invasion ignores the upheaval within the Peloponnesian alliance,
which had been going on since 371, and is contradicted by Xenophon's clear
testimony.

as arbitrators after Leuctra[16] but also from the following circumstantial evidence.

When the Thebans intervened in the Peloponnesus at the beginning of the winter of 370/369, the opposing allies are listed in the sources. The Achaeans are nowhere mentioned.[17] In fact, until Epaminondas implemented his plan to use the Achaeans as an instrument of Theban ambition in the Peloponnesus, there is no evidence that the Achaeans participated in the warfare of the early 360s or that any of the belligerents objected to their abstention.[18] The Spartans were not in a position to force their allegiance, and the Arcadian-Elean-Argive alliance may well have considered Achaean neutrality a blessing, since the geographical position occupied by the Achaeans to the north (and therefore on the opposite side of the Peloponnesus from Sparta) made them a potentially

16. See note 14 above. Note that Athens urged Sparta and Thebes to settle their differences through arbitration as early as 395 (Paus. 3. 9.11; Piccirilli, *Arbitrati*, vol. 1, no. 34).

17. For the Spartan allies, see Xen. *Hell.* 7. 1.1; Diod. 15. 67.1; Bengtson, *SVA*[2] no. 274 on Athens; see *Hell.* 7. 1.20; cf. 7. 1.28; Isoc. 6 [*Archid.*]. 62 on Dionysius of Syracuse; see *Hell.* 7. 2.2; cf. 6. 5.29 on Corinth, Epidaurus, Troezen, Hermione, Halieis, Sicyon, Pellene; but on Sicyon, see *Hell.* 7. 2.11 and note 15 above. For the Theban allies, see Diod. 15. 62.3; cf. Dem. 16 (*Megalop.*). 27; Bengtson, *SVA*[2] no. 273 on the Arcadian League; see *Hell.* 7. 5.4; Bengtson, *SVA*[2] no. 271 on the Phocians; *Hell.* 6. 5.22-23 on the Euboeans, Locrians, Acarnanians, Heracleots, Malians; *Hell.* 7. 1.18 on Elis, Argos.

18. See, for instance, E. Meyer, *Geschichte des Altertums*, vol. 5, new ed. (Stuttgart, 1937–39), 433; Beloch, *Griechische Geschichte*, vol. 3, part 1, 187; J. Roy, "Arcadia and Boeotia in Peloponnesian Affairs, 370–362 B.C.," *Historia* 20 (1971): 579. Contrary to the argument here and the consensus of earlier scholars, Buckler, *Theban Hegemony*, 187, denies that the Achaeans were neutral at the time of the Theban invasion. In his view, the Achaeans were still considered allies of Sparta and the Theban attack thus was justified because there is no evidence that the Achaeans ever separately concluded a formal peace with Thebes. For this reason, he concludes that despite "their relative inactivity after Leuktra, which did not technically constitute neutrality, they were still legally at war with the Boeotian Confederacy." The flaw in this argument is its rejection of the clear and unambiguous testimony of Xenophon in favor of an unrealistically strict interpretation of the "legalities" of the situation. There is no evidence that Epaminondas rejected (or even considered) the "legality" of the Achaeans' position. On the contrary, everything known about the Theban invasion indicates that Theban self-interest and the requirements of the overall strategy of achieving domination were the principal considerations behind the Theban decision to attack. Moreover, the combination of the "liberation" (as Diodorus calls it) of two Aetolian cities previously controlled by the Achaeans and disregard for Epaminondas' agreement with the Achaean aristocrats reinforces the perception that the Thebans were in no way prepared to restrain their foreign policy ambitions out of concern for loyalty and therefore refused to respect Achaean neutrality.

dangerous adversary at the Arcadians' rear if the Achaean aristocrats decided to support Sparta.[19]

C. NEUTRALITY IN 366

Among Sparta's traditional allies, Corinth, Phlius, almost certainly
Epidaurus, and perhaps one or more other, unnamed states broke
ranks in 366 and escaped from the continuing warfare between the
Spartan-Athenian and Theban-Arcadian alliances by independently
negotiating a peace with the Theban alliance. This release of Peloponnesian states from continued participation in the conflict with
Thebes is especially important to the present study because the
practical objective of the involved states was to convert their
unwanted, but obligatory, belligerency into formal neutrality.

Corinth was the first state to break away. During the five years
of warfare following Leuctra, the Corinthians had faithfully upheld
their obligations to the Spartan alliance and had been protected (in
theory anyway) by garrisons of Athenian troops stationed throughout their territory. In 366, however, reports arrived that the Athenians were planning to seize control of the state. To avert this danger,
the Corinthians immediately ordered the garrisons to withdraw,
and perhaps none too soon, for just as the Athenian troops were
gathered at Corinth for registration of any lawsuits arising from
their occupation, an Athenian fleet under Chares arrived at the
port of Cenchreae. Although the Athenians claimed that they had
come to prevent, and not precipitate, subversion, suspicion
remained, and the Corinthians appear to have believed, probably
with justification, that they were now threatened not only by their
declared enemies but also by untrustworthy allies. Accordingly,
they hastened to protect themselves not only by hiring a substantial
mercenary force to replace the Athenians but also by approaching
the Thebans and suing for peace (Xen. *Hell.* 7. 4.4–5).

These events, in both the apparent stop-at-nothing attitude of
the allies and the Corinthians' basic diplomatic goals, bear a striking resemblance to the abortive peace movement that arose at

19. Strategic potential was, according to Xenophon, the main reason why
Epaminondas conceived his plan to force the Achaeans into alliance with Thebes.
Nevertheless, Buckler, *Theban Hegemony*, 186, denies that the Thebans had any
hope of using the Achaeans as a counterpoise to the Arcadians and claims without
explanation that "topography was against this strategy."

Corinth during the early years of the Corinthian War (see 8.3.A above). But in this second effort the Corinthians succeeded. Xenophon reports that the Thebans were willing to negotiate a peace treaty with the Corinthians and allowed them to take the proposals to their allies "so that they might conclude peace with those who were willing and allow those who preferred the war to continue fighting" (*Hell.* 7. 4.7). The problem was, of course, that Corinth was still obligated to the Spartans.[20] So, according to Xenophon, the Corinthians went to Sparta and begged the Spartans either to join in the peace or to give their leave for the Corinthians to make peace separately. Given the Spartans' history of high-handed dealing with their allies, it may have come as somewhat of a surprise that although the Spartans refused to join in accepting peace, they nevertheless granted to the Corinthians and any other of their allies who wished the right to cease fighting and to negotiate a peace settlement for themselves.[21]

This was truly a ground-breaking diplomatic development. But a new problem arose immediately, when the Spartan allies returned to Thebes. In place of a simple peace treaty with the Theban alliance, the Thebans now pressured Sparta's allies not only to make peace but also to join in an alliance with Thebes. To this the Corinthians said flatly that acceptance of any kind of alliance with Thebes was out of the question because it would not bring peace but merely reversed alignment in the existing war (*Hell.* 7. 4.10). The Thebans, reportedly impressed by the Corinthians' determination not to become involved in hostility against their former benefactors (the Spartans), yielded and agreed to a simple treaty of peace.[22] The states from the Spartan alliance that joined Corinth in accepting the treaty were certainly Phlius, probably Epidaurus, and perhaps some of the other smaller cities whose names are not

20. On the obligations of members of the Peloponnesian alliance, see 3.5 above.

21. See Xen. *Hell.* 7. 4.6–11 (Corinth, Phlius); Isoc. 6. (*Archid.*). 13, 91 (Corinth, Phlius, Epidaurus). The details of the treaties are discussed by, among others, Ryder, Koine Eirene, 83, 137–39; Buckler, *Theban Hegemony* 198–201; but only Skalet, *Ancient Sicyon,* 75–76, makes the connection with neutrality, pointing out: "In 366/5 B.C. Corinth, Phlius and the cities of the Argolid coast concluded a partial peace with Thebes, or a treaty of neutrality on the principle that each should hold its own territory."

22. Bengtson, SVA² no. 285; Bengtson rightly rejects the notion (from Diod. 15. 76.3) that this was a Common Peace; see Ryder, Koine Eirene, 137–39.

recorded in the sources.[23] For all of these states the treaty represented an important victory in their long struggle, on the one hand, to conduct foreign policy more freely, and on the other, to secure for themselves recognized abstention from the continued warfare of the leading states.

For the Phliasians, the separate treaty meant escape from the virtually impossible situation that Sparta's weakened military power had created. Despite Xenophon's repeated praise of its loyalty during this period, Phlius plainly came under increasingly serious pressure from the attacks of hostile states that virtually surrounded the tiny *polis*.[24] The treaty with Thebes provided desperately needed immunity from further attack. But like Corinth, Phlius did not intend to change sides in the conflict. It was *philia* with all parties, and *symmachia* with none, that the Phliasians were attempting to negotiate.[25]

Epidaurus almost certainly also belongs in the list of Spartan allies that made peace in 366. Although Xenophon is silent, Isocrates appears to confirm this in a pamphlet written as a speech of Archidamus, the son of Agesilaus, responding to the allies' appeal to Sparta to join in making peace or allow them to proceed separately. Archidamus defends Sparta's determination to continue fighting and rejects any idea of peace until Messene has been recovered. No one, he argues, would reproach the Epidaurians,

23. Xenophon (*Hell.* 7. 4.10–11) names Corinth, Phlius, and "those who came with them." Isocrates (6 [*Archid.*]. 91) implies that Epidaurus was one of these states; of unnamed possibilities, Pellene, Troezen, Hermione, and Halieis could be mentioned; see *Hell.* 7. 2.2–3. A. Schaefer, *Demosthenes und seine Zeit*, vol. 1, 2d ed. (Leipzig, 1885), 114 n. 3, and Skalet, *Ancient Sicyon*, 75–76, include Sicyon on the grounds of the evacuation of Thyamia, a fortified position on the Sicyonian border; and both (Schaefer, 128 n. 3; Skalet, 76) reject as erroneous Diodorus' inclusion of Sicyon among the allies of Thebes in 362 (15. 85.2).

24. See Xen. *Hell.* 7. 2.1–2, 10–11, 17–20, 3.1.

25. It must be admitted that this policy was short-lived. Phlius seems to have abandoned its neutrality late in 362 and joined in a defensive alliance with Athens, the Arcadians, the Achaeans, and Elis (Tod, no. 144; Bengtson, *SVA*² no. 290). Some, including Bengtson, have dated the alliance before the battle of Mantinea (362); but Tod's arguments seem persuasive to me, especially given the absence of Phlius from the list of states present at the battle (also emphasized by Buckler, *Theban Hegemony*, 261). Moreover, on the basis of Xenophon's statement (*Hell.* 7. 5.27) that the battle of Mantinea produced more confusion and disorder than ever in Greece, it seems more likely that the change in Phliasian policy came in the unstable aftermath of the battle, when it became increasingly unclear whether the treaty with the Thebans would continue to afford protection against possible attack. Sicyon (see note 11 above) may also have entered into a new alliance about this time; see Bengtson, *SVA*² no. 285a, line 7 (p. 343).

Corinthians, or Phliasians for seeking by any means to escape destruction and save their own lives, but for Sparta, there can be no thought of safety if it means a loss of honor (6 [*Archid.*]. 90–91; cf. 12–13). Because the Epidaurians are not specifically said to have made peace but only to be blameless for desiring it, this reference is not conclusive by itself. However, when we consider Isocrates' linkage of Epidaurus, Corinth, and Phlius together with Xenophon's reference to other, unnamed states that concluded peace at the same time as Corinth and Phlius, there is no reason to doubt that Epidaurus was among the states that removed themselves from the war at this time. It also makes sense because Epidaurus was just as geographically isolated and, given Sparta's weakness, as militarily vulnerable as Corinth or Phlius.

None of these states is anywhere mentioned during the fighting that continued in the Peloponnesus after 366; and, most significantly, none is listed among the belligerent forces that fought at the great and critical battle at Mantinea in 362. For all of them involvement in the war ended with the peace negotiations of 366. From that date until after the battle of Mantinea they remained on the sidelines, passive bystanders, secure in their neutrality.[26]

D. THE PHOCIANS' REFUSAL TO INVADE THE PELOPONNESUS (362)

There is an interesting footnote to the use of neutrality during the 360s. When Epaminondas summoned the Theban allies for a joint invasion of the Peloponnesus in 362, the Phocians refused to participate on the grounds that their agreement with the Thebans was to help if anyone went against Thebes but not to march with them against other states.[27] The Phocian refusal is important because it

---

26. It should be added that under the year 366/365, Diodorus (15. 76.3) reports that the Persian king persuaded the Greek states to end the war with a Common Peace (*koine eirēnē*); see Bengtson, SVA[2] no. 282; Piccirilli, *Arbitrati*, vol. 1, no. 46. This led G. Glotz, *Histoire ancienne, Deuxième partie: Histoire grecque*, vol. 3 (Paris, 1926), 167, to argue that the Persian intention in seeking a Common Peace was to "neutralize" the Peloponnesus. But this surely inverts the true situation. The initiative for negotiating peace and neutrality in 366 did not come from the greater powers as a policy to be imposed on the weaker Peloponnesian states. Instead, it was, as the evidence gathered in this study attests, the final success of a movement that had been gaining force steadily throughout the fourth century. No theory of Persian involvement is necessary or justified.

27. Ἐπαμεινώνδας ἐξῆει, Βοιωτοὺς ἔχων πάντας καὶ Εὐβοέας καὶ Θετταλῶν πολλοὺς παρά τε Ἀλεξάνδρου καὶ τῶν ἐναντίων αὐτῷ. Φωκεῖς μέντοι οὐκ

reflects the ongoing struggle between the less powerful states, which fought to retain as much independent control as possible over their own foreign policy, and the hegemonial powers, which persistently pressured weaker states to contribute support in aggressive conflicts. By refusing to participate, the Phocians were expressing the same protest made by the Thebans themselves earlier in the century when they refused to join in the offensive campaigns of Sparta (see 8.2 above). But more importantly, by appealing to the specific terms of their agreement, the Phocians were forcefully reminding the Thebans that they were entirely within their rights to remain aloof, since the existence of a defensive alliance in no way abrogated the Phocians' legal right to pursue a neutral course in a situation where Thebes was the aggressor. This was, as we have seen, an old argument, repeatedly made and often ignored.

III. NEUTRALITY IN GREEK-PERSIAN RELATIONS (386–344/343)

A. THE COLLECTIVE DECLARATION DURING THE SATRAPS' REVOLT (362)

In the aftermath of the indecisive battle at Mantinea (362), the Greek states once again concluded a multilateral Common Peace, which only the Spartans refused to accept.[28] Apparently, it was soon after this that an embassy arrived in Greece from certain of Artaxerxes II's satraps who had revolted from the king and were seeking support from the Greek states.[29] Although little else is known about this mission, a fragmentary inscription found at Argos in the nineteenth century but now lost provides part of the

---

ἠκολούθουν, λέγοντες ὅτι συνθῆκαι σφίσιν ⟨σὺν⟩ αὐτοῖς εἶεν, εἴ τις ἐπὶ Θήβας ἴοι, βοηθεῖν, ἐπ᾽ ἄλλους δὲ στρατεύειν οὐκ εἶναι ἐν ταῖς συνθήκαις.   Xen. Hell. 7. 5.4 (Bengtson, SVA² no. 271)
3 σφίσιν ⟨σὺν⟩ αὐτοῖς Breitenbach: σφίσιν αὐτοῖς codd.: αὐτοῖς del. Cobet.

28. Bengtson, SVA² no. 292; Ryder, Koine Eirene, 140–44.
29. For details of the revolt, see W. Judeich, Kleinasiatische Studien: Untersuchungen zur griechisch-persischen Geschichte des iv. Jahrhunderts v. Chr. (Marburg, 1892), 190ff.; Meyer, Geschichte des Altertums, vol. 5, 473–478; Beloch, Griechische Geschichte, vol. 3, part 1, 213–17; 2, 254–57; R. P. Austin, "Athens and the Satraps' Revolt," JHS 64 (1944): 98; Olmstead, History of the Persian Empire, 411–422; Cook, Persian Empire, 220–22; M. J. Osborne, Naturalization in Athens (Brussels, 1981–83), D12.

joint reply given by the Greeks to the satraps' ambassador. The text follows.

----------------------- νου φυγ .....^{ca. 9}....

[-- ca. 18 - μετ]έχουσιν τῆς κοινῆς [εἰρήνης. δηλ]-
[ὦσαι δὲ τῶι παρὰ τ]ῶν σατραπῶν ἥκοντι διότ<ι> οἱ ["Ελληνες πρ]-
[εσβεύσ]αντες πρὸς ἀλλήλους διαλέλυνται τὰ <δ>[ιάφορα πρὸ]-
5 [ς κ]οινὴν εἰρήνην, ὅπως ἀπαλλαγέντες τοῦ π[ρὸς αὐτοὺς πολ]-
[έ]μου τὰς πόλεις ἕκαστοι τὰς αὐτῶν ὡς μεγί[στας καὶ εὐδαίμον]-
[α]ς ποιῶσιν καὶ χρήσιμοι μένωσιν τοῖς φίλο[ις καὶ ἰσχυροί.
[β]ασιλεῖ δὲ οὐδένα πόλεμον οἴδασιν ὄντα πρ[ὸς αὐτούς. Ἐὰν ο]-
ὖν ἡσυχίαν ἔχηι καὶ μὴ συνβάλληι τοὺς Ἕ[λληνας, μηδὲ τὴν ν]-
10 [ῦν] γεγενημένην ἡμῖν εἰρήνην ἐπιχειρῆ[ι διαλύειν τέχνηι μ]-
[ηδ]εμιᾶι μηδὲ μηχανῆι, ἕξομεν καὶ ἡμεῖς [τὴν ἡσυχίαν πρὸς β]-
[α]σιλέα· ἐὰν δὲ πολεμῆι πρός τινας τῶν [ὁμοσασῶν τὸν ὅρκον χ]-
[ρή]ματά τισι παρέχηι ἐπὶ διαλύσει τῆς εἰρή[νης τῆσδε, ἢ αὐ]-
[τὸ]ς ἐναντίον τοῖς Ἕλλησιν τοῖς τήνδε [τὴν εἰρήνην ποήσα]-
15 [σιν] ἢ ἄλλος τις τῶν ἐκ τῆς ἐκένου χώρ[ας, ἀμυνοῦμεν κοινῆι]
[πάντε]ς ἀξίως τῆς τε νῦν γεγενημένης ε[ἰρήνης καὶ ὧν πρὸ τ]-
[οῦ ἐπράξα]μεν. vacat
       τοῖς δικασταῖς τοῖς ἀπὸ τῶν [----------------]
[-- περὶ τᾶς] χώρας ἃς ἀμφιλλέγοντ[ι ----------------]
20 [--]ν ἐπὶ τούτοις διην ------------------------------
--- αντας ---------------------------------------
--³⁰

30. Tod, no. 145; Bengtson, SVA² no. 292; Piccirilli, Arbitrati, vol. 1, no. 48.
On the disputed date of the Greek declaration, see Tod, no. 145, followed here. It might be added to the arguments that have been put forth in favor of 362/361 that from the perspective of this study, 362/361 fits very well with the increased diplomatic use of neutrality, which occurred in Greek affairs generally during the 360s and in the formal relations of the major states, particularly Athens, with the Persian empire specifically (see 9.3.B below).
My text offers three new restorations:

1. In line 11, where Tod and others read [εἰρηνικῶς πρὸς β]/[α]σιλέα on the parallel of Isoc. 5 (Philip). 46 εἴτ' εἰρηνικῶς εἴτε πολεμικῶς αἱ πόλεις αὗται πρὸς ἀλλήλας ἔχουσιν, I read [τὴν ἡσυχίαν πρὸς β]. The context makes it quite clear that the Greeks intended to communicate the idea of neutrality. Expressions known to serve that purpose should therefore be considered preferable restorations if they fit the 14 or 15 letter spaces required for the accepted length of the line (46–48 letters). In fact, there are two possibilities. The most likely would be [τὴν ἡσυχίαν πρὸς β]/[α]σιλέα; see, for example, Diod. 11. 3.3 on the neutrals in 480 πρὸς δὲ τοὺς τὴν ἡσυχίαν ἔχοντας; cf. 13. 85.2 on Acragas in 406 and other expressions catalogued above on pp. 13–15 in chapter 1. It is also reassuring that this restoration echoes the phrasing of line 9, because the Greeks are formally demanding that the king remain neutral in Greek affairs, in return for which the Greek states pledge to remain neutral in Persian affairs. Thus the repetition is not only appropriate but actually strengthens the force of the decree by reflecting its insistence on reciprocity. It must be admitted, however, that a second reading, [τὴν εἰρήνην πρὸς β]/

[It is resolved by those] sharing in the Common [Peace to make it clear to the ambassador] coming [from] the satraps that the [Greeks, after sending ambassadors] to one another, have resolved their [disputes in the interest of] Common Peace, so that each (city-state), being rid of the war with [one another], may make itself as great as possible [and prosperous] and remain [strong] and useful to its friends. They know of no war existing between [themselves] and the King. [If], therefore, he remains at peace and does not come into conflict with the Greeks or endeavor [to dissolve] the peace that [now] exists among us either by stratagem or device, we will remain [*at peace with*] the King. But if he makes war on any [*of those who have sworn the oath (of peace) or*] furnishes [*money*] to anyone for the dissolution of [this] peace, [whether he sets himself] against those Greeks who [have made this peace] or someone else from his territory (does), [we will all defend ourselves together] in a manner worthy of the [peace] that now exists [and of what] we [have accomplished in the past].[31]

Despite its fragmentary condition and, in some places, less than certain restoration, this decree is a singularly crucial document for the study of neutrality during the fourth century. To begin with, it is not hearsay but an official, published document containing a formal declaration of neutrality by the Greek states participating

---

[a]σιλέα, cannot be ruled out, although I have not found it used with ἔχειν where the sense is clearly neutrality; cf. Diod. 13. 43.7 on Syracuse in 410 τηρεῖν ... πρὸς δὲ Καρχηδονίους τὴν εἰρήνην; cf. Diod. 19. 77.7 on the proposal to Sparta in 374, quoted on p. 15 in chapter 1.

2. In line 12, for [συσπόνδων ἡμιν] I read [ὁμοσασῶν τὸν ὅρκον] on the basis of Xen. *Hell.* 6. 5.2 ἐὰν δέ τις στρατεύῃ ἐπί τινα πόλιν τῶν ὁμοσασῶν τόνδε τὸν ὅρκον, βοηθήσω πάντι σθένει. This reading is supported in the historical sources, where "the oath" and "swearing" are used as pseudonyms for a specific Common Peace treaty; see, for instance, *Hell.* 7. 1.39; Diod. 15. 94.1; Isoc. 8 (*On the Peace*). 17; Dem. 23 (*Aristocr.*). 10.

3. In Lines 12–13, for [πρ/άγ]ματα I read [χ/ρή]ματα. There is abundant evidence that the king's "money" and its disruptive effect on interstate politics preoccupied Greek thinking during the first half of the fourth century; see, for example, on the Corinthian War, *Hell. Oxy.* 7(2). 2; Xen. *Hell.* 3. 5.1–2; Plut. *Ages.* 10.4, 14.2, 15.6; Paus. 3. 9.8; Polyaenus 1. 48.3; on the year 388, Lys. 33. 5; on 383, *Hell.* 5. 2.35; on 371, *Hell.* 6. 3.12; on 368, *Hell.* 7. 1.27; Diod. 15. 70.2; on 367, *Hell.* 7. 1.34–38; Dem. 19 (*False Leg.*). 137; Plut. *Pel.* 30.5–7; on 354, Dem. 14 (*Symm.*). 5, 29–31; on ca. 351, Dem. 15 (*Rhod.*). 23.

31. On the basis of Tod, no. 145; my italics reflect readings different from previous commentators (see note 30). Wickersham and Verbrugghe, *Greek Historical Documents*, no. 47, translate lines 9–11 "If he keeps the peace and does not invade Greece and does not seek to break the peace which now exists among us by any device or stratagem." However, as Tod, no. 145, points out, citing *LSJ*[9], s.v. *symballō* II:a, the sense here should be "embroil," not "invade."

in a Common Peace.[32] It involves not unilateral, but collective, adoption of neutral policy with the assumption that peaceful relations can be maintained even during warfare, under certain conditions. And it specifies, albeit in a threatening tone, exactly what the conditions for Greek neutrality will be during conflict between the Persian king and his satraps.

What the decree shows is that in their collective, as well as individual, diplomacy the Greek states continually recognized the desirability of having a formally accepted position of abstention. Despite the imprecision (by modern standards) of its nomenclature, the decree formally specifies this policy as best for the protection and preservation of the existing state of peace. Because the text is not the secondhand report of an individual historian or orator but preserves the exact words of the Greek response, it also provides valuable information about how contemporary diplomats communicated the idea of neutrality. It is reassuring to find that the authors of the decree use the same vocabulary found in nondocumentary sources. The decree also provides indisputable substantiation of the truly international character of diplomatic concepts— one of which, the idea of declared or negotiated neutrality, appears once again in relations between the Greeks and the Persians.

B. THE POLICY OF INDIVIDUAL STATES TOWARD PERSIA

Neutrality also repeatedly played a role in diplomatic relations between individual Greek states and Persia during the period between the Corinthian War (395–386) and the final recovery of Egypt by the Persians ca. 342. Athens and Sparta supply by far the best-documented examples, and a comparison of their respective diplomatic records is revealing.

Both Athens and Sparta gradually reversed their diplomatic policy toward Persia during the Corinthian War. Through the shrewd, if unprincipled, negotiation of Antalcidas, Sparta changed its rela-

---

32. This has long been accepted, see, among others, Jacoby, *FGH* IIIB Suppl. (to 328, Philochoros frag. 157), 531 n. 2: "Actually the answer of 362/361 equals a declaration of neutrality"; and Walbank, *Commentary on Polybius*, vol. 1, 482 (on Polyb. 4. 33.8–9): "They state their neutrality and intention to resist by force any attack by the Great King on any of their number." H. W. Parke, *Greek Mercenary Soldiers, From the Earliest Times to the Battle of Ipsus* (Oxford, 1933), 110 n. 2, argues that the satraps may be understood to be protected by a defensive alliance, according to the restoration of lines 10ff. of the decree, but his claim is groundless. This is another example of the confusion of *philia* with *symmachia*.

tionship with Persia from outright warfare to a mutually supportive accord that exploited the threat of a renewed Spartan-Persian alliance, which had been a decisive reality in the Peloponnesian War.[33] At the same time, Athens, which benefited early in the war from Persian aid brought by Conon, eventually provoked new Persian mistrust by coercing financial contributions from cities on the coast of Asia Minor, by sending aid to Evagoras (the rebellious ruler of Salamis in Cyprus), and finally by allying itself with the Egyptian king Nepherites (or Psammetichus, in Greek) in his revolt from the Persian empire.[34]

After the King's Peace, however, the Spartans gradually abandoned the cordial relationship with Persia established by Antalcidas and adopted a more definitely anti-Persian posture. Indications of this change can be seen first in 383, when the Spartans brought about the trial and condemnation of Ismenias, one of the leading democratic statesmen at Thebes, on the charge of medism, and then again, more unequivocally, in 380/379, when they agreed to ally themselves with Glos, a renegade Persian admiral, in his abortive attempt to detach part of western Asia Minor from the Persian empire.[35]

33. This was not an idle threat to those who could easily remember the Spartan-Persian alliance that brought about the final defeat of Athens in the Peloponnesian War (Bengtson, SVA^2 nos. 200–202). On the reversal of Spartan policy, see Lewis, *Sparta and Persia*, 145–47; Olmstead, *History of the Persian Empire*, 387–88. Xenophon (*Hell.* 5. 1.28) actually refers to the king as an ally (*symmachos*) of the Spartans in 387; but only the threat, not the existence, of a formal alliance has been recognized by scholars; e.g., Bengtson, SVA^2 (no alliance); Lewis, 147; Hamilton, *Sparta's Bitter Victories*, 305–6.

34. For a concise summary of Athens' reversal, see G. L. Cawkwell, *Philip of Macedon* (London and Boston, 1978), 69; on extortion in Asia, see Lys. 28 passim; Xen. *Hell.* 4. 8.30; Diod. 14. 99. 4–5; Nep., *Thrasyb.* 4.3; on Evagoras, see D. M. Lewis and R. S. Stroud, "Athens Honors King Euagoras of Salamis," *Hesperia* 48 (1979): 180–93; Lys. 19. 21–23, 43; Xen. *Hell.* 4. 8.24 ("the Athenians, though they had the king as a friend [*philos*], were sending aid to Evagoras, who was making war on the king"; cf. 27, where Athenian *philia* with the king is also mentioned); Dem. 20 (*Lept.*). 76; cf. Nep. *Chabr.* 2.2 (*Athenienses cum Artaxerxes societatem habebant*); on Nepherites-Psammetichus, see Ar. *Plut.* 178, a poor, but acceptable, source, given the Athenians' willingness to aid the revolt of Evagoras in Cyprus and Egyptian pretender Psammetichus' own eagerness to win Greek allies (see Lewis, *Sparta and Persia*, 147 n. 73). An earlier attempt by Egypt to aid Sparta (396) arose out of a Spartan proposal for reciprocal support (Diod. 14. 79.4–8; cf. Justin 6. 6).

35. On Ismenias, see Xen. *Hell.* 5. 2.35; on Glos, Diod. 15. 9.4, 18.1, 19.1; see also T. T. B. Ryder, "Spartan Relations with Persia after the King's Peace: A Strange Story in Diodorus 15.9," *CQ* 13 (1963): 105–9. Glos' father-in-law, Tirabazus, was earlier (385) accused of secretly using his *philia* with the Spartans to negotiate an alliance in support of an intended revolt; see Diod. 15. 8.4. That

During the same period, Athens shifted its official policy toward Persia in the opposite direction. Immediately after the King's Peace, the Athenians withdrew their support for the revolt of Evagoras in Cyprus; and they were subsequently careful to disassociate themselves officially from Chabrias when he enrolled as a mercenary commander for the rebellious Egyptian king Achoris (385–379).[36]

More of the Athenians' new position is revealed in an incident involving Chabrias' presence in Egypt. In 379, Pharnabazus sent an embassy to Athens and formally demanded that the Athenians either recall Chabrias immediately or risk becoming estranged from the king. In addition, Pharnabazus urged that Athens send Iphicrates to serve as a commander for the army he was gathering against Achoris. According to Diodorus, the Athenians were so eager to gain favor with the king and Pharnabazus that they complied on both counts.[37] Lurking behind these simple facts are subtle, but important, diplomatic distinctions. By allowing Chabrias to serve in Egypt as a private mercenary for Achoris, the Athenians continued to be troublesome to Persia without openly violating the officially peaceful relations that existed between the two powers. Pharnabazus countered this, however, by threatening that the king would not recognize any artificial distinction between the private and public actions of the Athenians but would hold the state accountable for Chabrias' actions, private or not. This was a clever and, in this case, successful negotiating tactic.

But even if a blurring of the distinction between public and private action gave Pharnabazus grounds for demanding the recall of Chabrias, it could hardly be used to summon Iphicrates. For

Sparta was the object of bitterness on account of medism is clear from Isoc. 4 (*Paneg.*). 175. Diodorus (15. 23.5) claims that at the height of Sparta's power (380/379), Persia sought an alliance. If so, it may have been aimed at precluding Spartan aid to Evagoras (Isoc. 4 [*Paneg.*]. 135; cf. 126); but the report is more likely apocryphal, and in any case, no alliance is known.

36. This point is emphasized by both Diodorus (15. 29.2: "[Chabrias], without having secured the permission of the people [*aneu tēs tou dēmou gnōmēs prosdexamenos*], accepted the command of the forces in Egypt") and Nepos (*Chabr.* 2). The latter even specifically contrasts Chabrias' private participation in Egypt with his public position in Cyprus: in Aegypto sua sponte gessit. nam Nectanabin adiutum profectus regnum ei constituit. fecit idem Cypri, sed publice ab Atheniensibus Euagorae adiutor datus (*Chabr.* 2).

37. Diod. 15. 29.3; cf. Nep. *Chabr.* 3.1.

this, Pharnabazus had to revert to traditional diplomatic principles and present the request for the general in terms of a friendly gesture. The hypocrisy of all of this is obvious enough, but in the context of contemporary diplomacy, there is really no contradiction. As far as the Persians were concerned, Chabrias' service to Achoris violated the spirit of friendly relations (i.e., *philia*) that existed, ostensibly, between Athens and Persia on the basis of the King's Peace. On the other hand, permitting Iphicrates to serve the king did not commit Athens officially, since it would be explained away in the same language used to defend Chabrias. And indeed, there is no evidence that Iphicrates' service involved any kind of official alignment with Persia on the part of the Athenians or was meant to alter the official relationship between the two states, although the Athenians obviously hoped that compliance might engender in the Persians some willingness to reciprocate the favor in the future. Moreover, by keeping their involvement on this level, the Athenians also protected their reputation, for they could easily repudiate the presence of Iphicrates as unofficial and thereby deny any accusations that they were medizing.[38]

What then was the official diplomatic relationship between Athens and Persia after the King's Peace? Both the incident involving Chabrias (379) and the clear rhetorical stance of the foundation decree of the Second Athenian Confederacy (378/377) suggest that the Athenians had, as of the peace in 386, reestablished formal diplomatic *philia* with Persia. Later, in 344/343, this is expressly mentioned as the official relationship; and Athens' cautious restraint toward Persia following the King's Peace points to ca. 386 as the

---

38. Contemporary speeches by Lysias (33 [*Olymp. Or.*], probably delivered in 388) and Isocrates (4 [*Paneg.*], dated 380) reflect popular hostility toward Persia, which orators exploited at every opportunity (cf. Ar. *Plut.* [as staged in 388] 170). Undoubtedly this rhetoric had some impact on public policy at Athens, as it appears to have had at Sparta (Diod. 15. 19.4; discussed by Ryder, Koine Eirene, 105). Moreover, it should be remembered from the recent incident in 383 involving Thebes (see 8.4.B above) that a state could prohibit its citizens from participating in a particular conflict in order to protect its neutrality and thereby demonstrate beyond question its commitment to the preservation of peaceful relations with the belligerents. Aeneas Tacticus, whose work on military affairs is roughly contemporary with these events, preserves just such an official decree, which proclaims: "The citizens are not to hire mercenaries or to hire themselves as mercenaries without the consent of the magistrates" (10. 7). Pharnabazus certainly would have known that the Greek states had this power; and he was acting accordingly.

date when *philia* was officially reestablished.[39] We have seen repeatedly that *philia* obligated states to refrain from injuring one another and could serve as the basis for negotiating mutual cooperation against a third party, yet it did not mandate cooperation and could be used as grounds for one state to refuse to join another in prosecuting a dispute with a third party (see 3.4 above). It therefore follows that if *philia* existed between Athens and Persia, the relationship restrained both states from directly supporting each other's enemies and thus provided some degree of security against either state interfering in the separate disputes of the other—a serious issue pressed home by Pharnabazus in 379.

This reconstruction is further supported by what we know of subsequent events. When Iphicrates fled from Persian service

39. On Chabrias, see above, with notes 36–37; on the decree, see especially lines 15–25 of *IG* II², 43 (Tod, no. 123; Bengtson, *SVA²* no. 257; Cargill, *Second Athenian League*, 16–27); cf. the alliance with the Chians (Tod, no. 118; Bengtson, *SVA²* no. 248). *Philia* existed at the outset of the Corinthian War (Xen. *Hell.* 4. 8.24, 27); for 344/343, see below, with notes 53–55. It may be reflected as early as 380 in Isoc. 4 (*Paneg.*). 155. Compare the establishment of "hereditary friendship" (*patrikē philia*) between Persia and Thebes in 367/366 (Plut. *Pel.* 30.5), and the alleged renunciation of "alliance and friendship" (*symmachia kai philia*) between Persia and Amphipolis ca. 366 (Dem. 19 [*False Leg.*]. 137). In *IG* II², 43, *philia* was, I believe, originally mentioned in line 13 but was later erased. Lines 12–14 have been carefully reexamined by Cargill, *Second Athenian League*, 28–32, who assumes—rightly I think—"that the intent was to erase certain phrases, not simply whole lines" (28). His conclusion is "that the King was mentioned, and that some sort of reference to the King's Peace was erased" (31); this has also been the consensus of other scholars. G. L. Cawkwell, "The Foundation of the Second Athenian Confederacy," *CQ* 23 (1973): 60 n. 1, dissents but bases his own restoration on a reading that Cargill shows to be orthographically "impossible" (30). Marshall, *Second Athenian Confederacy*, 16–17, sees an "uncomplimentary reference to Sparta's late high-handed proceedings" but offers no restoration in support. If these lines contained a reference to *philia* with the king, when and for what reason was it erased? No completely satisfactory answer can be given; but I believe it occurred much later (ca. 357) in connection with Athenian anger over the intrigue of Mausolus, the satrap of Caria, with Athens' allies. If so, erasure was propaganda—a public announcement of the potentially dire consequences of Mausolus' actions if the king was willing to support them. This would also explain the retention of the charter's original exclusion of states that belonged to the king (lines 17–18). Athens was warning the king, not throwing down the gauntlet. Erasure at the time of the war between Athens and her allies also helps to explain why the Athenians allowed Chares' overtly provocative aid to a rebel satrap. Given Mausolus' actions and Athenian resentment, Chares' service could be justified as simply tit for tat following the breakdown in diplomatic relations (see note 52 below for Isocrates' support of this reconstruction). The generally accepted date of 367/366 (Marshall, 16–17; S. Accame, *La lege ateniese del Secolo IV a.c.* [Rome, 1941], 149–50; Ryder, *Koine Eirene*, 81 n. 9; Cargill, 31–32, 167–68, 192) has against it the ignored testimony of Demosthenes that (also in 367/366) the Athenians ordered Timotheus not to violate the existing peace with the king when he was dispatched to aid Ariobarzanes (15 [*Rhod.*]. 9).

ca. 374 and Pharnabazus sent an embassy to Athens demanding that he be punished, the Athenians refused to do so on the grounds that he had broken no laws—that is, his private service as a mercenary violated no Athenian law, and his withdrawal was not a public issue (Diod. 15. 43.5–6). Significantly, Iphicrates' successor, Timotheus, entered the king's service only after the Athenians stripped him of his generalship. His service was, like that of Chabrias and Iphicrates, strictly unofficial and, if there is any truth in the accusations of the hostile speaker who prosecuted Timotheus upon his return to Athens (367/366), motivated purely by a combination of impending lawsuits and serious financial difficulties.[40] When the Athenians next dispatched Timotheus officially, it was to assist Ariobarzanes, the Persian satrap of Hellespontine Phrygia and an honorary citizen of Athens. Timotheus was, however, specifically instructed to do nothing in violation of the treaty with the king; when he learned that Ariobarzanes was in revolt, he gave him no support.[41]

What Timotheus did do was halt the recent Persian interference in the Greek islands and northern Aegean. He besieged Samos and expelled a Persian garrison installed there by Tigranes, another of the king's satraps. From Samos he sailed to the northern Aegean, where he took control of Persian-held Sestus and Crithote on the European side of the Hellespont and captured several other cities subject to the Chalcidian League.[42] Athenians looked back on Timotheus' successes with pride; but did they upset Athens' diplomatic relations with Persia? How should we interpret their diplomatic impact? Do these military operations represent "a period of intense conflict with the Persians," as J. Cargill argues?[43] If the original Athenian intent was to abide by the restraints of their relationship with the king, did Timotheus simply ignore official policy and run amuck or was it all part of a state-sponsored and -orchestrated anti-Persian campaign? Did the Athenians now con-

40. Xen. *Hell.* 6. 2.13; [Dem.] 49 (*Timoth.*). 4; Diodorus (15. 47.3) offers a false report of his reinstatement.
41. On the citizenship of Ariobarzanes, see Dem. 23 (*Aristocr.*). 141, 202; on Timotheus' expedition, Dem. 15 (*Rhod.*). 9.
42. On the siege of Samos and the campaigning in the northern Aegaean, see Dem. 15 (*Rhod.*). 9; Isoc. 15 (*Antid.*). 108, 111–14; [Arist.] *Oec.* 2. 23. 1350b4, b10; Deinarch. 1. 14; 3. 17; Diod. 15. 81.6; Nep. *Timoth.* 1.2; Polyaenus 3. 10.9–10, 15; Harp., s.v. Kyprothemis; cf. Parke, *Greek Mercenary Soldiers*, 108–10.
43. Cargill, *Second Athenian League*, 171.

sider themselves to be enemies of the king? Or was the former diplomatic relationship still in force?

The evidence for believing that Timotheus' actions either caused or reflected any fundamental change in Athenian-Persian relations is actually very weak. Since Samos was not a member of the Athenian Confederacy,[44] Tigranes' interference on the island was not a direct provocation of Athens; nor is there any good evidence that it constituted a violation of the terms of the King's Peace.[45] The reason for and the purpose of the garrison are unknown. Whether it was the official policy of the king or the kind of independent adventurism typical of the satraps' freedom of action within their satrapies is also uncertain. All we know is that Demosthenes later claimed the expulsion was not the basis of any hostility between Athens and the king (15 [Rhod.]. 10). The occupation of Sestus and Crithote may also have been less anti-Persian than thought. Ariobarzanes controlled these cities, and Timotheus may well have taken them from the rebel satrap not as payment (the claim of later sources) but as legitimate prizes seized from a party at war with the king, a ruler with whom the Athenians still, in legal fact, had peaceful and friendly relations.[46] If Athens was truly

44. This is generally agreed on the basis of negative evidence; see, for instance, Beloch, *Griechische Geschichte*, vol. 3, part 2, 163; Marshall, *Second Athenian Confederacy*, 91; Accame, *Lege ateniese*, 61 n. 1; Griffith, "Athens in the Fourth Century," in *Imperialism in the Ancient World*, 139–40; Cargill, *Second Athenian League*, 37.

45. Among sources for the King's Peace (Bengtson, *SVA²* no. 242), Isocrates (8 [*On the Peace*]. 16) mentions the removal of garrisons as a stipulation of the peace with the king of Persia. However, since it is not clear whether he means the King's Peace or its renewal in 375/374 (Bengston, *SVA²* no. 265), when the withdrawal of garrisons was definitely stipulated, we cannot say, as Marshall, *Second Athenian Confederacy*, 91, does that the Persian garrison on Samos was "in defiance of the terms of the Peace of Antalcidas" (i.e., the King's Peace). A Persian connection with the island's oligarchic elements is more likely; evidence of this connection goes back to the fifth century (Thuc. 1. 115); see Griffith, "Athens in the Fourth Century," in *Imperialism in the Ancient World*, 140.

46. See the decision that cargo seized from an Egyptian ship in 355 was a legitimate prize of war because Egypt was in revolt from the king (Dem. 24 [*Timoc.*]. 11–12). On the basis of this and the statement in Dem. 15 (*Rhod.*). 9, I reject the story in Nepos (*Timoth.* 1.3) that Timotheus received these places in lieu of cash payment for services rendered to Ariobarzanes in 366/365. It is especially suspicious that the king recognized Athens' claim to Amphipolis at this time—hardly the reaction one would expect if Athens was overtly hostile; see also Dem. 19 (*False Leg.*). 137 and [Dem.] 7 (*Halon.*). Perhaps the king was rewarding Athens for accomplishing what his own satraps had not been able to do, namely, deprive Ariobarzanes of his European possessions. Or perhaps Ariobarzanes may still have been loyal enough to surrender these places to Timotheus in accord with the supposed Common Peace (so G. L. Cawkwell, "The Common Peace of 366/5 B.C.," *CQ* 11 [1961]: 85).

hostile to the king, why did Timotheus refuse to aid the important city of Heraclea Pontica when it appealed to him during this period? In fact his refusal conformed exactly with the Athenians' insistence that he do nothing in violation of their agreement (*philia*) with the king.[47] Later these events may have been seen differently, but for contemporaries, they were defensible within the status quo.

Between 357 and 355, Athens fought a bitter war against several disaffected members of its confederacy who had seceded from the alliance with the encouragement and support of Mausolus, the satrap of Caria. How this may have damaged the official relationship between Athens and Persia can perhaps be seen in the erasure of the clause in the foundation decree of the Athenian alliance that related to the official obligations existing between Athens and Persia.[48] During the war, Chares, the Athenian commander, hired out the army under his command to the rebel satrap Artabazus and promptly won a major victory against the king's forces, which he boastfully called a second Marathon. In reaction, however, Artaxerxes Ochus sent an embassy to Athens and demanded Chares' recall with the threat that if he were not withdrawn, the Phoenician fleet would be sent to aid Athens' enemies. Faced with this ultimatum, the Athenians quickly backed away from their previous enthusiasm for Chares' anti-Persian exploits, ordered his immediate withdrawal, and hastily made peace with their allies.[49]

47. See Justin 16. 4; Justin also says that Thebes likewise refused to aid the Heracleans—a decision that fits well with the friendly relations existing between Thebes and Persia at the time. During this period the Egyptian king Tachos also appealed unsuccessfully for Athenian support for his revolt from Persia (*IG* II², 119). Chabrias was allowed to serve, but in an unofficial capacity; see Diod. 15. 92.3: Plut. *Ages.* 37.5; Nep. *Chabr.* 2–3; on Chabrias' status, see Grote, *History of Greece*, vol. 8, 345; Austin, "Athens and the Satraps' Revolt," 98–100; Parke, *Greek Mercenary Soldiers*, 111–12. Sparta, in contrast, sent Agesilaus officially; see Xen. *Ages.* 2.28–31; Diod. 15. 92.2–93.6; Plut. *Ages.* 36.1–40.2. Plutarch's assertion that Agesilaus served privately (36.1; cf. *Mor.* 214D) is contradicted by his own later statement (37.4–5). Austin concludes: "On the whole it seems certain that Athens, while officially remaining neutral (Beloch, *Gesch.*² III i 214), avoiding anything like an open breach with Persia, was making use of Persia's difficulties at this time to increase her influence in the Eastern Mediterranean" (100). Beloch, *Griechische Geschichte*, vol. 3, part 1, 214, states: "Athen blieb neutral, gestattete aber, dass Chabrias, dem Aegypten vor zwanzig Jahren die Abwehr des persischen Angriffs gegen Akoris zu danken gehabt hatte, in Tachos' Dienste trat, der ihm den Befehl über die Flotte übertrug."

48. See note 39 above.

49. On Mausolus, see Dem. 15 (*Rhod.*). 3, 27; Diod. 16. 7.3; on his role in precipitating the revolt, see S. Hornblower, *Mausolus* (Oxford, 1982), 206–18; Sealey, *History of the Greek City-States*, 440; Cargill, *Second Athenian League*, 178–79. On Chares, see Dem. 4 (*First Phil.*). 24; Diod. 16. 22.1–2, 34.1; cf. Parke,

Some have interpreted Athens' quick action to avoid direct conflict with Persia as a reversal of official policy.[50] But where is the evidence that Chares acted officially? Both Demosthenes and Diodorus state specifically that Chares acted without authorization and that the Athenians simply approved of the *fait accompli* with which they were presented.[51] The whole idea of Athens' policy zigzagging inconsistently and unpredictably is simply unfounded. Having a desperate need for money to continue the war, the Athenians chose to ignore (and perhaps even enjoyed) Chares' raising money any way he could; but the moment his actions brought the threat of open hostility with the king, they were repudiated officially.

Furthermore, soon after, in 354, the Athenians debated whether to send aid to Rhodes or to remain neutral in the island's struggle to free itself from Persian domination. Despite Demosthenes' eloquent plea for support, they refused to risk the possibility of conflict with Persia. On the contrary, cordial relations and even a grant of citizenship were negotiated with Orontes, the reinstated satrap of Mysia; and Athenian generals received substantial assistance from him during the attempt to save Olynthus from Philip II (349/348).[52]

As the Athenians became increasingly concerned about the growing power of Philip, they were careful not to injure their relationship with Persia. Fortunately, the official position can be seen in Didymus' quotation of Androtion, Anaximenes, and Philochorus about a Persian embassy to Athens in 344/343.[53] The comments of Andro-

---

Greek Mercenary Soldiers, 122–23; on the boast, Schol. Dem. 4. 19; Plut. *Arat.* 16.3; cf. Schol. Dem. 3. 31; on Artaxerxes' threat, Diod. 16. 22.2; on Athens' approval and reversal, Schol. Dem. 3. 31; Diod. 16. 22.2, 34.1; on the peace, Bengtson, *SVA*[2] no. 313; Cargill, 161–88.

50. E.g., Hammond, *History of Greece*, 516, who explains: "The plan was to join Artabazus, the satrap in revolt, draw pay for her mercenaries from him, and then ask the Great King to buy her neutrality by recalling Mausolus from operations in the Aegean."

51. See references to Chares above in note 49 and Isoc. 8 (*On the Peace*). 55.

52. For Demosthenes' appeal, see Dem. 15 (*Rhod.*); cf. the indications of improved relations with Persia elsewhere in Demosthenes (14 [*Symm.*]. 2–13, 29, 36; 24 [*Timoc.*]. 11–12) and Isoc. 8 (*On the Peace*). 16, which concerns the advantages of the restoration of officially cordial relations; 7 (*Areop.*). 8–9, 81, which describes the recent deterioration in relations. Note also Isocrates' complaint to Philip in 346 that despite his urging, Athens refuses to take the lead and pursue a Panhellenic crusade against Persia (5 [*Philip*]. 129–30). On Orontes, see Bengtson, *SVA*[2] no. 324; Beloch, *Griechische Geschichte*, vol. 3, part 2, 140; Hammond, *History of Greece*, 550.

53. Did. *In Dem.* 10. 34, col. 8, lines 7–8 = Jacoby, *FGH* 328, Philochorus frag. 157; ibid., 324, Androtion, frag. 53; ibid., 72, Anaximenes frag. 28. On the date of the embassy, see the discussion of Jacoby, *FGH* IIIB (Text), 533.

tion and Anaximenes are reported without distinction:

> When Philip sent to Athens regarding peace in the archonship of
> Lykiskos [344/343], the Athenians also entertained ambassadors
> from the King [Artaxerxes Ochus] but made a more contemptuous
> than useful speech to them; for [they said] that there would be peace
> with the King if he did not march against the Greek city-states.[54]

Philochorus is then quoted separately:

> In this year [344/343] when the King [Ochus] sent ambassadors to
> Athens and asked that the friendship (*philia*) of his fathers be
> maintained, they responded to the ambassadors that friendship with
> the King would continue if the King did not march against the
> Greek city-states.[55]

Although the two versions are in basic agreement, the reference to
long-standing (*patrōian*) *philia* between the Athenians and King
Artaxerxes in Philochorus' version of the embassy is especially
valuable because it specifies exactly what the diplomatic relationship was. This deserves emphasis. Since reference to maintaining
peaceful relations (*eirēneuein*) in Androtion and Anaximenes does
not in itself presuppose or even necessarily suggest the existence of
a formal diplomatic relationship, the existence of *philia* could be
justifiably doubted, especially in light of the minatory tone that
Androtion and Anaximenes attributed to the Athenians. Philochorus' clear statement is therefore extremely helpful.[56]

That neutrality was compatible with the *philia* between Athens
and Persia is corroborated by Diodorus, who also mentions the
incident reported by Didymus. He states that when the king sent
embassies throughout Greece to recruit troops for the campaign
against Egypt, "the Athenians and the Lacedaemonians said that
they continued to keep their friendship (*philia*) with Persia but
were opposed to supplying the commitment of an alliance (*sym-*

---

54. τοῦ Φιλίππου ἐπὶ ἄρχοντος Λυκίσκου Ἀθήναζε περὶ εἰρήνης πέμψαντος,
βασιλέως πρέσβ[ει]ς συμπροσήκαντο οἱ Ἀθηναῖοι, ἀλλὰ ὑπε[ρο]πτικώτερον
ἢ ἐχρῆν διελ[έ]χθησαν αὐτο[ῖ]ς. εἰρηνεύσειν γὰρ πρὸς α[ὐτὸν ἔφασ]αν,
ἐὰν μ[ὴ] ἐπὶ τὰς Ἑλλην[ίδας] ἴηι [πόλεις].   (Did. *In Dem.* 10. 34, col.
8)
55. Ἐπὶ τούτου βασιλέως πέμ[ψ]αντος Ἀθή[να]ζε πρέσβεις κἀξιο(ῦν)τος τὴν
[φι]λίαν [δ(ια)μένει]ν ἑαυτῶι τ(ὴν) πατρώιαν, ἀπε[κρί]νατο [τοῖς π]ρέσβεσιν
Ἀθήνησι διαμε[νεῖν] βασιλε[ῖ τὴν φιλ]ίαν, ἐὰν μὴ βασιλεὺς ἐπ[ὶ τὰς]
Ἑλληνίδ(ας) ἴηι πόλεις.   (Did. *In Dem.* 10. 34, col. 8)
56. Compare the joint response of the Greek states to the satraps (see 9.3.A
and note 30 above), in which peaceful relations are stressed, but the formal
relationship of *philia* is nowhere mentioned.

machia)."[57] No statement of the formal diplomatic distinction between *philia* and *symmachia* is any clearer than this. Since *philia* embodied no obligation of mutual support, the declaration of neutrality given here was perfectly legitimate and, in Athens' case, exactly in keeping with what we can see was its official policy toward Persia. Furthermore, Diodorus' mention of Sparta suggests that the Spartans had at last been freed from the rigidly anti-Persian policy championed by Agesilaus and had begun to pursue a more sophisticated diplomatic strategy modeled on that of Athens.[58] Ironically, Philip later complained that at this very time the Athenians also sought his support for a Panhellenic crusade against Persia if the king dared to interfere in Greece ([Dem.] 12 [*Philip's Letter*]. 6).

Neither Athens on its side nor the Persian king on his wanted war during the period between 386 and the late 340s. Yet the combination of competing ambitions, old hostility, and mutual mistrust created a situation in which true peace existed only on the diplomatic level. Behind the facade of officially friendly relations (i.e., *philia*) both parties remained suspicious and hostile. But unlike the cruder and more transparent diplomacy of Sparta, and even of Thebes,[59] Athenian relations appear upon close inspection to have been careful and consistent throughout the period. Despite troubled times and the ever-inflammatory rhetoric of the Athenian orators, the policy of official *philia* was protected whenever necessary by

57. ὁ δὲ βασιλεὺς ἐν μεγάλῳ τιθέμενος τὸ κρατῆσαι τῆς Αἰγύπτου διὰ τὸ πρότερον ἐλάττωμα πρεσβευτὰς ἀπέστειλε πρὸς τὰς μεγίστας τῶν κατὰ τὴν Ἑλλάδα πόλεων, ἀξιῶν συστρατεῦσαι τοῖς Πέρσαις ἐπ᾽ Αἰγυπτίους. Ἀθηναῖοι μὲν οὖν καὶ Λακεδαιμόνιοι τὴν φιλίαν ἔφασαν τὴν πρὸς Πέρσας τηρεῖν, συμμαχίαν δὲ ἀποστέλλειν ἀντεῖπαν (Diod. 16. 44.1); cf. Isoc. 12 (*Panath.*). 159; [Dem.] 12 (*Philip's Letter*). 6. This was official policy; unofficially, Diophantus, an Athenian, and Lamius, a Spartan, commanded the mercenary forces for the Egyptian king Nectanebos (Diod. 16. 48.2; Isoc. *Epist.* 8.8).

58. Isocrates unconsciously alludes to the change at Sparta in 12 (*Panath.*). 159, composed in 342. There he accuses both Athens and Sparta of seeking cordial relations with the king in the hope of individual gain.

59. Ca. 353; despite their *philia* with the king (Plut. *Pel.* 30.5), the Thebans sent Pammenes with 5,000 men to serve Artabazus (Diod. 16. 34.1–2), apparently to raise money for their ongoing war with the Phocians (Grote, *History of Greece*, vol. 8, 252); Grote comments: "The Thebans, it would seem, having no fleet and no maritime dependencies, were less afraid of giving offence to the Great King than Athens had been, when she interdicted Chares from aiding Artabazus." Pammenes served well, but Artabazus suspected his loyalty (Polyaenus 7. 33.2); and indeed, in 350, the king sent 300 talents to Thebes (Diod. 16. 40.1–2). Perhaps he was buying Theban neutrality in addition to mercenaries; at least that is suggested by Dem. 14 (*Symm.*). 33–34.

whatever actions or declarations were required. At the same time, a great deal of unofficial harassment was also carried on more or less surreptitiously by self-interested surrogates. The Athenians did nothing to interfere with the private mercenary service provided by their most talented generals to rebellious kings and satraps, and the Persian king allowed (and perhaps even encouraged) the intrigues of ambitious satraps who sought wherever possible to weaken the Athenian alliance. In reality, the situation amounted to a cold war conducted by shrewd and experienced adversaries, each determined to keep the other as weak as possible without risking the dangerous uncertainty of open warfare. And throughout this period, an essential diplomatic position adopted by both sides was the pretended noninvolvement of official neutrality during each other's independent conflicts.

IV. NEUTRALITY IN THE THIRD SACRED WAR (356/355–346)

Relations between the Phocians and Thebans deteriorated after the Phocians refused to join Epaminondas' last invasion of the Peloponnesus in 362 (see 9.2.D above). Not long afterwards, probably in 356, when the Thebans persuaded the Amphictyonic Council that protected the sanctuary of Apollo at Delphi to punish the Phocians for allegedly cultivating the sacred territory of Cirrha, the Phocians resisted.[60] Backed by a strong mercenary force under Philomelus, the Phocians occupied Delphi in the early spring of 355 and defiantly erased the decree of the amphictyony. The council in turn declared a "sacred war" against the Phocians and solicited contributions throughout Greece for the defense of the sanctuary.[61] Thus the

60. Concerning 362, see Xen. *Hell.* 7. 5.4; 9.2.D above; on the condemnation in 356, see Diod. 16. 23.3–5 (for other causes, see Jacoby, *FGH* 76, Duris frag. 2; Paus. 10. 2.1; Justin 8.1). On the chronology followed here, see Sealey, *History of the Greek City-States*, 463–68. In the beginning, the Phocians had a relatively good justification for their actions. Theban manipulation of the Amphictyonic Council was obvious, and the blatant injustice of the punishments must have aroused considerable sympathy among other states. After all, it was universally acknowledged that the sanctity of the oracle not only exempted Delphi from direct involvement in interstate politics but also obligated the sanctuary to that policy as a guarantee of its legitimately Panhellenic identity (see 3.1 above). By violating this basic mandate, the Thebans had destroyed the single most important force that protected the sanctuary. Phocian intervention could therefore be defended as a lawful restoration of the nonalignment and impartiality of the sanctuary after its role was perverted by Thebes' politicization of the Amphictyonic Council.

61. Diod. 16. 24.3–5, 28.4; Paus. 10. 2.2.

lines were drawn for a major power struggle in central Greece. The only question that seemed to remain was just how extensive the alignment of states would be.

According to Diodorus, Philomelus sent embassies to Thebes, Sparta, and Athens and "to the other most distinguished *poleis* throughout Hellas" to explain and defend his seizure of Delphi and to promise that he would give an account of his guardianship to anyone who wished it.[62] In addition, "he asked that if any cities were going to war with the Phocians on account of enmity or jealousy, they should far more preferably ally themselves with him, or, if not that, at least remain neutral."[63] Although Diodorus is vague about the exact outcome of these embassies, he later states that after Philomelus had been killed and had been succeeded in command by Onomarchus, the Thessalians were induced by bribery to become neutral; and echoing his earlier statement, just quoted, Diodorus adds that Onomarchus distributed the bribes primarily among leaders in the allied cities, but "he also corrupted many of the enemy, some of whom he persuaded to become allies and some of whom he required to remain neutral."[64]

Aside from the Thessalians, Diodorus names no states; but Justin (8. 4) accuses Philip II of receiving bribes for his promised neutrality, and at least two states, Sicyon and Megara, can tentatively be identified as neutral. According to C. H. Skalet, Sicyon must have maintained friendly relations with the Phocians because Sicyonians are listed among the sanctuary building commissioners (*naopoioi*) who served during the years of the occupation.[65] Legon concludes that "Megarian neutrality seems to have continued in the period after the Battle of Mantinea."[66] As evidence, he points to a passage in Isocrates' speech of 355, *On the Peace*, in which Isocrates cites the Megarians as a paradigm of political and diplomatic moderation (*sōphrosynē*) and contrasts them with the contentious and politically unstable Thessalians:

---

62. Diod. 16. 27.3–4.

63. ἠξίου δέ, ἄν τις δι' ἔχθραν ἢ φθόνον πολεμῇ Φωκεῦσι, μάλιστα μὲν συμμαχεῖν, εἰ δὲ μή γε, τὴν ἡσυχίαν ἄγειν (Diod. 16. 27.4); cf. Polyb. 9. 33.4.

64. διέφθειρε δὲ καὶ τῶν πολεμίων πολλούς, οὓς μὲν συμμαχεῖν πείθων, οὓς δὲ τὴν ἡσυχίαν ἔχειν ἀξιῶν (Diod. 16. 33.2); cf. H. D. Westlake, *Thessaly in the Fourth Century* (London, 1935), 172–74. Westlake believes only Pherae was actually corrupted through bribery (172 n. 1) but contradicts his own view (182).

65. Skalet, *Ancient Sicyon*, 76.

66. Legon, *Megara*, 278.

What are the reasons that the Thessalians, who inherited very great wealth and possess a very rich and abundant territory, have been reduced to poverty, while the Megarians, who had small and insignificant resources to begin with and who possess neither land nor harbours nor mines but are compelled to farm mere rocks, own estates which are the greatest among the Hellenes? Why is it that the Thessalians, with a cavalry of more than three thousand horse and light-armed troops beyond number, have their fortresses occupied from time to time by certain other states while the Megarians, with only a small force, govern their city as they see fit? And, again, why is it that the Thessalians are always at war with each other while the Megarians, who dwell between the Peloponnesians on the one hand and the Thebans and the Athenians on the other, are continually in a state of peace?[67]

This passage contains interesting echoes of the rhetoric used in the Corcyraean-Corinthian debate in Thucydides.[68] The Megarians' abstention from involvement in interstate conflict (their *sōphrosynē*) had been successful, and there is no good reason to think that they suddenly abandoned that policy to join in such an uncertain conflict as the Third Sacred War.

If history repeated itself, the Thebans and their allies might have accused neutral states of abandoning the "just" cause.[69] But the truth was that both the dubious legality of the provocative actions of members of the amphictyony and the reality of the Phocians' military strength must have made normally pacific states more hesitant to become involved than ever. The prominent accusations that neutrality was motivated by bribery reveal how the Phocians' opponents sought to shame neutrals into action. But the attractions of the policy were strong. The Phocians recognized this; and they might well have succeeded in their combined diplomatic and military offensive if it had not been for the unforeseen intervention of Philip II.

V. NEUTRALITY IN THE CONFLICT BETWEEN PHILIP II AND THE GREEK STATES (359–338)

Despite the fact that evidence is scanty and comes mostly from hostile sources, there can be no doubt that during the recurrent conflicts between the Athenians and Philip II neutrality had con-

67. Isoc. 8 (*On the Peace*). 117–18, trans. Norlin.
68. See chapter 2 above, and 5.3.C.
69. See the speech of Hermocrates in 7.2 above.

siderable appeal for many Greek city-states. Demosthenes unintentionally provides good evidence of this in his repeated outbursts of
acute frustration at the widespread adoption of neutral policy. For
example, in the *Third Philippic* (341) he complains:

> We are in such a miserable position, we have so entrenched ourselves
> in our different cities, that to this very day we can do nothing that
> our interest or our duty demands; we cannot combine, we cannot
> take any common pledge of help or friendship; but we idly watch
> the growing power of this man, each bent (or so it seems to me) on
> profiting by the interval afforded by another's ruin, taking not a
> thought, making not an effort for the salvation of Greece. For that
> Philip, like the recurrence of attacks of a fever or some other disease,
> is threatening even those who think themselves out of reach.[70]

The origins of Demosthenes' frustration can be seen in Philip's
shrewd manipulation of the widespread mistrust of Athens. In an
earlier speech supporting the Peace of Philocrates (346), Demosthenes described the situation vividly:

> If we should hereafter come to blows with Philip, about Amphipolis
> or in any private quarrel not shared by the Thessalians or the
> Argives or the Thebans, I do not believe for a moment that any of
> the latter would be dragged into the war. ... They would never
> make such a sacrifice unless the war had a common cause and
> origin. If we went to war again with the Thebans about Oropus or
> for some other private reason, I do not think we should suffer, for
> both their allies and ours would, of course, offer support, if their
> own territory were invaded, but would not join either side in aggres-
> sion. That is the way with every alliance worth considering, and
> such is the natural result. No individual ally is so fond either of us
> or of the Thebans as to regard our security and our supremacy in
> the same light.[71]

---

70. Trans. Vince.

οὕτω δὲ κακῶς διακείμεθα καὶ διορωρύγμεθα κατὰ πόλεις ὥστ' ἄχρι τῆς
τήμερον ἡμέρας οὐδὲν οὔτε τῶν συμφερόντων οὔτε τῶν δεόντων πρᾶξαι
δυνάμεθα, οὐδὲ συστῆναι, οὐδὲ κοινωνίαν βοηθείας καὶ φιλίας οὐδεμίαν
ποιήσασθαι, ἀλλὰ μείζω γιγνόμενον τὸν ἄνθρωπον περιορῶμεν, τὸν χρόνον
κερδᾶναι τοῦτον ὃν ἄλλος ἀπόλλυται ἕκαστος ἐγνωκώς, ὥς γ' ἐμοὶ δοκεῖ,
οὐχ ὅπως σωθήσεται τὰ τῶν Ἑλλήνων σκοπῶν οὐδὲ πράττων, ἐπεί, ὅτι
γ' ὥσπερ περίοδος ἢ καταβολὴ πυρετοῦ ἢ ἄλλου τινὸς κακοῦ καὶ τῷ
πάνυ πόρρω δοκοῦντι νῦν ἀφεστάναι προσέρχεται.   (Dem. 9 [*Third Phil.*].
28–29)

71. Trans. Vince.

ἐγὼ γάρ, εἰ γένοιθ' ἡμῖν πρὸς Φίλιππον πάλιν πόλεμος δι' Ἀμφίπολιν ἤ τι
τοιοῦτ' ἔγκλημ' ἴδιον, οὗ μὴ μετέχουσι Θετταλοὶ μηδ' Ἀργεῖοι μηδὲ
Θηβαῖοι, οὐκ ἂν ἡμῖν οἴομαι τούτων οὐδένας πολεμῆσαι. ... οὔκουν

This statement leaves no doubt that by 346 the days when the leading Greek states could expect the unhesitating support of their allies in any conflict were a thing of the past. Demosthenes lamented this change; but the majority of Greek states, including Athens' own allies, seemed to have welcomed it and to have made it clear that they would not support a war against Philip (or any other power) if they themselves were not directly threatened.[72] Years later, in 330, Demosthenes reflected on this refusal and attributed it to either baseness (*kakia*) or stupidity (*agnoia*) or both and concluded: "You [Athenians] were fighting a long and incessant war for purposes in which, as the event has proved, [the other Greek states] were all concerned, and yet they helped you neither with money, nor with men, nor with anything else."[73]

Granting then that neutrality was a very real, and perhaps even decisive, policy during the rise of Macedon, several important (but ignored) questions nevertheless remain. When Demosthenes condemns the neutral policy of other states, exactly which states does he mean? And just what did these states expect as a result of their neutrality? That is, were they confident that they could maintain their independence regardless of the outcome of the conflict between Philip and Athens? Or was neutrality, as Demosthenes claimed, merely a disguise for support of Macedonian conquest?

πρόοιντ' ἂν αὐτοὺς εἰς τοῦτο, μὴ κοινῆς τῆς ἀρχῆς καὶ τῆς αἰτίας οὔσης τοῦ πολέμου. οὐδέ γ' εἰ πάλιν πρὸς τοὺς Θηβαίους πολεμήσαιμεν δι' Ὠρωπὸν ἤ τι τῶν ἰδίων, οὐδὲν ἂν ἡμᾶς παθεῖν ἡγοῦμαι· καὶ γὰρ ἡμῖν κἀκείνοις τοὺς βοηθοῦντας ἂν οἶμαι, εἰς τὴν οἰκείαν εἴ τις ἐμβάλοι, βοηθεῖν, οὐ συνεπιστρατεύσειν οὐδετέροις. καὶ γὰρ αἱ συμμαχίαι τοῦτον ἔχουσι τὸν τρόπον, ὧν καὶ φροντίσειεν ἄν τις, καὶ τὸ πρᾶγμα φύσει τοιοῦτόν ἐστιν· οὐκ ἄχρι τῆς ἴσης ἕκαστός ἐστιν εὔνους οὔθ' ἡμῖν οὔτε Θηβαίοις, σῶς τ' εἶναι καὶ κρατεῖν τῶν ἄλλων, ... ἂν βούλοινθ' ... (Dem. 5 [*On the Peace*]. 14–17)

Cf. Aeschin. 2 (*On the Embassy*). 71.

72. For unsuccessful efforts to rouse support from other Greek states, among others, see Aeschin. 2 (*On the Embassy*). 57–60, 79–80; 3 (*In Ctes.*). 58, 64, 97–98; Dem. 2 (*Second Olynth.*). 11; 18 (*De cor.*). 20, 23–24, 44–45; 19 (*False Leg.*). 10, 16, 303. For the change in attitude toward the legal rights of states, see Isocrates' condemnation of the former policies of Sparta (12 [*Panath.*]. 45–46, 185–88; delivered in 342).

73. Trans. Vince and Vince: οἳ πόλεμον συνεχῆ καὶ μακρὸν πολεμούντων ὑμῶν, καὶ τοῦτον ὑπὲρ τῶν πᾶσι συμφερόντων, ὡς ἔργῳ φανερὸν γέγονεν, οὔτε χρήμασιν οὔτε σώμασιν οὔτ' ἄλλῳ οὐδενὶ τῶν ἀπάντων συνελάμβανον ὑμῖν (Dem. 18 [*De cor.*]. 20).

A. THE IDENTIFICATION OF NEUTRAL STATES

If we set aside as the product of patriotic exaggeration Demosthenes' categorical condemnation of all states that failed to join the Athenian alliance, other evidence, though severely limited, indicates that a surprisingly large number of states did not take part in the final conflict between Philip and the opposing Greek alliance. The examination of available evidence suggests many were formally neutral.

Argos. The Argives have been commonly identified as neutral; and three determinants of their policy have been suggested: (1) existing alliances with both belligerents, (2) their confidence in the goodwill of Philip, and (3) the potential blockade of the Isthmus by Corinth and Megara.[74] Supporting the first, the scholiast to Aeschines 3. 83 mentions an alliance made in 343/342 between Athens and the Achaeans, Arcadians, Argives, Megalopolitans, and Messenians; and this information has been seemingly confirmed by a fragmentary Athenian inscription that preserves the word "alliance" (*symmachia*) and the name of the Messenians.[75] Neither the exact historical context nor the terms of this alliance are preserved; but it seems likely at least that the various parties in the alliance had different goals—the Peloponnesian states were seeking protection against Sparta, and Athens support against Philip.[76]

On the other side, the case for an Argive-Macedonian alliance is entirely circumstantial. In 343, Demosthenes accused several Peloponnesian states, including Argos, of being infatuated with Philip. He does not, however, mention an alliance specifically, and it must be admitted that this is hard to explain, since it seems incredible that Demosthenes would have omitted mention of some-

---

74. See Grote, *History of Greece*, vol. 9, followed and elaborated by C. W. Roebuck, "The Settlements of Philip II with the Greek States in 338 B.C.," *CP* 43 (1948): 76, cf. 84–85.

75. *IG* II/III², 225; see Bengtson, *SVA²* no. 337.

76. See in support Paus. 4. 28.2 (which may refer to the alliance of 343/342, though Bengtson, *SVA²* no. 337, does not cite it). According to Pausanias, "the Messenians with Argos and Arkadia resisted [Sparta] in arms and asked the Athenians to come and fight for them; the Athenians said they would never invade Lakonia with them, but they promised to come if Lakonia started the war and attacked Messenia" (trans. P. Levi, Pausanias, *Guide to Greece*, vol. 2: *Southern Greece*, Penguin Classics [Harmondsworth, 1971], 167). On contemporary distrust of Sparta, see Diod. 15. 39; Isoc. 5 (*Philip*). 49; Dem. 16 (*Megalop.*). 22–23. On the military weakness of Argos at this time, see Isoc. 5 (*Philip*). 51–52.

thing as serious as a formal alliance, unless perhaps he still hoped
that if his rhetorical efforts succeeded, these states might be willing
to ignore past commitments and align themselves with Athens.[77]
As for the second factor influencing Argive policy, Argos' expectations of Philip and those of other abstaining states are best discussed
together and will be taken up in section B below.

Finally, the possibility of anti-Macedonian allies blocking the
movement of opposing troops at the Isthmus (realized when Corinth joined the Athenian alliance) presented a very real obstacle to
any Peloponnesian state seeking to join Philip. However, forces
could be ferried by sea. Still, since Argos lay on the southeastern
side of the Peloponnesus, the Argives would not only have to avoid
the hostile Athenian (and Corinthian?) fleets if they circumnavi-
gated the peninsula, but would also have to pass the hostile coast
of Achaea and disembark in the enemy territory of Locris or
Boeotia. Yet if Argos formally allied itself with Philip, it is very
strange that no source mentions it. This silence becomes entirely
understandable, however, if Argos simply remained neutral, not
only because the sources normally pay little attention to neutrals
but also because the policy itself is a common Argive posture.

Arcadia.   Included under this rubric are Tegea, Mantinea, Mega-
lopolis, and other smaller city-states of the central Peloponnesus.
Although the scholiast to Aeschines 3. 83 lists the Arcadians among
the states that allied themselves with Athens in 342, this seems
wrong. None of these states play any role on either side in the final
conflict of 340–338 or during the earlier warfare between Philip
and Athens.[78] Furthermore, Demosthenes (18 [*De cor.*].64) seems
to confirm their abstention in his restrospective lament that the
Arcadians together with the Messenians and the Argives did nothing to oppose Philip in the confident hope of selfish gain. The
Arcadians' diplomatic expectations and strategic considerations

77. Dem. 19 (*False Leg.*). 260–62. The existence of a formal alliance is generally
assumed (see, for example, Roebuck, "The Settlements of Philip II with the Greek
States in 338 B.C.," 76, 84), and Bengtson (commentary to *SVA²* no. 337) accepts
it, although he does not include it in his compilation, presumably because of the
lack of solid evidence.

78. Note Dem. 6 (*Second Phil.*). 25, in which Demosthenes expresses frustration
over the Arcadians' preference for peace; Roebuck, "The Settlements of Philip II
of Macedonia with the Greek States in 338 B.C.," 76, gives the same reasons as
Argos.

would have been essentially the same as those of the Argives and will be discussed below in section B.

Messene. The Messenians had been protected from Spartan aggression by Philip's threatened intervention in 344 and by their subsequent alliance with Athens in 342.[79] Pausanias alone reports that there was an alliance with Philip, but adds that "they [the Messenians] say this [alliance with Philip] is what prevented them from taking part in the battle the rest of Greece fought at Chaeronea: and of course they certainly had no intention of bearing arms on the opposite side to Greece."[80] What the Messenians said about their policy after the fact may have been self-serving, but neutrality resulting from conflicting alliances was not unprecedented in classical diplomacy (see 7.3 above). It also explains why Demosthenes bitterly criticizes the Messenians' lack of support (18 [*De cor.*].64) but never accuses them of failing to meet the obligations of their alliance with Athens.[81] Other strategic considerations encouraging abstention would have been essentially the same as those for Argos.

Elis. The policy of Elis appears to have been in large part dictated by intense internal conflict. About 344 an exiled faction of pro-Macedonian oligarchs carried out a bloody coup against the democratic government and entered into an alliance with Philip.[82]

79. On the connection with Philip, see Dem. 6 (*Second Phil.*). 9, 13, 25–26; cf. Roebuck, "The Settlements of Philip II of Macedonia with the Greek States in 338 B.C.," 76; with Athens, Bengtson, *SVA²* no. 337; cf. [Plut.] *X orat.* 851B (= *SVA²* no. 343), where the Messenians are wrongly listed as allies during the final conflict; see below, with the following note.

80. Paus. 4. 28.2, trans. Levi.

81. Note also that limitations on mutual support were becoming increasingly common in treaties of the fourth century; see, among others, Bengtson, *SVA²* nos. 290, 291, 293, 307, 318, 337, 340, in contrast to no. 308, for example (= Tod, no. 158, a treaty between Philip and the Chalcidian League in which no limitation on joint action is envisioned [lines 10–13]) and no. 345, where Aeschines (3 [*In Ctes.*]. 142) accuses Demosthenes of allowing terms in the alliance with Thebes that obligated Athens to aid Thebes in forcing any unwilling Boeotian cities to join the alliance with Thebes. Aeschines considers this outrageously unjust.

82. On the coup, see Dem. 19 (*False Leg.*). 260, 294; 9 (*Third Phil.*). 27; [Dem.] 10 (*Response to Phil.*). 10; Paus. 4. 28.4 ("which clearly derives from Demosthenes," so J. R. Ellis, *Philip II and Macedonian Imperialism* [London, 1976], 279 n. 103) and 5. 4.9; see also Beloch, *Griechische Geschichte*, vol. 3, part 1, 541. On the alliance, see Paus. 5. 4.9; cf. Dem. 9 (*Third Phil.*). 27. On the alignment of parties, we should remember Ellis' sensible warning (regarding the contemporary revolution at Megara) that "Demosthenes' picture of a pro-Athenian *demos* resisting a pro-Macedonian few is false" (278 n. 102). This surely applies also to foreign policy.

No subsequent Athenian alliance is attested; but some confusion arises from Aelian *VH* 1.6, where Elis is listed with states that opposed Philip at Chaeronea. However, the silence of other sources, particularly Demosthenes, certainly indicates that this is untrue; and modern commentators have dismissed the reference.[83] The truth seems to be accurately recorded by Pausanias, who attributes to the Eleans essentially the same apology put forth by the Messenians, namely that the Eleans "joined the Macedonian alliance, but they could not tolerate fighting on the anti-Greek side at Chaeronea, though they did take part in Philip's attack on Lakonia, because of ancient bitterness."[84] Though apologetic, this statement not only helps explain Elean policy but also suggests that Philip took the Eleans' neutrality in stride and harbored no resentment against them on account of it.

Sparta.   Despite an existing alliance with Athens, Sparta sent no troops to the allied army at Chaeronea. Lingering hatred of Thebes was, perhaps, one cause of this inactivity, but since Philip had also shown himself to be hostile to Sparta and a far more immediate threat to Spartan hopes for the recovery of Messene, the decision not to join the anti-Macedonian alliance was probably most influenced by Sparta's acute lack of manpower.[85] At the same time, Sparta's strategy for recovering its former power in the Peloponnesus appears to have rested on a long-range plan for rebuilding its former military strength by accumulating money from mercenary service; and it happened that in 338 Archidamus was serving in

83. E.g., Roebuck, "The Settlements of Philip II of Macedonia with the Greek States in 338 B.C.," 73 n. 1; N. G. L. Hammond and G. T. Griffith, *A History of Macedonia*, vol. 2: *550–336 B.C.* (Oxford, 1979), 604 n. 6; Aelian's list may, however, represent a genuine apologetic tradition that arose later to exonerate Elis from charges of pro-Macedonian complicity; see Polyb. 18. 14; Walbank, *Commentary on Polybius*, vol. 2, 566.

84. Trans. Levi.

Φιλίππου δὲ τοῦ Ἀμύντου οὐκ ἐθέλοντος ἀποσχέσθαι τῆς Ἑλλάδος, προσε-
χώρησαν μὲν ἐς τὴν συμμαχίαν τῶν Μακεδόνων οἱ Ἠλεῖοι στάσει κακωθέν-
τες ὑπὸ ἀλλήλων, μαχεσθῆναι δὲ οὐχ ὑπέμειναν τοῖς Ἕλλησιν ἐναντία ἐν
Χαιρωνείᾳ· τῆς δὲ ἐφόδου Φιλίππῳ τῆς ἐπὶ Λακεδαιμονίους μετέσχον κατὰ
ἔχθος ἐς αὐτοὺς τὸ ἀρχαῖον.   (Paus. 5. 4.9)

85. On the continuing suspicion of Thebes, see Isoc. 5. (*Philip*). 50. Sparta's manpower was, in fact, so severely depleted that the risk of yet another defeat in Central Greece was simply unthinkable (see Cartledge, *Sparta and Laconia*, 307–18).

Italy.[86] Given these disadvantageous circumstances, the Spartans were in no position to join the opposition to Macedon and risk retaliation from those Peloponnesian states whose sympathies were known to be with Philip. The policy failed, however, because of Philip's determination to solidify and protect the peace settlements of 338 by eliminating any possibility of Spartan resurgence. Still, it must be remembered that prior to his victory at Chaeronea, Philip's intentions toward Sparta remained unclear; and the Spartans, along with many other states, had reason to expect that their neutrality would be respected and would protect them from either hostility or intervention.

Possible Neutrals.   Sicyon and Phlius in the Peloponnesus, Cephallenia and the majority of Acarnanians in northwestern Greece, and Byzantium and Perinthus in the northeast all may have remained officially neutral during the conflict of 340–338.[87] Unfortunately, the evidence regarding the policy of these states is extremely meager. About Sicyon and Phlius there is no specific mention of policy; yet the known presence of prominent pro-Macedonian politicians in Sicyon suggests that its policy was the focus of an internal dispute that could have resulted in the city remaining neutral.[88] Similarly, the Phliasians may have followed the example of Argos, the Arcadian cities, and Elis but with so little ado that it left no impression in the sources.

The states of northwestern Greece had been threatened by Philip during his campaign into that region during 343. Demosthenes later boasted that his efforts at the time saved Ambracia and the Acarnanians from Philip; but it remains unclear whether or not these states subsequently joined the anti-Macedonian alliance.[89] Their absence from the lists of allies has led to ingenious explanations.

86. Beloch, *Griechische Geschichte*, vol. 3, part 1, 595, with n. 1.
87. However, the cities in Akte (Epidaurus, Troezen, and the island of Poros) joined the Greek alliance (Ael. *VH* 6. 1; Lycurg. *Leoc.* 42), as did Corinth and the cities of Achaea (Dem. 18 [*De cor.*]. 237).
88. Dem. 18 (*De cor.*). 48, 295; Skalet, *Ancient Sicyon*, 77.
89. Acarnania, unlike Leucas, is nowhere listed as a member of the Greek alliance. Aeschines (3 [*In Ctes.*]. 97–98) accuses Demosthenes of promising after his embassy in 340 that the Acarnanians would contribute 2,000 hoplites to the "Hellenic League"; but Aeschines adds in the next breath that this amounted to "hopes that were never realized and armies that were never assembled" (100)— a remark that does not seem to have been noticed by modern scholars, who have repeatedly assumed that the Acarnanians joined the alliance.

Perhaps, it is argued, the Acarnanians sent no official aid but allowed volunteers to serve in the allied army. But such an explanation is necessary only if we accept that there is some truth in Aeschines' scoffing reference to Acarnanian contributions, about which Demosthenes, who is especially eager to take credit for all such support, makes no mention.[90] It is simpler to assume that the northwestern Greek states, which are not specifically named as members of the Greek alliance, merely abstained. This would then apply also to Cephallenia, which is nowhere mentioned as an ally of either side. In this case, the silence seems especially suggestive, since both of the principal neighboring states, Corcyra and Leucas, are listed among the anti-Macedonian allies.[91]

Lastly, Byzantium and its neighbor Perinthus may also have refused either to join or to give official support to the anti-Macedonian alliance. Neither Demosthenes nor Aeschines mentions either state as an ally, and despite the recent aid that Athens had given them against Philip's aggression, which is known to have been gratefully received, there is no good evidence that either state joined the anti-Macedonian alliance.[92] Admittedly, the Byzantians appear

90. Tod, no. 178 (cf. Diod. 17. 3) records honors for Acarnanian individuals who served out of ancestral (lines 8–11) *philia* for Athens, but this does not mean that there was official commitment; the need to protect these loyal friends (lines 28–31) suggests the opposite. See Demosthenes' list of allies (18 [*De cor.*]. 237); Aeschin. 2 (*On the Embassy*). 57–60, 79–80; 3 (*In Ctes.*). 58, 64, 97–98; Bengtson, *SVA²* no. 343. Roebuck, "The Settlements of Philip II of Macedonia with the Greek States in 338 B.C.," 76 n. 16, includes Cephallenia in the Greek alliance "from our general knowledge of the situation in western Greece"; but given the uncertainty about the policy of nearby states, such a generalization is wholly unjustified.

91. Dem. 18 (*De cor.*). 237; cf. [Plut.] *Dem.* 17.

92. Byzantium was allied with Philip when he attacked in 340 (Dem. 9 [*Third Phil.*]. 35; 18 [*De cor.*]. 87) but had refused to join him in his campaigns against other Thracians. Demosthenes accuses Philip of disregard for international conventions, stating that the Byzantine refusal was justified on the grounds that their alliance included no obligation to join in offensive conflicts (18 [*De cor.*]. 87); that is, they had the right to remain neutral, and Philip violated that right. Grote, *History of Greece*, vol. 9, 447 n. 1, argues that the peace treaty that Diodorus (16. 77; under 340/339) says resulted from Philip's failure to take Byzantium and Perinthus was real, although the reference to participation by Athens was mistaken. This view has been abandoned more recently; Bengtson, for instance, omits the treaty from *SVA²*; G. T. Griffith, in Hammond and Griffith, *History of Macedonia*, 580, is a little more generous, observing, "Diodorus has made some muddle here; but I suppose that he made it out of something in his source(s), and did not invent it out of his own head." Still, he agrees with Schaefer, *Demosthenes und seine Zeit*, vol. 2, 488 n. 4, and others that Byzantium and Perinthus were subsequently in the Greek alliance. This conclusion is based on the crowns voted by these cities to Athens (Dem. 18 [*De cor.*]. 89–91; the decree in 90–91, however,

in one late list of allies who opposed Philip, but the same list
includes Messene, which clearly remained neutral, and the Locrians,
the inclusion of whom can only be explained on the assumption
that in fact the Amphissans specifically, and not the Locrians en
masse, are meant.[93] As a historical source then the list has no
credibility, particularly since later claims of participation in the
resistance to Macedonia would be especially self-serving and tempting if no record of activity existed to contradict such claims. It has
always been more glamorous to lie about one's war record than to
admit to having played no part at all.

B. THE ATTITUDE OF NEUTRAL STATES

Assessment of the expectations of neutral states is clouded by the
strong bias of the available sources. Demosthenes, in particular, is
absolutely uncompromising in his condemnation of statesmen who
opposed Athens' call for an anti-Macedonian alliance. To him and
his supporters, all resistance was attributable to venal "Philippizers" who had sold their loyalty for Macedonian gold.[94] This categorical accusation is obviously suspicious, but the outcome of
events made the charge credible, and the stigma lingered. There
were, however, some dissenting voices in antiquity. One critic of
Demosthenes' characterization is Polybius, who offers a detailed

---

is spurious), Demosthenes' reference to Byzantium fighting with Athens (230) and
to the Athenian-Byzantine alliance of 340 (254, 302; but omitted by Bengtson).
None of the aforementioned pieces of evidence is decisive. Decrees of thanks are
not the same as an alliance, which, if it existed at all, would not necessarily have
obligated Byzantium and Perinthus to join the Greek alliance. In addition, there
is no context for Demosthenes' reference to Byzantium fighting with Athens,
which makes it difficult to decide whether he means the final conflict of 339/338
or an earlier encounter (340). I believe we should return to Grote's interpretation
and accept the existence of a peace treaty between Philip and the Byzantians and
Perinthians (and perhaps the other states—Rhodes, Chios, Cos—that aided them)
that resulted in the neutrality of these states during the final conflict of 339/338.
Why else, we might ask, would it be necessary for Athens to dispatch its most
talented general (also the only one not suspected by Byzantium and Perinthus)
with a significant naval force to the Hellespontine region in the spring of 338
(Plut. *Phoc.* 14.8)? If Byzantium and Perinthus were allies, would they not have
been able to harry Macedonian shipping (as they had in the past [see Philip's
letter in Dem. 12. 2]) without taxing Athens so heavily?
    93. [Plut.] *X orat.* 851B; rejected by Roebuck, "The Settlements of Philip II
of Macedonia with the Greek States in 338 B.C.," 76 n. 16, and others.
    94. For typical accusations, see Dem. 9 (*Third Phil.*). 37–40, 53–69; [Dem.] 10
(*Fourth Phil.*). 4–5; 18 (*De cor.*). 18–19, 48, 61; 19 (*False Leg.*) 7–8; [Dem.] 7
(*Halon.*). 45. Aeschines restricts his accusations to Demosthenes.

defense of several of the accused politicians in a lengthy digression on treachery. They could not be called traitors, he argues, because they were fully justified in pursuing the best interests of their own states when they conflicted with those of Athens. Nor was there any treachery, he concludes, since their policy was aimed only at ending domination by the old hegemonial states of mainland Greece, not at transferring it to a new power.[95] Polybius may have his own prejudices, but his account must be closer to the truth than Demosthenes' sweeping image of the "crop of traitors". Indeed, aside from Demosthenes' mudslinging, there is nothing to suggest that states that failed to join the anti-Macedonian alliance, even if they welcomed Philip's intervention in Greece, ever imagined that the outcome of the conflict would be Macedonian supremacy.

But beneath the hostile complaints of the Attic orators lay a sinister reality that many states chose not to see. Even after the Peace of Philocrates, Philip continued to compaign tirelessly. In response, Demosthenes and his circle stepped up their efforts to expose what they believed to be Philip's secret ambition and thus win the support of uncommitted states. As early as 342, Hegesippus attempted to force Philip's intentions into the open by proposing that the guarantees of the Peace of Philocrates be extended to states outside of either the Athenian or the Macedonian alliance:

> As for the other amendment which you [Athenians] propose to introduce, that all the Greeks who are not parties to the peace should remain free and independent, and that if they are attacked, the signatories should unite to defend them, you considered it both fair and generous that the peace should not be confined to Athens and her allies on the one side and Philip and his allies on the other, while those who are allies of neither are exposed to ruin at the hands of their stronger neighbours, but rather that your peace should

95. Polyb. 18. 14.1–15; esp. 9–10, where Polybius remarks:

Had they in acting thus either submitted to have their towns garrisoned by Philip, or abolished their laws and deprived the citizens of freedom of action and speech to serve their own ambition and place themselves in power, they would have deserved the name of traitor. But if preserving the rights of their respective countries, they simply differed in their judgement of facts, thinking that the interests of Athens were not identical with those of their countries, they should, I maintain, not have been dubbed traitors for this reason by Demosthenes (trans. W. R. Paton, Polybius, *The Histories*, vol. 5, Loeb Classical Library [Cambridge, Mass., and London, 1926]).

extend its protection to them also, and that we should disarm and observe a real peace.[96]

With this proposal, Philip's opponents hoped to awaken uncommitted states to the threat of Macedonian imperialism. After all, if Philip truly intended no aggression, he could hardly object to allowing inclusion of these states in the existing peace. But if, as they alleged, he was plotting to conquer them, he could by no means agree to bind himself by oath to protect their independence. The surprise was that even though Philip refused to accept the amendment, his Athenian opponents nonetheless failed to win neutral states to the anti-Macedonian alliance.[97]

Demosthenes excused his own lack of success by blaming "Philippizers" and continued to argue that states remaining at peace would ultimately fall prey to Philip's aggression. In the *Third Philippic* (341), for example, Demosthenes cites the fall of Olynthus and upheavals in other cities and claims, "The patriots demanded a war-subsidy, the others denied its necessity; the patriots bade them fight on and mistrust Philip, the others bade them keep the peace, until they fell into the snare. Not to go into particulars, it is the same tale everywhere, one party speaking to please their audience, the other giving advice that would ensure their safety."[98]

96. Trans. Vince.

Περὶ δὲ τοῦ ἑτέρου ἐπανορθώματος, ὃ ὑμεῖς ἐν τῇ εἰρήνῃ ἐπανορθοῦσθε, τοὺς ἄλλους Ἕλληνας, ὅσοι μὴ κοινωνοῦσι τῆς εἰρήνης, ἐλευθέρους καὶ αὐτονόμους εἶναι, καὶ ἐάν τις ἐπ' αὐτοὺς στρατεύῃ, βοηθεῖν τοὺς κοινωνοῦντας τῆς εἰρήνης, ἡγούμενοι καὶ δίκαιον τοῦτο καὶ φιλάνθρωπον, μὴ μόνον ἡμᾶς καὶ τοὺς συμμάχους τοὺς ἡμετέρους καὶ Φίλιππον καὶ τοὺς συμμάχους τοὺς ἐκείνου ἄγειν τὴν εἰρήνην, τοὺς δὲ μήτε ἡμετέρους ὄντας μήτε Φιλίππου συμμάχους ἐν μέσῳ κεῖσθαι καὶ ὑπὸ τῶν κρειττόνων ἀπόλλυσθαι, ἀλλὰ καὶ τούτοις διὰ τὴν ὑμετέραν εἰρήνην ὑπάρχειν σωτηρίαν, καὶ τῷ ὄντι εἰρήνην ἄγειν ἡμᾶς καταθεμένους τὰ ὅπλα. ([Dem.] 7 [Halon.]. 30–31)

97. G. L. Cawkwell, "Demosthenes' Policy after the Peace of Philocrates," CQ 13 (1963): 133–34, points out that Philip actually turned the tables on his Athenian opponents in the negotiations of 344/343 first by rejecting all proposals because of the inclusion of the single issue of Amphipolis and then by coming back in 342 with his own version of the expanded guarantee, thus putting his opponents in the position of responsibility for the final collapse of efforts to create a system guaranteeing the peace and independence of the less powerful city-states—a characteristically shrewd diplomatic maneuver; for Athenian frustration, see, for example, in 341, Dem. 9 (*Third Phil.*). 118–19, 129–30; in 340, Aeschin. 3 (*In Ctes.*). 67–68.

98. Trans. Vince: εἰσφέρειν ἐκέλευον, οἱ δ' οὐδὲν δεῖν ἔφασαν· πολεμεῖν καὶ μὴ πιστεύειν, οἱ δ' ἄγειν εἰρήνην, ἕως ἐγκατελήφθησαν. τἄλλα τὸν αὐτὸν τρόπον οἶμαι πάνθ', ἵνα μὴ καθ' ἕκαστα λέγω· οἱ μὲν ἐφ' οἷς χαριοῦνται, ταῦτ' ἔλεγον, οἱ δ' ἐξ ὧν ἔμελλον σωθήσεσθαι (Dem. 9 [*Third Phil.*]. 64).

In the *Fourth Philippic* he criticizes neutral policy more explicitly, pointing out that "many so-called 'protectorates' are springing up everywhere, and all states are rivals for the leadership, but unfortunately some hold aloof, in mutual jealousy and distrust, and so each state has isolated itself—Argives, Thebans, Lacedaemonians, Corinthians, Arcadians, ourselves."[99]

But why did Demosthenes and his anti-Macedonian colleagues fail to win the support of nonaligned states? The answer evidently is that Philip made neutrality look very attractive. And this was shrewd diplomacy. From Philip's point of view encouragement of neutrality was the ideal tool for a policy of *divide et impera*. From the very beginning of his conflicts with the Greek city-states, Philip seems to have understood perfectly that, on the one hand, fragmenting his opposition was a vital military necessity and, on the other, achieving this end by exploiting the existing framework of Greek diplomacy offered legitimacy both for himself and his partisans. Philip also had an enormous advantage: his basic need was not for more allies but simply for fewer opponents. The only advantage of bilateral alliances lay in the creation of competing obligations that might result in the neutrality of a given state previously committed by alliance to states whose hostility Philip could not avoid. But more often states had no preexisting commitment that needed to be counteracted. Philip's goal was to make these states believe that their position was secure (or that some specific advantages would come to them) provided only that they refrained from opposing him. He must have known that if he succeeded in this, many states would turn a deaf ear to the appeals of his implacable enemies.

Between 340 and 338 Philip pursued this strategy with considerable success. For example, having seized the entire grain fleet as it left the Euxine in 340, he released all ships from states with which

99. Trans. Vince: ἔπειτα προστασίαι πολλαὶ καὶ πανταχόθεν γίγνονται, καὶ τοῦ πρωτεύειν ἀντιποιοῦνται μὲν πάντες, ἀφεστᾶσιν δ' ἔνιοι, καὶ φθονοῦσι καὶ ἀπιστοῦσιν αὑτοῖς, οὐχ οἷς ἔδει, καὶ γεγόνασι καθ' αὑτοὺς ἕκαστοι, Ἀργεῖοι, Θηβαῖοι, Λακεδαιμόνιοι, κορίνθιοι, Ἀρκάδες, ἡμεῖς ([Dem.] 10 [*Fourth Phil.*] 52). C. R. Kennedy, *The Olynthiac and Other Public Orations of Demosthenes* (New York, 1875), 143 n. 1, explains Demosthenes' critical reference to "protectorates" as follows: "Many states offer to come forward as protectors, but only on condition of taking the lead: they will not join the common cause on fair terms"; note the very similar and roughly contemporary comment of Aristotle in *Pol.* 7.14.1333b35–1334a2.

he was not in direct conflict.[100] Again in 339, having approached the Thebans with an offer of alliance, he conceded that if alliance was unacceptable, he would respect their neutrality providing only that they allowed him free passage through Boeotia.[101] Finally, also in 339, he called upon his allies in the Peloponnesus to send aid for the Amphictyonic War against Amphissa, when he found himself stalled at Elatea by a hostile coalition led by Athens and Thebes.[102] But few contemporaries would have been fooled into believing that Philip truly expected active support as a result of this appeal. His purpose was rather to manipulate public opinion by emphasizing his legal right (as appointed protector of the sanctuary at Delphi) and thereby increasing the pressure on abstaining states either to join him in defending the sanctuary or, at least, to continue avoiding the charge of supporting impiety. No action was taken by the Peloponnesian states discussed above. But at the time it is entirely possible that Philip's ambassadors made a compromise offer—like that just made to Thebes—of neutrality as an acceptable alternative. It was only when the new Hellenic League was founded at Corinth and the option of neutrality was officially precluded by the compulsion of majority rule that the other shoe fell and the neutrals saw clearly that they had lost their independence just as surely as the allies who fought and died at Chaeronea.[103]

SUMMARY

With the alignment of states during the conflict ending at Chaeronea, neutrality in the fourth century came full circle. In the last decade of the fifth century the Agrigentines had refused all assurances of respect for their neutrality when the Carthaginians invaded

---

100. Jacoby, *FGH* 328, Philochorus frag. 162; ibid., *FGH* 115, Theopompus frag. 292; see Griffith's excellent discussion in Hammond and Griffith, *History of Macedonia*, vol. 2, 575–78 (though the reference to Theopompus is incorrect [576 n. 2]).

101. Dem. 18 (*De cor.*). 213; for the pre-347 alliance with Thebes, see Bengtson, *SVA²* no. 327.

102. Dem. 18 (*De cor.*). 156, 158; noted by Griffith, in Hammond and Griffith, *History of Macedonia*, vol. 2, 592.

103. For details (unfortunately obscured by poor sources), see H. Schmitt, *Die Staatsverträge des Altertums*, vol. 3 (Munich and Berlin, 1969), no. 403; Ryder, *Koine Eirene*, 150–62; Hammond and Griffith, *History of Macedonia*, vol. 2, 623–46.

Sicily. Their refusal, after many years of successfully pursuing a neutral policy, is testimony to the severe uncertainty of the time and reflects the harsh reality that confidence in belligerents' respect for neutrality was neither absolute nor permanent. In mainland Greece, the situation was similar. The hegemony of Sparta created a difficult diplomatic situation in which virtually any form of abstention was interpreted as a statement of defiance or a provocative declaration of intended opposition. But the early fourth-century diplomatic situation was in no way static. The gradual weakening of the old hegemonial powers soon resulted in restored respect for the right of both the powerful and the weaker states to maintain neutrality without necessarily forfeiting their friendship (*philia*) or even alliance (*symmachia*) with states that became separately involved in conflicts with other states. Yet the very success and broader acceptance of neutrality also revealed its inherent vulnerability. Philip recognized, like the Persians, Athenians, Spartans, Carthaginians, and countless other conquerors, that neutrality had the potential to be a powerful weapon of subjugation. By convincing would-be adversaries that they would be respected (indeed protected) if they remained neutral, Philip strengthened Macedonian imperialism enormously. Hope, mingled with sheer exhaustion, had replaced the lessons of the fifth century as the guide for public policy in many of the Greek city-states; and it seems quite clear that even if they suspected what the true outcome of the struggle between the Athenian alliance and Philip would be, they nevertheless preferred to let events take their course and to accept the outcome as passive observers rather than active participants. In 338, it can be argued, neutrality worked; yet ironically, its acceptance in the diplomacy of the time resulted not in the preservation of the status quo but in the birth of a new age.

Conclusion

More than two hundred years separate the treaty-supported abstention of Miletus from the exhausted neutrality of a number of city-
states on the eve of Chaeronea. During this long period there are
numerous examples of states remaining uncommitted during wars.
There are also a number of instances where the issue of noninvolvement arose in such a way that it could not be ignored. When all
of these cases are carefully examined, they lead to the conclusion
that both belligerents and nonbelligerents alike recognized that a
neutral policy could be an alternative to alignment and that if such
a policy were adopted, certain rights and obligations should apply.
Unfortunately, there are serious deficiencies in the sources that
often make reconstruction of the exact details of any given state's
policy difficult.

Even in the case of the Peloponnesian War, for which the evidence is by far the best and most extensive, the sources repeatedly
neglect to identify specifically states that seem clearly to have
remained neutral (e.g., the Thessalians and the Cretans throughout;
the cities of Magna Graecia during the Archidamian War). Judging
from the sources' consistent lack of interest in states that successfully abstained from conflicts, we can only assume that the inactivity and detachment of bystanders normally made them unworthy
of notice unless they became involved in a conflict's main action
(consider, for example, Thucydides' concentration on Melos in 416,
Diodorus' focus on Acragas in 406, or Xenophon's sudden interest

in the position of Aegina in 389 and the Achaean cities in the 360s).

As we have seen, Thucydides can be an important exception to this generalization. But even he says nothing in his entire narrative of the Archidamian War (431–421) about the activities of neutral states such as Argos. His silence is especially frustrating because he seems otherwise to have recognized with brilliant insight that the fate of states that attempted to abstain from the conflict accurately reflected the war's harsh consequences and especially its destructive effect on respect for traditionally accepted customs and rules of interstate behavior.

What we have found is that the exact position of a state that sought to be neutral was not clearly defined. The rights and obligations of neutral states were not specifically stipulated in the way that terms for allies or belligerent parties were normally spelled out in alliances or peace treaties. This cannot simply be the result of a lack of specific terminology, for when it really mattered, as in the trial of the Plataeans in 427 or in the terms of the Peace of Nicias in 421, a very clear and legalistic notion of neutrality could be produced.[1] The hindrance to a definition of a neutral position, arose, I believe, from the persistent resentment of neutrality on several levels. For individuals, it conflicted with the commonly understood commitments between *philoi*. More broadly, refusal to participate undermined the whole heroic notion of *kleos*, which defined the individual and even the state in terms of successful military conflict and the renown (*kleos*) that was derived from the demonstration of competitive excellence and superiority over others. But worst of all, in a period in which, despite the aspirations of hegemonial powers, the balance of power was extremely precarious and could be decisively altered by the alignment of even a single previously neutral state (e.g., Corcyra in 433; see 5.3.C above), the existence of uncommitted third parties created serious strategic uncertainty that belligerents were reluctant to accept. None of these objections to neutrality is surprising. The problems faced by neutral states in classical Greece do not differ greatly from those that have plagued neutrals of the modern world. We might compare, for example, the sorry experience of Belgium in the First World War and Melos in the Peloponnesian War. The permanent neutrality of Belgium was recognized by the international com-

---

1. On Plataea, see 6.4 above; on the Peace of Nicias, 6.7.

munity of states from 1839, but in 1914, Germany ignored all
protest and occupied Belgium on the grounds of military necessity.[2]
Twenty-three hundred years before, Melos was crushed by the
Athenians on the excuse that Athenian security was threatened by
Melian nonalignment (see 7.1 above).

The rhetorical characterization of neutrality has also changed
little in over two thousand years. Take, for example, Churchill's
fiery condemnation of neutral states during World War II, Demosthenes' bitter abuse in the fourth century, or Hermocrates' hostile
moralizing in the fifth. During an address intended to prepare
public opinion for the Allied violation of the Scandinavian nations'
neutrality, Churchill heaped blame on neutral states in general and
accused them of inflicting a disadvantage on "the defenders of
freedom":

> We have the greatest sympathy for these forlorn countries, and we
> understand their dangers and their point of view; but it would not
> be right, or in the general interest, that their weakness should feed
> the aggressor's strength and fill to overflowing the cup of human
> woe. There can be no justice if in a mortal struggle the aggressor
> tramples down every sentiment of humanity and if those who resist
> him remain entangled in the tatters of legal conventions.[3]

Demosthenes laments the outcome Churchill claims to fear when
he speaks in retrospect about the neutral stance adopted by many
states throughout the struggle between the Athenians and Philip of
Macedon:

> Now what contributed to [Philip's] success, when he found you
> ready to fall into his trap almost eagerly, was the baseness, or, if
> you prefer the term, the stupidity, or both, of the other Greek states.
> You were fighting a long and incessant war for purposes in which,
> as the event has proved, they were all concerned, and yet they helped
> you neither with money, nor with men, nor with anything else.[4]

In words attributed to him by Thucydides, Hermocrates of Syracuse
also anticipates Churchill's moral posturing when he warns the
uncommitted Camarinaeans:

> No one should regard as fair to us, while safe for you, that prudent
> course of yours—to aid neither, forsooth, as being allies of both.

2. See, for example, P. Alemann, *Die Schweiz und die Verletzung der Bel-
gischen Neutralität im Weltkrieg 1914* (Buenos Aires, 1940), 64.
3. W. S. Churchill, "War Speeches," in *Into Battle* (London, 1941), 181–182.
4. Dem. 18 (*De cor.*). 20, trans. Vince.

Indeed it is not as fair in fact as the plea of right represents it. For if through your failure to take sides as allies the sufferer shall be defeated and the conqueror shall prevail, what else have you done by this selfsame standing aloof but refused to aid one to secure his salvation and to prevent the other from incurring guilt?[5]

The tension between belligerents and neutrals reflected in these statements transcends time and place and the presence or absence of international law.

But there is still the problem of legal definition. Many commentators have dismissed the study of ancient neutrality because of the lack of any well-developed international legal system in classical Greece;[6] and indeed, the absence of a body of statutes ratified by the international community of states is undeniable. Yet we may well remember that a precise, juridical definition of neutrality has also proven elusive in modern international law. The number of years that elapsed between the publication of Grotius' *De iure belli ac pacis* (Paris, 1625), in which neutrals are only vaguely referred to as *medii*, and E. Vattel's *Le droit des gens* (London, 1758), where this category of states receives specific legal definition, is close to the number of years that intervened between the defeat of Xerxes (480/479) and the battle of Chaeronea (338).[7] In both of these periods there was only very gradual acceptance of the indisputable existence of neutrals and in neither was a perfectly clear definition of the rights and obligations of neutrals established. Furthermore, during the nearly 250 years since Vattel, neutrality has not been a static concept but has evolved constantly.[8] The twentieth century, in particular, has demonstrated with devastating clarity that despite all attempts to achieve a universally accepted legal definition, in actual practice the "laws" pertaining to neutrality are constantly challenged, repudiated, and simply ignored by belligerents.[9] It there-

5. Thuc. 6. 80.1–2, trans. Smith.

6. See, for example, the studies mentioned above in the Preface.

7. See I. Brownlie, *International Law and the Use of Force by States* (Oxford, 1963), 315–16; Ørvik, *Decline of Neutrality*, 38–49.

8. Consider the debate over the policy of the United States toward conflicts in Latin America, see "Nonenforcement of the Neutrality Act: International Law and Foreign Policy Powers under the Constitution," *Harvard Law Review* 95 (1982): 1955–75.

9. See, for instance, P. Devlin, *Too Proud to Fight: Woodrow Wilson's Neutrality* (New York, 1975), 137, who concludes: "The history of international law in the twentieth century has been and will be the history of the withering away of neutrality." For similar conclusions, see Ørvik, *Decline of Neutrality*, Appendix VI, "Non-alignment and Neutrality since 1952," 279–302; J. W. Coogan, *The End*

fore seems fair to conclude—though perhaps it is hard to accept—
that the presence or absence of legal definition in the corpus of
international law is simply not the most critical requirement for
the successful existence of neutrality, ancient or modern.

Once we are able to pass beyond the misplaced stumbling block
of legality, important conclusions about the essential elements and
conceptual structure of neutrality in all periods begin to emerge.
Especially revealing is a comparison of classical Greek practices
involving abstention with their modern counterparts in international law. If we compare the substance of the nineteen specific
articles of neutrality adopted at the Hague Conventions of 1899
and 1907 with the evidence from the classical period, the basic
agreement is striking:

I.   *Neutral territory is inviolable and cannot be traversed or used
by belligerents for military purpose* (ARTICLES 1, 2, 3); *neutrals
have an obligation to prevent such passage or use* (ART. 5); compare
the Thessalians in the Peloponnesian War (431–404) (see 6.3); or the
Sicilian and South Italian city-states (415–413) (see 7.2).

II.   *Belligerents are not to recruit combatants in neutral territory* (ART. 4); *neutrals have an obligation to prevent such recruitment* (ART. 5); compare the Corcyraean speech in 433 (5.3.C); the
Theban decree ca. 383 (8.4.B); Greek regulation of service for Persia
and other belligerent states (389–344) (9.3).

III.   *Neutrals can allow the passage of individuals bound for
belligerent states, the export of goods (even military) to belligerent
states, the conduct of business by belligerents within their territory*
(ART. 6, 7, 8); *but whatever is allowed to one belligerent must be
allowed to the other* (ART. 9); compare the Corcyraean speech in
433 (5.3.C); Argos during the Archidamian War (431–421) (6.1);
Plataea in 429 (6.3); Corcyra in 427 (6.5); the Sicilian and South
Italian city-states (415–413) (7.2–3); small states in the Corinthian
War (395–386) (8.3.C–D).

IV.   *Defense of neutrality, even by force, cannot be regarded as
an act of hostility* (ART. 10); compare Corcyra in 427 (6.5); the
Sicilian and South Italian city-states (431–421) (6.2); (415–413)
(7.2–3); and Athens in 379 (8.4.C).

---

of Neutrality: The United States, Britain, and Maritime Rights, 1899–1915 (Ithaca,
N.Y., and London, 1981).

V. *Individuals cannot take advantage of their neutrality to commit hostile acts against a belligerent without liability to severe punishment* (ART. 17); compare the execution of Pollis of Argos in 429 (6.6); the Persian demand for the recall of Chabrias in 379 and of Chares in the 350s (9.3.B).

Naturally, there are noteworthy differences. Provisions for handling the wounded (ART. 14–15), the status of "native populations" within neutral states (ART. 16), and the requisition of railway property (ART. 19) have no ancient parallels. Nor is there any ancient parallel for the concept of internment (ART. 11–13) or the idea of establishing precedent through the publication of the decisions of prize courts established to adjudicate the disputes between belligerent and neutral parties (ART. 3 and 4 of those relating specifically to neutrality).[10] During the classical period, however, belligerents normally respected the right of neutral merchants to travel without restriction.[11] Nevertheless, true juridical treatment of the rights of neutral shipping appears to have come only during the Hellenistic period, with the widespread acceptance of the Rhodian sea law.[12]

The rules just enumerated applied to states that were seeking to be recognized as uncommitted bystanders during periods of warfare. While recognition could come as the result of a unilateral declaration, in many cases it was achieved through negotiation between the would-be neutrals and the belligerents. When negotiation was the means of recognition, the strongest support came from bilateral treaties, since neutrality could be bolstered by existing agreements that either dictated that a certain state would adhere to a neutral policy in certain circumstances or conceded the option of neutrality more generally. For instance, the Argives cited their treaty with Sparta at the outbreak of the Peloponnesian War (see 6.1), the Achaeans their *philia* with both sides (*ibid.*), and the

10. Nevertheless, these are differences in practice more than conception. I hope to show in a further study that the similarity of accepted practice as well as principle is not a matter of chance but a result of the strong influence of classical precedent on the formulation in the sixteenth to eighteenth century of international law dealing with neutrality.

11. See, for example, Jacoby, *FGH* 328, Philochorus frag. 162, on Philip's respect for neutral commerce (9.5.B); though see also Thuc. 2. 67; 3. 32 on the Spartans' violation of the rights of neutral merchants (see 6.6 above).

12. See Jados, *Consulate of the Sea*, xii, 191–94, no. 276; W. Ashburner, *Rhodian Sea Law* (Oxford, 1909).

Camarinaeans their *symmachia* with both sides (see 7.2). Until 389 Aegina appears to have had an agreement with Athens approved by the Spartans (see 8.3.D), and several Peloponnesian states may have claimed opposing agreements in defense of their neutrality in the conflict between Athens and Philip II (see 9.5.A).

Formal diplomatic connections obviously strengthened the position of neutrals; and indeed, unilateral declarations unsupported by formal obligations binding belligerents to restraint could be dangerous. The West Greek neutrals of 415–413 were respected (see 7.2), but when one faction gained control of Corcyra in 427 and issued a proclamation of neutrality, it was honored by no one (see 6.4). Likewise, Megara apparently kept itself out of the Corinthian War without formal agreements; but the Corinthians were unable to extricate themselves from the same conflict in 394 due to subversion of the movement by the belligerents (see 8.3.A).

These examples raise the issue of consistency. Even if we recognize that neutrality is found as a formal policy in the warfare of the classical Greek city-states, it does not necessarily follow that the practice was well enough established to be considered an institution in Greek diplomacy. To demonstrate institutionalization, evidence of universal recognition of the status is necessary. If that is present, then despite even blatant violations (e.g., Melos in the Peloponnesian War) and inconsistencies (e.g., Megara and Aegina accepted, Corinth subverted, in the Corinthian War) there should be no doubt that the concept of neutrality was recognized, even if its details remained largely undefined. After all, the history of neutrality in all periods is littered with violations, inconsistent practices, and disputed definitions.

There is, in fact, some evidence of institutional recognition of neutrality during the classical period. Take, for example, the Spartans' proposal in 429 that the Plataeans adopt a neutral position. There can be no doubt that neutrality was the policy specifically proposed. Moreover, when the Plataeans refused and were subsequently forced to surrender, the Spartans formally tried and condemned the captive Plataeans—primarily on the legal argument that they refused the Spartans' offer to respect their neutrality ("when, what they had later proposed to them before the siege, that the Plataeans be impartial (*koinous*) in accordance with the earlier agreement, had not been accepted" [Thuc. 3. 68.1; see 6.4 above]). Again, among the specified terms of the Peace of Nicias

(421), several Thracian city-states were designated as neutral with the stipulation that they were free to rejoin the Athenian alliance if they so desired and paid an annual tribute to Athens (see 6.7). This agreement presupposes that a neutral position was not only possible but could be defined and modified by treaty arrangement. Moreover, in another multilateral peace treaty, the first Common Peace of 371, the right of any state to refuse to become involved in subsequent conflict was expressly stated (see the terms in 8.5 above). Finally, in the declaration of Greek states sharing in the Common Peace to the ambassador of the satraps (probably 362), the Greeks assume that the Persian king will understand just as well as they do that their collective promise to preserve friendly relations during his conflict with the rebel satraps means that both parties will remain neutral during their separate conflicts (see 9.3.A).

The existence of an idea, however, does not guarantee its acceptance; and one of the findings of this study is that neutral states commonly were at pains to stress their diplomatic friendship (*philia*) for the belligerents. Although the evidence is widely scattered, there are also grounds for believing that interstate *philia* commonly served as the rhetorical trope and legal justification for neutrality. Like modern nonaggression pacts, *philia* treaties removed the threat of hostility but did not obligate the contracting parties to assist one another militarily. Thucydides makes this perfectly clear in his catalogue of allies at the outset of the Peloponnesian War when he explains that the majority of Achaean cities remained neutral because they had *philia* with both belligerents (2. 9.2). *Philia* is subsequently mentioned as the existing or desired relationship between neutrals and belligerents on numerous occasions, and understandably so.[13] By establishing formally, and emphasizing loudly, their *philia* for the belligerents, neutrals sought to preserve the respect and acceptance that in the absence of either statute or specific agreement the combatants might not otherwise feel toward uncommitted states.

This use of *philia* underlines the similarity between ancient and modern practice. Neutrals have virtually always stressed their friendship for belligerents. This attitude appears repeatedly in the writings of jurists of the sixteenth to eighteenth century and count-

13. See 3.4 above.

less times in the official rhetoric of modern neutral states.[14] To cite just one example from the foreign policy of the United States, in a proclamation on August 4, 1914, Woodrow Wilson stated that American citizens should "act and speak in the true spirit of neutrality, which is the spirit of impartiality and fairness and friendliness to all concerned."[15] If the legal protection of modern juridical neutrality were absolute, such a statement would obviously be unnecessary.

The identification of neutral states, the explanation of how neutrality was justified, and the reconstruction of what rights and obligations accompanied neutral status represent important parts, but not all, of what emerges from this study. Neutrality is an inherently fragile and vulnerable status during warfare. Consequently, an examination of how well or poorly it succeeded in successive conflicts, particularly where the evidence is best, that is, in the period between the city-states' successful defense of Greece against the Persians (480/479) and their defeat by the Macedonians (338), provides a realistic appraisal of changing attitudes toward the conventions of interstate affairs.

There are two important findings. The first involves the relationship between weak and strong states. Because neutrality is often the policy sought by the weak to avoid destructive involvement in the conflicts of the strong, it is valuable to see how respect for neutrality faded to near extinction during the fifth century only to reappear and gain increasing strength during the fourth. The celebrated "middle path" of fourth-century Megara contrasts sharply with the bitter fate of Melos in the fifth. Yet at the outset of the period, when Xerxes had been defeated and the neutrality of Argos and other states was angrily denounced and punitive action proposed, the majority of amphictyonic states voted it down, and in the following decades, despite a long (fourteen years at least) war between the major powers, no violent treatment of neutrals is recorded, and recognition of their position appears in the comprehensive multistate treaty that concluded the conflict.

14. See, among others, Ayala, *De iure et officiis bellicis et disciplina militari*, bk. 2, 18–19; A. Gentili, *De iure belli libri tres*, bk. 2 (Hanau, 1612), 22 (p. 438); Grotius, *De iure belli ac pacis*, bk. 2, 3.3; C. Bynkershoek, *Quaestionum iuris publici libri duo*, bk. 1 (Leiden, 1737), 1.2; Vattel, *Le droit des gens*, bk. 3, 103–35 (defined, 103).

15. *Foreign Relations Supplement*, 1914, 551–52; see also George Washington's remarks in his proclamation of neutrality, quoted on p. 10 in chapter 1.

It was only when the Peloponnesian War broke out that real erosion in the respect for neutral states began. By the end of that war there had been numerous violations not just of neutrality but of virtually every conventional rule of war. Still, neutrality was not dead. In the years immediately following the war, there were repeated attempts by a variety of states to abstain as new conflicts arose and former allies fell out. And there were some successes and some failures. Sparta's aggressive attitude toward its allies made the danger of retaliation for passivity very real, however well justified a state's abstention might have been. Phlius and Mantinea, for example, resorted to subterfuge in an effort to remain at peace and avoid confrontation with Sparta. Instead of refusing outright to participate in further military campaigns, they declared that sacred truces prevented their participation in the Corinthian War. In addition, despite postwar recriminations and reprisals, several of Sparta's closest Peloponnesian allies continued to agitate for formal exemption from participation in further offensive conflicts. In this, they were not seeking to support Sparta's enemies, but only to secure a neutral position in respect to Sparta's resolutely belligerent foreign policy (see 8. 1–4). In the wake of Sparta's disastrous defeat at Leuctra and the Theban intervention in the Peloponnesus, these states did finally extricate themselves from continued military involvement through a series of separate peace treaties with the Theban alliance. The intent of these treaties was clearly not the formation of an anti-Lacedaemonian coalition, but only the achievement of recognized neutrality in what the states concerned considered to be the pointless continuation of the struggle against the Theban alliance.

Once adopted, neutrality could be an extremely attractive policy. When Athens became embroiled in conflict with Philip II, no amount of Demosthenic rhetoric could dissuade many Greek states from the belief that if they simply remained neutral, they could successfully avoid injury and would not suffer any reprisal from either belligerent, regardless of the outcome. Philip skillfully manipulated the exhaustion and hopes of such states; but like Xerxes before him, he was not really interested in protecting any state's right to pursue an independent policy but rather in achieving a dominant position by fragmenting his opposition.

There is also a revealing difference between neutrality of the classical period and that which followed during the Hellenistic age.

In the roughly two hundred years between the death of Alexander the Great (323) and the Roman destruction of Corinth (146) a number of city-states adopted a position approaching the modern status of permanent neutrality. This represented a compromise that helped to mitigate the steep decline in the real independence and power of individual cities, even those that had dominated the international affairs of the classical period. These former hegemonial states no longer aimed for leadership but only for survival with dignity.[16] In most cases, the great powers of the period accepted this stance, either because they hesitated to appear as naked aggressors or because the steadfast neutrals played a valuable role by mediating in warfare between the Hellenistic leagues and monarchs.

It is this role of mediator between belligerents (also an important function of modern neutral states) that is surprisingly absent from neutrality of the classical period. But why? Why do we hear nothing about Argos attempting to mediate an end to the Archidamian War or Megara the Corinthian War or perhaps Elis the conflict between Athens and Philip II? The answer again, I believe, lies in the classical Greek mentality. The city-states of the sixth through fourth century were deeply competitive and lived with the basic assumption that the strong states would, if they could, dominate the weak.[17] Intellectuals like Plato and Isocrates may have sought to deflect this tendency by proposing to shift the direction of aggression toward the Persian empire, but on the whole they had little effect.[18] Classical neutrality has to be interpreted in this light. More often than not, neutrality represented passive resistance to the domination of powerful belligerents.[19] Hence the function of neutrals as mediators is completely absent, not because mediation was unknown but because the role of mediator was neither sought by neutrals nor,

16. E.g., Athens (Plut. *Arat.* 41; see W. S. Ferguson, *Hellenistic Athens* [London, 1911], 208); Rhodes (Diod. 20. 81).

17. See the study of H. Frisch, *Might and Right in Antiquity*, trans. C. C. Martindale (Copenhagen, 1949).

18. Pl. *Rep.* 471; Isoc. 4 (*Paneg.*) passim; cf. Arist. *Pol.* 7.2.5–6, 1324b; 2.4.9, 1267a; but also Diod. 15. 9.19. On the meaning of this rhetoric, see G. Murray, "Reactions to the Peloponnesian War in Greek Thought and Practice," *JHS* 64 (1944): 1–9; S. Perlman, "Panhellenism, the *Polis* and Imperialism," *Historia* 25 (1976): 1–30.

19. E.g., Melos in the Archidamian War (see 6.1 above); Camarina during the Athenian invasion of Sicily (see 7.3); Corinth, Thebes, and Athens (404–395) (see 8.2); Thebes in 383 (8.4.B); the Phocians in 362 (see 9.2.D).

it seems, desired by the belligerents. For a classical state, neutrality was a kind of formal escape aimed not at preserving commercial advantage or serving the cause of mitigating a conflict but only at avoiding the humiliation of domination by a stronger state or worse.

The truth is that in the majority of cases studied neutral policy was tolerated with reluctance and was seldom wholly successful. Throughout the classical period it occupied a grey zone between war and peace. Belligerents may have accepted the existence of neutral parties when necessity dictated, but all too often they seized the first opportunity to assail nonbelligerents and punish their lack of loyalty or commitment. Nor, in a culture that preferred action to inaction and aggression to passivity, was neutral policy often motivated simply by disinterest or true impartiality or pacifistic feelings. Neutrals mistrusted the aims of belligerents and feared that they could not be trusted to act with restraint. But equally belligerents suspected that neutrals sought to avoid war not because they wished to maintain peace but because they were waiting for the opportunity to enter the conflict under more advantageous circumstances. Until this mutual suspicion was resolved and the potentially decisive impact of neutral alignment diminished, the position of neutrals remained dangerously uncertain and was all too easily violated by nonbelligerents and belligerents alike.

Finally, in the classical period, hegemonial states proved to be the most determined opponents of neutrality, for they quickly realized its potential to erode their power base and limit their own superiority. Yet in a more sinister mind, they also wanted recognition of neutrality just as badly as the weak states did. The "fair phrases" (Thuc. 5. 89) of convention that defended neutrality could also be used to turn it into a weapon in the competition for hegemony. If carefully manipulated, recognition of neutrality could serve imperial ambition just as surely as its repudiation could (consider, for example, the diplomatic assurances of Xerxes in 480 [see 5.2] or the Carthaginian offer to respect the neutrality of Acragas [see 8.1]). But ultimately, in the aftermath of the Macedonian conquest, when the old city-state competition had become virtually pointless in the face of the overwhelming power of the newly evolved Hellenistic states, neutral policy reemerged and even flourished for a time as a respected diplomatic stance, serving not only to preserve old pride in the *polis* but also to facilitate negoti-

ated settlement of conflicts between the more powerful states.[20] In
the classical period, however, mutual suspicion, jealousy, and self-
interested ambition presented powerful obstacles to the acceptance
of neutrals and to the notion that neutrality was legitimate and
should be respected. As Thucydides warned in the context of
internal *stasis*, "those citizens in the middle [i.e., aligned with
neither faction] were destroyed by both sides" (3. 82.8). For the
states themselves, abstention from warfare also existed without
clear guarantees, for neither the certainty of legal protection and
redress nor the certainty of belligerent respect for neutrals could
be counted on in all situations. Pretexts for violence against nonbelligerents and the violation of their status were always easily found
and remained stubbornly common realities. In this too, the experience of classical Greece can offer both insight into and a warning
about the limitations of international law.

20. I am preparing a detailed study of Hellenistic neutrality from the death of
Alexander the Great to the Roman conquest of the Eastern Mediterranean
(323–167). Currently see P. Klose, *Die völkerrechtliche Ordnung der hellenistischen Staatenwelt*; A. Heuss, *Stadt und Herrscher des Hellenismus* (Leipzig,
1937).

Select Bibliography

Entries in the Bibliography are placed in conceptual or historical sections as seemed appropriate. For studies with a broad scope an arbitrary decision on placement has been made, but where historical investigation covers more than one period, the earliest period treated usually receives the entry.

NEUTRALITY, INTERSTATE POLITICS AND ANCIENT DIPLOMACY

Adcock, F. E. "The Development of Ancient Greek Diplomacy." *L'Antiquité classique* 17 (1948): 1–12.

Adcock, F. E., and D. J. Mosley, *Diplomacy in Ancient Greece*. New York and London, 1975.

Adkins, A. W. H. *"Polupragmosunē* and 'Minding One's Own Business': A Study in Greek Social and Political Values." *Classical Philology* 71 (1976): 301–27.

———. *Moral Values and Political Behaviour in Ancient Greece from Homer to the End of the Fifth Century*. London, 1972.

———. "'Friendship' and 'Self-Sufficiency' in Homer and Aristotle." *Classical Quarterly* 13 (1963): 30–45.

———. *Merit and Responsibility: A Study in Greek Values*. Oxford, 1960.

Allison, J. W. "Thucydides and *Polypragmosynē." American Journal of Ancient History* 4 (1979): 10–22.

Amit, M. *Great and Small Poleis: A Study in the Relations between the Great Powers and the Small Cities of Ancient Greece*. Brussels, 1973.

Andrae, H. H. "Begriff und Entwicklung des Kriegsneutralitätsrechts." Diss., Göttingen, 1938.

Ashburner, W. *Rhodian Sea Law*. Oxford, 1909.

Audinet, E. "Les traces du droit international dans l'Iliade et dans l'Odyssée." *Revue générale de droit international public* 21 (1914): 29–63.

Aymard, A. "La paix entre les cités grecques à la période classique (V^e–IVe siècles av. J.-C.)." *Recueils de la Société Jean Bodin* 14 (Brussels, 1962): 223–26.

Bacot, B. *Des neutralités durables: Origine, domaine et efficacité.* Paris, 1943.

Baudenet, A. H. d'. *Le développement de la neutralité de Grotius à Vattel.* Orléans, 1910.

Bengtson, H. "Zwischen staatliche Beziehungen der griechischen Städte im klassischen Zeitalter." *XIIe Congrès International des Sciences Historiques, Rapports IV, Wien 1965* (1966): 69–76.

Bierzanek, P. "Sur les origines du droit de la guerre et de la paix." *Revue historique de droit français et étranger* 4th ser., 38 (1960): 83–123.

Bikerman, E. "Autonomie: Sur un passage de Thucydide (I,144,2)." *Revue internationale des droits de l'antiquité* 3d ser., 5 (1958): 313–43.

———. "Remarques sur le droit des gens dans la Grèce classique." *Revue internationale des droits de l'antiquité* 4 (1950): 99–127 (also published in F. Gschnitzer, ed., *Zur griechischen Staatskunde*, Wege der Forschung 96 [Darmstadt, 1969], 474–502).

Bindschedler, R. L. "Neutrality, Concept and General Rules." In *Encyclopedia of Public International Law*, Installment 4, edited by R. Bernhardt, 9–14. New York, 1982.

Bleicken, J. "Zum sogenannten Stasis-Gesetz Solons." *Symposium für Alfred Heuss.* Frankfurter Althistorische Studien 12 (Kallmünz, 1986): 9–18.

Boesch, P. "Asylie, ein Beitrag zur Geschichte des Neutralitäts Gedankens." *Neue Züricher Zeitung* (21 December 1919).

Bottié, F. *Essai sur la genèse et l'évolution de la notion de neutralité.* Paris, 1937.

Brown, C. S. "Odysseus and Polyphemus." *Comparative Literature* 18 (1966): 193–202.

Buck, C. D. "The Interstate Use of the Greek Dialects." *Classical Philology* 8 (1913): 133–59 (also published in E. Olshausen and H. Biller, eds., *Antike Diplomatie*, Wege der Forschung 462 [Darmstadt, 1979], 57–90).

Burle, E. *Essai historique sur le développement de la notion de droit naturel dans l'antiquité grecque.* Trévoux, 1908.

Busolt, G., and H. Swoboda, *Griechische Staatskunde.* Vol. 2: *Darstellung einzelner Staaten und Zwischenstaatlichen Beziehungen*, 1240-64. 3d ed. Munich, 1926.

Calabi, I. *Ricerche sui rapporti fra le poleis.* Florence, 1953.

Calderini, A. *Trattati internazionali nell'antichità greca.* 2 vols. Milan and Venice, 1949.

Caldwell, W. E. *Hellenic Conceptions of Peace.* New York, 1919.

Carter, L. B. *The Quiet Athenian.* Oxford, 1986.

Cartledge, P. "The New 5th-Century Spartan Treaty Again." *Liverpool Classical Monthly* 3 (1978): 189–90.

————. "A New 5th-Century Spartan Treaty." *Liverpool Classical Monthly* 1 (1976): 87–92.

Cataldi, S. *Symbolai e relazioni tra le città greche nel v secolo a. C.* Pisa, 1983.

————. "Un regolamento ateniese sui misteri di Eleusi e l'ideologia panhellenica de Cimone." *Studi sui rapporti interstatali nel mondo antico* (Pisa, 1981): 73–146.

Ciccio, M. "Guerre, στάσεις e ἀσυλία nella Grecia del v secolo a. C.," *Contributi dell' Istituto di storia antica dell' Univ. del Sacro Cuore, Milano.* Vita e pensiero 10 (1984): 132–41.

Cohen, D. "'Horkia' and 'horkos' in the *Iliad*." *Revue internationale des droits de l'antiquité* 27 (1980): 49–68.

Collard, C. ed. Euripides, *Supplices.* 2 vols. Groningen, 1975.

Cybichowski, S. *Das antike Völkerrecht: Zugleich ein Beitrag zur Konstruktion des modernen Völkerrechts.* Breslau, 1907.

David, E. "Solon, Neutrality and Partisan Literature of Late Fifth-Century Athens." *Museum Helveticum* 41 (1984): 129–38.

Dieckhoff, M. *Krieg und Frieden im griechisch-römischen Altertum.* Lebendiges Altertum 10. Berlin, 1962.

Dienelt, K. *Die Friedens Politik des Perikles.* Vienna, 1958.

————. "Apragmosynē." *Wiener Studien* 66 (1963): 94–104.

Dover, K. J. *Greek Popular Morality in the Time of Plato and Aristotle.* Oxford, 1974.

Ducrey, P. "Aspects juridique de la victoire et du traitement des vaincus." In *Problèmes de la guerre en Grèce ancienne*, edited by J.-P. Vernant, 231–43. The Hague, 1968.

————. *Le traitement des prisonniers de guerre dans la Grèce antique.* Paris, 1968.

Ehrenberg, V. "*Polypragmosynē*: A Study in Greek Politics." *Journal of Hellenic Studies* 67 (1947): 46–67.

————. "When Did the *Polis* Rise?" *Journal of Hellenic Studies* 57 (1937): 147–59.

Ferguson, W. S. *Greek Imperialism.* Boston and New York, 1913.

Fernández Nieto, F. J. *Los acuerdos belicos en la antigua Grecia (época arcaica y clásica).* Vol. 1: *Texto.* Santiago de Compostela, 1975.

Figueira, T., and G. Nagy, eds. *Theognis of Megara: Poetry and the Polis.* Baltimore and London, 1985.

Finley, M. I. *The World of Odysseus.* 2d ed. New York, 1965.

Flaceliere, R. *Greek Oracles.* Translated by D. Garman. 2d ed. London, 1976 (originally published as *Devins et oracles grecs* [Paris, 1961]).

Flumene, F. *La "legge non scritta" nella storia e nella dottrina eticogiuridica della Grecia classica.* Sassari, 1925.

Forrest, W. G. "Colonisation and the Rise of Delphi." *Historia* 6 (1957): 160–75.

Fortuin, H. "Grotius et la neutralité." *Études internationales* 1 (1948): 425–45.

Frisch, H. *Might and Right in Antiquity.* Vol. 1: *Homer to the Persian Wars.* Translated by C. C. Martindale. Copenhagen, 1949.

Furlani, S. *I trattati internazionali nell'antichità*. Annuario de diritto comparato e de studi legislativi 31 (1951).

Garlan, Y. *War in the Ancient World: A Social History*. Translated by J. Lloyd. London, 1975 (originally published as *La guerre dans l'antiquité* [Paris, 1972]).

Garnsey, P. D. A., and C. R. Whittaker. *Imperialism in the Ancient World*. Cambridge, 1979.

Gauthier, Ph. *Symbola: Les étrangers et la justice dans les cités grecques*, Annales de l'Est. Nancy, 1972.

Gawantka, W. *Isopolitie: Ein Beitrag zur Geschichte der zwischenstaatlichen Beziehungen in der Antike*. Munich, 1975.

Gehrke, H.-J. *Jenseits von Athen und Sparta*. Munich, 1986.

———. *Stasis: Untersuchungen zu den inneren Kriegen in den griechischen Staaten des 5. und 4. Jahrhunderts v. Chr.* Vestigia 35. Munich, 1985.

Giovannini, A. *Untersuchungen über die Natur und die Anfänge der bundesstaatlichen Sympolitie in Griechenland*. Hypomnemata 33. Göttingen, 1971.

Glotz, G. "Le droit des gens dans l'antiquité grecque." *Mémoires présentés par divers savants à l'Académie des inscriptions et belles-lettres de l'Institut de France* 13:1 (1923): 91–103.

———. "Les lois de la guerre dans l'antiquité grecque." *Revue de Paris* 22, no. 17 (1 September 1915).

Grant, J. R. "A Note on the Tone of Greek Diplomacy." *Classical Quarterly* 15 (1965): 261–66 (also published in E. Olshausen and H. Biller, eds., *Antike Diplomatie*, Wege der Forschung 462 [Darmstadt, 1979], 99–109).

Greenhalgh, P. A. L. *Early Greek Warfare: Horsemen and Chariots in the Homeric and Archaic Ages*. Cambridge, 1973 (see especially the Appendix: "The Historical Basis of the Homeric Background Picture," 156–72).

Grossmann, G. *Politische Schlagwörter aus der Zeit des peloponnesischen Krieges*. Zürich, 1950.

Gschnitzer, F. *Ein neuer spartanischer Staatsvertrag und die Verfassung des peloponnesischen Bundes*. Beiträge zur klassischen Philologie 93. Meisenheim am Glan, 1978.

———. "Stadt und Stamm bei Homer." *Chiron* 1 (1971): 1–17.

———, ed. *Zur griechischen Staatskunde*. Wege der Forschung 96. Darmstadt, 1969.

Hammond, M. *City-State and World State in Greek Political Theory*. Cambridge, Mass., 1951.

Harding, P. "In Search of a Poly-pragmatist." In *Classical Contributions: Studies in Honour of Malcolm Francis McGregor*, edited by G. S. Shrimpton and D. J. McCargar, 41–50. Locust Valley, N.Y., 1981.

Havelock, E. "War as a Way of Life in Classical Culture." In *Classical Values and the Modern World*, edited by E. Gareau, 19–78. Ottawa, 1972.

Herman, G. *Ritualised Friendship and the Greek City*. Cambridge, 1987.

Hirata, R. "Die sogenannten Neutralitätsbestimmungen im Foedus Cassianum." In *Forms of Control and Subordination in Antiquity*, edited by T. Yuge and M. Doi, 96–104. Leiden, 1988.

Hirzel, R. Ἄγραφος νόμος. Leipzig, 1900 (also published in *Abhandlungen der königlichen Sächsischen Gesellschaft der Wissenschaften, Philologische-historische Klasse* 20:1 [Leipzig, 1903]: 1–98).

Hitzig, H. F. *Altgriechische Staatsverträge über Rechtshilfe.* Zurich, 1907.

Hönle, A. *Olympia in der Politik der griechischen Staatenwelt (von 766 bis zum Ende des 5. Jahrhunderts).* Tübingen, 1968.

Hunt, D. "Lessons in Diplomacy from Classical Antiquity." *Proceedings of the Classical Association* 79 (1982): 7–19.

Hutter, H. *Politics as Friendship: The Origins of Classical Notions of Politics in the Theory and Practice of Friendship.* Waterloo, Ont., 1978.

Jacobson, H. "The Oath of the Delian League." *Philologus* 119 (1975): 256–58.

Jados, S. S. *Consulate of the Sea and Related Documents.* Tuscaloosa, Ala. 1975.

Jankovic, B. "De la neutralité classique à la conception moderne des pays non-alignés." *Revue égyptienne de droit international* 21 (1965): 89–119.

Jessup, P. C. and F. Deák. *Neutrality: Its History, Economics and Law in Four Volumes.* Vol. 1: *The Origins.* New York, 1935.

Kahrstedt, U. *Griechische Staatsrecht.* Vol. 1: *Sparta und seine Symmachie.* Göttingen, 1922.

Karavites, P. "Diplomatic Envoys in the Homeric World." *Revue internationale des droits de l'antiquité* 34 (1987): 41–100.

Kelly, D. H. "The New Spartan Treaty." *Liverpool Classical Monthly* 3 (1978): 133–41.

Kiechle, F. "Zur Humanität in der Kriegführung der griechischen Staaten." *Historia* 7 (1958): 129–56 (also published in F. Gschnitzer, ed., *Zur griechischen Staatskunde*, Wege der Forschung 96 [Darmstadt, 1969], 528–77).

Kienast, D. *RE* Suppl. 13 (1973), 499–627, s.v. *presbeia.*

Kleen, R. *Lois et usages de la neutralité d'après le droit international conventionnel et la société des nations.* 2 vols. Paris, 1898–1900.

Kleve, K. "Ἀpragmosynē and Polypragmosynē: Two Slogans in Athenian Politics." *Symbolae Osloenses* 39 (1964): 83–88.

Konstan, D. "*Philia* in Euripides' *Electra.*" *Philologus* 129 (1985): 176–85.

Kussbach, E. "L'évolution de la notion de neutralité dans les conflits armés actuels." *Revue de droit pénal militaire et de droit de la guerre* 17 (1979): 19–36.

Lammert, F. *RE* Suppl. 6 (1935), 1351–62, s.v. *kriegsrecht.*

Larsen, J. A. O. *Greek Federal States: Their Institutions and History.* Oxford, 1968.

———. "Freedom and Its Obstacles in Ancient Greece." *Classical Philology* 57 (1962): 230–34.

———. "Federation for Peace in Ancient Greece." *Classical Philology* 39 (1944): 145–62.

———. "The Constitution and Original Purpose of the Delian League." *Harvard Studies in Classical Philology* 51 (1940): 175–213.

———. "The Constitution of the Peloponnesian League I." *Classical Philology* 28 (1933): 257–76.

———. "The Constitution of the Peloponnesian League II." *Classical Philology* 29 (1934): 1–19.

———. Sparta and the Ionian Revolt: A Study of Spartan Foreign Policy and the Genesis of the Peloponnesian League." *Classical Philology* 27 (1932): 136–50.

Lateiner, D. "'The Man Who Does not Meddle in Politics': A Topos in Lysias." *Classical World* 76 (1982): 1–12.

———. "Heralds and Corpses in Thucydides." *Classical World* 71 (1977): 97–106.

Leech, H. B. "Ancient International Law." *Contemporary Review* 43 (1883): 260–74; 44 (1883): 890–904.

Levine, D. B. "Symposium and the *Polis*." In *Theognis of Megara*, edited by T. Figueira and G. Nagy, 177–96. Baltimore and London, 1985.

Lonis, R. "La valeur du serment dans les accords internationaux en Grèce classique." *Dialogues d'histoire ancienne* 6 (1980): 267–86.

———. *Guerre et religion en Grèce à l'époque classique: Recherches sur les rites, les dieux, l'idéologie de la victoire*. Paris, 1979.

Luce, J. V. "The *Polis* in Homer and Hesiod." *Proceedings of Royal Irish Academy* 78 (1978): 1–15.

Machiavelli, *The Prince and the Discourses*. Translated by M. Lerner. New York, 1950.

MacQuelyn, M. J. *Dissertatio iuridica politica de neutralitate tempore belli*. Lyons, 1829.

Manicas, P. T. "War, *Stasis*, and Greek Political Thought." *Comparative Studies in Society and History* 24 (1982): 673–88.

Manville, B. "Solon's Law of *Stasis* and *Atimia* in Archaic Athens." *Transaction of the American Philological Association* 110 (1980): 213–21.

Martin, V. *La vie internationale dans la Grèce des cités (VIᵉ–IVᵉ s. av. J.-C.)*. Publ. de l'Inst. Univ. de Hautes Études Internationales, Genèves 21. Paris, 1940.

Massart, E. *Elementi di diritto internazionale nell'epos omerico*. Paris, 1933.

Meier, Ch. *Die Entstehung des Politischen bei den Griechen*. Frankfurt, 1980.

Missiou-Ladi, A. "Coersive Diplomacy in Greek Interstate Relations (with special reference to *presbeis autokratores*)," *Classical Quarterly* 37 (1987): 336–45.

Mosley, D. J. "Bericht über die Forschung zur Diplomatie im klassischen Griechenland." In *Antike Diplomatie*, Wege der Forschung 462, edited by E. Olshausen and H. Biller, 204–35. Darmstadt, 1979.

———. "Diplomacy and Disunion in Ancient Greece." *Phoenix* 25 (1978): 319–30 (also published in Olshausen and Biller, *Antike Diplomatie*, 145–63).

———. "On Greek Enemies Becoming Allies." *Ancient Society* 5 (1974): 43–50.

———. "Crossing Greek Frontiers under Arms." *Revue internationale des droits de l'antiquité* (1973): 161–69.

———. *Envoys and Diplomacy in Ancient Greece.* Wiesbaden, 1973.

———. "Diplomacy in Classical Greece." *Ancient Society* 3 (1972): 1–16. (Also published in Olshausen and Biller, *Antike Diplomatie*, 164–82.)

Nagy, G. "Theognis and Megara: A Poet's Vision of His City." In *Theognis of Megara*, edited by T. Figueira and G. Nagy, 22–81. Baltimore and London, 1985.

Neil, R. A., ed. *The* Knights *of Aristophanes.* Cambridge, 1901 (see especially Appendix II: "The Political Use of Moral Terms," 202–209).

Nenci, G. "Les rapports internationaux dans la Grèce archaïque (650–550 av. J.C.)." *Proceedings of the VIIth Congress of the International Federation of the Societies of Classical Studies*, edited by J. Harmata, vol. 1, 35–52. Budapest, 1984.

———. "La neutralità nella Grecia antica." *Il Veltro: Rivista di civiltà italiana* 22 (1978): 495–506.

Nestle, W. *Der Friedensgedanke in der antiken Welt.* Philologus Suppl. 31.1 (1938).

———. "Ἀπραγμοσύνη." *Philologus* 81 (1925): 129–40.

North, H. *Sophrosyne.* Ithaca, N.Y., 1966.

Numelin, R. *The Beginnings of Diplomacy: A Sociological Study of Intertribal and International Relations.* London and Copenhagen, 1950.

Olshausen, E., and H. Biller, eds. *Antike Diplomatie.* Wege der Forschung 462. Darmstadt, 1979.

Ørvik, N. *The Decline of Neutrality, 1914–1941.* 2d ed. London, 1971.

Ostwald, M. *Autonomia: Its Genesis and Early History.* American Classical Studies 11. Chico, Calif., 1982.

———. "Was There a Concept ἄγραφος νόμος in Classical Greece?" In *Exegesis and Argument: Studies in Greek Philosophy Presented to Gregory Vlastos*, edited by E. N. Lee, A. P. D. Mourelatos, R. M. Rorty, 70–104. Assen, 1973.

———. Nomos *and the Beginnings of Athenian Democracy.* Oxford, 1969.

Papageorgiou-Venetas, B. *Delos.* Paris, 1981.

Parke, H. W., and D. E. W. Wormell. *The Delphic Oracle.* 2 vols. Oxford, 1956.

Peek, W. "Ein neuer spartanischer Staatsvertrage." *Abhandlungen der Sächsischen Akademie der Wissenschaften zu Leipzig, Philologisch-historische Klasse* 45:3 (1974): 3–15.

Percorella Longo, Ch. "Sulla legge 'Soloniana' contro la neutralità." *Historia* 37 (1988): 374–79.

Perlman, S. "Panhellenism, the *Polis* and Imperialism." *Historia* 25 (1976): 1–30.

Phillipson, C. *The International Law and Custom of Ancient Greece and Rome.* 2 vols. London, 1911.

Piccirilli, L. *Gli arbitrati interstatali greci*. Vol. 1: *Dalle origini al 338 a.c.* Pisa, 1973.

Pistorius, T. *Hegemoniestreben und Autonomiesicherung in der griechischen Vertragspolitik klassischer und hellenistischer Zeit*. Europäische Hochschulschriften 3. Frankfurt, 1985.

la Pradelle, A. G. *The Evolution of Neutrality*. Bourquin, 1936.

Pritchett, W. K. *The Greek State at War*. 4 vols. Berkeley, 1974–85.

Raaflaub, K. *Die Entdeckung der Freiheit: Zur historischen Semantik und Gesellschaftsgeschichte eines politischen Grundbegriffs der Griechen*. Vestigia 37. Munich, 1985.

Raeder, A. *L'Arbitrage international chez les Hellènes*. Publications de l'Institut Nobel norvégien 1. Kristiania, 1912.

Rhodes, P. J. *A Commentary on the Aristotelian* Athenaion Politeia. Oxford, 1981.

de Romilly, J. *La loi dans la pensée grecque, des origines à Aristote*. Paris, 1971.

——. "Guerre et paix entre cités." In *Problèmes de la guerre en Grèce ancienne*, edited by J.-P. Vernant, 207–29. The Hague, 1968.

——. *Thucydides and Athenian Imperialism*. Translated by P. Thody. Oxford, 1963 (originally published as *Thucydide et l'imperialisme athénien* [Paris, 1947]).

Rostovtzeff, M. I. "International Relations in the Ancient World." In *The History and Nature of International Relations*, edited by E. A. Walsh, 31–65. New York, 1922.

Rougemont, G. "La hiéroménie des Pythia et les trêves sacrées d'Éleusis, de Delphes et d'Olympie." *Bulletin de correspondance hellénique* 97 (1973): 75–106.

Roux, G. "Politique et religion: Delphes et Délos à l'époque archaïque." *Proceedings of the VIIth Congress of the International Federation of the Societies of Classical Studies*, edited by J. Harmata, vol. 1, 97–105. Budapest, 1984.

——. *Delphes, son oracle et ses dieux*. Confluents 2. Paris, 1976.

Sastry, K. "A Note on Udasina: Neutrality in Ancient India." *Indian Yearbook for International Affairs* (1954): 131–34.

von Scheliha, R. *Freiheit und Freundschaft in Hellas*. Amsterdam, 1968.

Schwahn, W. *RE* 4 A (1931), 1102–34, s.v. *symmachia*.

Scott, J. B. *The Hague Conventions and Declarations 1899 and 1907*. London, 1909.

Sealey, R. *A History of the Greek City-States, 700–338 B.C.* Oxford, 1976.

Séfériadès, S. "La conception de la neutralité dans l'ancienne Grèce." *Revue de droit international et de legislation comparée* 16 (1935): 641–62.

——. *Principes généraux du droit international de la paix*. Academie de Droit International, no. 4, 1930 (see especially chapter 3: "Évolution historique du droit international," 216–33).

Shrimpton, G. S., and D. J. McCargar, eds. *Classical Contributions: Studies in Honour of Malcolm Francis McGregor*. Locust Valley, N.Y., 1981.

Siewert, P. "L'autonomie de Hyettos et la sympolitie Thespienne dans les *Helléniques* d'Oxyrhynchos." *Revue des études grecques* 90 (1977): 462–64.

Smertenko, C. E. "The Political Relations of the Delphic Oracle." In *Studies in Greek Religion*, edited by C. E. Smertenko and G. N. Belknap. Eugene, Oreg., 1935.

Smith, F. *International Law*. 5th ed. Revised and enlarged by C. Phillipson. London, 1918.

Sordi, M. *Santuari e politica nel mondo antico*. Milan, 1983.

Spahn, P. *Mittelschicht und Polisbildung*. Europäische Hochschulschriften 3. Frankfurt, Bern, and Las Vegas, 1977.

Starr, C. "The Early Greek State." *La parola del passato* 12 (1957): 97–108 (also published in A. Ferrill and T. Kelly, eds., *Essays on Ancient History* [Leiden, 1979], 122–33).

Steinwenter, B. *Die Streitbeendigung durch Urteil Schiedsspruch und Vergleich nach griechischem Rechte*. Münchener Beiträge zur Papyrusforschung und antiken Rechtsgeschichte 8. Munich, 1925.

de Taube, M. *Les origines de l'arbitrage international: Antiquité et moyen âge*. The Hague, 1932.

Ténékidès, G. "Droit international et communautés fédérales dans la Grèce des cités (Vème–IIIème siècles)." *Acad. de droit international de la Haye Recueil des cours* 90 (Leiden, 1956): 471–652.

———. *La notion juridique d'indépendance et la tradition hellénique: Autonomie et fédéralisme aux Ve et IVe siècles av. J.C.* Collection de l'Institut français d'Athènes 83. Athens, 1954.

Thomas, C. G. "Homer and the *Polis*." *La parola del passato* 21 (1966): 5–14.

Tod, M. N. *Ancient Inscriptions: Sidelights on Greek History*. Oxford, 1932.

———. *International Arbitration amongst the Greeks*. Oxford, 1913.

Triepel, H. *Die Hegemonie: Ein Buch von führenden Staaten*. 2d ed., 1943. Reprint, Aalen, 1961.

Vernant, J.-P., ed. *Problèmes de la guerre en Grèce ancienne*. The Hague, 1968.

Vinogradoff, P. *Outlines of Historical Jurisprudence*. Vol. 2: *The Jurisprudence of the Greek City*. London, 1922.

Walbank, M. B., *Athenian Proxenies of the Fifth Century B.C.* Toronto and Sarasota, Fla., 1978.

Wehrli, F. "Zur politischen Theorie der Griechen: Gewaltherrschaft und Hegemonie." *Museum Helveticum* 25 (1968): 214–25.

Weil, H. "*L'Iliade* et le droit des gens dans la vieille Grèce." *Revue de philologie* 9 (1885): 161–65.

Welwei, K.-L. *Unfreien im antiken Kriegsdienst*. Vol. 2: *Die kleineren und mittleren griechischen Staaten und die hellenistischen Reiche*. Wiesbaden, 1977.

Wéry, L.-M. "Le fonctionnement de la diplomatie à l'époque homérique." *Revue international des droits de l'antiquité* 14 (1967): 169–205 (also published in E. Olshausen and H. Biller, eds., *Antike Diplomatie*, Wege der Forschung 462 [Darmstadt, 1979], 13–53).

————. "Le meurtre des hérauts de Darius en 491 et l'inviolabilité du héraut." *L'Antiquité classique* 35 (1966): 468–86.

Westermann, W. L. "Interstate Arbitration in Antiquity." *Classical Journal* 2 (1907): 197–211.

Wheeler, E. L. "Sophistic Interpretations and Greek Treaties." *Greek, Roman and Byzantine Studies* 25 (1984): 253–74.

Wickert, K. "Der peloponnesische Bund von seiner Entstehung bis zum Ende des archidamischen Krieges." Diss., Erlangen-Nürnberg, 1961.

Wiesehöfer, J. "Die 'Freunde' und 'Wohltäter' des Grosskönigs." *Studia iranica* 9 (1980): 7–21.

Wogasli, D. *Die Normen des altgriechischen Völkerrechts* (Νόμοι κοινοὶ τῶν Ἑλλήνων). Diss., Freiburg in Breisgau, 1895.

Wüst, F. "Amphiktyonie, Eidgenossenschaft, Symmachie." *Historia* 3 (1954–55): 129–53.

ARCHAIC–PENTECONTAETIA

Andrewes, A. "Athens and Aegina, 510–480 B.C." *The Annual of the British School at Athens* 37 (1936–37): 1–7.

Balcer, J. M. "Separation and Anti-Separation in the Athenian Empire (478–433)." *Historia* 23 (1974): 21–39.

Beloch, K. J. *Griechische Geschichte*. 2d ed. Berlin, 1924–27.

Bengtson, H. *The Greeks and the Persians, From the Sixth to the Fourth Centuries*. New York, 1965.

————. "Themistocles und die delphische Amphiktyonie." *Eranos* 49 (1951): 85–92.

Boffo, L. "La conquista persiana delle città greche d'Asia Minore." *Memorie della Classe di Scienze morali e storiche dell' Accademia dei Lincei* 26:1 (1983).

Brunt, P. A. "The Hellenic League against Persia." *Historia* 2 (1953–54): 135–63.

la Bua, V. "La prima conquista persiana della Ionia." *Miscellanea di studi classici in onore di Eugenio Manni* 4 (Rome, 1980): 1267–92.

————. "Gli Ioni e il conflitto lidio-persiano." *Miscellanea greca e romana, Studi publicati dall' Ist. ital. per la storia antica* 5 (1977): 1–64.

Burn, A. R. *Persia and the Greeks: The Defence of the West, c. 546–478 B.C.* 2d ed. London, 1984.

————. *The Lyric Age of Greece*. London, 1960.

————. "The So-called 'Trade Leagues' in Early Greek History and the Lelantine War." *Journal of Hellenic Studies* 49 (1929): 14–37.

Busolt, G. *Griechische Geschichte bis zur Schlacht bei Chaeronea*. Gotha, 1893–1904.

Calderone, S. "Sybaris e i Serdaioi." *Helikon* 3 (1963): 219–58.

Cartledge, P. *Sparta and Laconia: A Regional History, 1300–362 B.C.* London, 1979.

Cook, J. M. *The Persian Empire*. London, 1983.

Cozzoli, U. "L'alleanza ellenica del 481." *Miscellanea greca e romana* 6 (1965): 31–51.

Craik, E. M. *The Dorian Aegean*. States and Cities of Ancient Greece. London, 1980.

Dunbabin, T. J. *The Western Greeks: The History of Sicily and South Italy from the Foundation of the Greek Colonies to 480 B.C.* Oxford, 1948.

Elayi, J. "Le rôle de l'oracle de Delphes dans le conflit gréco-perse d'après 'Les Histoires' d'Herodote." *Iranica antiqua* 14 (1979): 67–151.

Figueira, T. J. "Aeginetan Independence." *Classical Journal* 79 (1983): 8–29.

———. *Aegina: Society and Politics*. New York, 1981.

———. "Aeginetan Membership in the Peloponnesian League." *Classical Philology* 76 (1981): 1–24.

Forrest, W. G. *History of Sparta, 950–192 B.C.* London, 1968.

Glotz, G. *Histoire ancienne, deuxième partie: Histoire grecque*. 3 vols. Paris, 1925–36.

Graf, D. F. "Medism: The Origin and Significance of the Term." *Journal of Hellenic Studies* 104 (1984): 15–30.

Grote, G. *History of Greece, From the Earliest Period to the Close of the Generation Contemporary with Alexander the Great*. 10 vols. New ed. London, 1888.

Grundy, G. B. *The Great Persian War and Its Preliminaries*. London, 1901.

Hammond, N. G. L. *A History of Greece to 322 B.C.* 2d ed. Oxford, 1967.

Hammond, N. G. L., and G. T. Griffith. *A History of Macedonia*. Vol. 2: *550–336 B.C.* Oxford, 1979.

Hands, A. R. "On Strategy and Oracles 480/79." *Journal of Hellenic Studies* 75 (1965): 56–61.

Hanfmann, G. M. A. "Lydian Relations with Ionia and Persia." *Proc. Xth Int. Congr. Arch. Ankara-Izmir* (23–30 September 1973), edited by E. Akurgal, 25–35. Ankara, 1978.

Hignett, C. *Xerxes' Invasion of Greece*. Oxford, 1963.

Hill, G. F. *Sources for Greek History between the Persian and Peloponnesian Wars*. New ed. by R. Meiggs and A. Andrewes. Oxford, 1951.

Holladay, R. "Medism in Athens, 508–480 B.C." *Greece and Rome* 25 (1978): 174–91.

———. "Sparta's Role in the First Peloponnesian War." *Journal of Hellenic Studies* 97 (1977): 54–63.

How, W. W., and J. Wells. *A Commentary on Herodotus*. 2 vols. Oxford, 1912.

Huxley, G. "Corcyra and the Bones of Minos." *Kretologia* 8 (1979): 76–80.

———. *Early Sparta*. London, 1962.

Jeffery, L. H. *Archaic Greece: The City-States c. 700–500*. London, 1976.

Kagan, D. *The Outbreak of the Peloponnesian War.* Ithaca, N.Y., and London, 1969.

Karavites, P. "Ἐλευθερία and αὐτονομία in Fifth-Century Interstate Relations." *Revue internationale des droits de l'Antiquité* 29 (1982): 145–162.

Kelly, T. "The Traditional Enmity between Sparta and Argos: The Birth of a Myth." *American Historical Review* 75 (1970): 971–1003.

Knight, D. *The Foreign Policy of Pericles, 446–431.* Wiesbaden, 1970.

Lewis, D. M. "The Origins of the First Peloponnesian War." In *Classical Contributions: Studies in Honour of Malcolm Francis McGregor,* edited by G. S. Shrimpton and D. J. McCargar, 71–78. Locust Valley, N.Y., 1981.

———. *Sparta and Persia.* Leiden, 1977.

Lewis, N. *The Fifth Century B.C.: Greek Historical Documents.* Toronto, 1971.

Lonis, R. *Les usages de la guerre entre grecs et barbares, des genres médiques au milieu du IVème siècle av. J.C.* Paris, 1969.

Luria, S. "Zum Problem der griechisch-karthagischen Beziehungen." *Acta antiqua Academiae scientiarum Hungaricae* 12 (1964): 53–75.

Meiggs, R. *The Athenian Empire.* Oxford, 1972.

Meyer, E. *Geschichte des Altertums.* 5 vols. New ed. Stuttgart, 1937–39.

Myres, J. L. "*Akēryktos Polemos*: Herodotus v 81." *Classical Review* 57 (1943): 66–67.

Nesselhauf, H. *Untersuchungen zur Geschichte der delisch-attischen Symmachie.* Klio Beiheft 30. Leipzig, 1933.

Olmstead, A. T. *History of the Persian Empire.* Chicago, 1948.

Parker, H. W. "Croesus and Delphi." *Greek, Roman and Byzantine Studies* 25 (1984): 209–32.

Raubitschek, A. E. "Corinth and Athens before the Peloponnesian War." In *Greece and the Eastern Mediterranean in Antiquity and Prehistory, Studies Presented to Fritz Schachermeyr on the Occasion of His Eightieth Birthday,* edited by K. H. Kinzl, 266–69. Berlin and New York, 1977.

———. "Treaties between Persia and Athens." *Greek, Roman and Byzantine Studies* 5 (1964): 151–59.

Rawlings, H. R. "Thucydides on the Purpose of the Delian League." *Phoenix* 31 (1977): 1–8.

Robertson, U. D. "The True Nature of the Delian League, 478–461 B.C." *American Journal of Ancient History* 5 (1980): 64–96.

de Ste. Croix, G. E. M. *The Origins of the Peloponnesian War.* London, 1972.

Salmon, J. B. *Wealthy Corinth: A History of the City to 338 B.C.* Oxford, 1984.

Snodgrass, A. *Archaic Greece: The Age of Experiment.* London, 1980.

Steinbrecher, M. *Der delisch-attische Seebund und die athenisch-spartanischen Beziehungen in der kimonischen Ära (ca. 478/7–462/1).* Palingensia 21. Stuttgart, 1985.

Tomlinson, R. A. *Argos and the Argolid from the End of the Bronze Age to the Roman Occupation*. London, 1972.

Wallace, M. B. "Herodotos and Euboia." *Phoenix* 28 (1974): 22–44.

Walser, G. *Hellas und Iran: Studien zu den griechisch-persischen Beziehungen vor Alexander*. Darmstadt, 1984.

Westlake, H. D. "Ionians in the Ionian War." *Classical Quarterly* 29 (1979): 9–44.

Will, E. *Korinthiaka: Recherches sur l'histoire et la civilisation de Corinthe des origines aux guerres médiques*. Paris, 1955.

Wolski, J. "Μηδισμός et son importance en Grèce à l'époque des guerres médiques." *Historia* 22 (1973): 1–15.

THE PELOPONNESIAN WAR

Adkins, A. W. H. "Merit, Responsibility and Thucydides." *Classical Quarterly* 25 (1975): 209–20.

Amit, M. "A Peace Treaty between Sparta and Persia." *Rivista storica dell'antichità* 4 (1974): 55–63.

Anderson, J. K. "A Topographical and Historical Study of Achaea." *The Annual of the British School at Athens* 49 (1954): 72–92.

Andrewes, A. "Thucydides and the Persians." *Historia* 10 (1961): 1–18.

———. "The Melian Dialogue and Perikles' Last Speech." *Proceedings of the Cambridge Philological Society* 186 (1960): 1–10.

Bikerman, E. "La trêve de 423 av. J.-C. entre Athènes et Sparte." *Revue internationale des droits de l'antiquité* 1 (1952): 199-213.

Blamire, A. "Epilycus' Negotiations with Persia." *Phoenix* 29 (1975): 21–26.

Bruce, I. A. F. "The Corcyraean Civil War." *Phoenix* 25 (1971): 108–17.

———. "Plataea and the Fifth-Century Boeotian Confederacy." *Phoenix* 22 (1968): 190–99.

Brunt, P. A. "Spartan Policy and Strategy in the Archidamian War." *Phoenix* 19 (1965): 255–80.

Buchner, E. "Die Aristophanes-Scholien und die Frage der Tributspflicht von Melos." *Chiron* 4 (1974): 91–99.

Cogan, M. *The Human Thing: The Speeches and Principles of Thucydides' History*. Chicago and London, 1981.

———. "Mytilene, Plataea, and Corcyra: Ideology and Policy in Thucydides, Book Three." *Phoenix* 35 (1981): 1–21.

Connor, W. R. *Thucydides*. Princeton, 1984.

———. "Nicias the Cretan?" *American Journal of Ancient History* 1 (1976): 61–64.

Costa, E. A. "Evagoras I and the Persians, ca. 411 to 391 B.C." *Historia* 23 (1974): 40–56.

Eberhardt, W. "Der Melierdialog und die Inscriften ATL/A9 (*IG* I² 63 +) und *IG* I² 97 + : Betrachtungen zur historischen Glaubwürdigkeit des Thukydides." *Historia* 8 (1959): 284–314.

Eddy, S. "The Cold War between Athens and Persia, ca. 448–412 B.C."

Classical Philology 68 (1973): 241–58.

Fleiss, P. J. *Thucydides and the Politics of Bipolarity*. Nashville, 1966.

———. "Alliance and Empire in a Bipolar World: Athens' Imperialism during the Peloponnesian War." *Archive für Rechts- und Sozialphilosophie* 47:1–2 (1961): 81–103.

Gerolymatos, A. "Nicias of Gortyn." *Chiron* 17 (1987): 81–85.

Hans, L.-M. *Karthago und Sizilien: Die Entstehung und Gestaltung der Epikratie auf dem Hintergrund der Beziehungen der Karthager zu den Griechen und den nichtgriechischen Völkern Siziliens (VI–III Jahrhundert v. Chr.)*. Hildesheim, Zurich, and New York, 1983.

Hegyi, D. "Athen und die Achaemeniden in der zweiter Hälfte des 5. Jahrhunderts v.u.Z." *Oikumene* 4 (1983): 53–59.

Herman, G. "Nikias, Epimenides and the Question of Omissions in Thucydides," *Classical Quarterly* 39 (1989): 83–93.

Herter, H. "Pylos und Melos: Ein Beitrag zur Thukydides-Interpretation." *Rheinisches Museum* 97 (1954): 316–43.

Huss, W. *Geschichte der Karthager*. Handbuch der Altertumswissenschaft 3.8. Munich, 1985.

Kagan, D. *The Fall of the Athenian Empire*. Ithaca, N.Y., and London, 1987.

———. *The Peace of Nicias and the Sicilian Expedition*. Ithaca, N.Y., and London, 1981.

———. *The Archidamian War*. Ithaca, N.Y., and London, 1974.

Kelly, T. "Argive Foreign Policy in the Fifth Century B.C." *Classical Philology* 69 (1974): 81–99.

Kiechle, F. K. "Korkyra und der Handelsweg durch das adriatische Meer im 5. Jh. v. Ch." *Historia* 28 (1979): 173–91.

Laffi, U. "La spedizione ateniese in Sicilia del 415 a.C." *Rivista storica italiana* (1970): 277–307.

Levy, E. "Les trois traités entre Sparte et le Roi." *Bulletin de correspondance hellénique* 107 (1983): 221–41.

Liebeschuetz, W. "The Structure and Function of the Melian Dialogue." *Journal of Hellenic Studies* 88 (1968): 73–77.

———. "Thucydides and the Sicilian Expedition." *Historia* 17 (1968): 289–306.

MacDonald, B. R. "The Import of Attic Pottery to Corinth and the Question of Trade during the Peloponnesian War." *Journal of Hellenic Studies* 102 (1982): 113–23.

Macleod, C. W. "Thucydides' Plataean Debate." *Greek, Roman and Byzantine Studies* 18 (1977): 227-46.

Martin, T. *Sovereignty and Coinage in Classical Greece*. Princeton, 1985.

Meritt, B. D. "Greek Inscriptions." *Hesperia* 26 (1957): 198–221.

———. "Athens and Carthage." *Athenian Studies Presented to William Scott Ferguson*. Harvard Studies in Classical Philology. Suppl. 1 (Cambridge, Mass., 1940): 247–53.

———. *Documents on Athenian Tribute*. Cambridge, Mass., 1937.

Moxon, I. "Thucydides' Account of Spartan Strategy and Foreign Policy in the Archidamian War." *Rivista storica dell'antichità* 8 (1978): 7–26.

Podlecki, A. J. "Athens & Aegina." *Historia* 25 (1976): 396–413.

Pouncey, P. *The Necessities of War: A Study of Thucydides' Pessimism.* New York, 1980.

Seager, R. J. "After the Peace of Nicias: Diplomacy and Policy, 421–416 B.C." *Classical Quarterly* 26 (1976): 249–69.

Shrimpton, G. S. "When did Plataea Join Athens?" *Classical Philology* 79 (1984): 295–303.

Siewert, P. *Der Eid von Plataiai.* Vestigia 16. Munich, 1972.

Sjöqvist, E. *Sicily and the Greeks: Studies in the Interrelationships between the Indigenous Populations and the Greek Colonists.* Jerome Lectures 9. Ann Arbor, Mich., 1973.

Smarczyk, B. *Bündnerautonomie und athenische Seebundspolitik im Dekeleischen Krieg.* Beiträge zur Klassischen Philologie 177. Frankfurt, 1986.

Thompson, W. E. "The Athenian Treaties with Haliai and Dareios the Bastard." *Klio* 53 (1971): 119-24.

Treu, M. "Athen und Karthago und die Thukydideische Darstellung." *Historia* 3 (1954–55): 41–57.

———. "Athen und Melos und der Melierdialog des Thukydides." *Historia* 2 (1953–54): 253–73; 3 (1954–55): 58–59.

Wade-Gery, H. T. *Essays in Greek History.* Oxford, 1958.

de Waele, J. A. *Die historische Topographie der griechischen Akragas auf Sizilien.* Vol. 1. Archeol. Studien van het Nederlands Hist. Inst. te Rome 3. 's Gravenhage, 1971.

Wentker, H. *Sizilien und Athen: Die Begegnung der attischen Macht mit den Westgriechen.* Heidelberg, 1956.

Westlake, H. D. "Athens and Amorges." *Phoenix* 31 (1977): 319–29.

———. "Thucydides and the Uneasy Peace—A Study in Political Incompetence." *Classical Quarterly* n.s. 21 (1971): 315–25.

Whittaker, C. R. "Carthaginian Imperialism in the Fifth and Fourth Centuries." In *Imperialism in the Ancient World*, edited by P. D. A. Garnsey and C. R. Whittaker, 59–90. Cambridge, 1979.

Wick, T. E. "Athens' Alliance with Rhegion and Leontinoi," *Historia* 25 (1976): 288–304.

Wilson, J. *Athens and Corcyra: Strategy and Tactics in the Peloponnesian War.* Bristol, 1987.

THE FOURTH CENTURY

Accame, S. *Ricerche intorno alla guerra corinzia.* Naples, 1951.

———. *La lega ateniese del secolo IV a.c.* Rome, 1941.

Andrewes, A. "Spartan Imperialism?" In *Imperialism in the Ancient World*, edited by P. D. A. Garnsey and C. R. Whittaker, 91–102, 302–6. Cambridge, 1979.

Austin, R. P. "Athens and the Satraps' Revolt." *Journal of Hellenic Studies* 64 (1944): 98–100.

Aymard, A. *Le monde grec au temps de Philippe II de Macédonie et d'Alexandre le Grand (359–323 av. J.-C.).* Paris, 1948.

Beloch, K. J. *Die attische Politik seit Perikles.* Reprint. Stuttgart, 1967.

Bruce, I. A. F. *A Historical Commentary on the* Hellenica Oxyrhynchia. Cambridge, 1967.

———. "Athenian Foreign Policy in 396–395 B.C." *Classical Journal* 58 (1963): 289–95.

———. "Internal Politics and the Outbreak of the Corinthian War." *Emerita* 28 (1960): 75–86.

Buckler, J. "Alliance and Hegemony in Fourth-Century Greece: The Case of the Theban Hegemony." *The Ancient World* 5 (1982): 79–89.

———. *The Theban Hegemony, 371–362.* Cambridge, Mass., 1980.

———. "The Alleged Achaian Arbitration after Leuktra." *Symbolae Osloenses* 53 (1978): 85–96.

Cargill, J. "Demosthenes, Aischines, and the Crop of Traitors." *The Ancient World* 11 (1985): 75–85.

———. "Hegemony, not Empire: The Second Athenian League." *The Ancient World* 5 (1982): 91–102.

———. *The Second Athenian League: Empire or Free Alliance?* Berkeley, Los Angeles, and London, 1981.

Cartledge, P. *Agesilaos and the Crisis of Sparta.* London, 1987.

Cary, M. "The Alleged Achaean Arbitration after Leuctra." *Classical Quarterly* 19 (1925): 165–66.

Cawkwell, G. L. "The Decline of Sparta." *Classical Quarterly* 33 (1983): 385–400.

———. "The King's Peace." *Classical Quarterly* 31 (1981): 69–83.

———. "The Peace of Philocrates Again." *Classical Quarterly* 28 (1978): 93–104.

———. *Philip of Macedon.* London and Boston, 1978.

———. "The Imperialism of Thrasybulus." *Classical Quarterly* 26 (1976): 270–77.

———. "The Foundation of the Second Athenian Confederacy." *Classical Quarterly* 23 (1973): 47–60.

———. "Epaminondas and Thebes." *Classical Quarterly* 22 (1972): 254–78.

———. "Desmosthenes' Policy after the Peace of Philocrates." *Classical Quarterly* 13 (1963): 120–38, 200–213.

———. "The Common Peace of 366/5 B.C." *Classical Quarterly* 11 (1961): 80–86.

Cloché, P. *Isocrate et son temps.* Annales littéraires de l'Université de Besançon 54. Paris, 1963.

———. *La politique étrangère d'Athènes de 404 à 338 av. J.-C.* Paris, 1934.

———. "La Grèce de 346 à 339 av. J.-C." *Bulletin de correspondance hellénique* 44 (1920): 108–59.

———. "La politique thébaine de 404 à 396 av. J.-C." *Revue des Études grecques* 31 (1918): 315–43.

Crum, R. H. "Philip of Macedon and the City-State: A Study of Theopompus, Aristotle, Polybius and Panaetius." Diss., Columbia University, 1966.

Dobesch, G. *Der panhellenische Gedanke im 4. Jh. v. Chr. und der "Philippos" des Isocrates.* Vienna, 1968.

Ducat, J. "La confédération béotienne et l'expansion thébaine à l'époque archaïque." *Bulletin de correspondance hellénique* 97 (1973): 59–73.

Dugas, Ch. "La campagne d'Agesilas en Asie Mineure (395): Xénophon et l'Anonyme d'Oxyrhynchos." *Bulletin de correspondance hellénique* 34 (1910): 58–95.

Dušanic, S. "Le médisme d'Isménias et les relations gréco-perses dans la politique de l'Académie platonicienne (383–378 av. J.C.)." *La Béotie antique, Lyon-Saint-Étienne, 16–20 May 1983* (Paris, 1985): 237–46.

Ellis, J. R. *Philip II and Macedonian Imperialism.* London, 1976.

Fredricksmeyer, E. A. "On the Final Aims of Philip II." In *Philip II, Alexander the Great and the Macedonian Heritage*, edited by W. L. Adams and E. N. Borza, 85–98. Lanham, Md., New York, and London, 1982.

Fougères, G. *Mantinée et l'Arcadie orientale.* Bibliothèque des écoles françaises d'Athènes et de Rome 78. Paris, 1898.

Funke, P. *Homónoia und Archē: Athen und die griechische Staatenwelt vom Ende des peloponnesischen Krieges bis zum Königsfrieden (404/3–387/6 v.Chr.).* Historia Einzelschrift 37. Wiesbaden, 1980.

Garnsey, P. D. A., and C. R. Whittaker, eds. *Trade and Famine in Classical Antiquity.* Proceedings of the Cambridge Historical Society. Suppl. 8. Cambridge, 1983.

Gray, V. *The Character of Xenophon's Hellenica.* London, 1989.

Grenfell, B. P., and A. S. Hunt. *The Oxyrhynchus Papyri.* Part 5. London, 1908.

Griffin, A. *Sikyon.* Oxford, 1982.

Griffith, G. T. "Athens in the Fourth Century." In *Imperialism in the Ancient World*, edited by P. D. A. Garnsey and C. R. Whittaker, 127–44. Cambridge, 1979.

———. "Philip of Macedonia: Early Interventions in Thessaly (358–352 B.C.)." *Classical Quarterly* 20 (1970): 67–80.

———. "The Union of Corinth and Argos (392–386)." *Historia* 1 (1950): 236–56.

Hack, H. M. "Thebes and the Spartan Hegemony, 386–382 B.C." *American Journal of Philology* 99 (1978): 210–27.

———. "The Rise of Thebes: A Study of Theban Politics and Diplomacy, 386–371 B.C." Diss., Yale University, 1975.

Hahn, I. "Foreign Trade and Foreign Policy." In *Trade and Famine in Classical Antiquity.* Proceedings of the Cambridge Historical Society, Suppl. 8, edited by P. D. A. Garnsey and C. R. Whittaker, 30–36. Cambridge, 1983.

———. "Die Hellenisierung Karthagos und die punisch-griechischen Beziehungen im 4. Jahrhundert v.u.z." *Hellenische* Poleis (Berlin, 1974): 841–54.

Hamilton, C. D. "Agesilaus and the Failure of Spartan Hegemony." *The Ancient World* 5 (1982): 67–78.

———. *Sparta's Bitter Victories: Politics and Diplomacy in the Corinthian*

War. Ithaca, N.Y., and London, 1979.

——. "Spartan Politics and Policy, 405–401 B.C." *American Journal of Philology* 91 (1970): 294–314.

Hampl, F. *Die griechischen Staatsverträge des 4. Jahrhunderts v. Christ Geb.* Leipzig, 1938. Reprint. Rome, 1966.

Harding, P. "The Purpose of Isokrates' *Archidamos* and *On the Peace*." *California Studies in Classical Antiquity* 6 (1973): 137–49.

Hark, H. M. "Thebes and the Spartan Hegemony, 368–382 B.C." *American Journal of Philology* 99 (1978): 210–27.

Hirsch, S. W. *The Friendship of the Barbarians: Xenophon and the Persian Empire*. Hannover and London, 1985.

Hornblower, S. *Mausolus*. Oxford, 1982.

Ilari, V. *Guerra e diritto nel mondo antico*. Vol. 1: *Guerra e diritto nel mondo greco-ellenistico fino al III secolo*. Publ. Ist di dir. rom. e dei. dell' oriente mediterr. 56. Milan, 1980.

Judeich, W. *Kleinasiatische Studien: Untersuchungen zur griechisch-persischen Geschichte des IV. Jahrhunderts v. Chr*. Marburg, 1892.

Kagan, D. "Corinthian Politics and the Revolution of 392 B.C." *Historia* 11 (1962): 447–57.

——. "The Economic Origins of the Corinthian War (395–387 B.C.)" *La parola del passato* 16 (1961): 321–41.

Karavites, P. "The Political Use of ἐλευθερία and αὐτονομία in the Fourth Century among Greek City-States." *Revue internationale des droits de l'antiquité* 31 (1984): 167–91.

Kelly, K. H. "Agesilaus' Strategy in Asia Minor." *Liverpool Classical Monthly* 3 (1978): 97–98.

Kennedy, C. R. *The* Olynthiac *and Other Public Orations of Demosthenes*. New York, 1875.

Lazillotta, E. "Le città greche dell'Asia Minore dalla battaglia di Cnido alla pace di Antalcida." In *Scritti sul mondo antico in memoria di Fulvio Grosso*, edited by L. Gasperini, 273–88. Rome, 1981.

Legon, R. P. *Megara: The Political History of a Greek City-State to 336 B.C.* Ithaca, N.Y., and London, 1981.

——. "Phliasian Politics and Policy in the Early Fourth Century B.C." *Historia* 16 (1967): 324–37.

Lehmann, G. A. "Spartas *archē* und die Vorphase des korinthischen Krieges in den *Hellenica Oxyrhynchia* I–II." *Zeitschrift für Papyrologie und Epigraphik* 28 (1978): 109–126; 30 (1978): 73–93.

Levy, E. *Athènes devant la défait de 404*. Athens, 1976.

Lewis, D. M., and R. S. Stroud. "Athens Honors King Euagoras of Salamis." *Hesperia* 48 (1979): 180–93.

Luccioni, J. *Démosthène et le panhellénisme*. Paris, 1961.

McKay, K. L. "The Oxyrhynchus Historian and the Outbreak of the Corinthian War." *Classical Review* n.s. 3 (1953): 6–7.

McKechnie, P. R., and S. J. Kern, eds. Hellenica Oxyrhynchia. Wiltshire, 1988.

Marshall, F. H. *The Second Athenian Confederacy*. Cambridge, 1905.

Martin, V. "Le traitement de l'histoire diplomatique dans la tradition littéraire du IVe siècle avant J.-C." *Museum Helveticum* 1 (1944): 13–30.

Meyer, E. *RE* 15 (1932), 152–205, s.v. Megara.

Milne, J. G. "Trade between Greece and Egypt before Alexander the Great." *Journal of Egyptian Archaeology* 25 (1939): 177–83.

Mitchel, F. W. "The Rasura of *IG* II^2 43: Jason, the Pheraian Demos and the Athenian League." *The Ancient World* 9 (1984): 39–58.

Montgomery, H. *The Way to Chaeronea: Foreign Policy, Decision Making and Political Influence in Demosthenes' Speeches.* Oslo, 1983.

Mosley, D. J. "Theban Diplomacy in 371 B.C." *Revue des Études grecques* 85 (1972): 312–31.

———. "Athens' Alliance with Thebes, 339 B.C." *Historia* 20 (1971): 508–10.

———. "Diplomacy in 371 B.C." *Proceedings of the Cambridge Philological Society* 188 (1962): 41–46.

Moysey, R. A. "Chares and Athens' Foreign Policy." *Classical Journal* 80 (1985): 221–27.

Murray, G. "Reactions to the Peloponnesian War in Greek Thought and Practice." *Journal of Hellenic Studies* 64 (1944): 1–9.

Osborne, M. J. *Naturalization in Athens.* 2 vols. Brussels, 1981–82.

———. "Athens and Orontes." *Annual of the British School at Athens* 66 (1971): 297–321.

Park, H. W. *Greek Mercenary Soldiers, From the Earliest Times to the Battle of Ipsus.* Oxford, 1933.

———. "The Development of the Second Spartan Empire." *Journal of Hellenic Studies* 50 (1930): 37–79.

Payrau, S. "*Eirenika.* Considérations sur l'échec de quelques tentatives panhelléniques au IVe siècle avant Chr." *Revue des études anciennes* 73 (1971): 24–79.

———. "Sur un passage d'Andocide." *Revue des études anciennes* 63 (1961): 15–30.

Perlman, S. "Greek Diplomatic Tradition and the Corinthian League of Philip of Macedon." *Historia* 34 (1985): 153–74.

———. "Athenian Democracy and the Revival of Imperialistic Expansion at the Beginning of the Fourth Century B.C." *Classical Philology* 63 (1968): 257–67.

———. "The Causes of the Outbreak of the Corinthian War." *Classical Quarterly* 14 (1964): 64–81.

———. "A Note on the Political Implications of the Proxenia in the Fourth Century B.C." *Classical Quarterly* 8 (1958): 185–91.

Prandi, L. "La fides punica e il pregiudizio anticartaginese." *Contributi dell'Istituto di storia antica dell' Università del Sacro Cuore, Milan* 6 (1979): 90–97.

———. "La liberazione della Grecia nella propaganda spartana durante la guerra del Peloponneso." *Contributi dell' Istituto di storia antica dell' Università del Sacro Cuore, Milan* 4 (1976): 72–83.

Prunner, I. *Die Rolle Delphis in der griechischen Geschichte des 4. and 3. Jhdts. (mit monumentalen Zeugnissen).* Diss., Vienna, 1981.

Reid, C. "Ephorus, Fragment 76, and Diodorus on the Cypriote War." *Phoenix* 28 (1974): 123–43.

Rice, D. G. "Xenophon, Diodorus and the Year 379–378 B.C.: Reconstruction and Reappraisal." *Yale Classical Studies* 24 (1975): 95–130.

Roberts, J. T. *Accountability in the Athenian Government.* Madison, Wis., 1982.

Roebuck, C. W. "The Settlements of Philip II with the Greek States in 338 B.C." *Classical Philology* 43 (1948): 73–92.

de Romilly, J. "Les modérés Athéniens vers le milieu du IVe siècle." *Revue des études grecques* 62 (1954): 323–33.

Roux, G. *L'amphictionie, Delphes et le temple d'Apollon au IVe siècle.* Collection de la maison de l'Orient Mediterraneen. Série archéologique 6. Paris, 1979.

Roy, J. "Diodorus Siculus XV 40—the Peloponnesian Revolutions of 374 B.C." *Klio* 55 (1973): 135–39.

————. "Arcadia and Boeotia in Peloponnesian Affairs, 370–362 B.C." *Historia* 20 (1971): 569–99.

Ruchenbusch, E. "Tribute, etc." *Zeitschrift für Papyrologie und Epigraphik* 53 (1983): 125–43.

Ruzicka, S. "Clazomenae and Persian Foreign Policy, 387/6 B.C." *Phoenix* 37 (1983): 104–8.

Ryder, T. T. B. "Desmosthenes and Philip's Peace of 338–7 B.C." *Classical Quarterly* 26 (1976): 85–87.

————. Koine Eirene: *General Peace and Local Independence in Ancient Greece.* Oxford, 1965.

————. "Athenian Foreign Policy and the Peace Conference at Sparta in 371 B.C." *Classical Quarterly* 13 (1963): 237–41.

————. "Spartan Relations with Persia after the King's Peace: A Strange Story in Diodorus 15.9." *Classical Quarterly* 13 (1963): 105–9.

————. "The Supposed Common Peace of 366/5 B.C." *Classical Quarterly* 7 (1957): 199-205.

Schaefer, A. *Demosthenes und seine Zeit.* 3 vols. 2d ed. Leipzig, 1885.

Schmitt, H. *Die Staatsverträge des Altertums.* Vol. 3. Munich and Berlin, 1969.

Seager, R. J. "Agesilaus in Asia: Propaganda and Objectives." *Liverpool Classical Monthly* 2 (1977): 183–84.

————. "The King's Peace and the Balance of Power in Greece, 386–362 B.C." *Athenaeum* 52 (1974): 36–63.

————. "Thrasybulus, Conon, and Athenian Imperialism, 396–386 B.C." *Journal of Hellenic Studies* 87 (1967): 95–115.

Seager, R. J., and C. J. Tuplin. "The Freedom of the Greeks of Asia: On the Origins of a Concept and the Creation of a Slogan." *Journal of Hellenic Studies* 100 (1980): 141–54.

Sealey, R. "Callistratus of Aphidna and His Contemporaries." *Historia* 5 (1956): 178–203.

Sinclair, R. K. "The King's Peace and the Employment of Military and Naval Forces, 387–378." *Chiron* 8 (1978): 29–54.

Skalet, C. H. *Ancient Sicyon, with a* Prosopographia Sicyonia. Baltimore, 1928.

Smith, R. E. "The Opposition to Agesilaus' Foreign Policy, 394–371 B.C." *Historia* 2 (1953–54): 274–88.

————. "Lysander and the Spartan Empire." *Classical Philology* 43 (1948): 145–56.

Sordi, M. "La pace di Atene de 371–370 a.c." *Rivista di filologia* 29 (1951): 34–64.

Thompson, W. E. "Arcadian Factionalism in the 360's." *Historia* 32 (1983): 149–60.

————. "Isocrates on the Peace Treaties." *Classical Quarterly* 33 (1983): 75–80.

————. "The Politics of Phlius." *Eranos* 68 (1970): 224–30.

Tuplin, C. J. "The Date of the Union of Corinth and Argos." *Classical Quarterly* 32 (1982): 75–83.

————. "The Athenian Embassy to Sparta, 372–371 B.C." *Liverpool Classical Monthly* 2 (1977): 55–56.

Underhill, G. E., and E. C. Marchant. *Commentary on Xenophon's* Hellenika. Oxford, 1906.

Wankel, H. *Demosthenes Rede für Ktesiphon über den Kranz.* Heidelberg, 1976.

Whitby, M. "The Union of Corinth and Argos: A Reconsideration." *Historia* 33 (1984): 295–308.

Wickersham, J., and G. Verbrugghe. *The Fourth Century B.C.: Greek Historical Documents.* Toronto, 1973.

Woodhead, A. G. "IG II^2 43 and Jason of Pherae." *American Journal of Archaeology* 61 (1957): 367–73.

Wüst, F. R. *Philip II von Makedonien und Griechenland in den Jahren von 346 bis 338.* Munich, 1938.

Zahrnt, M. "Hellas unter persischen Druck? Die griechisch-persischen Beziehungen in der Zeit vom Abschluss des Königsfriedens bis zur Gründung des korinthischen Bundes." *Archiv für Kulturgeschichte* 65 (1983): 249–306.

General Index

Index Locorum